D0611270

Clinician's Guide to Child Custody Evaluations

Marc J. Ackerman

JOHN WILEY & SONS, INC.

New York • Chichester • Brisbane • Toronto • Singapore

Library of Congress Cataloging-in-Publication Data:
Ackerman, Marc J.
    Clinician's guide to child custody evaluations / Marc J. Ackerman.
        p.   cm.
    Includes index.
    ISBN 0-471-05252-3 (cloth)
    1. Custody of children—United States. 2. Custody of children—
Psychological aspects. 3. Children of divorced parents—
Psychology. 4. Psychology, Forensic.   I. Title.
KF547.A925   1995
346.7301 7—dc20   94-14859
[347.30617]

Printed in the United States of America
10   9   8   7   6   5   4   3   2   1

And the king said: "Divide the living child in two, and give half to the one, and half to the other." Then spoke the woman whose living child was unto the king. . . , and she said, "Oh, my lord, give her the living child, and in no wise slay it." But the other said: "It shall be neither mine or thine, divide it." Then the king answered and said "Give her the living child." . . . and all Israel heard of the judgment . . . and they saw the wisdom of God was in him, to do justice.

This book is dedicated to judges who employ the wisdom of Solomon; to parents who do not subject their children to Solomon's sword; and to children who suffer under their parents' use of Solomon's sword.

and

To Stephanie, Scott, and Melissa

Contents

Acknowledgments   ix

Preface   xi

1. Introduction   1

2. Psychologist's Responsibilities   10

3. How Divorce Affects Families   34

4. Interviews, Behavioral Observations, and Collateral Information   82

5. Psychological Testing   100

6. Ackerman-Schoendorf Scales for Parent Evaluation of Custody (ASPECT)   119

7. Guidelines for Evaluating Parents' Behavior   142

8. Abuse Allegations   160

9. Reporting the Results   196

10. Surviving Your Day in Court   210

APPENDIXES

A. Glossary of Legal Terms   237

B. Ethical Principles of Psychologists and Code of Conduct   240

C. Specialty Guidelines for Forensic Psychologists   255

D. Guidelines for Child Custody Evaluations in Divorce Proceedings   266

E.   Academy of Family Mediators Standards of Practice for
     Family and Divorce Mediation   276

F.   American Professional Society on the Abuse of Children
     Guidelines for Psychosocial Evaluation of Suspected
     Sexual Abuse in Young Children   285

References   292

Author Index   305

Subject Index   308

Acknowledgments

A number of individuals must be acknowledged for their support and contribution in this endeavor. First and foremost, I would like to acknowledge Andrew W. Kane, Ph.D., as a friend and collaborator. He provided significant contributions to Chapter 2 as well as invaluable feedback and input to enhance the quality of other chapters. It is through Andy's continual striving for excellence that my work reaches the plateau that it does.

I would also like to thank the law offices of James and Peggy Podell for their continued support. Specifically, I would like to thank Attorney Nina Vitek for the legal research that she performed and Joann Stern for the secretarial support that she provided.

In addition I would like to acknowledge the insights shared by Attorney Susan Hanson and Mary Zosel, Ph.D., in the preparation of these materials. Sue Hanson's experience as a preeminent guardian ad litem and Mary Zosel's experience as one of the most highly regarded psychologists in the Milwaukee metropolitan area were extremely helpful in formulating many of the ideas for this book.

Last, I would like to thank my wife, Stephanie S. Ackerman, and my office manager, Lynn Spencer, for the editing, typing, and revising of this manuscript. They dealt with the deadlines, responded to my anxieties, and provided endless support throughout this project.

Preface

As society becomes more litigious, psychological services are being requested more frequently as part of legal cases. This book not only presents the professional literature as it applies to these cases but also offers insights associated with the experience of having participated in more than 1,000 divorce-related cases during the past decade.

Chapter 1 offers the reader information about how to get started as a mental health practitioner operating in the legal arena. The different roles that psychologists play in these cases is discussed.

Chapter 2 addresses the ethical considerations and responsibilities that must be faced when involved in legal cases. The issues of confidentiality, content of the evaluation, and the application of the American Psychological Association *Ethical Principles of Psychologists and Code of Conduct* are discussed.

Chapter 3 covers the dynamics of custody action, the mediation process, and how divorce affects children at different developmental milestones. It also presents considerable research concerning how divorce affects families. In addition, sample custody and placement schedules are provided.

Chapters 4 through 8 discuss the evaluation process in detail. Chapter 4 provides information about interviewing children and family members, gathering information from collateral contacts, and utilizing behavioral observations in the evaluation process.

Psychological testing is an important component of the custody evaluation process. Chapter 5 addresses the standards applicable to custody evaluations, how the information derived from each of the tests can be interpreted to enhance the evaluation process, and which are the best tests to use.

Chapter 6 discusses in detail the utilization of the Ackerman-Schoendorf Scales for Parent Evaluation of Custody (ASPECT) in custody evaluation cases. It is the only test that has been developed that measures most of the important variables that are incorporated in custody decision making.

Chapter 7 provides a subjective overview of the behaviors that parents should and should not engage in during the divorce process. Those parents who are engaging in more of the "Do's" and less of the "Don'ts" are more likely to make better placement parents.

Unfortunately, as time goes on, abuse allegations are becoming more and more a part of child custody litigation. More than half of the custody cases include some form of physical, psychological, and/or sexual abuse allegations. Chapter 8 addresses these issues and helps the reader understand the dynamics associated with these allegations.

Once the interviewing has occurred, the testing has been performed, and the allegations have been dealt with, the evaluator must report the results. Chapter 9 provides information about writing reports, drawing conclusions, and rendering opinions.

After the entire evaluation process has been completed, it is likely that the psychologist will be called upon to testify either in deposition or a courtroom setting. Chapter 10 gives information on the psychologist's role in the court process. The most frequently used strategies of attorneys, and how to deal with them, and what the psychologist needs to do to prepare for the courtroom setting are covered.

In all, this book addresses the custody evaluation process from beginning to end. It not only provides relevant research but also draws on the vast experience of the author and many other individuals cited in the acknowledgments section. The appendixes of the book include the relevant guidelines, codes, and documentation necessary to perform these evaluations most effectively.

CLINICIAN'S GUIDE TO CHILD CUSTODY EVALUATIONS

CHAPTER 1

Introduction

HISTORY OF CUSTODY DECISION MAKING

The decision-making process in custody disputes was not always as difficult and challenging as it is now. Prior to the 1900s, custody of children was automatically given to fathers, because it was assumed that they were in a better position to support the children financially, and children were viewed more as property. In the event a mother gained custody, the father was no longer financially responsible for the support of the children. The Industrial Revolution brought an increasing awareness of the mother's role in caring for her children and gave rise to the "tender years" doctrine, which assumed that children, particularly young children, fared better in the mother's care. This resulted in a switch to automatically favoring mothers in custody disputes. The women's movement from the 1960s to the present has called attention to the inequity of custody decision making based solely on the gender of the parent, and focus began to shift to "the best interest of the child" (Goldstein, Freud, & Solnit, 1973).

In the early 1970s, the Uniform Marriage and Divorce Act (UMDA) was developed and subsequently adopted by most states. The UMDA focuses on the best interest of the child and provides several factors that may be considered in establishing the best interests. These factors include:

1. The wishes of the parents regarding custody.
2. The wishes of the child.
3. The interaction and interrelationships of the child with the parents, siblings, and anyone else who significantly affects the child's adjustment to home, school, and community.
4. The mental and physical health of the parties.
5. Other factors that may be deemed relevant to each individual case.

Over the past 25 years, courts, attorneys, and mental health professionals have been attempting to measure the variables put forth in UMDA. Al-

1

though they are not established as the sole criteria, they are often used as such.

As society has moved into the 1990s, mothers still receive placement of children 90% of the time in all divorce actions and 60% of the time in contested divorce actions.

COMPONENTS OF THE CHILD CUSTODY EVALUATION

All parties involved in the direct care of the children should be evaluated as part of the child custody evaluation. This includes the natural parents as well as significant others. "Significant others" can include stepparents, live-in partners, grandparents who are responsible for day-to-day care, and live-in help.

The evaluation process should include interviews, behavioral observations, tests of cognitive functioning, and tests of personality functioning. In addition, collateral information should be obtained through school records, medical records, legal and court records, and from relevant people.

The types of tests that are administered, the extent of the interviews, the focus of the behavioral observations, and the utilization of collateral material will all be discussed in detail in subsequent chapters.

What to Evaluate

Since none of the traditional tests of psychological functioning yields a profile of a "fit parent," other variables need to be addressed. In subjectively evaluating the "fitness" of a parent, there are many factors to assess. The overall stability of a parent, measured in terms of emotional stability, job stability, and stability of residence, is an important component. From the psychological point of view, the evaluator must review psychiatric hospitalizations, the use of psychiatric medication, the reason for and outcomes of psychotherapy, and the occurrence of any alcohol- or drug-related problems. Within the family structure, the evaluator addresses such questions as which parent can more likely support the children academically, and which parent provides support for activities of daily living such as hygiene, medical care, car pools, school conferences, and household chores.

Determining which parent is less likely to obstruct time with the other parent is another important component to evaluate, along with identifying which parent has been more cooperative with existing court orders. In addition, extended family relationships should be evaluated to see how they would impact the children. The cooperativeness with the evaluation process and the appropriateness of behavior during the evaluation also need to be considered. Furthermore, the parents' social skills, social judgment, and common sense, from a practical application standpoint, also need to be addressed. The interaction between the child and the parent, negative feelings toward the parent, openness of communication between parent and child, and the quality of communication between the parents should also be assessed.

All of these subjective factors and objective test data have been incorporated in the only instrument currently available to provide a broad-based measure of fitness as a placement parent—the Ackerman-Schoendorf Scale for Parent Evaluation of Custody (ASPECT). This instrument is discussed in greater detail in Chapter 6.

Who Performs the Evaluation?

In a mental health community with a dwindling market of indemnity insurance companies, an increase in managed health care programs with reduced fees, and a greater need to find alternative sources of income, forensic psychology in general, and child custody evaluations specifically, are viewed by many as an attractive and easy income alternative. However, not all psychologists are qualified to perform child custody evaluations. Specifically, psychologists who have little or no training in child psychology and function primarily or exclusively as adult and/or adolescent psychologists, should not be performing child custody evaluations if children under 12 or 13 are involved. Many adult psychologists circumvent this problem by involving a child psychologist to perform the evaluations of the children, resulting in a collaborative report.

Generally, collaborative reports are not the most effective way to perform child custody evaluations; if possible, a single professional should render an opinion. In addition, collaborative reports can double the cost to the parties at the time of trial if both the adult and child psychologist are subpoenaed to testify. Certainly, the adult psychologist can rely on the information obtained from the child psychologist through the hearsay exception and/or the common practice of having a psychometrician do part of the test administration. However, that does not prevent the attorneys from subpoenaing both individuals. It would also be unusual to have both the adult psychologist and child psychologist agree on all points of view. As a result, contradictory and, therefore, confusing testimony could subsequently occur during trial proceedings.

WHO HIRES YOU AND WHAT TO DO

Historically, when psychologists initially became involved in child custody evaluations, the mother's attorney and the father's attorney would each hire an expert. Invariably, the mother's psychologist would recommend for the mother and the father's psychologist would recommend for the father. Subsequently, the court would appoint a psychologist to serve as a "tie breaker." This approach was not only cumbersome and costly, it was unnecessary.

Instead of becoming a custody trial, this approach usually engendered a battle of the experts. Courts soon realized that one of the best ways to circumvent this problem was to begin with a court-appointed psychologist, giving either or both parents the right to obtain second opinions if they did not agree with the court-appointed psychologist's conclusions and recommendations.

Upon entering a custody dispute, psychologists must be certain that they are there to aid the *trier of fact* in determining placement of the children and are not the triers of fact themselves. The trier of fact is either a judge or jury (see Appendix A for a glossary of legal terms). The psychologist can be brought into a custody dispute in many ways. These are described in the next section.

Court or Guardian ad Litem Appointed

Probably the purest way to be involved in a child custody evaluation is to be appointed by the court or guardian ad litem. The psychologist properly operates as a teammate of the guardian ad litem. Both are obligated to make recommendations based primarily upon the best interest of the child(ren) and, secondarily, on other issues. As a result, the psychologist and guardian ad litem should work closely with one another in performing this process. The psychologist who is brought into a case by a guardian ad litem is often viewed as a court-appointed psychologist, since the guardian ad litem is also appointed by the court. In some cases, however, the court appoints a psychologist who is different from the one appointed by the guardian ad litem.

A number of years ago, a court appointed the present author in a case that had previous reports from 11 mental health professionals regarding whether or not child sexual abuse had occurred. The recommendations of the reports were from one end of the continuum to the other. The judge asked this psychologist to review all of the mental health professionals' materials, interview the parents, and report back to the court as to what it all meant. This is another way in which the psychologist may function as a consultant to the court.

Mother's or Father's Attorney

When the mother's or father's attorney retains a psychologist as an independent expert, there is immediate danger of being perceived as a "hired gun."

One appropriate role for a psychologist is as a consultant to an attorney. It is appropriate for an attorney to send a client to a psychologist for a partial evaluation, for example, a Minnesota Multiphasic Personality Inventory (MMPI) outside of the custody evaluation process, in an effort to determine the stability of the parent and whether it would be reasonable or unreasonable to pursue custody. If this is the understanding of the psychologist's role prior to performing the evaluation of one parent, it is not necessary to provide information to all of the attorneys in the case. It is likely that if this evaluation has negative implications, the attorney will discourage the client from pursuing custody of the children. It is also possible, however, that the results will indicate that there are no psychological concerns that would interfere with the parent's ability to function as a placement parent, and as a result, the attorney can in good faith proceed to seek custody on behalf of the client. Ethically, a psychologist who has evaluated only one parent cannot make a recommendation about placement of children. One may only specify whether that parent would or would not make an appropriate custodial parent, and why.

The most appropriate way to perform a full evaluation, when hired by the mother's attorney or the father's attorney, is to indicate that the results will be shared by the psychologist with all three attorneys regardless of what the conclusions are. This must be stated to the attorneys prior to performing the evaluations, so there is no confusion when results unfavorable to a parent are shared with the attorney on the other side. One should also discuss this with each parent prior to the evaluation and get a signed "informed consent" from each parent acknowledging that discussion and knowledge.

Mother and/or Father Without an Attorney

A number of individuals represent themselves in divorce actions. This representation is referred to as *pro se*. Parents choose to represent themselves for a variety of reasons: they may feel that they cannot afford the cost of an attorney; they may feel they can represent themselves better than could an attorney; they may be attorneys who want to represent themselves; or they may have utilized four or five attorneys in the past, none of whom were able to provide the outcome that the parent desired, and cannot find another attorney who would be willing to take the case. This author will rarely become involved in a case when retained by a pro se parent, since they generally have little understanding of legal implications, are blinded by their own obsessions in the case, and do not appreciate the psychologist's ethical obligations. They are often litigious beyond reasonableness, may be members of fringe groups, and are usually difficult to work with. This author has been involved in cases where parents who represented themselves sued judges, attorneys, psychologists, and the attorney general; made threats requiring restraining orders; and, in one case, murdered someone.

Second Opinion Expert

Second opinion experts have the greatest danger of appearing like hired guns. If an attorney is going to bring a second opinion expert into court to testify, that expert is going to agree with that attorney's position, or the attorney would not use the expert. This leaves the courts with the old dilemma of a battle of the experts. The following approach to performing second opinion evaluations safeguards against appearing to be a hired gun. When a referral is made for a second opinion, the second opinion expert informs the attorney that the same procedure will be used as if a first opinion evaluation was being performed. The results of the evaluation will be reported to all three attorneys in the case, regardless of the outcome. It will not be a situation in which the opinion will only be used if it agrees with the attorney who hires the expert. Attorneys agreeing to this approach will inform their clients that if the second opinion agrees with the initial opinion, there will be no contest in court. However, when the second opinion disagrees with the first opinion, a child custody contest may ensue. When full evaluations are performed by qualified evaluators, in most cases the second opinion evaluation will essentially agree with the original evaluation.

Second opinion evaluations are important in situations where incomplete evaluations have been performed or complete evaluations have been performed incompetently. When any of the ethical standards that should apply to child custody evaluations are violated (see Chapter 2), or when psychologists render an opinion based on administration of one test and/or one hour-long interview, a second opinion evaluation also becomes essential. However, just because an incomplete evaluation was performed initially does not necessarily mean that the second opinion conclusion will be different.

Rebuttal Witness

Psychologists and other mental health professionals also can be hired as rebuttal witnesses for the explicit purpose of rebutting the testimony of other expert witnesses. It is virtually impossible to serve as a rebuttal witness and not look like a hired gun. The rebuttal witness is often asked to sit through the testimony of other experts, review the depositions of other experts, and provide contradictory testimony to these experts. Again, serving as a rebuttal witness can be useful in circumstances where ethical codes or standards of practice have been violated, blatant misinterpretations of test material have occurred, and/or bias has been demonstrated. When serving as a rebuttal witness in these situations, it is important to have supporting documentation of your position, not just to present your personal opinion. The courts will look upon psychologists as being more credible witnesses if supporting documentation is presented from what the legal system refers to as "learned treatises." To avoid being pinned down by the opposing attorney, it is recommended that the expert have two or more references for each major point. Otherwise, the opposite counsel may try to suggest that the psychologist accepts everything in a single reference, and will try to trip up the expert by quoting various statements from that text out of context.

Consultants

A mental health professional may be called upon to serve as a consultant in a case without providing direct testimony. This role can include reviewing documents prepared by other mental health professionals, reviewing depositions, providing questions for attorneys to ask in examination and cross-examination, and providing supporting documentation for hypotheses that have been generated. The roles of the consultant and expert witness are separate from one another. It is the expert witness's responsibility to be impartial and objective in providing court testimony. However, the consultant's role is to attempt to help the attorney build her or his case. When a consultant ceases the role of consultant and becomes an expert witness, there is a greater likelihood of being viewed as a hired gun.

Mediator

The mediator's role in child custody evaluations is distinct from either the evaluator's role or the therapist's role. In many states, the mediator is not allowed to testify about the content of the mediation without written consent of all parties involved. This is done in an effort to prevent parents from misusing the mediation process to build a case. If an individual tries to serve as both an evaluator and a mediator, it will likely be viewed as a dual relationship. However, this author does not believe that it is a dual relationship for the psychologist to act as a mediator in a custody matter once the evaluation is complete, particularly if mediation has a significant likelihood of preventing a court battle. Because the ethical imperative is to serve the best interest of the child, the individual who conducted the evaluation may be in the best position to help avoid going to court, thereby decreasing the animosity between the parents, which in turn would benefit the child.

There are times following a psychologist's divorce/custody evaluation when parties decide to mediate rather than litigate the visitation/placement issues. It is not unusual for the psychologist who has performed the evaluations to be asked to provide this mediation service, based on his or her familiarity with the case and the existing working relationship with the parties and their attorneys. Having the evaluator become the mediator can be effective if appropriate precautions are taken.

All parties and all attorneys must be aware that if the psychologist becomes a mediator in the case, it is likely that he or she will no longer be sufficiently independent to be available for court testimony. There is no way that the psychologist can forget information that was obtained during mediation and segregate it from information obtained during evaluation. All attorneys and parties should sign a statement acknowledging that they understand and accept the psychologist's change of roles and, further, understand that the psychologist will no longer be available to testify in the case—and that the attorneys, therefore, will not ask the psychologist to do so.

Following this approach, the possibility of a conflict of interest or dual relationship is avoided. If the mediation process breaks down, the attorneys must be aware that it will be necessary to find a new psychologist to perform independent evaluations.

Getting Involved

Psychologists must make careful decisions about getting involved in child custody evaluations. Any state association ethics committee, licensing board, or other regulatory body will report that one of the largest number of complaints generally occurs in child custody evaluation situations. Unlike other work that psychologists do, no matter how good the work product is, someone is going to be dissatisfied with one's results and conclusions. The better the work product, the more likely that it will be attacked in the courtroom setting. This runs counter to the way mental health professionals are trained.

Mental health professionals are trained as "helping professionals." Once they enter the legal system, however, they are entering an adversarial process. It is often difficult to blend the helping and adversarial approaches to help the client as much as possible. Nevertheless, psychologists have both an ethical and moral obligation to make this adversarial process as helpful as possible. One means of doing this is to work as diligently as possible to try to prevent a case from resulting in testimony in open court, where the mother and father may testify about how bad the other parent is. These kinds of wounds are very difficult to heal, as are the wounds from hearing the psychologist testify about the psychological status of each parent.

Due to the stress, risk factors, and energy required to perform child custody evaluations, not many psychologists are willing to take on this responsibility. As a result, once the legal community knows that a psychologist is willing to perform these evaluations, a substantial referral base can be quickly established. This can easily be done by sending a letter to local family law attorneys introducing yourself and identifying your willingness to perform child custody evaluations. Offering to give presentations to local bar associations or writing articles for community newspapers can also be helpful.

It is during the psychologist's initial entry into this system that a reputation is established that the psychologist will have to live with for many years to come. Since attorneys spend much of their time standing around courtrooms and in courthouse hallways waiting for cases to be called, they also spend a considerable amount of time talking with one another about divorce-related issues, including experts. It is through this network of attorneys talking with one another about what they can expect from psychologists performing these evaluations that psychologists' reputations are discussed.

When a referral comes to one's office for a custody evaluation, it is important to check with all of the parties involved, in advance of any work, regarding what questions are to be addressed by the evaluation. It is not unusual for one of the parents to make the initial appointment and to provide a scenario that is contrary to what the guardian ad litem, other attorneys, or the other parent is interested in having done. The psychologist is much more likely to provide a meaningful report if it is understood in advance what types of information are desired from the evaluation. Thus, as part of the initial contact with an individual, it is important to get releases to speak to all of the attorneys in the case to make sure that the desired work is performed.

During the initial evaluations, when a psychologist is too eager to please the initial referral sources and appears as a hired gun, that reputation will follow the psychologist. A psychologist who maintains the position of always recommending based on what is best for the child(ren), regardless of who has brought the psychologist into the case, will enjoy a long-standing, positive reputation.

It is clear that psychologists should understand their role in the custody evaluation process. Although they can become involved in many different ways, psychologists must always function in the best interests of children. Many factors need to be considered during the custody evaluation process. The remainder of this book devotes itself to looking at those factors and how to incorporate them into a meaningful report and testimony.

CHAPTER 2

Psychologist's Responsibilities

CODE OF ETHICS AND STANDARDS OF PRACTICE

Ethical guidelines and standards of practice, propounded by all professions, are an essential part of maintaining the integrity and cohesiveness of a profession (Keith-Spiegel & Koocher, 1985). They are a primary ingredient in the professionalization of an occupation, in part because society accords professionals special privileges that it does not offer to commercial enterprises. People expect professionals to be more trustworthy, competent, and error-free than the average businessperson. There is a fiduciary relationship between professionals and their patients and clients (Pope & Vasquez, 1991). The trust given to professionals by society and by clients and patients is a source of power, as is the requirement that most professionals be licensed. "Licensed professionals are permitted to engage in certain activities that are prohibited to others who do not possess the license" (Pope & Vasquez, 1991, p. 36). This has led professionals to institute ethics codes as mechanisms to balance the self-interest of the individual professional against the interests of the people with whom the professional works. These ethics codes function as moral guides to self-regulation and help to ensure the appropriate use of skills and techniques (Keith-Spiegel & Koocher, 1985).

TESTING

Requirement to Use Best Methods Available

Ethics guidelines may also require that the psychologist use the best methods available.

The best methods are those that do two things: (1) they promote the principles of objectivity and scientific competence, and (2) they provide data that are as relevant as possible for the questions faced by the court. . . . [In general,] standardized methods promote objectivity better than non-standardized methods. . . . Among other things, standardization means that the examiner has less opportunity to be swayed by personal bias or simple error in seeking information about a parent or child.

A method does not have to be a "test" to be standardized. There are standardized interview schedules that may be used. . . . Moreover, a method does not have to be "published" in order to be standardized. . . . If [used] consistently from one case to another, then they can be said to have this quality of standardization. . . . On the other hand, the most common standardized methods now used in custody evaluations are our traditional clinical psychological tests. (Martindale, Martindale, & Broderick, 1991, p. 488)

This raises questions about the use of a test designed for one purpose, in a setting calling for the most relevant information possible for the court.

Some newer evaluation methods may provide more obviously relevant information than do common psychological tests, but these newer methods also lack the time-tested validity and reliability of the psychological tests. The expert needs to weigh all these factors, selecting those tests and other instruments that are as valid, reliable, and relevant as possible to the task at hand.

Relevancy is the underlying predicate for all expert testimony. . . . Courts have not seemed inclined to limit the use of forensic instruments or psychological tests, so long as their relevance to the legal standard can be demonstrated. Such demonstration could be made in the report itself or during direct testimony. This could be considered part of the ethical obligation incurred by a psychologist, working in a forensic context, to provide a "full explanation of the results of tests and the bases for conclusions . . . in language that the client can understand." (Heilbrun, 1992, p. 257)

The 1992 revision of the *Ethical Principles of Psychologists and Code of Conduct* (see Appendix B) requires that "(a) [p]sychologists do not base their assessment or intervention decisions or recommendations on data or test results that are outdated for the current purpose. (b) Similarly, psychologists do not base such decisions or recommendations on tests and measures that are obsolete and not useful for the current purpose" (American Psychological Association [APA], 1992).

This is particularly relevant to intelligence tests. With each revision of the Wechsler Adult Intelligence Scale (WAIS), Wechsler Intelligence Scale for Children (WISC), and other intelligence tests, there is also a revision of the normative standards, based on an updated normative population. Once this is available, older forms of the test should no longer be used. An exception is possible for neuropsychological testing, where well-established norms for the assessment of brain damage are not necessarily significantly altered by the updating of the test.

An exception to the above guideline would be the use of the MMPI instead of the MMPI-2, even though the MMPI-2 has been published for more than five years. The controversy surrounding this issue is discussed in Chapter 5.

Informed Consent

Psychologists are obligated to obtain informed consent for all professional activities, including informing "consumers as to the purpose and nature of an evaluative ... procedure" (APA, 1992). The psychologist must ensure that any party to the custody action old enough to understand the explanation knows who requested the psychologist's services, who is paying the fees, and whether the psychologist is representing one of the parents, has been appointed by the court, or has been retained by the guardian ad litem. The psychologist should inform the individual whether the report will go to only one of the attorneys, who may or may not use the information, or whether it will go directly to the court. Although people are not likely to refuse to participate in an evaluation, because it will give the appearance they have something to hide, once informed of the limits of confidentiality, individuals do retain the right to disclose or not disclose any information they wish. It should be kept in mind, however, that a skilled examiner may create an environment that feels therapeutic, in which the individual may forget that he or she has been warned about the lack of confidentiality (Schetky, 1992).

If an expert is asked to evaluate one parent and one or more children in an actual or potential custody case, the psychologist should determine whether it is both legal and ethical to do so in each particular case. "In some states, a noncustodial parent may not legally seek services from a psychologist for a child without permission from the custodial parent or by court order. However, to avoid a charge of unethical behavior, the psychologist should notify the custodial parent, regardless of the statute" (Boyer, 1990, p. 8). If the parents are informally separated, getting the consent of the other parent is still strongly recommended. If formally separated, it is critical to have that consent. Prior to agreeing to conduct the evaluation, the noncustodial parent should be informed of the need of notice to the custodial parent. Even though not required by law, ethical codes generally require that the expert clarify the nature of relationships when multiple parties are involved. Because the custodial parent could be affected by the results of the evaluation, that parent is a party to the request for the evaluation and should be notified.

Requirement That Tests Be Correctly Administered

Psychologists are responsible for ensuring that tests are correctly administered. They must ensure that the correct instructions are used, that the environmental conditions are appropriate, and that the patient/client personally responds to all of the test items. The *Casebook for Providers of Psychological Services* indicates that:

> [w]hen the psychologist does not have direct, firsthand information as to the conditions under which a test is taken, he or she is forced . . . to assume that the test responses were not distorted by the general situation in which the test was taken (e.g., whether the client consulted others about test responses). Indeed, the psychologist could have no assurance that this test was in fact completed by the client. In the instance where the test might be introduced as data in a court proceeding, it would be summarily dismissed as hearsay evidence. (APA, 1984, p. 664)

Further, Standard 6.2 of the *Standards for Educational and Psychological Testing* (APA, 1985) indicates that "[w]hen a test user makes a substantial change in test format, mode of administration, instructions, language or content, the user should revalidate the use of the test for the changed conditions or have a rationale supporting the claim that additional validation is not necessary or possible" (p. 41).

To be absolutely certain that tests are correctly administered, the psychologist should administer the tests personally. This ensures that correct procedures are used, that extratest behavior (reactions, expressions, and side comments, for example) is noted, and that the entire realm of test-taking behavior is considered in the interpretation done by the psychologist (Berman, 1986).

> If any circumstances might have affected the results of psychological testing, such as dim lighting, frequent interruptions, a noisy environment, or medication, or if there is doubt that the person being tested shares all relevant characteristics with the reference groups on which the norms are based, these factors must be taken into account when interpreting test data and must be included in the formal report. (Pope & Vasquez, 1991, pp. 99–100)

As reported in the July 1993 American Psychological Association *Monitor*, the APA's Ethics Committee was requested "to address whether it is a per se violation of the *Ethical Principles of Psychologists and Code of Conduct* to send a Minnesota Multiphasic Personality Inventory home for administration" (p. 41). The response of the Ethics Committee was that this would not automatically be an ethics violation, and that each case would be considered individually.

In the past, the Committee has found it to be a violation to write a report based on information from a test that was sent home. "The reasons for the violation involved failure to protect the security of the test, failure to adequately supervise the testing, particularly when reservations about reliability and validity are not stated [in the report], and impairment of the welfare of the client" (APA, 1993, p. 41).

The Committee endorsed the following points in its response to the question:

1. Nonmonitored administration of the MMPI generally does not represent sound testing practice and may result in invalid assessment for a variety of reasons (e.g., influence from other people, completion of the test while intoxicated, etc.).

2. Test security cannot be guaranteed when the MMPI is allowed outside the clinical setting.

3. There is debate as to whether there are even any circumstances in which it might be reasonable and appropriate to allow an MMPI to be completed away from the clinical setting. In cases where the psychologist allows an MMPI to be completed away from the clinical setting, the burden would lie with the psychologist to demonstrate that the welfare of the client, or other extenuating circumstances, necessitated the nonmonitored administration, and reasonable efforts were made to maintain test security (Ethical Standard 2.10). Furthermore, in such circumstances, it would be incumbent upon the psychologist to consider the nonstandard conditions under which the test was completed in interpreting and reporting the results (Ethical Standard 2.05).

4. These issues are not unique to the MMPI, but must be considered in conducting any assessment.

5. In judging the ethicality of at-home administration of tests, it is important to consider such things as the nature and purpose of the test and available information regarding reliability, validity, and standardization procedures. Relevant statements of the test authors and other experts in this regard must be considered seriously. However, the final responsibility for the appropriate use of any assessment instrument lies with the psychologist who administers it.

Test Integrity

Psychologists are obligated to maintain the integrity of the tests they use, both by ethical requirements and by contractual agreements with the publishers who hold the copyrights on those tests. It would be a violation of those ethical and contractual requirements for the psychologist to submit to an attorney or to the court raw data, answer sheets, or other information that would compromise both the validity of the test and its utility for others, though (with patient/client consent or a court order) the information could be released to another psychologist (Stromberg et al., 1988).

There is no simple solution to the dilemma posed if a psychologist's test records are subpoenaed. The ethical and contractual obligation is to refuse disclosure, although there is an obvious personal danger for the psychologist to be held in contempt of court if the records are not disclosed. It would be hoped that discussions between the psychologist, the judge, and the attorneys could resolve the matter without forcing the psychologist to violate ethical and contractual obligations (Weithorn, 1987). At a minimum, it may be possible for the subpoena to be narrowed sufficiently for the psychologist to be able to respond without ethical or contractual breaches (Stromberg et al., 1988).

A recent Illinois statute, found at Illinois Revised Statutes chapter 91, paragraph 803, and effective January 1991, provides protection from disclosure in court for psychological tests. The statute specifies that only licensed psychologists may have access to test questions, scoring sheets, and an individual's responses in judicial, administrative, and legislative proceedings. It is the intent of the law to preserve the validity and reliability of assessment tools by keeping them out of public records. The law states that:

> Psychological test material whose disclosure would compromise the objectivity or fairness of the testing process may not be disclosed to anyone including the subject of the test and is not subject to disclosure in any administrative, judicial or legislative proceeding. However, any recipient who has been the subject of the psychological test shall have the right to have all records relating to that test disclosed to any psychologist designated by the recipient. (APA, 191, p. 22)

Test publishers have been tightening the requirements on psychologists who wish to purchase various instruments. The most recent catalog from The Psychological Corporation, for example, explicitly states, under the heading "Maintenance of Test Security," that:

> Access to test materials must be limited to qualified persons with a responsible, professional interest who agree to safeguard their use.

> Test materials and scores may be released to persons qualified to interpret and use them properly.

> No reproduction of test materials is allowed in any form or by any means, electronic or mechanical. (1994 *Assessment and Related Products for the Development of Human Resources*, The Psychological Corporation, Harcourt Brace and Company, San Antonio, 1994, at 86)

Psychologist's Need for Data

A psychologist is obligated to identify all the major factors that need to be addressed prior to stating an opinion and to refuse to do an evaluation (or to limit the scope of an evaluation) if those factors cannot, for whatever reason, be addressed adequately. This would apply, for example, to the situation where the psychologist may not have access to all the parties in the custody action. It would also apply if any medical, school, social service, or other records were refused. For the evaluation to be adequate, it is essential that many sources of data be consulted, including records, psychological tests, and interviews of the parties and others who have potentially relevant input.

In addition, a low and arbitrary limit placed on the number of hours a psychologist may devote to data gathering and analysis would mean that factors may not be addressed adequately. Although there need not be a blank check, any limits on time need to be liberal if the best interests of the child are to be served. One author suggests that "sixteen hours can be considered a minimum amount of time for a study involving two parents and one child. For each additional child or stepparent to be interviewed two hours could be added. These estimates do not include 'mulling it over' time but rather represent direct involvement hours" (Skafte, 1985, pp. 25–26). These figures also leave out time to write a report, deposition time, and court time. A psychologist who cannot devote that amount of time, or who has a client who is unwilling to retain the psychologist for enough hours to do the job right, has an obligation to refuse the task. It should be added that psychologists are ethically required to do some work pro bono, so the issue of adequate time spent is not necessarily a financial question.

Limits on Going Beyond the Data

As clinicians and scientists, psychologists are well trained to gather and interpret data, whether from observations, interviews, psychological testing, medical or school records, or other sources. The data gathered and analyzed may relate to abilities, attitudes, thoughts, feelings, behaviors, and relationships. The psychologist is also trained to organize the data from disparate sources into a meaningful whole, which may then be presented as part of the legal inquiry. In addition, psychologists are trained to be able to elaborate on those aspects of functioning of each parent that relate to the unique needs of each child. Ethically, however, psychologists must limit how far beyond the data they go in speculating about the future, and must clearly distinguish between those conclusions that are based on hard data and those that are not.

A different way to address the same question is in reference to how validly the psychologist can make statements in response to each of several types of questions asked. If the question is about the individual's current psychological functioning, existing psychological tests permit a number of statements to be made validly and reliably. Examples would include statements regarding an individual's level of intelligence as measured by the Wechsler Adult Intelligence Scale-Revised (WAIS-R) or personality as described by the MMPI. More difficult are questions regarding the presence of a particular state or condition, for example, a formal diagnosis of a mental disorder, because the criteria for making the diagnosis are less explicit than are test results. That is, the psychologist must infer rather than simply report. More difficult yet are responses to questions involving potential dangerousness to self or others, or future parenting quality. Here the inference is clouded by the substantial influence that environmental factors can have on the way an individual responds to future situations. The quality of possible predictions is at best equivocal and must be made with a variety of qualifying statements to have any validity at all. In other words, the psychologist should not claim certainty about these tenuous factors (Weiner, 1989).

Requirement to Report All the Data

Psychologists are ethically obligated to report *all* the data they have that relate directly to the purpose of an evaluation.

> They provide thorough discussion of the limitations of their data, especially where their work touches on social policy or might be construed to the detriment of persons in specific age, sex, ethnic, socioeconomic or other social groups. In publishing reports of their work, they never suppress disconfirming data, and they acknowledge the existence of alternative hypotheses and explanations of their findings. (APA, 1992)

"If a psychologist is appointed by the court, he may feel more independent. Nevertheless, an expert is professionally obligated to state his findings and opinions truthfully and without bias—regardless of who engaged him" (Stromberg et al., 1988, p. 646). The psychologist is also obligated to try to prevent distortion of his or her own views. This point is underscored by Bazelon's statement that:

> conclusory statements are bad enough when they merely propound the scientific gospel. They become positively dangerous when they verge into naked pronouncements on the ultimate issue faced by the decision maker. . . . What the public needs most from any expert, including the psychologist, is a wealth of intermediate observations and conceptual insights that are adequately explained. Only then can his or her contributions be combined with the communal sense of right and wrong to produce a decision. (1982, pp. 115–116)

Thus, the expert's task may be seen as the utilization of special skills to generate a representative sample of data to supplement and complement data the parties will produce. The evaluator might also indicate whether various factual allegations of the parties are consistent with the data developed in the evaluative process. The court may then assign relative weights to these independent sources of data to arrive at an ultimate decision (Stone & Shear, 1988).

Limits on Predictions

Although the body of research regarding the effects of divorce on children is substantial and growing, there is a "lack of any methodologically sound empirical evidence allowing psychological predictions as to the effects of various types of custodial placements on children, or whether joint custody, in general, is a better option than single-parent custody" (Weithorn, 1987, p. 161). Thus, the psychologist may use the data from his or her evaluation to make statements "to a reasonable degree of professional certainty" about the past and present; however, any statements about the future must be stated as opinions, the psychologist noting the limitations of the testimony and being willing and able to identify the bases for those opinions.

Limits on Predictions from Tests

Very few of the tests used by psychologists have been specifically validated for use in custody proceedings, making it necessary for the psychologist to report (a) what the test *does* validly address, and then (b) how that intermediate factor would be expected to impact both the ability of an individual to parent well and the needs of the child. For example, if a child is determined to have a very substantial need for nurturing, while a given parent is found to have a severe narcissistic personality disorder or frequent, ongoing major depressive episodes, it is reasonable to conclude that there is a poor fit between this need of the child and the ability of the parent to address the need—not because the test showed the degree of fit, but because the test yielded information that could be analyzed and addressed in drawing this conclusion (Weithorn, 1987).

Because the recommendations made by the expert in a custody case may be given great weight by the judge, the life of the family and each individual in it will be affected for years by the recommendations made. With such great power, the expert must be especially cautious (Deed, 1991).

Limits on Custody Recommendations

Psychologists are to consider all factors that may potentially affect their own opinions and recommendations and to try to avoid situations wherein there is a significant potential for misuse of those opinions and recommendations. One consequence is that a psychologist is potentially compromising ethical standards when hired by one parent in a custody evaluation, rather than serving as a court-appointed expert or, at the least, as an independent expert retained by both parents jointly. It would be an ethical violation to draw *any* conclusions about which parent would be the better custodial parent unless the psychologist has assessed *both* parents. Similarly, it would be an ethical violation to indicate that *either* parent would be the better custodial parent unless the expert has evaluated each child for whom that statement is to be made, because the better custodial parent for one child may not be better for another child.

Further, the psychologist's primary responsibility is to the child (by virtue of the requirement that the decision ultimately made be in the best interest of the child), a fact that may become cloudy if the psychologist is retained by only one parent. It does not serve the best interests of the child if the psychologist appears to be a hired gun, and even the most ethical psychologist may feel some pressure to shade the results of the evaluation in the direction of the parent who is paying the bill. "Even merely the fact of being employed by one side or the other will create a tendency toward bias or somewhat diminished objectivity, sometimes even without awareness on the part of the expert that such a tendency is operating" (Ziskin, 1981, p. 37).

These factors do not preclude a psychologist from being retained by one parent in a custody matter. They *do*, however, point out the ethical traps inherent in doing so, and the extreme caution a psychologist must exercise in making any statements at all about one or some, but not all, of the parties involved in the custody action (Weithorn, 1987).

Types of Bias

Noting that everyone is subject to bias in the manner in which information is processed, Williams (1992) describes several types of bias that the expert must avoid to the degree possible.

Confirmatory bias, Williams indicates, occurs when the expert looks for and emphasizes information that supports his or her position as opposed to information that does not. Experience increases, rather than decreases, the degree to which this is done, Williams asserts.

Anchoring, giving excessive weight to initial information, is considered a type of confirmatory bias. This may particularly be a problem when the plaintiff's attorney indicates that his or her client has the worst case of [name of disorder] he or she has ever seen, or when the defense attorney indicates that the patient has no weaknesses whatsoever.

Availability refers to how easy it is for given information to be brought to mind. People tend to remember things that are vivid or dramatic.

Illusory correlation occurs when a relationship between events or characteristics is claimed, even though no objective data indicate that the relationship exists.

Hindsight bias is a tendency to conclude, when the outcome of some event is known, that it could have been identified in advance more easily than was actually possible. As an example, Williams indicates that if a clinician is aware of a previous diagnosis, she is more likely to come to the same diagnosis than if the evaluation was being done totally independently. Similarly, an expert may give too much weight to certain data, like a high score on the MMPI's Depression Scale, if she knows that the patient later committed suicide.

Brodsky concludes that biases like those described "constitute a far greater hazard to impartiality than the mythical bought witness. Their impact is gradual and beyond the immediate awareness of the expert. These influences are sufficiently powerful that they may be the single greatest threat to expert integrity" (1991, p. 9). Grisso (1990, p. 37) agrees, noting that "the issue is not one of the 'hired gun.' Any well-meaning and reputable clinician can be seduced by collaborative relationships having a subtle and almost irresistible pull toward advocacy. Often this will be at the expense of the objective attitude for which clinicians must strive, as required by their professional ethical principles."

To counter these biasing tendencies, Williams (1992) recommends that experts use explicit decision rules (e.g., the specific criteria for each disorder in DSM-IV) to make diagnoses, and that only the most valid data be used. One must also avoid making generalizations based on studies involving small numbers of subjects. It is vital to know the base rates in the population for the disorders or problems being addressed, because predictions for low base-rate disorders or events (e.g., suicide) are very difficult.

Further, Williams suggests that the clinician identify potentially relevant diagnoses and then seek evidence for each one. The expert might also ask himself or herself how the data would be viewed if the expert were retained by opposing counsel in the case. Other possible explanations for the data should also be reported.

Reliance on one's memory is a poor practice in most cases. Clinicians tend to "remember" symptoms that were not actually present but are consistent with their diagnosis. They also tend to forget symptoms that are not consistent with their diagnosis. To counter this problem, it is recommended that the expert report separately symptoms that were present and those that were not.

The clinician must also know the sensitivity and the specificity of the tests used and diagnoses made, Williams indicates. *Sensitivity* is the ability of a test or a diagnostic process to identify those people who have a given condition. *Specificity* is the ability to avoid false positives, that is, identifying someone who does not have a given condition as having that condition.

Quoting a study by Needell, Sparr and Boehnlein indicate that:

inaccuracy and bias may assume three major forms: (1) experts who offer biased opinions, based on either calculated or unconscious prejudices; (2) physicians lacking in psychiatric sophistication who offer expert psychiatric testimony; or (3) fully qualified experts who, through inadvertence or laziness, perform examinations that do not serve as a professionally adequate basis for their conclusions. (1990, p. 283)

With regard to custody evaluations, one may identify both theoretical and practical biases:

Examples of theoretical bias include favoring a particular custody arrangement without research basis for the point of view, theoretical overreaching which ignores the family's social, economic, and legal realities, lack of training in the dynamics of child sexual abuse and spouse abuse, [and] falling into counter-transference traps. Practical biases include ignorance about the practical and legal consequences of the custody recommendations, failure to understand long-standing inequities between men and women in the court system, the assumption that both parents contribute equally to a custody dispute, and participating in dual relationships. Many of these pitfalls can be avoided if the custody evaluator takes care not to go beyond the data. (Deed, 1991, p. 76)

Distortion of Test Results

It should be kept in mind that test results, though relatively objective evidence, can be distorted, consciously or unconsciously, by the professional using them. This includes the psychologist who administers and interprets the test and the psychiatrist, social worker, or other professional who may use information from tests in forming or defending an opinion. The distortion can range from the choice of tests to the specific operations necessary to administer and score the test (Melendez & Marcus, 1990).

Podboy and Kastle (1992) write about the misuse of psychological testing in complex trial situations. They point out that there are both intentional and unintentional misuses of psychological instruments. Psychologists can *unintentionally* misuse psychological tests when they lack the knowledge necessary to administer and interpret the test appropriately. Unintentional errors can also occur when psychologists place undue reliance on a single, relatively brief test. A third typical error arises when an intelligence test is only partially administered, thus reducing the reliability of the results.

Podboy and Kastle also address *intentional* misuse that can occur at the hands of psychologists. They point out that outright fraud appears to be rare; however, some intentional misuses still need to be addressed. One such misuse occurs when a psychologist, or other mental health professional, has inadequate training in the field of assessment and relies on computerized interpretations without fully understanding the information. A second source of error occurs when overgeneralizations are used in interpreting Rorschach data. The authors are also concerned about overuse of the Post-traumatic Stress Disorder diagnosis. They identify this as a third problem area and indicate that even minor injuries are often reported as causing Posttraumatic Stress Disorder. The last intentional misuse that the authors discuss occurs in the field of neuropsychology. One form of this error is administering a wide variety of neuropsychological tests and using results of some of the tests as indicating deficiencies, even though other test results may not so indicate. The authors state that the context of the evaluation is also relevant in performing neuropsychological evaluations.

In a study (Podboy & Kastle, 1992) in which 120 psychological reports in mental disability cases were reviewed, only five (4%) of the reports "were considered to be free of errors, biases, or slanted points of view." Twenty-three of the reports evidenced problems because the evaluator did not have adequate credentials to administer the tests used. Seventy-six had problems with the specific test battery used, including utilization of batteries inadequate to the task, violation of standardization norms, violation of test instructions, violation of scoring procedures, or other problems. Eighty-seven had problems involving test interpretation, including interpretive selective data, making contradictory statements, making errors in interpretations, and ignoring indicators of invalidity of results. Seventy-one of the reports were judged to offer exaggerated or biased diagnoses, and 10 others used diagnoses that did not meet DSM-III-R criteria. Therefore, it is critical that the evaluator be carefully chosen and that all tests used be properly administered and interpreted.

Conclusions on Matters of Law

Being relatively naïve about the legal process, a psychologist may draw conclusions on matters of law rather than solely provide data and recommendations that may be used by the judge in making the determination of what would be in the best interests of the child. Although psychologists can and should provide data regarding the positive and negative aspects of parenting by each parent, and the quality of the "fit" between the needs of the child and the abilities of the parents, it goes beyond the present ability of any psychologist to predict with certainty which parent would be the better custodial parent in all circumstances. The psychologist is obligated to acknowledge in stating opinions this lack of ability to identify a threshold below which custodial rights should be denied. That judgment belongs to the court. This does not necessarily mean that a psychologist must not render an opinion regarding type of custody arrangement, visitation, or similar issues. Rather, that opinion must be labeled as an opinion. It should also be noted that some state laws oppose recommendations from experts regarding the ultimate disposition of the case, while laws of other states (e.g., Wisconsin) permit such recommendations to be made. Some judges feel that they (or a jury) need the expert's opinion on the ultimate issue to come to a fair decision. Experts are expected to have such opinions and to offer them if asked. None of the major mental health professional organizations has formulated a position regarding whether an evaluator should make a recommendation regarding the ultimate issues. The attorney should advise the psychologist regarding what the relevant statute in the particular state requires or permits.

RIGHTS AND PROTECTION

Affirmative Duty to Promote Client and Patient Welfare

Most professional codes of ethics mandate that the welfare of the consumer is paramount and that the services of the professional must be used in a responsible manner. It would be a violation of these requirements to simply point out the nature of the problems in the person or people being evaluated, without also identifying strengths and recommending means of improvement. In a child custody case, for example, the expert should analyze the strengths of each parent, the developmental needs of the children, and the requirements for promoting new family structures. In so doing, the advantages and disadvantages of various alternatives must be weighed.

Duty to Warn or Protect

Case law has firmly established the responsibility of psychotherapists to at least warn responsible parties if a patient or client makes a threat, if not take a number of actions to try to protect the threatened party. These requirements initially stemmed from the *Tarasoff* case in California.

Howell and Toepke (1984) suggest that the same responsibility to warn or protect may be present if an expert is doing an evaluation in which a threat is made against someone. The basis for this responsibility is that a special relationship exists between the evaluator and the people who are evaluated, much as there is a special relationship between a therapist and a patient or client. Howell and Toepke cite the well-known fact that violence in family disputes, including custody battles, is not uncommon. It is therefore a small step, they suggest, from the requirement to warn or protect in psychotherapy to the same requirement when evaluations are done. For psychologists, this responsibility could fall under the ethical requirement to "respect and protect human and civil rights" (APA, 1992).

Reporting Child Abuse

The laws in most states require psychologists to report suspected child abuse. The *Ethical Principles of Psychologists and Code of Conduct* and the *General Guidelines for Providers of Psychological Services* reinforce that requirement. If a psychologist who is conducting any part of a custody evaluation suspects child abuse, he or she is obligated to report that suspicion to the designated social services agency, except in those few states that have an exemption from disclosures made in voluntary treatment sought by an abuser (Miller, 1992).

Preservation of Legal and Civil Rights

Forensic psychologists are required to make a reasonable effort to ensure that their services are used to promote the preservation of the legal rights of the parties to a legal proceeding. They are also obligated to understand the civil rights of parties to those proceedings and in no way to diminish or endanger those rights (APA, 1992).

Need to Avoid Iatrogenic Harm

Iatrogenic illness refers to "an illness unwillingly precipitated, aggravated, or induced by the physician's attitude, examination, comments, or treatment" (Stone & Shear, 1988, p. 80). In the course of conducting an evaluation, a mental health expert could do a number of things that would harm the individuals involved in the process. The expert must be cognizant of ways in which this could occur and make every effort to avoid doing harm (Stone & Shear, 1988).

Forensic psychologists are required to "ensure that their services and the products of their services are used in a forthright and responsible manner," that is, a manner that minimizes the probability of an iatrogenic injury (APA, 1991, II.B).

In a custody battle, it is likely that each family member is going through a personal crisis engendered by the divorce and custody dispute. It is essential, therefore, that the evaluator do everything possible to minimize the stress involved in the process. One means of doing so is to discuss the nature of the evaluation process so that the individual can anticipate what to expect. Another is to avoid probing in areas that are only marginally relevant to the questions that must be answered in the evaluation (Stone & Shear, 1988).

In the custody evaluation, it would also be harmful in most cases to directly ask a child which parent the child wishes to live with, implying that the choice belongs to the child. "Assigning a child this responsibility invariably provides the child a destructive misperception of omnipotence and potentiates a sense of betrayal and ultimately guilt" (Stone & Shear, 1988, p. 54).

It would also be destructive of the relationship between a parent and a child to indicate, unless absolutely necessary, that negative conclusions about the parent are based directly on statements made by the child. Although the expert has the obligation to disclose the bases of conclusions and recommendations, discretion must be used in an attempt to effect the best outcome for the child and the family and to avoid this type of iatrogenic injury (Stone & Shear, 1988).

If the evaluator is seeing only one of the parents, along with the children, it is likely that the anxiety of the children will be increased. This is true whether the other parent is aware of the evaluation but refuses to participate or is unaware of the evaluation and the children are being asked to keep it a secret from that parent. In either case, the relationship between the children and the noninvolved parent will be strained, with the psychologist as a "party to the crime."

A dilemma can occur when an expert is asked to evaluate a victim, with the knowledge that discussion of the victimization could precipitate a negative psychological reaction potentially as severe as suicidal acting-out. The expert must ethically respond first as a mental health professional, protecting the individual from harm, and only secondarily as an expert hired in a legal matter.

LEGAL ISSUES

Avoiding Dual Relationships

Psychologists must "make every effort to avoid dual relationships" (APA, 1992); that is, to avoid situations where loyalty is owed to more than one person or institution or that may otherwise compromise the quality of one's judgment by involving a conflict of interest. In a custody case, the primary loyalty is owed to the "best interests of the child," but loyalty is also owed to the psychologist's other clients: the court, each person evaluated, and, unless court-appointed, to one or more attorneys. The psychologist is, therefore, obligated to abide by ethical obligations regarding informed consent for those assessed, confidentiality, clarification of any matters related to fees, and so forth. "As adjuncts to the fact-finding process, psychologists must internalize the court's concern for objectivity, fairness, and the well-being of the child" (Weithorn, 1987, p. 193).

A dual relationship is automatically involved when a psychologist is both the therapist for any party to a custody action *and* an expert who is to offer information (and possibly recommendations) to the court. If either parent is the psychologist's patient/client, the psychologist may have a conflict of interest in that the best interests of the child and those of the patient/client may not be the same. If the psychologist believes the patient/client *would* be a good custodial parent, this potential conflict of interest may be avoidable. If the *child* is the patient/client, it may irreparably damage the progress of therapy if the psychologist is required to testify in open court regarding his knowledge and opinions. Doing so could create a conflict between the role of the child as patient/client on the one hand (including the issue of confidentiality) and the obligation of the psychologist to advocate for the best interests of the child on the other. This conflict may be resolvable only by having the psychologist meet in chambers with the judge and the attorneys, with the testimony being unavailable to the parents until therapy ends (Weithorn, 1987, pp. 196–97).

Having pointed out in an evaluation that one or more parties to an action should have individual or conjoint psychotherapy, it is not unusual for the independent or court-appointed evaluating psychologist to be asked to be the therapist for the party or parties, given that he already knows the family members well. If the request is for therapy to begin prior to the end of the custody matter, it would be unethical (as a dual relationship problem) for the psychologist to agree. If therapy is to begin after the custody matter is settled, there would no longer be a dual relationship and therapy could proceed. Therapy should proceed, however, only if all parties and attorneys agree that the psychologist's role as an independent evaluator has terminated and that the psychologist will no longer be required to fulfill the role of an independent expert in the case. Alternatively, the parties and their attorneys could stipulate that the psychologist remain an independent expert even though he is working with the couple on joint issues (as therapy or mediation). Once the psychologist becomes a therapist, his independent status is largely relinquished. It would not be unethical for a psychologist to evaluate a single parent or child and proceed to become the person's therapist while the custody matter is still under way.

It is always better to evaluate both parents, either through appointment by the court or agreement by the parents to jointly retain the expert for that purpose. Part of the reason is that the clinician is likely to feel "a subtle and almost irresistible pull toward advocacy . . . at the expense of the objective attitude for which clinicians must strive" (Grisso, 1990, p. 37). Second,

> some of the most important information obtained in custody cases is about the relationships between the parents. An arrangement that often does not give us access to both parents and the child places severe limits on what we can offer the court. . . . It is not clearly unethical for an examiner to be retained by one side, as long as the examiner restricts testimony to the narrow opinions formed with such limited information. (Grisso, 1990, p. 37)

Informal Discussions

There are no official procedural or ethical guidelines that prevent an expert from consulting with a peer or even talking with an attorney for "the other side" about a case in which the expert has been retained as an educator or a testimonial witness. Informally, however, attorneys have a norm that requires the attorney who retained the expert to be consulted prior to any discussions with that attorney's expert by opposing counsel. If an attorney used information from an informal encounter with an expert against the adverse party, any sanctions that may be imposed would be imposed on the attorney or the parties, not the experts. If a specific jurisdiction differs in any way from these conclusions, it is important for the attorney to so advise any experts he or she retains.

Appearance of Duality

The expert must also avoid the appearance of a dual relationship as much as possible. One way to do so is to limit phone calls from litigants, requesting that if they have information to add to what has been said during the evaluation that they write it down and mail it. Any expressed need for counseling should, of course, be referred to another professional. The expert should make notes on all phone calls received because they are part of the relevant clinical records. Through these processes, it should not appear as if the expert is favoring one of the parents in a custody suit or a particular litigant in a personal injury suit.

Fees

The evaluator must make it clear from the onset what fees will be charged for the services rendered. Consideration must be given to testing time, interpretation time, report writing time, consultation with attorneys, and testimony. It is general practice to include testing, interpreting, and report writing time in the evaluation fee. Some individuals prefer to charge a flat fee for the entire evaluation of each individual, and others prefer to charge on an hourly basis. Some evaluators charge the same flat fee for all individuals involved in the evaluation; others charge different fees for parents, children, and significant others, based on the amount of time that is put into evaluating each of these individuals.

A payment schedule should also be identified from the onset. The safest way for the evaluator to proceed is to request that the entire estimated amount of the evaluation be paid in the form of a retainer, escrowed in a trust account, or placed in the guardian ad litem's trust account to be paid upon completion of the evaluation. It is best to structure the fee schedule in a manner that requires all fees for the evaluation be paid prior to the distribution of the report. Since the APA *Ethical Principles of Psychologists and Code of Conduct* does not allow psychologists to withhold information for lack of payment, it is best to receive the entire retainer before the evaluation.

Psychologists who have agreed to wait for payment of fees generally find that their accounts receivable escalate rapidly and are difficult to collect for these cases. This will be particularly true of the fees due from the parent against whom the evaluator has recommended.

Fees for testimony should also be paid in advance. The evaluator should estimate the amount of time, including travel and preparation, that will be required for a court testimony. This axiom would hold whether applied to deposition testimony or court testimony. When the testimony fees are paid in advance, it is less likely that the witness will feel the need to unconsciously slant testimony in the direction of the individual paying the fee. A witness will perform better when he or she is not thinking, "I hope that the person who is supposed to pay my fee is impressed enough by my testimony to actually pay me when this is over." Advance payment also decreases the likelihood of being labeled a hired gun, since one can testify that payment is in no way contingent upon content of testimony.

It is not unusual for court proceedings to be canceled. This author informs individuals that the entire estimated amount of court time must be paid seven days in advance of the court date. In the eventuality that the court date is canceled less than seven days before trial, those portions of the fee collected that represent hours that the psychologist is able to fill with other income-producing work will be refunded or kept as a credit balance for future testimony. Those portions of the fee that represent time that cannot be filled will be kept by the psychologist.

Unfortunately, there are times when psychologists go to court, having blocked out a half day of their schedule, fully expecting to testify, only to learn that their testimony has been delayed to the next day. It becomes necessary for the psychologist to charge for both the unused and used time.

Although this may appear unfair to the individuals paying for the witness's time, attorneys and courts fully understand that when mental health professionals operate in the legal arena, it is necessary to take this position. As a result, complete preparation for court appearances and time in court may end up being paid for two or three times before the witness is finally permitted to testify.

On occasion, an attorney will ask the witness to block out a half day, a whole day, or several days. If a psychologist averages 10 hours of therapy a day, and he or she is asked to block out a full day, he or she should charge 10 times the hourly rate. Likewise, when psychologists generally work six hours a day, six times the normal hourly rate should be billed. Some individuals prefer to charge more per hour than their therapy hour rate, since legal time is billed on a clock hour, not a 50-minute hour, or because legal cases frequently involve numerous brief phone calls or other tasks for which one would not bill separately. The difference between the therapy hour rate and the legal hour rate should be proportionate.

Although psychologists generally do not charge for telephone time, brief consultation time, or brief review time, in the legal arena the psychologist should not be reluctant to charge for this time when substantial periods are involved. Attorneys use this method of billing and expect that other individuals will also. When getting involved in custody evaluation cases, the psychologist quickly becomes aware of the fact that the 15 to 20 minutes here and there can add up to hours of time that should be billed for. As a rule of thumb, one might charge for calls or other tasks involving 15 minutes or longer but consider brief calls and tasks part of the basic fee.

Contingency Fees

The expert needs to be independent to maximize objectivity. This independence is seriously compromised if the expert is not paid for each phase of the evaluation process as it is completed and would be even more seriously compromised if the expert worked on the basis of a contingency fee. Thus, the *Specialty Guidelines for Forensic Psychologists* (see Appendix C) state that:

> forensic psychologists do not provide professional services to parties to a legal proceeding on the basis of "contingent fees," when those services involve the offering of expert testimony to a court or administrative body, or when they call upon the psychologist to make affirmations or representations intended to be relied upon by third parties. (Committee on Ethical Guidelines for Forensic Psychologists, 1991, IV.B)

Similarly, the American Academy of Psychiatry and the Law (AAPL) *Ethical Guidelines for the Practice of Forensic Psychiatry* state that "contingency fees, because of the problems that these create in regard to honesty and striving for objectivity, should not be accepted. On the other hand, retainer fees do not create problems in regard to honesty and striving for objectivity and, therefore, may be accepted." If a retainer has not covered the cost of producing a written report, the report should not be furnished until the expert has been paid for all the work that led to its production (Blau, 1984).

Personal Notes/Work Product

Many evaluators believe in error. The notes they write during or following an evaluation are not subject to discovery.

> Notes taken during the course of an examination or interview for the purpose of recording relevant aspects of the individual's demeanor, verbal behavior and so forth are not considered personal notes. . . . Personal notes include only notations made for the personal use of the evaluator (e.g., hunches, speculations, areas to pursue) and which do not function as a basis, whether partial or otherwise, for the evaluator's professional product, testimony, or other evidence. (Golding, Grisso, & Shapiro, 1989, p. 9–10)

Hearsay

Experts may generally testify regarding things told to them in the course of their evaluations and research. However,

> While hearsay or otherwise inadmissible evidence may form the partial basis of their opinion, evidence or professional product, [psychologists] actively seek to minimize their reliance upon such evidence. Where circumstances reasonably permit, forensic psychologists seek to obtain independent and personal verification of data relied upon as part of their professional services to the court or to a party to a legal proceeding. . . . When data . . . has not been corroborated, but is nevertheless utilized, the forensic psychologist has an affirmative responsibility to clarify its evidentiary status and the reasons for relying upon such data. (Committee on Ethical Guidelines for Forensic Psychologists, 1991, VI.F)

Limits on Competency of Psychologist

No expert can claim to know everything of possible relevance to a case or to have done all possible research in the course of an evaluation. Therefore,

> Forensic psychologists have an *obligation* to present to the court, regarding the specific matters to which they will testify, the boundaries of their competence, the factual bases (knowledge, skill, experience, training, and education) for their qualifications as an expert, and the relevance of those factual bases to their qualification as an expert on the specific matters at issue. (Committee on the Ethical Guidelines for Forensic Psychologists, 1991, III.B)

A psychologist will be in violation of Principle A and Ethical Standard 1.04 of the *Ethical Principles of Psychologists and Code of Conduct* if he or she claims "expertise without sufficient training or experience, or engages in professional relationships with clients without sufficient training or experience and fails to adequately protect the welfare of their clients" (Blau, 1984).

Confidentiality Issues

The American Psychological Association clearly states guidelines for confidentiality in its *Ethical Principles of Psychologists and Code of Conduct* (see Appendix B). However, when an individual is involved in a custody dispute or personal injury suit, the aspects of confidentiality change substantially. If the evaluation is court ordered, individuals must understand that what occurs during the evaluation may not be confidential.

Generally, activity that takes place between a psychologist and a client is considered privileged communication. The information can only be supplied to others if a *release of information* form is signed by the parties involved. A client/patient can legally waive privilege, and, in some circumstances, a court can order the removal of privilege. Information is generally either privileged or not privileged. A psychologist should be careful about release authorizations that attempt to limit disclosure to just one person.

When utilizing a release of information form as part of a legal case, it is generally a good idea to have each individual sign a release, officially allowing the psychologist to talk with all the attorneys and any other evaluators. If other significant individuals would need to be contacted, then releases for these individuals should also be signed. This allows the psychologist to speak to all parties involved in the custody or personal injury matter, maximizing the accuracy and thoroughness of the evaluation. The release of information form should be stated in such a way that it allows for an *exchange* of information between the evaluator and the other parties. Furthermore, the release of information form should state if and when the release expires and that the individual has the right to withdraw the release at any time.

When an individual is seen in psychotherapy by a therapist and chooses not to have the content of that therapy process disclosed in the custody dispute or personal injury case, that individual may invoke privilege, and the therapist, in most states, may invoke it on behalf of the patient (at least if the therapist is a psychologist or psychiatrist). Social workers seldom have privileged communication status. It is important for the individual to realize, however, that privilege is an all or none situation—the therapist may not be allowed to disclose certain information and withhold other information. If the individual's psychological status is at issue in a personal injury case, the individual waives the privilege automatically.

Privileged Communication

Knapp and Vandecreek (1985), experts in the area of privileged communication, point out many concerns that have surfaced around the issue of confidentiality and privileged communication. The laws regarding privileged communication vary from state to state. Knapp and Vandecreek point out:

> only doctors can practice medicine, and only lawyers can practice the law. Psychiatrists, psychologists, social workers, mental health counselors and pastoral counselors, however, all provide psychotherapy.... Privileged communication laws often apply to psychiatrists and psychologists qualified for private practice, but less frequently for other mental health professionals who are likely to work in community mental health centers. (1985, p. 405)

The authors also emphasize that there needs to be a balance between what the court requires and what the psychotherapist requires. Both are working for the best interests of the children. At times, however, attorneys and judges feel pressure to discover everything about a particular case, while psychotherapists may be reluctant to disclose certain pieces of information because of the therapeutic harm that could come to the child or family. In sensitive situations, it can be suggested that the judge screen records privately in chambers before allowing open testimony in court. This may protect individuals from being required to expose irrelevant, potentially harmful information.

It is also the ethical obligation of the psychologist to inform the participants at the beginning of the evaluation (preferably in writing) regarding the nature of the evaluation, the extent of the evaluation, the cost and fee arrangements of the evaluation, and the amount of time the evaluation should take. The psychologist should also inform the parties of what will be done with the information after the evaluation process has been completed.

Maintaining Records

Although a specific standard has not been statutorily set for maintaining records in most states, the American Psychological Association Committee on Professional Practice has developed guidelines. They state that the complete record should be kept for 3 years after the last contact with the client. After that time, the complete record or a summary must be kept for another 12 years. Records involving minor children must be kept for 3 years after the child reaches maturity. The content of these records should include identifying data, dates of service, types of service, fees, assessment plans, summary reports, and/or testing reports and supporting data as may be appropriate, and any release of information obtained (APA, 1993).

ETHICAL DO'S AND DON'TS

This summary is based on a review of the American Psychological Association *Ethical Principles of Psychology and Code of Conduct*, the *Specialty Guidelines for Forensic Psychologists*, and other professional writing in this area. These principles require that psychologists follow the standards of practice. Although specific references to issues may not be identified in the Code, if they are presented in other official documents that represent the standard of practice, they must be followed. This section is not meant to be prescriptive in nature, as exceptions to any rule could occur. Each statement below is followed by a reference to the principle or standard that applies. The American Psychological Association *Ethical Principles of Psychology and Code of Conduct* will be referred to as the "Code" and the *Specialty Guidelines for Forensic Psychologists* will be referred to as "Guidelines."

- Do not transcend the boundaries of your expertise.
  (Code—Principle A; Standard 1.04(a))
- Do not misrepresent your qualifications.
  (Code—Principle B; Standard 1.04(a); 3.01(a); 3.03)
- Avoid dual relationships.
  (Code—Principle B; Standard 1.17(a, b); 7.03; Guidelines—IV, D (1,2))
- Discuss fees from the onset.
  (Standard 1.25(a, d, e))
- Do not release raw data to unqualified individuals.
  (Standard 2.02(b))
- Do not use obsolete tests.
  (Standard 2.07(a, b))
- Do not violate test security.
  (Standard 2.10)
- Inform patient/client of limits of confidentiality.
  (Standard 5.01(a); 5.05(a, b); Guidelines V, B)
- Report previously unreported child abuse.
  (Standard 5.05(a))
- Understand state laws of duty to warn and protect.
  (Standard 5.05(a))
- Do not withhold records for lack of payment.
  (Standard 5.11)
- Do not make recommendations without seeing both parents.
  (Standard 7.02(a, b, c); 7.04(b); Guidelines VI, H; *American Psychological Guidelines for Child Custody Evaluations*)
- Do not work on a contingency fee basis.
  (Guidelines IV, B)

In addition to the general ethical principles and conduct codes summarized in the preceding list, clinicians performing custody evaluations should adhere to the specific guidelines set forth in the APA *Guidelines for Child Custody Evaluations*. See Appendix D for a full summary of these guidelines.

CHAPTER 3

How Divorce Affects Families

DECISIONS TO DIVORCE

It appears that during the past two decades there has been a breakdown in the commitment of individuals to long-term relationships: Fewer people are staying with the same employer for the duration of their working years; moves from neighborhood to neighborhood and city to city are far more common; and there has been a steady increase in the divorce rate.

Today's laws make it relatively easy to obtain a divorce; in fact, many states have no-fault divorce laws. People seem to be choosing to divorce for less significant reasons. For example, an informal survey of therapists by the author indicates that some couples are divorcing because they are not good sexual partners or because their interests do not match perfectly with each other. A generation ago these were considered conflicts to be resolved within the marriage relationship, not reasons for terminating it. Unfortunately, the children of today's marriages are modeling their parents' behavior and are likely to reflect the same feelings their parents have toward interpersonal and marital relationships.

Divorce has increased significantly in the past 10 to 15 years. A study by Schwartz (1985) cited U.S. government data noting that the divorce rate increased from 0.3 per thousand population in 1867 to 5.0 per thousand in 1982. The rate almost doubled between 1968 (2.9 per thousand) and 1982. Schwartz also noted that the number of children affected by divorce increased dramatically: from 6.3 per thousand children under 18 years of age in 1950 to 18.7 per thousand in 1981.

ADVERSARIAL DIVORCE

One of the factors blamed for the rising divorce rate is the effect of the feminist movement on women. Women who may have previously allowed unreasonable domination by their husbands discovered a new assertiveness, thus changing the rules on which their relationship was based. When one's attitudes and views change, the spouse must be willing to adjust and change as well or the marriage will be in trouble.

One question that often arises is whether the couple should stay together for the sake of the children. Views on this issue have changed in the last decade or two. More than a generation ago, the notion was that people should remain married for the sake of the children no matter how bad the marriage was. But research has indicated that couples who stayed together for the sake of the children often ended up with maladjusted children. As a result, divorcing couples are likely to be less concerned about how the divorce affects the children. Unfortunately, research has shown that children can suffer maladjustment as a result of their parents' divorce as well.

Today, the question must be asked: When is it better to stay together for the sake of the children and when is it better to get divorced for the sake of the children? When answering this question, parents must realize that divorce adversely affects children. Parents consulting a therapist may say, "We are getting divorced and we want to do it in a way that won't upset our children," but there is no way for parents to divorce without initially upsetting their children and adversely affecting their children's future. When the parents' relationship is destructive, however, staying married has a greater adverse effect on the children than terminating the marriage. Examples of destructiveness in a marriage include verbal, physical and/or sexual abuse, frequent inappropriate expressions of anger, and continually involving the children in unresolved conflicts. Although parents may have fallen out of love, if they can cohabitate without exhibiting destructive behavior, breaking up the home will generally have a greater adverse effect on the children than staying in a home with parents who do not love each other (Wallerstein, 1986). Consequently, the parents' ability to control their feelings determines how much a divorce will affect their children adversely.

Adversarial versus Cooperative Divorce

Once parents have decided to divorce, many concerns must be addressed. The first concern is whether the divorce will be cooperative or adversarial. A *cooperative divorce* is one in which the parties are willing to meet, discuss, and resolve the issues without requiring a court battle. In cooperative divorces, attorneys generally encourage the mediation process, facilitate reaching a stipulation, and participate in negotiations when necessary. An *adversarial divorce* is one that leads to a legal contest or a court battle and involves attorneys assuming opposing positions in court. The adversarial divorce generally occurs when individuals are initially unwilling to enter into a cooperative process or when the cooperative process breaks down. It is important for attorneys today to be able to participate in both cooperative and adversarial divorce processes. A cooperative divorce will help children adjust; an adversarial divorce will be harmful.

DIVORCE MEDIATION

Divorce mediation has become relatively popular in recent years. Because many individuals present themselves as divorce mediators, it is important for anyone seeking mediation to select an individual who is qualified to be a divorce mediator. At this time, the Academy of Family Mediators accredits individuals based on their training and experience as mediators. Criteria for admission to the Academy of Family Mediators include at least 40 hours of mediation training, review of mediation agreements from at least 15 successfully completed mediations, and documentation from an already experienced mediator that the individual is qualified. (See also Appendix E.)

The mediation process can involve either one or two mediators. A divorce can be either fully mediated—resolving custody and placement issues, financial issues, division of property, and other related issues—or partially mediated.

One advantage of the mediation process is that when participants are cooperative, they can resolve divorce issues quickly, including custody concerns. A second advantage is that the mediation approach generally costs a fraction of the adversarial approach. In addition, the mediation approach has demonstrated that it leaves far fewer scars on the family members involved than the adversarial approach (Ellison, 1983). Furthermore, mediated divorces are much less likely to be relitigated than adversarial divorces (Erikson, 1984).

It is important to note that the mediation process is not designed to exclude attorneys from the divorce process; indeed, most mediators are either attorneys or psychotherapists with some level of training. However, some attorneys perceive their role as mediator to violate the Code of Professional Responsibility, because they perceive it as providing legal representation to both parties.

When a mediation agreement is reached, the parties submit it to their respective attorneys. The attorneys then will advise their clients as to the legality of any of the items agreed to and will make sure that the agreement is read into the court order as agreed upon. The court must then accept or reject the agreement.

THE ADVERSARIAL APPROACH

When the cooperative divorce process breaks down, the divorce process becomes more and more adversarial, resulting in less direct communication between the parties. Consequently, they have less direct control over the eventual outcome, which is vividly apparent when a judge, who is a relative stranger to the case and familiar with the situation for only a few hours at best, becomes responsible for making a decision that will affect the divorcing couple and their children for the rest of their lives.

ARBITRATION

Another approach that can be used to aid conflict resolution is arbitration. Arbitration can be either binding or nonbinding. *Binding arbitration* obligates the parties to follow the arbitrator's recommendations, but *nonbinding arbitration* allows the parties to disagree with the arbitrator and find remedies for their disagreement through other avenues. The author considers binding arbitration to be the best approach.

An arbitrator can be used in a number of different ways. For example, a retired judge may be appointed as an arbitrator to resolve small technical issues and avoid the necessity of going to court. Nonjudges can also serve as arbitrators for a number of different issues.

Sometimes, the mediation process allows resolution to a certain point, only to break down with a few minor details left unresolved. This may happen when the parties need to continue to fight with one another, unconsciously perceiving that battling the ex-spouse is a way of being able to maintain their relationship. The mediation process may need to end in arbitration when small issues cannot be resolved. For example, when all of the major marital property has been divided, but a list remains of items valued at less than $1,000 total, an arbitration approach can be used productively. The mediator may state, for example, that these issues will be mediated for three more sessions. If resolution has not been reached after the three sessions, the mediator becomes the binding arbitrator and determines who gets which pieces of property.

Although this approach can be used to wind up the mediation process, it can also be court ordered when the small issues remain unresolved and would only take up unnecessary court time. This approach alerts the parties that unless they find a way to reach a resolution themselves, the decision-making power will be taken out of their hands and given to someone else. This almost always serves to increase the parties' motivation to reach resolution.

JOINT VERSUS SOLE CUSTODY

Another issue that must be decided is whether to enter into a joint custody agreement or designate one of the parents as sole custodian. In a *joint custody* arrangement, both parents have equal legal rights with regard to their children's education, religious upbringing, and medical treatment. Joint custody, however, does not necessarily mean that the children will spend an equal amount of time with both parents. It is the placement decision that determines how much time the children will live with each parent. In a *sole custody* arrangement, the sole custodian holds all of the legal rights to decision making about the children's development and future. Joint custody is generally best for the parents and the children because it keeps both parents actively involved in the development of their children (Shiller, 1986). Steinman (1981) notes that joint custody arrangements done privately break down less frequently than joint custody arrangements ordered by the court. Pearson and Thoennes (1990) report that parents with joint custody felt they had better cooperation with ex-spouses and greater financial resources available to them than those with sole custody.

Joint custody works most effectively when the parents can communicate with one another. Practically speaking, it is likely that the couple was unable to communicate effectively while they were married; otherwise, they may not have divorced in the first place. When parents demonstrate that despite a considerable amount of effort and intervention, they cannot cooperate with each other even for the sake of their children, it may become necessary to designate a sole custodian. If a custody dispute ensues, it often forces the parties to become adversaries, each trying to demonstrate the incompetence of the other parent and the expertise of his or her own parenting skills. This process is usually destructive and tends to leave wounds that are very difficult to heal. It is ironic that, following an extended custody dispute that may include a considerable amount of mud-slinging, judges often conclude a case by stating, "The parties must now communicate effectively with one another for the sake of the children."

Several factors need to be considered when deciding whether joint or sole custody should be sought. First, can the parents sustain the communication that is necessary to maintain joint custody? Second, what kinds of children do well in a joint custody arrangement? Joint custody generally benefits younger children, because there are more ongoing issues that need to be discussed between the parents. Parents who can separate their own needs from their children's needs are much more likely to make good joint custodial parents. Joint custody should not be used as a compromise when no other solution can be achieved. The success or failure of joint custody will depend primarily on the parents' ability to communicate effectively with one another (Ilfeld, Ilfeld, & Alexander, 1982).

Kline, Tschann, Johnston, and Wallerstein (1989) studied how children adjust to joint versus sole custody situations. They found that there was no difference between children's adjustment to sole custody versus joint custody arrangements. However, they did find that "joint custody children had contact with both parents significantly more often than sole custody children" (Kline et al., 1989, p. 435). They concluded that despite having more access to both parents, joint custody children showed neither less disturbance nor better social and emotional adjustment after divorce than sole custody divorces.

Goldstein dealt with the concept of the best interest of the child in works published in 1973 and 1979. He is currently taking a retrospective look at the concept of best interest, based on the years of study since his original works were written. He takes a psychoanalytic point of view regarding visitation, custody arrangements, and related matters. He believes that courts should not force visitations, should leave the decisions of whether visits take place up to the noncustodial parent, and should not forcibly remove children from the custodial parent who refuses to cooperate with court orders. His final conclusion is that although judges may believe they are making decisions in the best interest of the children, they may indeed be putting children in harmful situations (Goldstein, 1991).

Gardner (1991) reminds the reader that joint custody is not for everyone. He identifies advantages to joint custody but also points out that there may be times when joint custody is harmful:

> It increases the chances that the children will be used as weapons or spies in parental conflicts; because no restraints are placed on the children, such use of the children is likely. . . . Automatic awarding of joint custody seldom takes into consideration the logistics of school attendance, and, therefore, it may cause problems in the educational realm as well, and . . . it may be confusing for the child to be shuttled between two homes—especially when there are different lifestyles, disciplinary measures, rules, and even socioeconomic conditions. (p. 90)

Gardner (1991, p. 91) identifies the following criteria as necessary when parents are considering joint custody:

1. Both parents [must be] reasonably capable of assuming the responsibilities of child rearing—their involvement with the children and affection for them [must be] approximately equal. When there is a significant difference between the parents in these areas, another custodial arrangement should be considered.

2. The parents must have demonstrated the capacity to cooperate reasonably and meaningfully in matters pertaining to raising their children. They must show the ability to communicate well and be willing to compromise when necessary to ensure the viability of the arrangement. The key words here are *cooperation* and *communication*.

3. The children's moving from home to home should not disrupt the school situation. Accordingly, the arrangement generally is possible only if both parents are living in the same public school district or reasonably close to the child's private school.

Gardner further states that parents who cannot communicate, cannot cooperate, or are actively involved in litigating sole custody should be considered poor candidates for joint custody.

Sorenson and Goldman (1989) performed research on the criteria used in deciding who will be the placement parent. Ninety-six judges were sampled in this research project. The research demonstrated that there were seven factors that derived from analysis of the data:

The first factor, Social Deviance, included criteria stating that the primary residential parent must: have no felony convictions; have no previous psychiatric treatment or hospitalization; and have no history of alcohol or drug abuse. The second factor, Parental Supports, describes the resources of the home environment, enough money to support the child, seeking a two-parent home, practicing their religion, and having community support groups to help in raising the children. The third factor, Tradition, includes criteria which in the past have been considered important for the child but are no longer part of the Florida Statutes in determining the custodian: the mother, if the child is 12 years or younger, the same sex as the child, biologically related to the child, and having held physical custody of the child from the separation to the divorce. The fourth factor includes only the child's wishes (Child's Wishes), while the fifth factor includes only the evaluation by an expert witness and a friend of the court (Psychological Evaluation). The sixth factor, Quality Time, is comprised of criteria that determine the time the custodian has available for the child: having evenings and weekends free for the child and not living with someone with whom the custodian is romantically involved. Finally, the seventh factor, Family Unity, consists of criteria describing who makes up the family unit: access to relatives and keeping siblings together. (Sorenson & Goldman, 1989, p. 77)

A significant majority of the judges in this study still favor the mother as custodial parent, believing that the mother is better able to provide for the needs of the children.

PHYSICAL PLACEMENT AND VISITATION SCHEDULES

In divorce situations, another important issue to decide is the physical placement of the children. Even when joint custody is awarded, one parent generally becomes the primary placement parent and the other, the secondary placement parent. Sometimes, *shared placement* is arranged, which allows the parents to have either an equal or approximately equal amount of time with their children. Traditionally, a placement parent and a "visiting parent" are designated. Because the term "visitation" has certain connotations that have become distasteful over the years, the new terminology is "periods of physical placement."

Hodges (1991, pp. 171–172) has presented guidelines for helping determine the most appropriate visitation patterns. He states that although they are not exhaustive, the following guidelines can be very helpful.

1. If the child is an only child and there are no special considerations, consider the developmental guidelines [see the discussion following this list].
2. If the parents have tried a developmentally inappropriate pattern with apparent success over some reasonable period of time, consider that

the child may be very adaptable. Evaluate whether there are symptoms or problems that are ignored by parents, such as difficulty at transfer, unusual levels of dependency, unusual levels of detachment or spaciness. If no symptoms are present, and the pattern is not widely divergent from the guidelines, acceptance of the deviation might be appropriate.

3. If the child shows symptoms of attachment problems, consider evaluation by a mental health professional.

4. If the child shows symptoms at transition from leaving one parent, consider (a) that visitation problems may exist (e.g., psychological abuse, sexual abuse, neglect, conflict); (b) that the child may attempt to please the parent who is being left; and (c) that the child may find leaving the parent less painful if everyone is upset and angry.

5. If the child shows symptoms at transition from leaving both parents, consider that the child (a) has difficulty with loss; (b) is trying to please both parents; and (c) has a difficult temperament and has difficulty with any change.

6. If an older sibling is present for parent access times and the child has bonded with the sibling, consider longer duration visits.

7. If the child is not bonded with the sibling(s) consider the developmental guidelines.

8. If the parents have chronic conflict, consider (a) third party transfer; (b) sole custody; (c) regular predictable visits; and (d) reduced frequency of transfers.

9. If the non-primary parent is psychopathological, consider reducing visitation frequency and duration. Also consider supervision or termination of parent access.

10. If the non-primary parent is an abuser, consider supervision or termination of parent access.

11. If the child has a difficult temperament, consider longer visitation duration and fewer changes. Consider providing stability in terms of where the visitation occurs.

12. If the child is severely alienated from the parent, consider very brief visits (one half-hour to one hour) with or without supervision.

13. If there is a great geographic distance between parents, consider frequent visits if the child is young, provided such visits are financially feasible. Half the time, have the primary parent take the child to the non-primary for visits with nightly return to the primary parent. Half the time, have the non-primary parent travel to the city of the primary parent. Avoid long visits for very young children. For children over seven, long visits tend to be better tolerated.

14. If there has been a long break in parent access with a wish to reinstate contact, consider phasing in a schedule to let the child get used to

the formerly absent parent and rebuild trust. If trust is absent in the child or the primary parent, consider a phase-in with supervision.

15. If the custodial parent is socially isolated, is under stress, has few friends or relatives available to share child care, and has low income, consider increasing visitation duration with the non-custodial parent to relieve the custodial parent from constant child care responsibilities.

16. If the child has an easy temperament and the parents want to change the guidelines, consider such compromises, but evaluate the effect on the child. Often, visitation schedules are related to convenience rather than to the child's welfare.

Hodges also provides developmental guidelines to help in the determination of an appropriate amount of visitation. He states:

> For infants from birth to six months, a frequent and predictable visitation pattern is recommended. The more frequently the non-custodial parent can be available, the longer the duration should be. For infants who can be visited only once or twice a week, visitations should not exceed one or two hours. (1991, p. 174)

He concludes, "If the six to 12 month old child has had little prior contact with the non-custodial parent, visitations should be short and frequent to provide familiarity and comfort for the infant" (p. 175). When children are 18 months to three years of age, they can handle less frequent visits than infants, "but consistency and frequency are still important. Long visitations during summer vacations are not recommended. Although the exact length of long visitation for this age child is not known, a child familiar with and bonded to the non-custodial parent can handle three to four days" (p. 177). Hodges believes that "for preschool children, professionals should take into account that conflict between parents and high quality parenting may be more important than the pattern of visitation. . . . Children from three to five benefit from highly predictable visits. Support of more frequent visitation should be the next level of priority after consistency" (p. 177).

As children move into the primary school age, Hodges believes that:

> [the] visitation pattern should minimize the interference with peer relationships. . . . If the parents have a reasonably cordial relationship, visitation more frequent than every other weekend may be desirable. At seven or eight years of age, children who have contact with non-custodial parents several times a week are the most content with visitation. . . . At ages 10 to 11, boys in particular seem to prefer less contact, perhaps only every other week with the non-custodial parent. . . . Long visitations during the summer are acceptable, but some contact with the non-custodial parent either through visitation or phone is desirable. (p. 179)

Finally, Hodges states that "visitation for adolescents should take into account that teenagers do not need contact for long duration with either parent. Weekend visitation may interfere with developmental needs to separate from both parents. Contact once or twice a week for an hour or more may be enough contact" (p. 180).

Hodges addresses the issue of long visitation for young children. Although it may be ideal for children under seven years of age to have shorter visits, it is not always practical. When long visitations are necessary, Hodges provides several guidelines. He indicates that an increase of object constancy is necessary for the young child. "[W]ith long separations, the child has increasing difficulty in maintaining an image of the absent parent. Photographs of the parent, cassette tapes of the favorite bedtime stories in the parent's voice, and frequent phone calls can help bridge the memory of the absent parent for the young child" (p. 185). This object constancy can also be maintained by bringing familiar objects such as dolls, toys, and blankets when the child visits the other parent. Whenever possible, the receiving parent should maintain the same routines for mealtimes, bedtimes, and discipline.

Periods of physical placement can vary. The traditional arrangement allows for an 11/3 split. This generally allows the primary parent to have the child(ren) 11 of every 14 days and the nonprimary placement parent to have them 3 of every 14 days. Generally, the 3 days involve a Friday night and Saturday one week and Friday night to Sunday the alternate week. Placement can be on an 11/3, 10/4, 9/5, 8/6, or 7/7 basis. These decisions generally depend on the availability of parents, the input from professionals, and the parents' desire to be involved in the upbringing of their children.

One of the more popular recent arrangements is the 9/5 split, which gives the secondary placement parent one overnight one week and a four-day weekend the alternate week. The four-day weekend is generally from Thursday night to Monday morning or Friday night to Tuesday morning. This allows the secondary placement parent to do more than visit with the children and to become actively involved with childrearing. It also requires active communication between parents. The 8/6 and 7/7 (or other 50/50 schedules) should not be considered unless parents communicate well.

This plan is nothing more than an extension of the traditional visitation schedule of alternating weekends. However, instead of the weekend being a Friday night to Sunday afternoon, it is a four-day weekend. With the long weekend, the parent will be required to help with homework, take children to lessons, take children to sporting activities, and provide discipline. This also reduces the likelihood that a parent will become a "Disneyland parent."

HOLIDAYS

When working out an arrangement for placement schedules, the common practice is to alternate holidays. The preference, however, is to share rather than alternate holidays. This, of course, depends on whether the parents are living in the same city. When holidays are alternated, the children miss spending each holiday with half their extended family. Not only do they miss visiting with one parent, they also miss visiting with the aunts, uncles, cousins, and grandparents on that side of the family. Provided the parents are living in the same city, most major holidays provide an opportunity for sharing. The author recommends the following plan for sharing holidays.

Thanksgiving

If one family has Thanksgiving dinner early in the day, the other family can have their Thanksgiving dinner late in the day. The children can eat Thanksgiving dinner with one family and have dessert with the other family. The parents can alternate having the children for dinner from year to year.

Christmas

The children can spend Christmas Eve with one parent and Christmas Day with the other parent. If both parents wish to have Christmas Eve or Christmas Day, then the Christmas Eve/Christmas Day placement can be rotated annually. This allows the children to spend part of Christmas with each family.

When children reach school age, the issue of Christmas/winter break becomes part of the holiday planning. Parents may wish to take a vacation with their children at Christmastime but are unable to do so because of the restrictions of the visitation schedule. One alternative allows the parents to share the winter break each year. For example, in odd-numbered years, the mother could have the children from the beginning of the vacation through Christmas Eve, and the father would have the children from Christmas Day until school starts again. During even-numbered years, the father would have the children from the beginning of the vacation through Christmas Eve, and the mother would have the remainder of the vacation. Thus, each year one of the parents would have a majority of the break and the other would have a shorter portion, but they would both be able to spend holiday-related time with their children.

Easter

The children can spend Easter morning and Easter brunch with one family and Easter dinner with the other family.

Fourth of July

Many activities take place on the Fourth of July, generally starting in the morning and ending with evening fireworks. The day can be divided so that the children go to the morning parade and have a picnic lunch with one family and then have dinner and fireworks with the other family. If both parents have the same preference, the arrangement can be rotated on an annual basis.

Other Holidays

The children should spend Mother's Day with their mother and Father's Day with their father, regardless of the established visitation schedules. On each parent's birthday, the children should also be available to visit that parent.

Because children's birthdays are seldom celebrated on the actual birth date, one parent can plan a birthday celebration for the child on the weekend prior to the actual birth date, with the other parent arranging a celebration for the weekend following the actual birth date.

Memorial Day and Labor Day are considered minor holidays and can either be alternated or shared, as the parents wish.

Several rules of thumb should be utilized as part of visitation and holiday schedules. They include:

1. Holiday placement supersedes regular placement schedules.
2. Whoever has the children at 6:00 p.m. is responsible for feeding the children.
3. The receiving parent will transport the children. This reduces concerns about parents being late in dropping off or picking up children.
4. Flexibility is necessary, with no requirement for parents to balance out hours that have been gained or lost. It is important for parents to understand that throughout the course of their children's minority, the time will even out.

JOINT CUSTODY/SHARED PLACEMENT: THE ACKERMAN PLAN

When parents divorce, often they both qualify as reasonable custodial parents and desire placement of the children. Unfortunately, in making decisions about sharing placement, judges sometimes fail to consider what is psychologically best for the children. Judges have issued orders requiring children to spend the first half of the week in one household and the second half of the week in the other household, alternating weeks, alternating every two weeks, alternating months, even alternating years. Orders have been issued allowing the mother to have the children on Monday, Wednesday, and Friday of one week; on Sunday, Tuesday, Thursday, and Saturday of the following week; and alternating that plan every two weeks. The problem with all of these alternating plans is that they do not provide the children with a sense of home and a secure base from which to operate. Now there is a plan that provides the parents with relatively equal time with the children throughout the year and at the same time allows the children a sense of security. The plan is a 9/5–10/4 flip-flop arrangement. Deciding that this was a mouthful, Judge Patrick Madden in Milwaukee County Circuit court labeled it the *Ackerman Plan.*

This plan allows one parent to have primary placement during schooltime (September 1 to June 1) on a 9/5 basis, as described previously. The other parent then would have the children for primary placement on a 10/4 basis during nonschool time. In this way the second parent would have the children 10 out of every 14 days, during which time the first parent has the children for a three-day weekend one week and an overnight the alternate week. Nonschool time is defined as June 1 to September 1, a week at Thanksgiving, two weeks at Christmas, and a week at Easter. This allows the 10/4 parent to have the children on a 10/4 basis 4 out of the 12 months of the year, and the 9/5 parent to have the children on a 9/5 basis 8 of the 12 months of the year. When all is tallied, the 9/5 parent has the children approximately 20 days more than the 10/4 parent.

One objection to the Ackerman Plan is that the 10/4 parent always has the children during holiday times. It must be noted that the 9/5 parent still has four days during these blocks of time in which to spend holiday time with the children. In addition, each parent can be allowed two or three weeks of uninterrupted time during the course of the year to allow for vacations.

When deciding which parent will have the children 9/5 during schooltime and which one will have the children 10/4 during nonschool time, several things must be considered. Generally, the parent who is better able to support the children academically should be the 9/5 parent during schooltime, and one who can provide and support recreational activities should be the 10/4 parent during nonschool time. Accordingly, child support should be established to reflect that the parents have the children on a nearly equal basis.

OTHER PLACEMENT SCHEDULES

The Ackerman Plan is only one example of a placement schedule. Cohen (1991) also provides several suggestions of samples of joint custody placement. Although alternate (50/50) placement schedules are not considered appropriate in most cases, the following plans can be considered if necessary (see figure 3.1).

	Mon.	Tues.	Wed.	Thur.	Fri.	Sat.	Sun.
Every Week	X	X	X／Y	Y	Y	Y	Y／X

X represents days spent at the father's home
Y represents days spent at the mother's home

	Mon.	Tues.	Wed.	Thur.	Fri.	Sat.	Sun.
Week I	Y	Y	X	X	X	X	X
Week II	Y	Y	X	X	Y	Y	Y
Week III	Y	Y	X	X	X	X	X
Week IV	Y	Y	X	X	Y	Y	Y

X represents days spent at the father's home
Y represents days spent at the mother's home

	Mon.	Tues.	Wed.	Thur.	Fri.	Sat.	Sun.
Week I	Y	Y	Y	Y	Y	X	X
Week II	Y	Y	Y	Y	Y	Y	Y
Week III	X	X	X	X	X	Y	Y
Week IV	X	X	X	X	X	X	X

X represents days spent at the father's home
Y represents days spent at the mother's home

Figure 3.1   Other placement schedules.

FACTORS AFFECTING ADULTS

Undoubtedly, divorce has a financial impact on a family, and it may be necessary for the mother to work outside the home after the divorce. Research clearly demonstrates that if the mother has worked before divorce, continuing to work after the divorce will not negatively affect the children. However, when a mother who did not work prior to the divorce is forced to get a job after the divorce, it will affect the children negatively. They will perceive this as a second loss: first Dad left, and now Mom is leaving also.

When parents cannot agree on custody and/or placement arrangements, it is often left to professionals to determine who would make the best custodial parent. Many factors can influence this decision, including psychological evaluations. Research has identified the following characteristics that are important in the custodial parent (Ackerman, 1984). Generally, the parent who is able to provide a more stable environment will make a better custodial parent (Roseby, 1984). A stable environment is generally defined by the number of times a parent has moved, employment history, and the physical setting in which the children will reside (Ackerman, 1984). The better custodial parent is the one who will be more sensitive to the developmental needs of the children and able to identify their current and future needs (Bronfenbrenner, 1979). Research has further demonstrated that the custodial parent of choice is less authoritarian, has a greater capacity to communicate, and generally provides appropriate intellectual stimulation in the home environment (Roseby, 1984).

POSITIVE ADJUSTMENT FOLLOWING DIVORCE

Many factors have been identified as leading to a relatively positive adjustment to the divorce process. Wallerstein and Kelly (1980) and Stolberg and Anker (1984) report that little change in financial stability leads to a positive adjustment. Wallerstein and Kelly (1980) and Hetherington, Cox, and Cox (1978) identify several variables that affect adjustment, including the emotional adjustment of the custodial parent, low levels of conflict between parents prior to and during the divorce process, and cooperative parenting following the divorce process. In addition, Wallerstein and Kelly believe that the approval and love from both parents and the availability of regular visitation from the noncustodial parent are also important factors. Kurdek and Berg (1983) point out that children adjust better, depending upon their age at the time of the marital rupture, if they have a high level of interpersonal understanding and if they have a high level of internal locus of control. The latter means that they are self-directed.

Neal (1983) identifies several stages a child must go through before fully adjusting to the divorce. They include:

1. Acknowledging the reality of the marital rupture.
2. Disengaging from parental conflict and distress in assuming customary pursuits.
3. Accepting the loss.
4. Resolving anger and self-blame.
5. Accepting the permanence of the divorce.
6. Achieving realistic hope regarding relationships.

Parents' Relationship Postdivorce

Masheter (1990, 1991) wrote two papers on the relationship between ex-spouses following divorce. In one study, she looked at friendly versus hostile feelings toward the ex-spouse and found that "contact was friendlier and quarreling was less frequent for those without children than with children. Lower well-being was associated with quarreling and pre-occupation, whereas contact frequency and affect had no relationship to well-being" (1991, p. 103). Masheter concludes:

> Children of divorced couples need on-going contact with both parents. There-fore, divorced parents, though they may dislike or be indifferent to each other, must not let these feelings interfere with their children's relationships with both parents. The implication is that former marriage partners must cooperate sufficiently to permit on-going contact between each parent and the children. Such cooperation implies some sort of relationship between ex-spouses, though it may not be pleasant or easy. (1990, p. 118)

Maccoby, Depner, and Mookin (1990) attempted to examine coparenting dynamics during the second year after divorce. It is generally agreed that the first year after divorce carries with it a significant number of adjustment problems. Maccoby et al. looked at children living either with mothers or fathers or having dual residences. They reported that the residential place-ment of the children had little bearing on the amount of conflict between the divorced parents. They did note that although the residential arrange-ment did not appear to affect the amount of acrimony between parents, the initial level of discord between parents had a noticeable impact on the subsequent quality of coparenting.

PARENTAL FACTORS

Effect of Divorce on Fathers' Roles

A number of researchers have evaluated the specific effect of divorce on fathers' roles. These studies looked at the differences between joint custody and noncustodial fathers, frequency of visitation, the attitudes of the single custodial father, and the relationships between single fathers and their chil-dren.

Greif and DeMaris (1990) studied 1,132 single fathers in an effort to identify their characteristics. They concluded that single fathers should be considered in the same context as single mothers. The same social dynamic issues must be addressed with single fathers as single mothers. In another study, Greif and DeMaris (1992) conclude that fathers no longer must have significant financial means to obtain custody. Furthermore, fathers should not be discouraged from pursuing placement of children based exclusively on the age of the children.

Facchino and Aron (1990) found that "single parent fathers were likely to be better adjusted if they were older and had completed college, if they had older children and had greater percentages of custody, and if they were dating" (p. 45).

According to Arditti (1992), joint custody fathers "saw their children more frequently, showed greater satisfaction with their custody arrangement, and had more education than fathers without custody" (p. 186).

Seltzer (1991) looked at the relationships between fathers and children who live with their mothers. She found that fathers who visit with their children are more likely to pay child support and be influential in child-rearing decisions. Richards and Goldenberg (1986) reported that fathers continue to feel hostility toward their ex-spouses, because they have reduced responsibilities within the family. Healy, Malley, and Stewart (1990) found that both frequency and regularity of fathers' visits positively correlate with their children's self-esteem. A reduction in the frequency or regularity of visits is also related to an increase in behavior problems for young children.

Effect of Divorce on Mothers' Roles

A number of researchers have specifically looked at the effect of divorce on mothers and their children. Greif (1987) surveyed 517 mothers without custody. He found that noncustodial mothers needed to improve their self-esteem, define themselves in roles broader than that of being a mother, and provide children with models when appropriate. Schachere (1990) researched the relationships between working mothers and their infants. She concluded, "[p]oor marital quality compounded by long working hours has produced the problems in attachment between working mothers and their infants. . ." (p. 31). Denham (1989), not too surprisingly, found that maternal emotions affected the emotions of their toddlers. The lower the mother's psychosocial functioning, the more negative the toddler's behavior. Greene and Leslie (1989) studied the mother-son relationship following divorce. They found that "a mother's attitude toward her former mate is related to how supportive and coercive her son reports her to be in their relationship. Likewise, how coercive the mother is perceived to be is related to the son's level of aggression in school" (p. 235).

Effects of Divorce on Homosexual Parents

Until recent years, a parent's acknowledged homosexuality led to almost immediate exclusion from consideration as a placement parent. As society in general and courts in particular have become more open-minded and understanding, the sexual preference of the parent has become less and less of an issue. Instead of looking at sexual preference as a primary issue, the parent's acceptance of his or her own sexual preference, how the sexual relationship is presented to the children, and the children's overall response to the homosexual parent's sexual preference are more important indicators. These parents today tend to be evaluated more on general factors than sexual preference factors. Kirkpatrick, Smith, and Roy (1981) compared children living with lesbian mothers and children living with heterosexual mothers. They found that the lesbian mothers placed greater concerns on providing appropriate adult male role models for their children than did the heterosexual mothers. In general, the children of lesbian mothers were as well adjusted as children of heterosexual mothers. Hoeffer (1981) found few differences between children of lesbian mothers and children of heterosexual mothers. It appeared as if the lesbian mothers had little negative impact upon the boys' behaviors.

Most of the studies have looked at the relationships between lesbian mothers and their children. Few studies have addressed homosexual fathers and their children. Studies that have been performed indicate that sons of homosexual fathers tend not to become homosexual themselves.

In Hodges's (1991) book on custody evaluations, he states that:

> in any family, it is important to evaluate that a child is not being exposed to sexually explicit material or to adults' sexual behavior. Questioning may need to be more explicit in an evaluation with a homosexual parent, because norms concerning parenting behavior are less well defined and the "coming-out" behavior (and concomitant increase in self-esteem) may conflict with "hiding" something about the homosexuality from the children. (p. 115)

Effects of Divorce on Parents

Wallerstein (1986) believes that women who are younger at the time of divorce (less than 40 years of age) generally are happier and have greater psychological growth. One-third of men never remarry. Individuals in their twenties at the time of divorce are considered to be the most vulnerable. Of those, 43% are still struggling financially 10 years later, 60% have an unstable residence, 30% have irregular employment, and more than 40% have a living standard that has declined in the past five years.

At the time of divorce, there is often a massive ego regression on the part of parents. People who had previously behaved reasonably well will behave poorly at this time. A spilling of aggressive and sexual impulses, in addition to intense depression, can occur. Much of this is based on the fact that most divorces are unilateral decisions. This results in a "narcissistic injury" of being rejected. Because a shared identity exists during the marriage, anxiety occurs based on the question "Who am I without the marriage?" This is similar to the identity crisis experienced by adolescents. Intense loneliness and diminished capacity can also occur in conjunction with ego regression.

Diminished Capacity of Parent

Diminished capacity goes hand in hand with the crisis in the adult. This diminished capacity can exhibit itself in many ways, including reduced sensitivity, poorer judgment, and less awareness of the children. It is difficult to maintain discipline in a family because parents do not want the child to become angry and reject them. There is an unconscious feeling that because the marriage contract has been broken, the parent does not have to be as attentive to the concerns of the children. This diminished capacity occurs at the time when the children's needs are greater and much more important than before. Diminished capacity can also lead to either a wish to abandon children or a greater dependency on them. This is one reason that many separations and divorces are precipitated by the birth of a child and the unconscious need to abandon the responsibility.

Parent Anger

It is difficult to divorce without anger arising between the parents. Ten years after the divorce, 40% of the women and 80% of the men are still as angry as they were at the time of the divorce. However, there appears to be no relationship between the persistence of anger and success in a remarriage. Therefore, the therapeutic adage that anger must be resolved prior to the commencement of a successful relationship does not necessarily hold true.

Much of the anger is associated with the traditional complaints that mothers have more time with children and fathers have a greater earning capacity. Anger is perpetuated when the mother becomes upset over the father's disposable income and the father becomes upset about the amount of time the mother has with the children. Each parent then tends to manipulate the visitation or money issue, which, in turn, interferes with the psychological well-being of the child.

Child Support

Because 88% of children of divorce live with their mother, and most fathers are required to provide child support, the research looks at fathers providing support. The father's continued payment of child support correlates with the psychological intactness of the father-child relationship, the full employment of the father, and the visiting pattern of the father. Visiting pattern does not refer to frequency as much as it does consistency. There is no correlation between the continued payment of child support and whether the father remarries. Fathers are likely to continue child support when they remarry unless they have lost contact with their children and have emotional ties with children from the second marriage.

Child support is generally not affected by a decline in the mother's socioeconomic circumstances, illness of the mother, or a downward socioeconomic move on the part of the mother. However, child support *is* affected by an increase in the mother's socioeconomic status: Support tends to go down if the mother starts making more money.

College Education

College education is something that is generally not included in the divorce agreement. So many issues need to be resolved at the time of divorce that attorneys are generally reluctant to add issues that are not relevant until the children reach adulthood. Unfortunately, as a result, college education is often not planned for in divorce situations. Even though the fathers could afford to pay for college, they often respond, "I have been an honorable man and paid my child support all these years and fulfilled my legal obligations. As a result, it is now the mother's responsibility to pay for the college education." This is often impossible, because the mother's earning capacity is generally significantly less than the father's.

Wallerstein studied 49 college-aged children. Only half the children attended college. Forty-two percent ended their education without a two-year degree. Only 20% of the children attended college with full support. The children tended to feel bitter and betrayed and a victim of their parents' divorce.

GRANDPARENTS' VISITATION

To date, all 50 states have passed laws giving grandparents the right to petition the court for legally enforced visitation privileges with their grandchildren (Thompson, Tinsley, Scalora, & Park, 1989, p. 1217), even over parental objections, under certain conditions. Research indicates that grandparents affect the development of their grandchildren by caregiving and providing both cognitive and social stimulation. In addition, they serve as an important resource of social support for the parents. Grandparents can act as historians, transmitting family values and traditions to succeeding generations. They also influence the grandchildren through their relationships with the adult children. Interestingly, the relationship between grandparents and grandchildren is shaped by the grandparents' relationship with their children. When separation and divorce occur, maternal grandparents tend to see the children more frequently and assume more of a parental role in their child's life by assisting the mother both financially and in other ways. By contrast, the paternal grandparents generally experience less contact with their grandchildren.

Grandparents generally turn to the courts for visitation rights only when no agreement between the parents can be reached. The existence of grandparent visitation statutes changes the grandparents' leverage over the child's parents when intergenerational disputes regarding the grandchildren occur. Some questions that remain unanswered at this point include whether grandparents should be notified of all changes regarding residence, visitation, and placement. One of the more common problems that occur with grandparent visitation is when the grandparents are allowed to see the children but the parent(s) is(are) not. Because of their sense of loyalty, the grandparents may allow the nonpermitted parent to visit the children, which becomes a loyalty issue between the grandparents and their children.

Grandparents' visitation may need to be restricted or eliminated altogether if they use their visitation time to brainwash the grandchildren in favor of one parent. Grandparents should not engage in destructive comments like, "Why does your mother keep accusing your father of . . . ," or "Things would be much better if your father would pay the child support he's supposed to." The very special relationship between grandparents and their grandchildren should be unencumbered by unwarranted pressure on the children.

Grandparents' Roles

Wallerstein (1986) believes the role of grandparents in the divorce process can be very important. When grandparents are committed to helping their grandchildren, it is a tremendous support during the divorce process. However, if grandparents choose to become part of the fight, it has an even greater adverse effect on the children. Grandparents can help counterbalance the problems occurring between the parents. They can help maintain a sense of family and self-esteem. Unfortunately, grandparents are available for support in only 25% of divorces.

FACTORS AFFECTING CHILDREN

Problems Children Experience

Researchers have predicted what proportion of children will be affected by divorce in the future. Hetherington, one of the most prominent and first researchers on divorce, estimated that 40% to 50% of children born in the 1970s will spend some time living with a single parent (Hetherington, 1979). Reports show that 28.5%, or 18 million of the 63 million children in the United States under 18 years of age, live in single-parent households (*Newsweek*, 1986).

Parents should be aware of several distinct problems that their children may confront following a divorce. It is unusual for children to experience divorce without some degree of difficulty.

Guilt and withdrawal of affection often cause children particular difficulty. Children, especially those five to seven years of age, may believe they caused the divorce (Wallerstein, 1986). A child may think, "If only I had been better," or "If only I had not made Mommy and Daddy scream so much, they would not be getting divorced." If children have been told that Mom and Dad divorced because they no longer love each other, they may reason that Mom and Dad no longer love them. The children should be told that adults had to fall in love, so they can fall out of love. In contrast, parents have *always* loved their children, so parents cannot fall out of love with them.

In a meta-analysis, Amato and Bruce (1991) reviewed 92 studies that evaluated how divorce affects children. They addressed the issues of parental absence, economic disadvantage, family conflict, and other related issues, with several interesting results. The authors conclude that "children who experience parental death tend to be better off than children who experience divorce" (1991, p. 39). When examining socioeconomic factors, the hypothesis that children are better off living with stepfathers rather than with single mothers was not supported, except among boys. However, "some support was found for the hypothesis that children have a higher level of well-being in father-custody families than mother-custody families" (p. 40). The authors' meta-analysis supported the conclusion that family conflict remains a significant factor in how children function. The impact of postdivorce conflict between parents was strongly associated with children's maladjustment, receiving the widest support among the general concerns.

Kalter, Kloner, Schreier, and Okla (1989) discussed the predictors of postjudgment adjustment. They found that parents' adjustment directly affects children's adjustment. They also report that negative changes in the mother's life negatively affect boys' adjustment to divorce, and the severity of problems negatively affects girls' adjustment to divorce.

Demo and Acock (1988) determined that a child's emotional adjustment, gender role identification, and antisocial behavior appeared to be affected by the divorce process. However, other dimensions of a child's well-being remain unaffected. Like other authors, Demo and Acock concluded that the level of family contact may also be a factor in the adjustment of children.

The divorce process necessitates a complex adjustment for both parents and children. Parents who think life will be much simpler when the divorce is final must remember that they will be required to have a relationship with their former spouse as long as their children are minors. In addition, adjusting to the demands of the divorce itself may take six months to a year (Wallerstein, 1986).

The adjustment period after the divorce is just as important for the children as it is for the parents. Furthermore, both parents and children must deal with the concerns of moving to a new neighborhood, going to a new school or job, getting used to new relationships, and becoming familiar with the visitation schedules.

Preschool Years

In establishing the placement arrangements, several considerations must be taken into account. The author believes that children under two years of age should generally not have overnight visitations. Franke states, "In visitation, a baby under two should not be moved back and forth between the homes of his divorced parents, for example, but should stay put in one place and have the parents visit him" (1983, p. 70).

> "It's too hard for the young mind to integrate that lack of constancy," says Frank Williams at Thaliens Community Mental Health Center in Los Angeles. "A baby needs not only the familiar shapes of the room and his own crib to make him feel secure. Not until the child is at least two years old does he or she have the maturity to tolerate spending alternate weekends or a summer stint as long as two weeks away from the familiarity of 'home.' In the interim, the baby will benefit from as much visitation as possible from the noncustodial parent." (Franke, 1983, p. 70)

The concern for very young children has been addressed by Ware (1982), who points out that children under two years of age should sleep in the same home to establish a home base. She suggests that the other parent visit on Monday, Wednesday, and all day Saturday.

Because young children need to have a home base, a 50/50 arrangement is usually not in the young child's best interest. A 50/50 arrangement should never be allowed when the parents live in different states, because it would require the children to continually move and adjust to different homes, schools, and neighborhood environments. A 50/50 arrangement can work effectively only when both parents live within the same school district and relatively close to one another. This affords the children the opportunity to attend the same school and maintain the same neighborhood friends while staying with either parent. This arrangement, of course, presupposes that the parents can communicate effectively with one another.

Franke (1983) looks at the way children of different ages respond to the process of divorce. She refers to the preschool years as the "age of guilt" (p. 73). During this period children feel guilty about their parents' divorce. They may think, "If I had been a better child, my parents would not have gotten divorced." It is important for parents of preschool children to explain the process of divorce in simple terms. In doing so, make sure that they understand that their behavior did not cause the divorce. Parents must strive to act in an adultlike manner in the presence of their children. If their anger causes them to react childishly, it will only confuse their preschool-aged children and make their adjustment to the divorce more difficult (Franke, 1983).

Gottman and Fainsilber-Katz (1989) performed research on four- and five-year-old children in an effort to determine how divorce affected the children's behavior. They found that marital discord negatively affected the children's level of play, their peer interaction and their physical health, and increased children's susceptibility to physical illness.

Elementary School Years

Franke (1983) refers to the years between six and eight as the "age of sadness" (p. 90). Children at this age have come to rely on the security of the family structure and interpret disruption of that structure as a collapse of their entire protective environment. Their emotional immaturity prevents these children from protecting themselves against these losses. The child's survival is threatened because "loss of one parent implies the loss of the other as well." Franke states that:

> anger, fear, betrayal, in the disruptive post-divorce household, and a deep sense of deprivation are the characteristic responses of children this age to divorce. But above all, the children feel sad, a persistent and sometimes crippling sadness that, even a year after the divorce, they have only been able to mute to resignation. (1983, p. 90)

The following example shows how this sadness pervades the child's life:

> Jacob is kicking a soccer ball around his backyard. In the garage he can see the oil stain where his father's car used to be and the hook where his father's golf bag used to hang. There are still a lot of tools on his father's workbench, but Jacob isn't allowed to touch them unless his father is there. And his father hasn't been there for six months. They were going to build a bicycle rack together, but that was before his father left. Now they probably never will. Jacob halfheartedly kicks the ball again. But it isn't fun. Nothing seems to be fun these days. (Franke, 1983, pp. 90–91)

Middle School Years

The period from 9 to 12 years of age has been called the "age of anger" (p. 112). This is a particularly crucial period of time in the child's life. It is essential to resolve the anger that is experienced during this period. Otherwise, it will be carried forward into later childhood and early adulthood and be extremely disruptive to relationships. Franke states:

> The bad news follows naturally from much of the good news. As team players, children have a very strict sense of fairness, of what is right and what is wrong. . . . Children live by a rigid code of ethics that stresses black and white definitions of loyalty and behavior. When the very parent who taught the child these rules does not abide by them, the child becomes angry—very angry. It is this deep and unrelenting anger that most characterizes the reaction to divorce of late latency-age children. Unlike younger children, who fight against feelings of anger toward a parent, these children often seek it out. Often the child chooses between the "good" and "bad," reserving so much hostility for the latter that visitation with the noncustodial parent sinks to an all-time low, especially for boys. (1983, p. 113)

The author believes that defusing the anger the child feels toward the parent is extremely important. Although it is tempting for the angry custodial parent to take advantage of the child's angry feelings, creating an alliance that may make the parent feel triumphant may prevent the child from resolving the divorce and moving on. Furthermore, this has a tendency to backfire in adolescence. The child may become angry with the custodial parent for encouraging his anger toward the noncustodial parent during the late latency years. He may even go as far as accusing the custodial parent of preventing a relationship with the other parent. Psychotherapy can help deal with these extraordinarily volatile feelings.

Shybunko (1989) researched the effect of divorce on middle school children. He found that "for this particular age group, after a period of at least two years, the divorce process does not necessarily produce impaired parent-child relationships or impaired child adjustment" (p. 309). The results did suggest, however, that children of divorced families were more inattentive, aggressive, or socially unpopular in school settings.

Sandler, Wolchit, Braver, and Fogas (1991) studied 206 children, aged 8 to 15. They concluded, "In predicting children's self-reported maladjustment (a) stable, positive events but not changes in positive events were related to lower maladjustment; (b) increased negative events were related to higher maladjustment; and (c) change for the worse was related to higher maladjustments" (p. 501).

High School Years

Franke (1983) refers to the teenage years as the "age of false maturity" (p. 150). She feels that the developmental tasks of adolescence are both exaggerated and blurred by the divorce process. It is "during the teens, when a child begins to act and think as an adult, that the lasting effect[s] of a badly resolved divorce—parental abandonment, inattention, or overdependence—suddenly jump to the fore" (p. 152). It is less difficult to help teenage children through divorce than younger children, because teens have already begun gaining independence from their parents and have some stability of their own. Nevertheless, it is important to be totally honest with the teenage children as to why the marriage failed. If it was caused by extramarital affairs, alcoholism, mental illness, or abuse, the teenagers should be told, sparing them the gruesome details. If they sensed that any of these issues had become a problem, they will be glad to know that their perceptions were accurate. Because teenagers are entering the age when meaningful heterosexual relationships are likely to develop, it is extremely important to handle these issues properly at the time of divorce. If teenagers emerge from the divorce feeling that interpersonal relationships are not worth the effort, their own meaningful relationships will be disrupted. On the other hand, if teenagers realize that the dissolution of the parents' marriage was related only to the relationship between the two and is not a generalization applicable to all relationships, they are more likely to be able to sustain meaningful relationships. It is especially important, even with teenagers, to reassure children that their parents still love them and that they did not cause the divorce.

Forehand et al. (1991) studied the functioning of adolescents for a two-year period after divorce. They studied 112 adolescents and found that adolescents from divorced families did not function as well as adolescents from intact families. The study examined the relationships in these adolescents' lives and found that the more conflict between the children's parents, the greater the likelihood of problems in the parent-adolescent relationship. In turn, problems in the parent-adolescent relationship were predictors of difficulties in adolescent functioning.

Frost and Pakiz (1990) studied 382 15-year-olds. They found that "those who experience parental separation more recently were most likely to be adversely affected, and that girls from recently disrupted families were more likely than boys to experience problems in emotional and behavioral functioning and were likely to express dissatisfaction with available levels of social support" (p. 544).

Carlson (1990) specifically looked at how observing marital violence can affect adolescents. She studied 101 adolescents from residential treatment centers, approximately half of whom had witnessed marital violence. They found that many of the adolescents who had witnessed marital violence reported being depressed, running away, hitting their parents, and being struck by a parent's dating partners.

College Years

Cain (1989) is one of the few researchers to examine the effects of parental divorce on college-aged children.

> Preliminary findings suggest that young adult offspring are likely to deny their parents' impending divorce, are more likely to ascribe blame to one parent than blame themselves, to use aggressive morality as a conduit for rage, to experience a series of role realignments post-parental divorce, and to demonstrate altered attitudes toward romantic love and marriage following their parents' mid-life divorce. (Cain, 1989, p. 135)

Bonkowski (1989) studied young adults between 18 and 21 years of age. She reported that when young adult children experienced their parents' divorce, they had difficulty establishing a separate relationship with each of the parents. Furthermore, they had a greater difficulty establishing a relationship with the father than the mother, possibly because fathers tended to be blamed for the divorce more frequently than mothers. Bonkowski concludes that although there was a lingering sadness in these adult children, most of them were able to overcome these concerns and progress in a developmentally appropriate way.

Lopez, Campbell, and Wadkins (1988) studied the relationship between parent divorce and college students' development. They compared 255 individuals from intact homes with 112 from divorced homes and found that college-aged children of divorce reported greater independence from their parents. As a result, they also demonstrated lower conflict with fathers.

Franklin, Janoff-Bulman, and Roberts (1990) performed two studies with college-aged children. They concluded that although college-aged children of divorce did not differ from intact family children on measures of depression and eight hypotheses tested, they were less optimistic about the success of their own future marriages and reported less trust in their future spouses.

Glenn and Kramer (1987) attempted to determine statistically the differences between subsequent divorces of children of divorce compared to children living with both parents. They studied gender, racial, and age differences and identified a "parental divorce effect," especially in white females. However, across all of the groupings, there did not appear to be as much of a familial trend in divorces as expected.

Barber and Eccles have reviewed the recent divorce research literature. They looked at a number of different variables and concluded:

[I]n summary, past research that has focused on the negative outcomes of divorces has been inconclusive. Although there seemed to be some small differences between children of divorced and intact families cognitive performance, delinquency, and self-esteem, these differences frequently disappear when confounding and mediating variables are controlled. The research on children of divorces is frequently flawed by serious methodological problems, reducing the generalized reliabilities of findings and leading to the possibility that the negative outcome attributed to divorce may, in fact, be due to economic struggle or parent conflict. Although it may be generally true that two parents can do a better job of raising children than one parent, it does not follow that all children are better off if their parents stay together. First, the negative consequences of being raised in a conflictual family may be averted if parents separate. Second, there may be some advantages to the socialization experienced by children growing up with their single mothers. Children in single-parent, female-headed families may develop a greater sense of personal responsibility and self-esteem, and girls and boys may develop less gender-role stereotyped occupational aspirations and family values, which could lead to their increased success in the labor market. (1992, p. 122)

Kaye (1989) performed research on 234 children of divorce, comparing them with 223 children from intact families. Grades and achievement test scores in a variety of academic areas were recorded for five consecutive years. He reports:

[T]he results showed that children had poor achievement test scores in the immediate aftermath of divorce. Their grades, on the other hand, did not seem to be adversely affected. By the fifth year following divorce, sex differences were pronounced with divorce adversely affecting the grades and achievement test scores of boys but not girls. (p. 283)

Kaye also found that the poor academic performance in children of divorce lasted approximately two to three years. In addition, they found that the younger the child, the more likely that divorce would adversely affect academic performance. Looking at content-specific areas, Kaye found that children of divorce show poorer quantitative skills than children from intact families.

Bisnair, Firestone, and Rynard (1990) studied factors that affected academic achievement in children following parental separation. They concluded:

> Elementary school children who maintained their academic performance following separation of their parents were compared with levels of those who declined. No single measure could accurately predict children's academic adjustment. Those who maintained performance level spent significantly more time with both parents. . . . In summary, 30 percent of the children in the present study experienced a marked decrease in their academic performance following parental separation, and this was evident three years later. Access to both parents seemed to be the most protective factor, in that it was associated with better academic adjustment. (p. 75)

In addition, Bisnair et al. found that the less time the mother spent at work and the more time the child spent with the noncustodial parent, the more academically competent the child was.

Mulholland, Watt, Philpott, and Sarlin (1991) reported similar results. They found that children of divorce showed academic deficits when compared with children from intact families even several years after the separation. They found "significant performance deficits in academic achievement, as reflected in grade point average and scholastic motivation in the middle school, but not in nationally normed tests of scholastic aptitude and other less direct measures of behavioral conformity" (p. 268).

Gender Differences

Zaslow (1988, 1989) wrote about gender differences throughout divorce, looking at a number of different variables. Her 1988 study concluded, as many other projects had, that boys are generally more negatively affected by divorce than girls. The second part of her study develops some hypotheses: "that boys do indeed respond more negatively to parental divorce, both immediately and over a period of years if they are living with an unmarried mother; whereas in post-divorce families involving a stepfather or father custody, girls fare worse" (1989, p. 136).

A study by Welch stated the following: "Experiencing parental divorce was associated with a greater tendency to join in coalition with mothers, the custodial parent in the present study, against fathers and a tendency to blame fathers for the divorce. A lasting negative effect of parental divorce on the father-child relationship was also found" (1991, p. 1).

Abandonment/Rejection

Another area of concern occurs when the children experience feelings of abandonment and/or rejection. Children often perceive that the noncustodial parent has left the home and abandoned them. A child who has relied on the noncustodial parent for certain things over time now finds this parent unavailable to provide those things. Even children who are capable of understanding that the separation may be court ordered and against the will of the noncustodial parent will usually feel abandoned and rejected. This seems to be especially true of children between the ages of five and seven. They are more likely to perceive the divorce as abandonment/rejection, because of their perception that they may have caused the divorce.

Powerlessness/Helplessness

Feelings of powerlessness and/or helplessness may result when children experience many changes in their lives and are unable to control them. For example, in a relatively short period of time, the household breaks up, the noncustodial parent must find a new dwelling, the custodial parent and the children may be required to move, the children find themselves in a new neighborhood and a new school, and there is a definite change in the financial status of the family. All of these major changes take place without the advice or consent of the children. Because these undesired changes are forced on the children, it leaves them feeling powerless and helpless.

During and shortly after the divorce, children may exhibit a greater need for nurturing or dependency than before. Having lost close contact with one parent, they are often concerned that the other parent may leave them too. It takes children of divorce a long time to understand that because one parent has left does not mean the other will leave them as well.

Insecurity

The feelings of guilt, abandonment/rejection, powerlessness/helplessness, and the need for nurturing/dependency can collectively lead to the larger problem of a child's becoming very insecure. The thought process may be, "All right, Mom just kicked Dad out of the house. How do I know she's not going to kick me out of the house, too?" When a custody battle is part of the divorce, there is good reason for feelings of insecurity. For example, "Mom and Dad and their lawyers are arguing about which parent I'm going to live with. I don't know what school I'll go to. And I don't know what neighborhood I'll live in and what friends I'll play with."

Children often feel that nothing is left of their former life, which may be an accurate conclusion. The children's activities, school, peer relationships, and family relationships may all remain unknown for a prolonged period, possibly six months to a year, until the custody battle is resolved. This uncertainty can lead to a noticeable insecurity on the part of the children.

Following a court decision determining where and with whom the child will live, new insecurities will almost certainly arise. The child may think, "OK, I'm going to move now. How do I know if I will do well in the new school? How do I know if I'm going to find friends in the neighborhood? How do I know things are going to work out? How do I know I'm not going to move again in another six months?"

A court decision may be only the beginning of a child's insecurity. If the noncustodial parent claims, "I'm going to appeal the decision," it prolongs the period of insecurity for the child. In the author's experience, the more often the custody issue is taken back to court, the longer the child experiences feelings of insecurity and the more likely these feelings will result in long-term psychological problems.

Regressive Behavior

Children may react to divorce by exhibiting regressive behavior. Generally, *regressive behavior* means a reversion to a former development level by adopting a previous habit. For example, children who have stopped thumb-sucking may go back to it. Children who have stopped wetting their pants or their beds (enuresis) or soiling their pants or their beds (encopresis) may revert to these behaviors. Just about any type of behavior that occurred in earlier childhood can recur during these regressive stages.

Several general rules should be considered when deciding whether professional intervention for regressive behavior is necessary. In many cases, children exhibit regressive behaviors in response to *any significant life changes*. A *significant life change* can be a change of school, a death in the family, a serious illness, a divorce, a marriage in the family, or a change in the composition of the household. In the author's experience, regressive behavior that lasts less than two weeks does not warrant intervention unless it is dangerous to the child. If all of the regressive behaviors lasting less than two weeks were addressed in therapy, children would be in and out of counseling for much of their childhood. Generally, if nonharmful regressive behavior lasts for a two- to four-week period, the parent(s) should consider the options in dealing with that behavior. If, during this two- or four-week period the behavior gradually subsides, there is little need to be concerned. However, when regressive behavior continues beyond four weeks, therapeutic intervention may be advised.

Acting-Out Behavior

Acting-out behavior frequently results from the child's sense of frustration and anger over the changes in his or her life. It is not unusual to see children of divorce, who were formerly well behaved, suddenly become involved in vandalism, shoplifting, or alcohol or other drug use or abuse. The degree of acting-out behavior tends to vary as a function of the divorce process.

As the issues become more immediate, such as court dates or interviews with attorneys, the acting-out behavior will likely increase. When a lull in the divorce process occurs, the acting-out behavior tends to subside.

Repetitive Behavior

Repetitive behavior can also be observed at the time of a divorce. *Repetitive behavior* is an act a child does repeatedly, such as asking the same question over and over or continually playing with the same toy. A child may be attempting to maintain or establish some kind of control over his or her life. The child may think, "Okay, I can't control what the courts say I have to do. I can't control which parent I'm going to live with. I can't control what house I'm going to live in, who my friends are going to be, and what school I'm going to go to. But maybe through some repetitive behavior I can demonstrate some control over my life." Although not this clearly defined, the child's thought process does follow a similar course. Prohibiting a child from engaging in repetitive behavior at this time may be somewhat dangerous. It may be the only "glue" holding the child together during the divorce process.

Of the problems just described, three or four appear to be deep-seated psychological problems that may require short-term or long-term therapeutic intervention. The author describes short-term intervention as treatment that takes six months or less, and long-term intervention as treatment that takes more than six months. Often, short-term intervention requires only a half dozen or fewer sessions. Usually, feelings of abandonment, powerlessness/helplessness, and insecurity can be dealt with just by helping the child understand the significant changes in his or her life.

Guilt

One problem that may require long-term intervention is guilt, which may come from many sources. Children may feel guilty because the parents are getting divorced, guilty because they cannot do anything to bring the parents back together, guilty because they perceive that some action of theirs led to the divorce, or they just have unexplained feelings of guilt. As a result, children will often find a concrete example on which to blame their abstract feeling, as illustrated in the following:

A 56-year-old man had been in therapy for over a year. He was staying in a terrible marriage and a terrible job experience. It came to the point that the man and the therapist felt that there was some underlying need to punish himself that kept him in these situations. At one point, the subject of his mother's death came up. His mother had died when he was 10 years old. When talking about his mother's death, he suddenly remembered the day his mother died. He was walking home from school and saw a baseball lying on somebody's front lawn. He took the baseball and walked home with it. When he got home he found out his mother had died. That night he decided that his mother died because God was punishing him for stealing the baseball.

This belief was born out of a 10-year-old's need to find a concrete reason for an abstract feeling.

Unresolved Anger

Two other problems that arise during the process of divorce are most important: unresolved anger and depression. In this author's experience, a child of divorce usually displays either unresolved anger, depression, or both. "The hapless child's fear of being overwhelmed by the intense feelings of sorrow, anger, rejection and yearning further block the acknowledgment of the family rupture" (Wallerstein, 1983, p. 234). This is of such great importance because people do not like to deal with anger, either their own or another's. In group or individual therapy, it is the most difficult problem for people to deal with and resolve. This author has observed that a child's anger following divorce is directed at almost everyone. Children are angry with their mother for kicking Dad out of the house, with Dad for doing the bad things that got him kicked out of the house, with themselves for whatever they perceived they did wrong that caused the divorce, with the people they think should have supported them through the process and did not, and with everyone who was less understanding than the children expected or wished them to be.

Sometimes, the anger is copied from the parents' example. The children may not know why the parents are angry, but they observe that their mother and father are angry and believe that is how they should act during the process of divorce.

Although often related to depression, anger has many specific associated problems. It can lead to acting-out behavior or *somatizing*, which involves converting psychological problems into bodily complaints. The following example provides an illustration of somatizing:

A nine-year-old child was referred for therapy because of stomach pains. She was using the stomach pains as an excuse to avoid participating in all activities. The pains had reached such severity that at times she was unable to stand erect. It must be noted that the girl was not merely using these pains as an excuse, but was really feeling the pain. In the first two therapy sessions, it became apparent that she was angry about the divorce that her parents had recently gone through. The therapist merely stated that it was okay to be angry and described different ways of expressing the anger appropriately as well as inappropriately. The pain symptoms subsided rather quickly at that point and did not return.

When this nine-year-old girl learned that it was acceptable to express the anger she had been suppressing, her physical symptoms disappeared.

Unlike younger children who generally fight the anger they feel toward a parent, many middle-aged children (ages 6 to 12) seem to seek it out. Often, the child, especially a boy, chooses hostility toward the noncustodial parent when visitation with the parent sinks to an all-time low. In many cases, young adults carry this unresolved anger with them into adulthood, and it becomes much more difficult to undo 20 years of repressed and unresolved feelings than to cope with new feelings. Often, the therapy process for young children involves providing a stable, reasonable, accepting adult who is not emotionally involved in the divorce process. This is not to suggest that anything is psychologically wrong with the parents. However, because of the emotional stress associated with divorce and the volatility of both parents' lives at that point, it is often difficult for them to provide the child with an objective viewpoint. As a result, the child comes to therapy, discovers that not all adults are experiencing what his parents are experiencing, and learns that it is all right to get angry without fear of reprisal.

Depression

Depression in children is the most frequently undiagnosed problem, sometimes because a child's acting-out behavior often masks depression. The diagnosis can be missed if the evaluator is a therapist who works primarily with adults. Children do not necessarily exhibit the classic signs of depression that adults exhibit; in fact, those symptoms are usually absent unless the child happens to be severely depressed. When a child is severely depressed, the diagnosis is relatively easy.

It should be pointed out that depression and unresolved anger are very closely related: Depression is often anger turned inward. Therefore, one way children learn to relieve their depression is by dealing with it indirectly, through outbursts of anger, rather than directly. Following these outbursts, the depression may subside somewhat. The symptoms of depression in children can be identified relatively easily in evaluations performed by psychologists who are trained to work with children.

The depressed child may be overlooked in school. This child usually sits quietly in the back of the classroom and causes no problems for the teacher. Genuine suicidal thoughts, a common characteristic in depressed adults, are relatively rare in depressed young children. Consequently, depression is often difficult for parents and teachers to recognize.

Preoccupations with death and loss may be an indication of depression. Inability to get along with friends, which was not a problem previously, may be another sign of depression. The desire to spend more time alone and not participate in family, school, or neighborhood activities may also be warning signs. And, certainly, obvious behaviors such as increased crying, serious suicidal talk, and noticeable loss of appetite should not go ignored.

Children need to be told that it is acceptable to be sad about what they are experiencing. They must be permitted to express their feelings. However, parents often will not allow their children to do so, not out of maliciousness, but more likely out of frustration. For example, after two weeks of listening to her child cry, the mother might yell, "Quit that damn crying already. You're driving me nuts." The child perceives that he is not allowed to feel sad or to express those feelings. Following the divorce, the child may actually experience a type of grief reaction. The grief process can follow the loss of a pet, a loved relative, or an object of affection. It can also occur when a friend moves away or the child suffers a similar loss. It is essential that the child have the opportunity to talk these feelings through.

Research on the Effects of Divorce on Children

A considerable amount of research has been done on how divorce affects children. A comprehensive study was done by Guidubaldi, Cleminsaw, Perry, Nastasi, and Adams (1984) at Kent State University. The study included 699 children from 38 states and was designed as a two-year longitudinal examination. All of the children were evaluated with regard to the effects of divorce at least two years after it occurred (Time 1); two years later the same children were reevaluated to determine their level of adjustment (Time 2). The Time 1 and Time 2 evaluations looked at intelligence scores, achievement scores, social behavior rating, school behavior rating, peer acceptance or rejection rating, and parent and teacher ratings. These variables were viewed on the basis of the child's grade, sex, race, occupation of parent, family income, and length of time in a single-parent household. Children from single-parent divorced homes were compared with children from families intact since birth.

The Time 1 study indicated that the physical health of children was significantly poorer in divorced homes than in intact homes. It further found that divorced-family male children were most adversely affected by the time they reached fifth grade. These children had significantly greater anxiety, were significantly more withdrawn, had physical acting-out behavior, had feelings of blame, were impulsive, talked irrelevantly, had significantly poorer reading and spelling achievement, had significantly greater referrals to the school psychologist, and had significantly greater nonregular classroom placements. Divorced-family male and female children in first grade showed these same differences between divorced and intact families. However, by fifth grade, divorced-family females were similar to intact family males and females at the same age levels. In other words, between first grade and fifth grade divorced-family female children were able to adjust, but divorced-family male children were not.

Two years later (Time 2), the average time since the divorce was 6.2 years. Again, the results were relatively similar. Divorced-family boys achieved significantly lower on 10 of the 46 variables measured, but girls were significantly lower on only one variable. When the children's adjustment was compared with intelligence, those individuals with lower intelligence had significantly poorer adjustment. When adjustment was compared to mental health variables, male children were significantly lower on six mental health variables. These studies suggest that girls are more stable over time and that boys manifest greater variability.

The children's home environment was evaluated to determine its effect on their adjustment. Higher-income families had significantly better adjustment than lower-income families. In addition, the quality of the relationship with the noncustodial parent predicted adjustment better than did the quality of the relationship with the custodial parent. Permissive child-rearing styles yielded better adjustment for girls but significantly poorer adjustment for boys.

The children's classroom setting was also evaluated. Four variables were identified as being important: (a) a safe and orderly environment, (b) high expectations, (c) the use of reinforcement practices, and (d) monitoring of progress. Children of divorce in a classroom that provided a safe and orderly environment showed significantly better adjustment than children of divorce in a less orderly classroom. For boys, frequent monitoring of school progress was negatively correlated with adjustment. However, the use of positive reinforcement practices did provide a positive correlation for adjustment with boys.

Judith Wallerstein's Research

Perhaps the most widely known research in the area of how divorce affects children has been performed by Judith Wallerstein. A compilation of more than 15 years of her research is presented here from a number of research journals and part of a weeklong seminar at the Cape Cod Institute.

Criticisms have been leveled against some of Wallerstein's research; claims have been made that she has generalized too much from the data presented, has used too small a sample to support her conclusions, and has not been entirely in step with the generalizations she has made. It must be noted that Wallerstein is a pioneer in the area of longitudinal studies, having presented the only information on a group of children who have been followed for up to 15 years. Certainly, future research will be performed that may demonstrate tighter research design methods. However, as a pioneer in the field, Wallerstein's conclusions are extremely important to understanding the effects of divorce on children.

Wallerstein found that the most vulnerable group at the time of separation was preschoolers. The second most vulnerable group was adolescents. At the 1-year mark, the girls had recovered, but many of the boys had worsened. At the 5-year mark, the boys were still much worse, with significantly higher learning and social problems. At the 10-year mark, this changed directions. The most psychologically vulnerable group at the entry into young adulthood was young women. These 19- to 23-year-old women were suffering much more from interpersonal relationship problems than young men of comparable age.

Children who are older at the time of the marital rupture typically respond worse than those who are younger. What affects the children most is not the marital rupture itself but the postmarital course in that family.

Young children do not see divorce as a time-limited behavior. The feeling is that it is going to last forever and that their life will be permanently changed. Young children of divorce do not use their peers for support at the beginning of the divorce process, because they feel they are betraying the confidence of the family in doing so. When children reach older adolescence, they are finally able to use each other for peer support. Siblings also provide support for each other unless they identify with a different parent.

Eighty percent of preschool children are not told that their parents are divorcing; they just wake up one morning to find a parent gone. The process of adjusting to divorce is more difficult when this occurs. It must also be noted that adjusting to divorce is different from adjusting to the death of a loved one. At the time of bereavement, for instance, the family rallies around and everybody comes together to support each other. However, during separation for divorce, the families tend to split apart.

Boys

The boys' relationship to their fathers is an important component of the divorce process. Studies show that boys are the saddest children initially. They also tend to worry more about whether they will be thrown out next and see themselves as being left with a powerful mother. Older boys worry more about whether they will find someone to love them.

Boys seek to be with fathers when they are living with a psychologically deteriorating mother or perceive a lack of warmth from the mother; when they are looking for a more permissive home; and when the father is not yet prepared to take responsibility for rearing a child. A particularly important finding is that the psychological adjustment of boys is related to the quality of the relationship with the father, not the frequency of the visits.

Girls

As girls grow older, they experience a greater degree of anxiety, because they are concerned about repeating their parents' experiences. They have a fear that no one will love them. In one-third of the cases studied, the level of anxiety reached the point of "derailing" the girl in forming relationships, going on to school, choosing a career, being social, and forming an independent life. One-third of the women approaching adulthood left home to live with a man shortly before or after high school graduation. They tended to be drifting, did not have as much interest in economic support as emotional support, and chose older men. They were afraid they would end up marrying a man like their father and were concerned about the problems associated with it.

Adolescence

Wallerstein found that boys need more contact with their fathers during adolescence. This appeared to be more critical for their overall psychological functioning than it was for girls. However, it is still a serious consideration for both boys and girls. She found that adolescent girls want acknowledgment from their father regarding their looks, their emerging womanhood, and their accomplishments. Rejection by the father at this critical stage of development led to further adjustment problems later.

Birth Order

Wallerstein noted that the oldest children in the family tend to do less well than younger children. When there are two children in the family, the younger of the two tends to do better. Being the oldest child in a divorced family places that child at greater risk for all types of problems. That child is required to take more responsibility for the absent parents' tasks. The custodial parent tends to depend on the older child more than on the younger children in the family. However, the youngest children are most frightened of being abandoned physically, a result of the emotional abandonment by the absent parent, and, as mentioned previously, are also more likely to feel that they caused the divorce.

Change of Placement to Father

Most of the research discusses placement with the mother because 88% of the children studied still live with their mothers. When children want to change placement to live with their father, it is often a difficult task. There is fear of moving toward the father and the unknown of never having lived alone with the father previously. Furthermore, this topic is very difficult to discuss with the mother, who is generally reluctant to enter into discussions about changing placement. Both parents are generally unaware of the child's fear and, as a result, cannot respond appropriately to it.

Overburdened Child

The concept of being overburdened refers to children who are required to deal with more, psychologically and developmentally, than they are prepared for at their stage of development. Wallerstein's work on the overburdened child is based on research performed with 700 individuals.

One type of overburdened child is required to take too much responsibility for growing up. The parent generally reneges on many of the parenting roles and leaves the child to fend for himself. A second type of overburdened child is responsible for maintaining the psychological functioning of the parent. If the parent demonstrates a diminished capacity to function as a result of the divorce, the child often ends up having to parent the parent.

Children in this category feel that it is their responsibility to ward off the parent's loneliness, depression, fear of disintegration, and other serious psychological concerns. A third situation that leads to overburdening the child occurs when the parents fight over the children and their affection, time, and alliance. It often occurs when parents cannot reconcile the fact that being divorced means they will spend less time with the children, whether or not they are the primary placement parent. The overburdening remains unresolved as more litigation and relitigation occur.

Young children are more vulnerable to overburdening than older children. A child is more likely to become overburdened if he or she is an only child. Parents also contribute to overburdening the child when they distort the child's role by taking the child to adult functions and even allowing the child to sleep with the parent.

Partly because of the experience of being overburdened, there is a 45% chance that children of divorce will also divorce. There is a 30% chance that these children of divorce will remarry and a 20% chance that they will be divorced a second time.

Five-Year Follow-Up Study

At the five-year mark in Wallerstein's research, those children who did poorly were in families where the fighting between the parents continued as if the divorce had never occurred. This was true with one-third of the children. They also did poorly when parenting skills remained diminished, when there had been a disruptive relationship with one parent, and when the child was left in the care of a psychologically ill parent. In general, these children experienced an overall diminished quality of life.

The children who did well at the five-year mark were those in situations where the diminished parenting had improved, where the parental fighting had significantly decreased, and where the contact with the father had been maintained. These were also children who had been separated from an emotionally disturbed parent, had grandparents who had been warmly involved, and in which the overall quality of life, including economics, had been reconstituted.

Thirty percent of the children five years after the divorce were still somewhat fixated developmentally where they were at the time of the divorce. They were still angry at their father and had established a closer relationship with their mother. Even adolescent males, who at this point would have normally moved in the direction of their fathers, were still fixated at the developmental age of relating more closely to the mother.

There was an increase in suicidal ideation in children at the five-year mark. Although 34% of the children were doing well, 37% of the children were clinically depressed. This was characterized by parents who continued to fight, parents who were more concerned about meeting their own needs than the needs of their children, and parents who were more concerned about developing their own interests. Furthermore, these children had parents who visited more capriciously.

Ten-Year Follow-Up Study

Wallerstein's 10-year study included 131 children, mostly middle class and mostly white, in Marin County, California. At the 10-year mark, 90% of the children were successfully contacted for the follow-up study. The children in the 10-year study were seen at the time of separation, 1 year after separation, 5 years after separation, and 10 years after separation. The benchmark date was separation, not divorce, because the psychological impact of divorce takes place in children at that time.

At the 10-year mark, the children who were young at the time of divorce were doing better because the postdivorce course for these children was easier. Younger children did not have vivid memories of the divorce process, whereas children who were nine years old or older at the time of divorce had vivid negative memories of the divorce and separation process. The older group tended to feel that their entire childhood and adolescence was spent in the shadow of their parents' divorce; they felt they had sacrificed a significant part of their carefree childhood through their parents' divorce. It was also noted at the 10-year study that hardly any of the children were aligned with one parent over the other. Furthermore, very few parents were still fighting with each other. This was in part because most of the children had reached adulthood and the issues over which they would have been fighting were no longer relevant.

Ten years after the divorce, women were generally economically worse off than their former husbands. However, they were less socially isolated than they had been.

Wallerstein noted a difference between the way boys and girls responded to divorce. A considerable amount of research has demonstrated that boys from divorced families do worse in every way than boys of intact families, whereas girls have reactions indistinguishable from those in intact families. However, Wallerstein's research demonstrates that when girls reach young adulthood, they have trouble trusting the reliability of their partner. They have great anxiety with regard to the relationship as a whole, with regard to the sexual aspects of the relationship, and with regard to trust. One of the implications that can be drawn from this research is that boys act out during childhood in response to the divorce. However, in doing so, they resolve their feelings about the divorce. On the other hand, girls tend to repress their concerns, which do not emerge until young adulthood when they attempt to establish meaningful relationships with others.

Fifteen-Year Follow-Up Study

Wallerstein has continued to enlighten the professional community with her insights about the long-term effects of divorce on children. A recent compilation of research in this area has been published in several sources. A summary of these findings follows.

Wallerstein states, "[T]he visiting-father relationship has no counterpart in the familiar family structure. We do not know the potentialities or limitations of the visiting-parent role in the psychological, social, or moral development of the child" (1991a, p. 349). In looking at long-term studies, Wallerstein points out that "the history of the pre-divorced family, the nature and events of the separation, all remain relevant to the outcome for adults and children alike" (1991a, p. 350). Wallerstein quotes the long-term Berkeley study that reports, "[B]y the time the marriage breaks down, many children have spent years feeling relatively unsupported by their parents in a home that they regard as ill-tended or conflict ridden. This experience of many years surely contributes to the anxiety, the vulnerability, and the symptoms of children as the difficulties rise to a crescendo" (1991a, p. 351). In Wallerstein's own 15-year follow-up study, she stated:

> [I]t is apparent that the third decade of life of many of these young people is critical for working out issues of man-woman relationships. A significant number entered psychotherapy, where they worked hard on issues of trying at long last to separate themselves from identification with the mother or the father or their guilt of having attained what a parent failed to achieve. Several young women reported that establishing a realistic view of the father enabled them for the first time to make a heartfelt commitment to a man within a loving relationship. (1991a, pp. 353–354)

She also found that half the children emerged as compassionate and competent people, but almost half were worried, underachieving, and self-deprecating.

In reviewing early research performed by many researchers, Wallerstein concluded, "[I]t is reasonable to assume that the psychic threat to the child is heightened when the parental conflict centers specifically on the child and when the parents engage in a continuing tug of war with the child as the object" (1991a, p. 354). This information is closely linked with a 1991 study done at Stanford, which demonstrates that girls are more likely to feel caught in the middle of the divorce process than boys. In addition, "[I]t is likely that the sense of the adolescent of being caught in the parental conflict is associated with feeling safe nowhere, and that the feeling of being used in the parental conflict is that of being exploited by those primarily charged with his or her welfare" (Wallerstein, 1991a, p. 355). Wallerstein also reports on a 1976 study by Furstenberg, in which "the researchers concluded that 'marital disruption effectively destroys the ongoing relationship between children and the biological father living outside the home in a majority of families" (1985, p. 356).

Wallerstein summarizes the current status of long-term research by stating:

There is no long-term study of patterns of overnight visiting for infants and toddlers, although the courts have issued orders for these very young children, including nursing babies. There is no long-term study of the psychological effects of the major divorce-related economic issues: the decline in family income; greater economic insecurity of the child; child support that ends when the child reaches age 18; and significant economic discrepancies between the parents' households over the post-divorce years. Much of the psychological research in divorce has dealt with white middle-class families. There is a pressing need to expand the database to include families at different socio-economic levels from diverse ethnic and racial populations. (1991a, p. 358)

Wallerstein also concludes:

Despite the complexity of the research, we have obviously learned a great deal. The earlier view of divorce as a short-lived crisis understood within the familiar paradigm of the crisis theory has given way to a more sober appraisal, accompanied by rising concern that a significant number of children suffer long-term, perhaps permanent detrimental effects from divorce, and that others experience submerged effects that may appear years later. This reappraisal has gone hand in hand with an increasing body of knowledge that shows that parental divorce does not fall neatly under the rubric of a circumscribed childhood trauma whose effects may or may not be sealed over at some subsequent time. Instead, from the child's perspective, divorce represents an ongoing condition of family life that gives rise to a series of particular experiences and multiple life changes throughout childhood, adolescence, and often extending into adulthood. (1991a, p. 358)

Wallerstein (1991a), at the Colorado Bar Association's annual conference, reflected on her years of work and research on divorced families. She made a number of observations. She indicated that 40% of the children had been surprised to find out that their parents were getting divorced. Furthermore, noting that boys have more difficulty at the time of divorce, Wallerstein feels that this is based on the boys entering the divorce experience with consolidated emotional difficulties. Because they are depleted in their capacity to deal with new trauma, they become symptomatic. This is in part because father-son relationships have generally started to deteriorate prior to the divorce. This was not true of father-daughter, mother-son, or mother-daughter relationships. She also noted that it was not the quantity of time that the father spent with the children during visitations that was important but the quality of the relationship.

Wallerstein also addressed the issue of females' responses. She stated that young women tended to be preoccupied with two fears as they approached adulthood: "He'll betray me, or he'll abandon me." She found that the divorce rate for young women from divorced families was 60% higher than the rate for young women from intact families. On the other hand, when boys reach young adulthood, the central issue is, "When she gets to know me, will she love me?" Wallerstein points out that parents staying together for the sake of the kids put too much pressure on the kids to be "perfect." It is not fair to the kids. Wallerstein concluded her comments by summarizing all of her years of experience: "Children of divorce do not need anything more than children of intact families; it's just harder to give them what they need."

FAMILY FACTORS

A number of factors affect the family as a whole and not just the children or the parents. Gardner's Parental Alienation Syndrome and many of the myths associated with divorce are discussed in this section.

Parental Alienation Syndrome

Gardner has been involved in divorce-related research and publications for several decades. In a recent publication, he describes *parental alienation syndrome*: "a disturbance in which children are preoccupied with deprecation and criticism of a parent—denigration that is unjustified and/or exaggerated" (1989, p. 266). Gardner believes there are two major reasons for the prevalence of parental alienation syndrome. He notes that although courts previously operated under the concept of acting in the best interest of the child, joint custody arrangements have become more popular in the last decade, resulting in more equal time shared with each parent. Gardner believes that these changes have placed women at a disadvantage in custody disputes, and, as a result, they are more likely than fathers to attempt to alienate their children from the other parent.

"Typically, the child is obsessed with hatred of a parent. These children speak of the parent with every vilification and profanity in their vocabulary—without embarrassment or guilt" (Gardner, 1989, p. 228). In an effort to justify the alienation, children will use trivial reasons for hating the other parent. They may actually become somewhat manipulative in this process, voicing their hatred of the other parent only in the presence of the "loved" parent. Children will avoid family therapy situations, because their manipulations may be revealed. Unfortunately, the hatred often extends to the child's grandparents, aunts, and uncles and any close friends of the hated parent. The child may not acknowledge greeting cards, may refuse presents, and may hang up on phone calls. These children tend to blindly accept the allegations of the loved parent against the hated parent.

Gardner identifies another symptom of parental alienation syndrome: lack of ambivalence. These children tend to look at both their hated parent and their loved parent in a black or white perspective.

Gardner identifies many factors that contribute to the development of parental alienation syndrome. The first factor is brainwashing, which he defines as "conscious acts of programming the child against the other parent" (1989, p. 233). He says that "the loved parent embarks upon an un-relenting campaign of denigration and, . . . at times, the criticism may even be delusional" (1989, p. 233). Gardner states, for example, that mothers may complain so much about the lack of financial support from the father that the children may actually fear going without food, clothing, and shelter. This, in turn, increases their hatred toward the father. Mothers may even exaggerate the minor problems of the father, such as identifying an infrequent drinker as an alcoholic or the husband who has moved out as abandoning the family. Gardner points out that when the brainwashing reaches delusional levels, the mother may actually pretend to have been hit when she was not or pretend that the father said things that he actually did not.

Mothers involved in brainwashing will use sarcasm by making statements like "After all these years, he's finally gotten around to taking you to a ball game" (Gardner, 1989, p. 236). Mothers can also distance the father by refusing to share school reports or refusing to allow the father to attend teachers' conferences and then complaining to the children that the father is not interested in the child's school performance.

Harassment is often used as an excuse for alienating a parent. An unfortunate cycle develops when the alienated father increases his efforts to communicate with his children but these efforts are met with accusations of harassment. It may appear that everything the children are doing takes priority over speaking with the father. The mother will interfere with the phone contacts by saying the children are busy, eating, watching television, or doing homework.

Gardner also points out that mothers may program their children against their fathers in subtle and unconscious ways. By using the subtle manner, she can then proclaim innocence to any accusations of brainwashing. These subtle criticisms often take the form of indirect communications, such as, "There are things I could say about your father than would make your hair stand on end; but I am not the kind of person who criticizes a parent to his children" (1989, p. 233). Or "What do you mean you are going to your father's house? Oh, what am I saying, that's wrong, I shouldn't have said that. I shouldn't discourage you from seeing your father" (1989, p. 239). Parents who allow children to make the decision regarding visitation may indirectly tell them not to visit. Or a mother may say, "You have to go see your father. If you don't, he'll take us to court" (1989, p. 239). This is all done without mentioning any positive benefits that may result from visiting with the father.

Another indirect way of alienating the father occurs when the mother moves a considerable distance away for no other reason than to be far from the father. It must be noted that these mothers are much less loving of their children than their actions would indicate, because a loving parent appreciates the importance of a relationship with the noncustodial parent.

Gardner identifies emotional factors within the child that may lead to parental alienation syndrome. For instance, the child's psychological bond with the loved parent may simply be stronger than the bond with the hated parent. If the child fears that this bond will be disrupted and that the preferred parent will become angry, the child may love the "loved" parent more and hate the "hated" parent more. Because he already feels abandoned by one parent, the child is unwilling to risk being abandoned by the other parent. "This fear of the loss of mother's love is the most important factor in the development of the symptoms . . . of parent alienation syndrome" (Gardner, 1989, p. 246). What fathers do not realize is that this obsessive hatred is really a disguise for deep love; the child does not hate the father but is afraid of losing the mother's affection. Although Gardner does not use the term, this is often described as a loyalty issue.

Finally, Gardner identifies situational factors that can contribute to parental alienation syndrome. He points out that the longer a child remains with a particular parent, the more the child will resist moving to the other parent. Another common situation is one "in which the child will develop complaints about the "hated' parent in which the child has observed a sibling being treated harshly or even being rejected for expressing their affection for the 'hated' parent" (1989, p. 249).

Gardner classifies parent alienation syndrome into severe, moderate, and mild cases and identifies several recommendations for dealing with parental alienation syndrome. In severe cases, "the mothers of these children are often fanatic. They use every mechanism at their disposal (legal and illegal) to prevent visitation. They are obsessed with antagonism towards their husbands. In many cases they are paranoid" (1989, p. 361). Unfortunately, these mothers do not respond to logic or appeals to reason. Children of these mothers end up being equally fanatic as a result of modeling their behavior. As a result, children can become panic-stricken when asked to visit their fathers. These panicked states become so severe as to render the possibility of visitation improbable. Unfortunately, cases of severe parental alienation syndrome do not respond to traditional therapeutic approaches. Traditional therapy for the children is also not beneficial because:

> [the] therapeutic exposure represents only a small fraction of the total amount of time of exposure to the mother's denigrations of the father. This is a sick psychological bond here between the mother and children that is not going to be changed by therapy as long as the children remain living with the mother. (Gardner, 1989, pp. 362–363)

Gardner believes that the first step in the treatment of children in this situation is to remove them from the mother's home and place them with the father. He also identifies very structured and drastic recommendations to facilitate this process:

> [F]ollowing this transfer, there must be a period of decompression and debriefing in which the mother has no opportunity at all for input to the children.

The hope here is to give the children the opportunity to reestablish the relationship with the alienated father, without significant contamination of the process by the brainwashing of the mother. Even telephone calls must be strictly prohibited for at least a few weeks, and perhaps longer. Then according to the therapist's judgment, slowly increasing contacts with the mother may be initiated. (1989, p. 363)

Gardner notes that, in some cases, the children may eventually be returned to the mother. However, if the mother continues to alienate the children, it may be necessary to consider never returning the children to the mother.

The fathers in these situations also need to be involved in individual therapy. The fathers must understand that the children do not sincerely hate them. A strong, healthy bond was established when the children were much younger, and the current allegations of hatred are merely a facet of a loyalty issue.

In moderate cases of parental alienation syndrome, the mothers are not as fanatic:

[T]hey are able to make some differentiation between allegations that are preposterous and those that are not. There is still, however, a campaign of denigration and a significant desire to withhold the children from the father as a vengeance maneuver. They will find a wide variety of excuses to interfere with or circumvent visitation. (Gardner, 1989, p. 365)

The children in this category are also less fanatic than those severely affected. Although they are likely to vilify the father in the presence of the mother, they are likely to give up this attitude in the father's presence.

Gardner believes that these families should be seen in family therapy by one therapist rather than several therapists. The likelihood of manipulation may actually increase if several therapists take part. The therapist involved in this type of case must not succumb to the notion of "respecting the wishes" of the children and may actually have to be quite directive. The therapist must also be aware that "the older children may promulgate the mother's programming down to the younger ones" (1989, p. 368). The pathology extends itself when the mother relies on the older children to make sure that the younger children act accordingly with the father. If this becomes an ongoing problem, it can be recommended that the older children visit separately from the younger children.

If transition from the mother to the father becomes difficult, a neutral place, such as the therapist's office, the guardian ad litem's office, or a social service agency office, can be used for the transfer of children. It is also important for the therapist to understand that the mother may be continuing the acrimony in the relationship as a way of remaining in a relationship with the former husband, although it may appear to be a sick reason for doing so. It becomes the therapist's obligation, if this is occurring, to help the mother move beyond that type of thinking.

In cases of moderate parental alienation syndrome, the fathers must learn not to take the children's vilifications too seriously. When the children engage in this type of denigration, the father must be encouraged to help avert their attention to healthier interchanges. The entire therapy process can be aided if a therapist can "find some healthy 'insider' on the mother's side of the family" (Gardner, 1989, p. 372). For example, "the mother's mother can become a very powerful therapeutic ally if the therapist is able to enlist her services" (1989, p. 372). Last, Gardner suggests that with moderate cases, the therapist must be a strong individual who is not psychoanalytically oriented but can be directive and structuring when necessary.

In mild cases of parental alienation syndrome, mothers are generally more psychologically healthy than the mothers in the moderate or severe cases. They recognize that alienation from the father may not be in their children's best interest, and they are less likely to become involved in ongoing litigation. These mothers also recognize that protracted litigation could cause everyone in the family to suffer. Nevertheless, there may still be some minor acts of programming, but without paranoia. Children of these mothers tend to be more interested in strengthening their position with their mother than in openly denigrating their father. When a final court order results in primary placement with the mother, the fear of being transferred to the father is reduced, and the parental alienation syndrome generally disappears.

Gardner points out "that without the proper placement of the child (for which a court order may be necessary) treatment may be futile" (1989, p. 374).

Gardner also states that the guardian ad litem's role in these cases can be very important. He sees the guardian ad litem as being a potentially powerful ally for the therapist in working with families where parental alienation syndrome is present. He cautions, however, that if the guardian ad litem is not familiar with the consequences of parental alienation syndrome, the guardian ad litem may become manipulated into "supporting the children's positions" to their actual detriment. Because guardians ad litem are assigned to act in the best interest of their wards, they may have great difficulty in supporting "coercive maneuvers" such as "insisting that the children visit with the father who they profess they hate" because "it goes so much against the traditional orientation to clients in which they often automatically align themselves with their client's cause" (1989, p. 375).

ADDED PROBLEMS OF DIVORCE

This section reflects a combination of 20 years of experience by this author in working with divorce cases. Many of the problems reported are also reported by other therapists and research.

During the divorce process, it is not only the parents who are getting divorced. The child gets divorced, too, even though the legal document does not specifically record the child's name. Interest in normal childhood activities decreases at this time. It is almost as if the child is saying, "What's the use? Mom and Dad are getting divorced, so why should I worry about something as trivial as school?" The child becomes preoccupied with the divorce and, as a result, may be distracted easily. This preoccupation is manifested in feelings of anger, helplessness, and insecurity. The child's teacher may be trying to explain an important concept, but the child is wondering how much longer he or she will be in that school or neighborhood. Often, academic performance can be a barometer of how the divorce is affecting the child. When a former A/B student suddenly becomes a C/D student, the divorce is obviously having a dramatic effect on the child.

Children of divorce often carry with them the magical wish that their parents will get back together again. In a significant number of cases, this wish is carried into adulthood. Unfortunately, this issue is frequently ignored by the parents. As a result, it remains unresolved in adulthood. When one of the parents decides to date or to remarry, this unresolved issue may cause problems. A child may try to interfere with the parent's decision, not because he or she dislikes the new person, not because he or she cannot get along with the new person, but because the new person is interfering with the fantasy that the natural parents will get back together. The child reasons, "If Mom marries this man, then she cannot remarry Dad." In this situation, children may consciously or unconsciously act inappropriately in an effort to sabotage the upcoming marriage.

Another problem associated with divorce is that the child may not have an appropriate sex role model. This tends to be a problem more often with male children than with female children. Most frequently the mother becomes the custodial parent and the female child has an appropriate sex role model. It is very important for a male child to have a strong male role model available. This is particularly true during the onset of pubescence and adolescence. An uncle, an older cousin, or an organization like Boy Scouts or Big Brothers can provide this type of role model. Although the Big Brother organization can be beneficial, there is one key concern with this group—it requires only a one-year commitment. Consequently, just as the child is becoming comfortable with his new Big Brother, the Big Brother may leave his life. This may be interpreted as additional abandonment/rejection that the child must resolve.

In addition to not having an appropriate sex role model, the child may not have an appropriate heterosexual relationship model. After the divorce, it can be important for children to see their parents experience anger and then resolve it. It is also important for children to see their parents hug and kiss another adult in a meaningful relationship or sit close to another adult on the sofa. Furthermore, it is extremely important for children to witness the process of resolving disagreement. This scenario is often absent in a divorce situation. Immediately prior to the divorce, children may see only the arguing but no resolution. They do not have the opportunity to see their mother and father interacting positively as husband and wife. As a result, their last male/female relationship model has been a negative one.

When this type of positive model is absent, children may have difficulty in establishing their own relationships as they approach adulthood. They may not know how to establish good, healthy heterosexual relationships because they never witnessed one during their childhood. Typically, divorces beget divorces. When these children get married and have difficulties within their marriages, they see divorce as the means of resolving these difficulties rather than developing interpersonal communication skills.

When parents separate, one parent stays home and the other parent finds an alternate living situation. It is particularly important for children to see where the noncustodial parent is living as soon as possible after the separation, because the children are still concerned about both parents. They want to know that the noncustodial parent still has a place to sleep, a stove to cook on, and a bathroom to use. Young children are very much at the primary needs level and want to make sure that the noncustodial parent's primary needs of eating, sleeping, and eliminating are being met. If this opportunity is not provided, children often entertain the fantasy that the noncustodial parent has been kicked out of the house and has only the car to live in. This process may be particularly difficult for children if the non-custodial parent is required to move from a large house to a small efficiency apartment.

It is helpful when divorced parents continue to be involved in the children's educational and sporting events. Parents should be able to put aside their differences long enough to attend parent conferences together at school. If they attend school plays or athletic events, it is not necessary for them to sit with each other. However, it may be very important for the child to know that both parents are present. It is unfortunate when one parent states that he or she will not be present if the other parent is going to be there. If parents decide to attend parent conferences together, they should avoid using these occasions as arguing grounds or as a means of expressing anger toward each other.

In the first two chapters, the reader was introduced to the concepts of custody evaluations and the psychologist's responsibilities. This chapter has addressed decisions that parents need to make as part of the divorce process and the effects of the divorce process on children, parents, and the families as a whole. Professionals should be sensitive to the factors discussed in these chapters as they perform custody evaluations. Chapters 4 through 8 discuss the evaluation process, which will rely heavily on the preceding information.

CHAPTER 4

Interviews, Behavioral Observations, and Collateral Information

INTERVIEWS

The interview is an integral part of any evaluation process. The length and the extent of the interview varies from evaluator to evaluator. The evaluator must realize when beginning the evaluation process that the most frequent complaint that parents have about their evaluations is not having sufficient time to "tell their story." The evaluator may have performed hundreds of custody evaluations, but, in most cases, this is the only custody evaluation that the parent has participated in. Even when evaluators attempt to shorten the interview process by providing extensive questionnaires, parents still do not feel that they have had enough time to tell their story unless there is sufficient face-to-face time. Keilin and Bloom's (1986) study reported that the average evaluator spends approximately two hours of interview time with each parent and an hour and a half of interview time with each child.

There generally is not a correct or incorrect way to conduct the interview process; however, several factors can be useful in structuring the interview. Some psychologists prefer to interview the parents completely before they interview the children, whereas others prefer to divide the interview time so that the parents and children are interviewed on a staggered basis, with follow-up interviews after everyone has had an initial interview. Since each of the parties in the custody evaluation is likely to be making statements about other parties, it is essential that the concerns generated during the initial interviews be clarified during subsequent interviews. As a result, it is good practice to interview the mother and father individually for an hour or more each, followed by interviewing the children, followed by reinterviewing the parents for an hour each. It may be necessary, after interviewing the parents for a second time, to reinterview the children.

The content of the interview also varies from evaluator to evaluator. Some interviewers feel that it is essential to engage in an exhaustive interview process that details all personal history from birth to the time of the evaluation. Other evaluators feel that it is only necessary to interview individuals about those areas that are specifically relevant to the custody evaluation. In the latter case, introductory questions would be asked about the subject's various developmental stages. When nothing relevant is generated by the initial questions, additional detailed information is not sought. This streamlines the interview process, saving both time and money.

Interviewing Parents

This author commences every interview with the same open-ended statement: "I guess the best place to start would be for you to tell me a little bit about what you know about why we are meeting today." This allows interviewees to start at any point that they feel comfortable with. Clinically, the first thing the parent brings up is often of significance.

When basic demographic information has not been obtained through a questionnaire, it should be obtained during the interview process. In addition, information in several areas should be pursued, including:

1. Place of residence. The interview should also address the number of times that the individual has moved and what the current living environment is like.

2. Place of employment. This section should also discuss job satisfaction, ability for promotion, and duration of employment.

3. Employment history. The employment history does not need to include part-time jobs held during school. However, if the interviewee has only had part-time jobs, then considerable discussion should clarify why. Similarly, if an individual has changed jobs more than once every few years, that should be discussed, with consideration given to calling former employers to verify information.

4. Educational history. This portion of the interview can be very straightforward but may require extensive discussion if the interviewee has dropped out of school, failed out of school, or not completed any high school or college degree program that was begun.

5. Names and ages of children, and whether the children are living at home. In the case where children are residing in another residence, either exclusively or on a primary placement basis, discussion should include why, for how long, and the quality of contact.

6. Previous psychological or psychiatric treatment. Releases should be sought from all previous or present therapists, counselors, or physicians who have prescribed psychiatric medications. This portion of the interview should discuss whether the treatment was inpatient or outpatient, what the diagnosis and treatment were, what the outcome was, and what the individual learned from the therapeutic process. It can also be beneficial to determine if the therapy was terminated by mutual agreement, by the therapist, or by the client/patient leaving prematurely. Furthermore, this section should also discuss whether any psychiatric medications have been taken previously or are currently being taken.

7. *Alcohol or other drug use/abuse history.* Although some individuals consider alcohol and other drug abuse as falling under the category of psychological or psychiatric treatment, it is frequently viewed as a separate category. It is important to obtain the parents' perceptions of the quantity of drinking and whether drinking has ever interfered with employment, school, social relationships, or familial relationships. Discussions should also include whether the individual has ever been involved in any alcohol or other drug abuse treatment. When the answer is affirmative, it is essential to determine if the parent is still involved in aftercare. One of the most frequent indications of relapse in alcohol and other drug abuse patients is termination of aftercare less than two years posttreatment.

8. *Problems with the law.* Ordinarily, this portion of the interview would not include problems that the parent had during teenage years or minor problems during college years. However, when there is a considerable history of difficulty with the law during childhood and adolescence, this area needs to be explored in further detail. One of the more important components to be identified during this portion of the interview is whether these problems were isolated or are related to a chronic behavior pattern. When an individual has had three or four arrests for the same or similar crimes, it is significant, even when these arrests may have been spread over a period of 20 or 25 years. The evaluator must also determine if the problems with the law were in any way related to psychological problems and, if they were, whether treatment was sought.

9. *Information about the family of origin.* Questions in this area would include whether parents are living or deceased and if deceased, when they died and how the parent grieved the loss. Familial histories of alcoholism, suicide, mental illness, divorce, and other serious concerns should be discussed in detail. The types of occupations or professions the individual's parents had and the relative success of their employment careers should also be discussed. As part of discussions about the family of origin, ages of siblings, marital status of siblings, and closeness with siblings should also be discussed.

10. *Any problems with developmental milestones.* Not only should the parents be interviewed about whether they had problems with any developmental milestones but, also, whether the children who are subjects of the custody evaluation had any problems with developmental milestones. It can be particularly interesting if the parents have different perceptions of the developmental milestones and any related problems that their children had. History of walking, talking, toilet training, eating patterns, sleeping patterns,

unusual childhood illnesses, and seizure disorders would be of particular interest.

11. History of sexual abuse or assault. Since sexual abuse or sexual assault can have a profound, long-term negative impact on individuals, it is essential that this area be explored in detail when parents answer in the affirmative. Questions in this area should include particulars about when the abuse or assault occurred, who the perpetrator was, what the resolution was, if Protective Services was involved, whether any legal action was taken, and whether the individual sought any therapeutic relief following the abuse or assault.

12. Current medical problems. When the medical problems are serious in nature, discussion must include how it is being treated and if the illness affects the parent's activities of daily living.

13. Major stressors in parents' lives. Does the parent perceive that there are currently any major stressors in his or her life, other than the divorce or postjudgment dispute? Again, when the answer is affirmative, detailed questions must be asked about how these stressors affect the parent, the child(ren), employment, and/or social relationships.

14. Previous marriage history. When parents have been previously married, the evaluator must determine whether there were children from that marriage. Questions should be asked about where those children are residing. If they reside with the parent being interviewed, questions should also address how much time the other parent is spending with the child(ren), what the parent being interviewed feels about the relationship of these children with the other parent, and questions that would identify any other problems. In the case where the children are living with the other parent, questions should address how much time the parent being interviewed spends with those children and, specifically, whether any problems are associated with those contact times. If so, additional questioning should ensue. In cases where the parent being interviewed did not receive custody or placement of the children from a previous marriage, that parent should be questioned about whether placement was determined by a court order or stipulation, or through mediation. When the court ordered that the child be placed with the other parent, details should be sought as to why the court made that decision. It is not necessary to obtain detailed information as to why the previous marriage ended in divorce, but summary information would be beneficial. However, when there were major problems with the previous marriage, further questioning would be beneficial.

All parent interviews end with the same question, that is, "In thinking about coming in here, is there anything you wanted to tell me that I haven't asked you about?" This allows the parent to cover any issue areas that may not have been adequately covered in the interview. It is not unusual for parents to respond to this question by merely summarizing the points of concern that had been generated earlier.

Outside Activities

Although the outside activities that the individual engages in are not central to the decision-making process in child custody evaluations, they do help provide a picture as to how broadly based the parent's activities are. These questions should ask about organizations that the parent belongs to, hobbies, skills, interests, and generally how free time is spent. A well-rounded person will have some outside activities and will be a better role model, all things being equal.

Custody/Placement

In addition to background questions, several questions should be asked about the current divorce situation. They would include questions addressing the following issues:

 1. *Problems with visitation or periods of physical placement.* When problems have occurred, details should be sought identifying the cause of the problems, remedies that have been sought for the problems, and what the parent feels he or she has contributed to the problem(s).

 2. *Reasons the parent feels he or she would make the best custodial or placement parent.* When addressing this issue, the parents may need to be redirected. They often have the need to spend time explaining what is wrong with the other parent, when they have basically been asked to explain why he or she would make the best custodial or placement parent. Those parents who require frequent redirecting on this issue are likely to be ones who are overly zealous in their efforts to denigrate the other parent.

 3. *Reasons the parent feels that the other parent would* not *make an appropriate custodial or placement parent.* Several interesting situations may arise in answering questions in this area. The evaluator is likely to be prepared to receive a lengthy list of problems with the other parent, especially since they are involved in a custody determination dispute. Generally, these lists are either very short or not forthcoming. A noticeable number of parents will also respond by making a statement similar to "I am not here to bad-mouth the other parent" or "I am uncomfortable criticizing the other parent" or "I am not saying that he shouldn't be the placement parent, I am only saying that I feel that I would make a better placement parent." When parents respond in this manner, it is a very positive sign. Any issues that the parent identifies as being a concern should be questioned in detail. These questions would try to determine the exact nature of the concerns and to identify any collateral source that could provide additional information to support the concern. For example, when a parent states, "I'm concerned

about the children driving in the car with him because he always drinks and drives," follow-up questioning would include whether the other parent has ever been arrested for driving under the influence of alcohol or received alcoholism treatment, and related questions.

4. Concerns that the parent feels that the other parent has about him or her. It is particularly important for people to recognize their own shortcomings. In addition, when parents are able to identify the other parent's concerns, it demonstrates that they are clearly in touch with what the process is about and are more likely to be able to make necessary changes. It is also of note when a parent identifies a problem that he or she feels the other parent is concerned about, if the other parent does not raise that same issue.

5. What the parent considers the ideal placement schedule to be. The response to a question addressing placement schedules can help the evaluator determine how reasonable the parent being interviewed will be with time the children spend with the other parent. When a parent states, for example, "I should get 95% of the time and he should get 5% of the time," this represents a parent who does not understand the importance of contact between the children and both parents. This "ideal placement" question should also address the issues of the variability in placement schedules during the school year as compared to nonschool time (vacations, summer). Last, this area should also identify the amount of time the parent is willing to allow the children to have with the other parent.

6. Reason for the current divorce. When the child custody evaluation is the result of a postjudgment action and the parties are already divorced, this question should address the reason for the divorce when it occurred. It is not necessary to cover every small detail as to why the divorce occurred. However, issues of concern should be pursued with follow-up questioning.

7. Living environment. Questions about the living environment that the parent will provide for the child(ren) should include questions about place of residence, school, use of day care, use of baby sitters, neighborhood setting, and other related issues. The evaluator should determine whether the parent has identified a sufficient number and range of support system elements to ensure the child(ren) will be well cared for.

8. Description of child. Questions should be asked to determine how aware the parent is of the interests, activities, and general life of the child. These questions should be related to school, likes and dislikes, outside activities, strengths and weaknesses, and peer and family relationships of each of the children.

9. Discipline. Questions about what the parent considers appropriate discipline should be pursued. Instead of asking parents if they spank their children, which is likely to be answered in the negative, it may be more beneficial to ask the question in the form of "How often do you spank your children?" In the latter format, the parent is more likely to respond honestly.

A series of open-ended or projective questions are also beneficial in identifying potential areas of concern. These questions include:

1. If you had three wishes, what would your three wishes be? Reality orientation, preoccupation with the concerns being addressed in the evaluation, and ability to deal with an open-ended question of this nature are important to assess.

2. If you could live anywhere in the world, where would you want to live?

3. If you could be anybody in the world, living or dead, who would you want to be? This question often addresses issues about self-esteem and role identification.

4. What do you like best about [name of other parent]? It is generally a negative indicator for placement when a parent cannot identify any positive attributes of the other parent.

5. If you could change one thing about the other parent, what would you want to change? If details in answering this question have not come forth during the general interview, they should be asked at this time.

6. The same questions of What do you like best about . . ? and What would you like to change about . . ? should be asked about each child, stepparents (if any exist), and the individual being evaluated.

7. A series of feeling-related questions should be asked, including, Tell me something that makes you happy, Tell me something that makes you sad, Tell me something that makes you mad, Tell me something that you worry about, and Tell me something that you are afraid of.

8. The last series of questions involves future orientation. These questions include What would you like to be doing in 5 years?; What would you like to be doing in 10 years?; and What would you like to be doing in 25 years? These questions can be beneficial to determine the future orientation of the individual. In addition, the answers will also provide information regarding the reality base from which the parent operates. Parents who are not able to provide answers to these questions are less likely to be able to model future orientation for the children.

In relatively uneventful life histories, all of these areas can easily be covered within two hours. Where there is extensive history in many of these areas, the interview process could last for as long as four to six hours spread over several interviews.

In follow-up interviews, it is always important to address issues that the other parent or the children have raised during their interviews. In doing so, it is helpful to attempt to avoid putting the other parent on the defensive.

Instead, indicate that you are only requesting that they respond to the concern generated by the other parent, to "hear both sides of the story."

Child Interviews

All children three years of age and older should be interviewed individually. Certainly the younger the child is, the less involved the interview process is likely to be. With very young children, interviews may actually be relatively short due to language limitations, lack of awareness of problems within the family, or unwillingness to respond. Even so, the attempt should be made.

Although children three to five years old may wish to have a parent present during the interview process, it is generally not a good idea to use this format. Any time a parent is in the interview room with the child, the child is likely to respond to questions in the direction that the child perceives the parent wishes. There is no harm in having the parent bring the child to the interview room and leave prior to the content-related questions. In situations where the child is unwilling to allow the parent to leave the evaluation room, it may be helpful to have the other parent bring the child on a different occasion and have that parent attempt to leave the child. It is of clinical significance, and should be noted, when the child is willing to be left with the psychologist by one parent but not the other. In situations where the child refuses to be left after this process has been attempted a number of times on several different occasions, it is appropriate to abandon attempts to interview that child. It is also of note when a child older than four or five years of age demonstrates the problems just described with younger children. When this is the case, it becomes essential for the interviewer to attempt to determine what has occurred in the childrearing practices that has resulted in this immature behavior.

It is inappropriate to ask a child where he or she would like to be placed. Not only does this empower the child, it can also lead to feelings of guilt and confusion. Just as we do not allow children to choose bedtimes, meals, and whether or not they will attend school, we must not let them choose regarding this important issue. However, as part of the evaluation process, we are concerned about how the child perceives each of the parents and environments. A series of questions can be helpful in this regard. They include:

1. How would you feel if the judge said you should live with your father? and next, How would you feel if the judge said you should live with your mother? When the child responds in either the affirmative or the negative, follow-up questions should be asked to clarify the reason for the response, unless the child has already given a detailed response in the original answer. When the child gives an ambivalent response, care must be taken to avoid putting too much pressure on the child

by requiring them to answer the question when they really do not want to.

2. As a follow-up to the above area, children can be asked, Would you like to see your mother/father more time, less time, or about the same amount of time? The answer should be explored in detail, especially if the child wants more or less contact when they have an ample amount of time or the answer is "about the same" if they do not have much time at present.

3. When you do something bad, how does your mother/father punish you? When children respond with answers that suggest physical punishment, it is essential to query about the extent of the punishment, the implements used for punishment, and whether any injury has resulted from the punishment. Certainly, if previously undisclosed physical abuse is identified at this time, it becomes necessary for the evaluator to report the findings to the Child Protective Services agency in one's community. As a follow-up to the discipline/punishment questions, a series of questions such as Did your mother/father ever hurt you? would be asked. Again, if the answer is in the affirmative, details should be sought.

4. While talking about the subject of hurt or injury, questions like Did your mother ever hurt your father? or Did your father ever hurt your mother? should also be asked. In asking these questions, the examiner would have the opportunity to pursue any details that may be clinically significant.

5. One of the areas of concern is whether either or both of the parents coached the child to say something that would be advantageous to that parent's case. Generally, this can be dealt with by asking the question, What did your mother/father tell you to be sure to tell me today? Coaching is generally easy to discern. In those cases where coaching has not taken place, the child is likely to look at the evaluator in a confused manner and say things like "I don't know" or "nothing" or "just be honest." However, in those instances where the parent has actually encouraged the child to share certain information, the child generally will respond with a long, rather well-rehearsed litany of statements. When asked to discuss this again at some point later in the interview, the child is likely to repeat the same information either verbatim or almost verbatim.

6. Concerns are often raised about substance abuse on the part of the parents. As a result, this author has recently started to include the question, Have you ever seen your mother/father drunk? as part of the interview process. A yes answer would be followed by questions about frequency and behavior of the parent when under the influence of alcohol.

7. Each child should be asked if he or she has talked about the divorce with anyone. This provides the examiner with the opportunity to determine if either or both of the parents are sharing inappropriate information with the child. Since it is disadvantageous for the children to know more information than is necessary, parents sharing such information would be a negative indicator.

8. A series of questions should be asked about parental involvement with the child. Not only should these questions deal with discipline, addressed earlier, but they should also include questions like:

   • What kinds of activities does your mother/father do with you?
   • Who takes you to school?
   • Who goes to school conferences?
   • Who drives car pools?
   • What activities do you go to with your grandparents/aunts/uncles/cousins?
   • Who helps you with homework? Who takes you to the doctor?
   • What are the household rules and who enforces them?
   • Do you go to religious school and, if so, who takes you?

All of these questions can be used as part of the determination of which parent is more actively involved with the child(ren). It is not unusual, once the custody dispute has commenced, for a previously relatively inactive parent to suddenly become active. As a result, it can be helpful to ask children if there has been any change in the activity of either of the parents recently. This can be accomplished by asking, Has your mother/father started doing anything now that he/she has not done before?

Abuse Allegations

In recent years, abuse allegations have occurred in significant proportions in child custody evaluations. If they are not directly made, they are often indirectly alluded to by one or both of the parents, knowing the impact they are likely to have on the custody determination. As a result, this author has recently included abuse-related questions in all interviews. The initial questions include "good touch/bad touch" questions, for example, Do you know what a good touch and a bad touch is? In most cases, the child will respond correctly. When the child does not respond correctly, it is important for the evaluator to provide some information about good touches and bad touches. When a child states that he or she knows what good and bad touches are, the evaluator states, "Give me an example of a good touch" and "Give me an example of a bad touch." At that time, the child should be asked if anyone has ever "bad touched" him or her. If the answer is yes, then considerable further inquiry is necessary.

In those instances where the child has indicated that a bad touch has occurred or a sexual abuse allegation has been made prior to the evaluation process, a series of guidelines should be followed. When the allegation occurs outside the context of the evaluation, the interview should be conducted as soon as possible after the allegation has been made. Johnson and Howell (1993, p. 221) have provided guidelines for interviewing in sexual abuse allegations. They state:

1. The interview should be conducted as soon as possible after the allegation of abuse has been made. This reduces the likelihood of contamination of the information and allows the child to share the information as quickly as possible.

2. The interview should be conducted in a neutral setting that is physically comfortable. Not only should the setting be neutral, but neither of the parents should be present during the interview process. This is likely to contaminate the situation if it occurs.

3. The person who conducts the interview should not confuse the roles of therapist and investigator. It is important to note that often the therapist cannot serve in the role of an investigator without interfering with the therapeutic process.

4. The reality-testing of the child should be evaluated at the onset to determine whether perceptual disturbances may have influenced accurate encoding in the original memory trace. Since we know that younger children are likely to have incomplete memories, this is particularly important.

5. The evaluator must be aware that young children do not understand temporal and/or sequential concepts very well. As a result, although it may be felt that the information provided is not very accurate, it is instead the result of developmental concerns.

6. The evaluator must be aware that preschoolers are especially susceptible to suggestion. When the initial statement in an interview, whether conducted by a mental health professional or law enforcement agency, is, "Show me on these dolls where your daddy touched you," the entire process from that point forward has been contaminated and can, unfortunately, allow for a perpetrator to escape prosecution.

7. The evaluator must be aware of the cognitive and semantic levels of the child. Since younger children operate at a very concrete level of functioning, the examiner must be aware of children's understanding of words to be able to adequately interview them.

When sexual abuse allegations occur, it is generally unwise for the guardian ad litem to be performing the sexual abuse allegation evaluation. The primary reason for this approach is that attorneys cannot testify in cases. When a child discloses sexual abuse to the guardian ad litem and then refuses to discuss it with anyone else, that information cannot be used in court testimony. Again, as a result, a perpetrator may be able to avoid findings of abuse. It is also the evaluator's obligation to try to ensure that as few interviews as possible are conducted, since an increased number of interviews can be disadvantageous to the mental health of the child. It is also not an automatic first step to remove the alleged perpetrator from the alleged victim. It can be an easy out for social service agencies to state, "Do not let him visit" or to get a restraining order. Initially, however, many times the alleged perpetrator can be allowed to remain in the household provided that there are appropriate safeguards against future possible perpetration.

The interview process should proceed from general to specific. To avoid the possibility of suggestibility, general questions should be asked without direct allusion to sexual abuse allegations. However, as the interview progresses, it becomes necessary to have the questions become more specific, particularly if all of the general questions are asked and nothing is stated about the abuse allegations. These can be asked in the manner of, "I heard that [blank] happened; can you tell me about it?" The sexually anatomically correct dolls should *not* be used in the interview process at any point. However, when the entire sexual abuse allegation evaluation process has been completed, the sexually anatomically correct dolls may be used in an effort to corroborate what has been previously stated. When the sexually anatomically correct dolls are used too early in the evaluation, they provide a concrete focus for the child that may interfere with the memories of the actual events.

Guidelines for sexual abuse evaluations from the American Professional Society on the Abuse of Children are provided in Appendix F. It is generally important to follow those guidelines as closely as possible. In addition, nearly all individuals who have researched the problem of sexual abuse allegations suggest that more than one interview, on more than one occasion, is necessary to evaluate the consistency of the story, encourage the child to share more information as he or she becomes more comfortable with the examiner, and further evaluate the likelihood of whether or not the abuse has occurred.

Last, word-for-word notes should be kept. When this is not possible, an audiotape should be made of the interview, with written parental permission. In court cases, the judge's or jury's findings often turn on one or two words that have been found in the interview notes. It is extremely important to have accurate interview notes. Therefore, in sexual abuse allegation cases, the more copious the notes, the more accurate the notes, and the broader the base of data, the greater the likelihood of making an accurate and defensible determination of whether or not the abuse has occurred.

Concluding the Child Interview

It is not unlikely that a child will provide inaccurate or incomplete information during the interview process. This can occur when the child is reluctant to share information, does not know the information, or is somewhat shy and withdrawn. Since relevant issues may be raised as part of the interviews of the parents, it is important to check out these issues with the child. It is appropriate, at this time, to confront the child with information that the evaluator has which contradicts what the child has stated. This confrontational component of the interview should be at the very end of the interview process, to avoid interfering with the free flow of information during other portions of the interview.

BEHAVIORAL OBSERVATIONS

Many formats can be utilized during the behavioral observation component of the evaluation. It is important to note that there is no "correct" model for these observations. Evaluators tend to develop their own formats for behavioral observation. What is essential, however, is that some form of observation occur, whether formal or informal.

Often the greatest source of observational information occurs when the parents are observed informally in the waiting room with one or more of the children. This can be particularly beneficial in situations where the children act out, make unreasonable requests, or are generally disruptive in the waiting room. It can be helpful if this informal observation can occur surreptitiously. It can also be helpful if support staff has sufficient understanding of the dynamics of the evaluation and can report back to the evaluator when grossly inappropriate behaviors have occurred. The evaluator is not relying on the support staff to provide interpretation of the behavior but only to describe it.

Formal Observations

Generally, in cases that involve more than one child, it is most productive to observe each child alone with each parent. It can also be beneficial to observe each parent with all of the children together. When the children are only observed alone with the parent, the interactional affect among the children is lost, and the opportunity to observe the parents dealing with the children as a group is also lost. Some parents can very adequately handle their children on a one-on-one basis, but their parenting ability deteriorates when required to handle all of the children together.

Examiners generally choose one of two formats during the observation. One format would be a structured observation with the evaluator providing a task for the parent and child(ren) to accomplish. This could include requesting that the parent and child(ren) plan an activity together or even do something as structured as build something with Legos™, play a game provided by the evaluator, or engage in drawing tasks.

Other evaluators prefer to have the observation unstructured. This puts the onus on the parent to provide the stimulation and structure during the observation. It also provides the evaluator with the opportunity to see how the parent handles unstructured activities. The unstructured observation makes it more difficult for the parent to hide behind the structure of the activity and makes it easier for the evaluator to see if that individual's parenting is effective.

The evaluator should be in the background as much as possible during the observation portion. The evaluator has already had ample opportunities to interact with the parents and child(ren) and does not need the observation for additional factual information. Of particular note is when the child(ren) interact with the evaluator during the observation instead of with the parent who is present, even when the evaluator has requested that the child(ren) interact with the parent.

When there are major concerns about the interaction between the parent and child(ren), it can be helpful to have a combination of both types of observations, an unstructured observation followed by a structured observation. Attorneys are often concerned about how the children will act if brought in by one parent as opposed to the other. In the situation where formal observations occur, this mitigates the effect of having one parent bring in the child or the other.

It is not unusual during the evaluation process to have one parent subject to a restraining or "no-contact" order. This author's position is that the restraining and/or no-contact order must be waived during the evaluation process. Ethically, it would not be possible for a psychologist to provide a recommendation without the opportunity to include all necessary components of the evaluation process. The evaluator can ensure that there will be no contact between the parent and the child(ren) without the evaluator being present. This can be accomplished by having the parent who is subject to the restraining or no-contact order wait in another room until the child(ren) is (are) in the evaluator's office. The subject parent can be brought into the observation room after the child(ren) are present and leave the observation before the child(ren) do. It is also essential for the evaluator to try to safeguard children from contact outside of the office setting. This can generally be accomplished by explaining to the parent who is the subject of the restraining and/or no-contact orders the implication should inappropriate contact take place outside of the office setting, especially if this parent takes manipulative advantage of this opportunity.

Some evaluators think that it can be helpful to observe both parents with all of the children. It is this author's perception that this provides undue pressure and is not necessary. The evaluator already knows the parents do not deal effectively with one another, are angry with one another, and are involved in a major dispute. This additional observation is not necessary to validate that. Furthermore, it is likely to put undue stress on the children. The children need to perceive the evaluator's office as being a relatively comfortable, safe place to be, not one where major confrontations are likely to occur.

COLLATERAL INFORMATION

When addressing the issue of collateral contacts, several questions must be answered. They include What collateral contacts will be made?; Who will make the collateral contacts?; and What will the form of the contacts be? The answers to these questions vary, based on whether or not a guardian ad litem is involved in the case. When a guardian ad litem is involved, the gathering of information becomes a shared responsibility. If the psychologist has already worked on a number of cases with a particular guardian ad litem, it may not be necessary to plan in advance the division of labor. However, in those cases where the guardian ad litem and the psychologist have not worked together previously, an initial contact can help decide how the information will be obtained and which person will obtain which information.

Stepparents

A custody evaluation should never be performed without contacting stepparents. It is assumed that if the children are going to live with a natural parent who has remarried, then the stepparent will have an influence over the children's lives. As a result, to ignore this important component of the evaluation process is to perform an incomplete evaluation. At times, both parents will be found to be relatively equal in the custody determination investigation, and it is the stepparent's influence that "breaks the tie" in one direction or the other. As discussed in other chapters, there is a question as to whether it is necessary to perform a complete evaluation with a stepparent or only a partial screening evaluation. In any case, questions should be asked about previous marriages, the relationship between the stepparent's ex-spouse and their children, the relationship between the stepparent and the ex-spouse, and reasons for the initial divorce. It is also appropriate to obtain police records, treatment records, and job-related records for stepparents.

Other Relatives

It is of questionable value to request each parent to provide testimonials from relatives as to their perceptions. Like all letters of recommendation, these testimonials tend to be self-serving. It is unlikely that a parent will provide the name of an individual whom they perceive will give a negative report. As a result, this author rarely uses information from relatives as part of the evaluation process. The exception would be relatives who have been involved in ongoing child care over a considerable period of time. When that has occurred, their input could be germane and valuable.

When a parent lives with one or both grandparents, they represent significant others and should be evaluated in much the same fashion as a stepparent would. This also holds true if a relative is going to provide day care on a full-time basis.

Home Visits

Home visits are generally performed by the guardian ad litem or social worker rather than the psychologist. When home visits are conducted, it can be advantageous to have both an announced and unannounced visit. The purpose of the home visit is not only to assess the living environment but also to observe the familial interactions within the home environment.

Therapists

Records should be obtained from all previous therapists regardless of how long ago the therapy took place. The evaluator then should discriminate which records are relevant and which are not, as one does with police records. The frequency of hospitalizations, the nature of the hospitalizations, and the outcome should be assessed.

The client/patient has the right to invoke privilege with regard to therapeutic records. The problem associated with invoking privilege is that it gives the appearance that the individual is attempting to hide something, although this may not be the case. As a therapist, be aware that invoking privilege is an absolute. It is not permissible for a person to invoke privilege in one setting and release information in another setting.

When psychiatric hospitalizations have occurred, it is incumbent upon the psychologist to evaluate the outcome of the treatment, medication compliance (when relevant), and follow-up outpatient therapy. One of the questions often asked following psychiatric hospitalizations is, How long after the hospitalization will we know that the parent is emotionally stable? This depends on treatment outcome, medication compliance, and outpatient follow-through. The more times the individual has been hospitalized, the less the compliance with treatment, and the more severe the diagnoses, the less effective a parent will be. This relates to the concerns generated by Wallerstein, discussed in Chapter 3, about overburdened children.

In the event that a child has been hospitalized on a psychiatric unit, it is also the evaluator's responsibility to get those records. This principle would apply to both inpatient and outpatient therapy. As part of this component of the evaluation, the evaluator should peruse the treatment notes for any indication of cooperation or lack of cooperation on the part of the parent(s) during the treatment process. This information can be obtained not only from reviewing the treatment notes but also from talking directly to the treating therapist(s).

Other Collateral Contacts

The evaluator should consider contacting any other individuals who would have significant input to the evaluator or significant contact with the parents and/or child(ren). Depending on circumstances, these could be day-care workers, baby-sitters, lifelong friends, former spouses, or anybody else deemed relevant.

School Records

Since child custody evaluations always involve children, obtaining school records is an essential component of any evaluation. As part of obtaining school records, the evaluator should both contact the teacher and obtain a copy of the school transcript. Discussions with the teacher should include the teacher's perceptions of the behavior of the child in school, the cooperativeness of each of the parents, information regarding who attends conferences, whether there is a difference in the child's preparedness when living with one parent as opposed to the other parent, and how each of the parents aids the child with homework completion. When a child's academic performance has diminished since the onset of the divorce or since a change of placement, this information would be of particular concern. If the guardian ad litem has pursued these avenues, it is not necessary for the psychologist to duplicate the effort.

Police Records

In any situation where a parent has a police record, the records should be obtained. It is best to obtain all the records all the way back to the person's youth if permitted by law and decide on one's own the relevancy of the records, as opposed to just requesting recent records. Again, this is information that could be obtained by the guardian ad litem but should be shared with the evaluator. The evaluator should look for frequency of offenses, duration between offenses, recidivism, whether there was prison time or not, whether there were parole violations, and the nature of the crime. Crimes against persons are viewed as being of greater concern in custody evaluations than crimes against property.

The interview process is an integral part of the evaluation. Parents, children, and collateral sources are interviewed as part of the evaluation. In addition, formal or informal observations of the children with the parents also provide useful information. Individuals who have significant roles in the lives of any of the family members would be considered collateral sources and should be incorporated into the evaluation process.

CHAPTER 5

Psychological Testing

CHILD CUSTODY EVALUATION PRACTICES

The American Psychological Association Committee on Professional Practice and Standards appointed a committee to develop child custody evaluation guidelines, which were approved by the APA in February 1994. (Appendix D) The guidelines are divided into three sections.

The first section addresses the purpose of the child custody evaluation. The instruction to the psychologist is to determine what is in the best psychological interest of the child, understanding that the child is the primary client. Even if a parent hires the psychologist, the child remains the primary client. The focus of the evaluation is on parenting capacity and the psychological and developmental needs of the child. As a result, a functional evaluation of each parent is performed to determine if each is able to meet the needs of the child. The psychopathology of the parent is not the primary focus of the evaluation; it is relevant only to the degree it is expected to have a negative influence on the child.

The second section of the guidelines deals with the general guidelines themselves. The role of the psychologist is that of a professional who takes an impartial stance. Although it is necessary for the psychologist to have specialized competence in evaluating children, adults, and families, that is not sufficient. The evaluating psychologist must also understand developmental needs, be familiar with laws that pertain to evaluations, and use up-to-date professional knowledge. If there are allegations of child abuse, neglect, or violence, additional training is necessary in these areas in order for the psychologist to perform the evaluation competently. As part of this process, the psychologist must be aware of personal and societal biases and take care not to discriminate as a result of these biases. Last, the psychologist is to avoid multiple relationships. When the psychologist has previously served as a therapist for one of the parties or is a mediator for the parents, the psychologist should not do a custody evaluation.

The third section in the guidelines deals with how to conduct custody evaluations. The scope of the evaluation should be determined by the request that is made. The psychologist obtains informed consent of all participants, including informing the participants of the limits of confidentiality. In addition, multiple avenues of data gathering must occur, followed by conservative interpretation. The psychologist must avoid giving an opinion about someone who has not been personally evaluated. Recommendations that are made must be based on the best interests of the child. In addition, the psychologist must clarify financial arrangements for the evaluation and maintain adequate written records.

STAGES OF THE PSYCHOLOGICAL EVALUATION

A psychological evaluation of children or adults is generally performed in three stages. The first stage involves gathering information as discussed in Chapter 4.

The second step of the evaluation is the processing stage. During this stage, all the information that is gathered through interviews, tests, or collateral sources is synthesized and processed by the examiner. It is the examiner's responsibility to score and interpret all tests administered. This information is then integrated with information obtained through interviews and supporting documents. The examiner should separate the more important information from the extraneous or irrelevant material. Then the examiner is ready to write a report.

The last stage of the evaluation involves preparing the report, which will be discussed in Chapter 9.

TEST ADMINISTRATION

Before administering the evaluation, the evaluator should locate an appropriate setting, one that is quiet, free from distractions, and comfortable. It is generally not a good idea to perform evaluations in the home of the participants, as the neutrality of the setting is lost. It is important that the evaluator establish rapport with the individual being tested. As part of this process, the evaluator can give a brief description of the evaluation process in a manner that is designed to put the individual at ease. An experienced examiner can usually establish rapport in a relatively short period of time. However, it may be difficult to establish rapport with young children who are fearful. In such instances, occasionally a parent requests permission to sit in on the evaluation with a child. This is generally not recommended, as a parent may unknowingly provide additional stress for the child or may inadvertently attempt to aid the child or, at the least, may distract the child.

When the examiner notes a significant amount of reticence on the part of the child, the examiner should invite the parent to accompany the child to the testing room and to leave shortly after the child is settled.

The most important requirement for the examiner during the psychological evaluation is that the tests be administered correctly. With tests that are standardized, individuals who read or interpret the results of an evaluation assume that the standard instructions were given. Whether the examiner agrees or disagrees with the prescribed format used in instructing the individual being tested, the directions must be given verbatim. If examiners used their own stylized version of the directions, the standardization of the test would be in jeopardy, and the results would need to be interpreted with skepticism. When an examiner finds it necessary to deviate from the established directions for legitimate reasons, the reason must be indicated in the report along with a statement regarding whether the nonstandard instructions are believed to affect the test results in any way, and, if so, how. Acceptable reasons for deviation include visual, auditory, physical, and/or mental impairment.

Many psychologists permit individuals to take certain tests home, to be completed at the subject's leisure. This procedure may work when individuals are coming solely for therapy, though it is not recommended. Moreover, in the circumstances of a custody evaluation, it is essential to ensure that the answers were provided by the subject and were not the result of collaborative work or another source of misinformation. This can be a particular problem when both a parent and a stepparent are filling out the same instruments at home and may collaborate, compare answers, or put down inaccurate statements knowing his or her spouse may see the answers given.

Criteria for the Use of Testing

Heilbrun ("The Role of Psychological Testing in Forensic Assessment," in *Law and Human Behavior,* 1992) suggests a very conservative set of criteria for the use of psychological testing in forensic assessment. They are:

1. The test is commercially available and adequately documented in two sources. First, it is accompanied by a manual describing its development, psychometric properties, and procedure for administration. Second, it is listed and reviewed in *Mental Measurements Yearbook* or some other readily available source. . . .

2. Reliability should be considered. The use of tests with a reliability coefficient of less than .80 is not advisable. The use of less reliable tests would require an explicit justification by the psychologist. . . .

3. The test should be relevant to the legal issue, or to a psychological construct underlying the legal issue. . . . Such justification should be made in the report, clarifying the evaluator's reasoning for selecting

a given test on relevancy grounds. A justification can be made on theoretical grounds; if there is no research evidence with which to evaluate the accuracy or strength of the connection between psychological construct and legal issue, then the court should be so informed. . . .

4. Standard administration should be used, with testing conditions as close as possible to the quiet, distraction-free ideal. . . .

5. Applicability to this population and for this purpose should guide both test selection and interpretation. . . . The closer the "fit" between a given individual and the population and situation of those in the validation research, the more confidence can be expressed in the applicability of the results. . . . Under some circumstances, the best data source may involve the use of specific information obtained and tabulated under clinical conditions, so-called "quasi-experiments in real-life settings. . . . "

6. Objective tests and actuarial data combination are preferable when there are appropriate outcome data and a "formula" exists. . . . If no "formula" exists, then we have no alternative but to use our heads. . . .

7. Response style should be explicitly assessed using approaches sensitive to distortion, and the results of psychological testing interpreted within the context of the individual's response style. When response style appears to be malingering, defensive, or irrelevant rather than honest/reliable, the results of psychological testing may need to be discounted or even ignored and other data sources emphasized to a greater degree. . . . The only psychological test with extensive empirical support in measuring response style is the MMPI. . . . Unless response style is explicitly measured and demonstrated to be honest. . . . the interpretation of the results of psychological tests may be impossible." (pp. 264–268)

In an ideal world, all Heilbrun's criteria could be fully met. In practice, psychologists may use a test that does not quite meet the ideal. For example, a test may be too new to appear in the *Mental Measurements Yearbook* or published research. The psychologist is responsible for acknowledging this fact, however, and for indicating how a given test addresses the psychological and legal issues.

Order of Test Administration

In general, the least-structured psychological tests should be administered first, for example, the Rorschach, the Thematic Apperception Test (TAT), and sentence completion tests. The somewhat structured tests, for example, the Minnesota Multiphasic Personality Inventory (MMPI, MMPI-2), should be given next. The last to be given should include the most-structured tests, those that clearly have right and wrong answers, for example, the intelligence tests (Lundy, 1988).

The Rorschach may be an exception to the preceding rule. Exner and Clark indicate that the Rorschach should normally be given last, as it "is usually the most ambiguous test given in a battery and for this reason may prove to be the most threatening and disruptive to the subject" (Exner & Clark, 1978, p. 155). They indicate that differences have been found in intelligence test performance when the Rorschach precedes the intelligence test. Some psychologists disagree, feeling that the Rorschach should be administered first so that there is minimal interference from other tests and procedures.

If one test is administered a significant amount of time before another, for example, a week or more, the order of administration is much less likely to be significant. So, for example, the Wechsler Adult Intelligence Scale-Revised (WAIS-R) could be administered during the first evaluation session without necessarily having a negative effect on the results of tests administered a week later. Within a single session, however, the effect can be substantial if the administration of structured tests precedes that of unstructured ones.

Frequency of Use of Testing

A 1986 study of 190 psychologists, psychiatrists, and master's-degree-level mental health practitioners showed that the majority of the mental health professionals were retained by the attorney for one side but that they generally preferred to be appointed by the court (Keilin & Bloom, 1986). In the evaluation procedure, all the evaluators interviewed the mother and the father individually, taking approximately two hours for each individual. Almost all interviewed each child individually, taking approximately 1.5 hours for each interview. Seventy-five percent of the evaluators administered psychological tests to the parents and the children, taking approximately 2.5 hours each. Approximately 70% of them observed the interaction between each parent and each child for slightly less than an hour. Only half of the individuals observed the mother and father together or had conversations with significant others (friends and relatives). Thirty percent made school visits or home visits; of those who did, the average duration was more than an hour. In addition, the average report writing took 2.8 hours, the average consultation with attorneys took 1.4 hours, and the average court testimony took 2.3 hours, for an average total of 18.8 hours.

As shown in Table 5.1, the most frequently used instruments in testing adults in child custody evaluations were the MMPI, the Rorschach, the TAT, and the WAIS-R. Table 5.2 shows the frequency of use of psychological tests of children and adolescents in child custody evaluations.

TABLE 5.1.   Frequency of Use of Psychological Testing of Adults in Child Custody Evaluations

Psychological Test	% Respondents Using Test	Mean % Cases in Which Test Is Used[a]
Minnesota Multiphasic Personality Inventory	70.7	87.8
Rorschach	41.5	67.3
Thematic Apperception Test	37.8	67.3
Wechsler Adult Intelligence Scale	29.3	66.8
Bender-Gestalt	12.2	82.5
Adult Sentence Completions	12.2	76.0
Draw-a-person	6.1	81.0
Miscellaneous Projective Drawings	6.1	80.0
Sixteen Personality Factor Questionnaire	6.1	60.0
California Psychological Inventory	4.9	86.3
Clinical Analysis Questionnaire	3.7	70.0
House-Tree-Person Projective Technique	3.7	46.7
Miscellaneous Projectives	3.7	45.0
Kinetic Family Drawings	2.4	97.5
Parent-Child Interaction Test	2.4	52.5
Personality Inventory for Children	2.4	35.0
Other Tests[b]	19.5	

[a] Includes only those respondents who reported using the test.

[b] Tests used by one respondent only.

Source: Keilin & Bloom, "Child Custody Evaluation Practices: A Survey of Experienced Professionals," 17 *Professional Psychology: Research and Practice* No. 4, at 341 (1986). Copyright 1986 by the American Psychological Association. Reprinted by permission.

The MMPI was used with adults by 71% of the evaluators, who used it 88% of the time; the Rorschach was used by 42% of the evaluators, 67% of the time; the TAT was used by 38% of the evaluators, 67% of the time; and the Wechsler Adult Intelligence Scale was used by 29% of the evaluators, 67% of the time. All other tests were used by 12% or fewer of the evaluators.

When testing children and adolescents in child custody evaluations, a wider range of tests was used. Intelligence tests (WISC-R, WAIS, and Stanford-Binet) were used by 45% of the respondents, who used them 85% of the time. The Thematic Apperception Test or Children's Apperception Test was used by 39% of the respondents, 75% of the time. Projective drawings were used by 33% of the respondents, 86% of the time, while the Rorschach was used by 29% of the respondents, 78% of the time. The Bender-Gestalt, the Wide Range Achievement Test, and the Draw-A-Person Test were used on average by approximately 20% of the respondents, on average approximately 80% of the time. All the rest of the instruments were used 12% of the time or less.

TABLE 5.2.   Frequency of Use of Psychological Testing of Children and Adolescents in Child Custody Evaluations

Psychological Test	% Respondents Using Test	Mean % Cases in Which Test Is Used[a]
Intelligence Testing (WISC, WAIS, Stanford-Binet)	45.1	85.1
Thematic Apperception Test or Children's Apperception Test	39.0	74.7
Miscellaneous Projective Drawings	32.9	85.7
Rorschach	29.2	77.9
Bender-Gestalt	23.2	81.3
Wide Range Achievement Test or other achievement test	20.7	76.0
Draw-a-person	19.5	79.4
Children's sentence completions	12.2	70.5
House-Tree-Person Projective Technique	9.8	82.5
Kinetic Family Drawings	8.5	94.3
Peabody Picture Vocabulary Test	8.5	71.4
Roberts Apperception Test	8.5	54.3
Family Relations Test	7.3	90.0
Minnesota Multiphasic Personality Inventory[b]	7.3	48.3
Tasks of Emotional Development Test	3.7	81.7
Miscellaneous anxiety inventories	3.7	73.3
Strange Situation Test	2.4	56.0
Other	15.9	

[a] Includes only those respondents who reported using the test.
[b] Tests used by one respondent only.

Source: Keilin & Bloom, "Child Custody Evaluation Practices: A Survey of Experienced Professionals," 17 *Professional Psychology: Research and Practice* No. 4, at 341 (1986). Copyright 1986 by the American Psychological Association. Reprinted by permission.

Keilin and Bloom reached several conclusions:

1. Child custody evaluators generally prefer to serve in an impartial capacity.
2. Child custody evaluations typically include interviews, testing, and gathering of additional information.
3. Evaluators generally spend an additional six to seven hours in related activities (report writing, consultation with attorneys, and court testimony).
4. Evaluators spend an average of 18.8 hours in the various phases of a custody evaluation, excluding testimony.
5. The evaluator may consider requiring advance payment of fees, particularly before court testimony.
6. In the process of recommending a single custodial parent, the evaluators considered the following factors to be most important: the

expressed wishes of the older child, one parent attempting to alienate the child from the other parent, the quality of the emotional bonding between the child and each parent, the psychological stability of each parent, and the parenting skills of each parent.

7. Evaluators consider the following factors to be most important in deciding between joint and single-parent custody: the wishes of the older child, the quality of the relationship the child has with each parent, the parent's willingness to enter into a joint custody agreement, the psychological stability of the parents, the ability of the parents to separate their interpersonal difficulties from their parenting decisions, and the amount of anger and bitterness between parents.

8. In single-parent custody, custodial recommendations generally stipulate that all children will remain together with the same parent.

9. Evaluators generally do not see joint custody as being a fantasia for all disputed custody cases. (Keilin & Bloom, 1986, p. 334)

Incomplete Evaluations

One of the most frequent criticisms leveled against individuals performing custody evaluations involves incomplete evaluations. When an examiner administers a Rorschach and an incomplete sentences test and performs a clinical interview, the information garnered will not be sufficient to provide adequate information for decision making. Among other problems, when no objective tests are administered, it allows the evaluator to form subjective opinions that may or may not be supported by independent data. To be adequate, an evaluation must include objective testing such as achievement testing, intelligence testing, and an objective personality inventory. The conclusions drawn will otherwise be difficult to substantiate and are unlikely to hold up under cross-examination.

INTELLIGENCE TESTING

Tests of cognitive functioning are an integral part of child custody evaluations. Many different intelligence tests can be utilized in child custody evaluations. For adults, they would include the Wechsler Adult Intelligence Scale-Revised (WAIS-R) as the preferred choice and the Stanford-Binet-4th Edition (SB:FE) as a secondary source. When testing school-age children, the Wechsler Intelligence Scale for Children-3rd Edition (WISC-III) is generally the test of choice. However, the Kaufman Assessment Battery for Children (K-ABC) or the SB:FE are reasonable alternatives. In addition, the Wechsler Preschool and Primary Scale of Intelligence-Revised (WPPSI-R) and the McCarthy Scales of Children's Abilities (MSCA) can be used with preschool age children.

The primary purpose of administering intelligence tests is to determine if the parent is going to be able to academically support the children. To be able to do this, it is important for the parent's intelligence to be relatively equal to or higher than the children's intelligence. A parent with an IQ of 82 is not going to be able to adequately support the academic work of a child with an IQ of 124.

Full intelligence tests can also be beneficial in helping evaluate the parent's level of social comprehension, arithmetic reasoning, conceptual ability, and general knowledge.

Some psychologists feel that it is necessary to utilize full intelligence tests with every individual evaluated. However, it may be unnecessary to administer intelligence tests at all to adults who are trained at the doctoral level (physicians, lawyers, Ph.Ds). It is safe to assume that if an individual is qualified enough to be trained at the doctoral level, they are cognitively able to provide academic support for their children.

When the examiner is not sure whether it is necessary to administer a complete intelligence test, one of the brief paper-and-pencil tests could be used, such as the Kaufman Brief Intelligence Test (K-BIT), the Shipley Hartford, or the Slosson. When concerns are generated by these brief intelligence tests, then it would be advantageous to administer the full intelligence tests.

ACHIEVEMENT TESTS

Achievement tests are given for much the same reason as intelligence tests. It is generally not necessary to give a full achievement battery. A test like the Wide Range Achievement Test—3rd Edition (WRAT3) will generally suffice. The WRAT3 provides a grade equivalent for achievement. Generally, when parents show evidence of achieving at the ninth-grade level or higher, they will have the capacity necessary to support the child academically.

PERSONALITY TESTING

A number of paper-and-pencil personality tests have been developed over the years. They include tests like the Minnesota Multiphasic Personality Inventory (MMPI), the Minnesota Multiphasic Personality Inventory-2nd Edition (MMPI-2), the Minnesota Multiphasic Personality Inventory-Adolescent (MMPI-A), the Millon Clinical Multiaxial Inventory-2nd Edition (MCMI-II), the Personality Inventory for Children (PIC), the California Personality Inventory (CPI), and the 16-Personality Factors Test (16-PF).

MMPI/MMPI-2

The MMPI has been in existence for more than 50 years and has been examined in more than 12,000 articles and books to date. It is clearly the most widely researched of all personality tests. Given its nearly universal acceptance as a central part of evaluations, a psychologist who does not utilize the MMPI or MMPI-2 should be questioned about this omission.

The MMPI-2, published in 1989, was initially met with considerable controversy. There were issues concerning the standardization sample, the comparison between MMPI and MMPI-2 scores, the elimination of the Wiggins Content scales, and the arbitrary moving of the cutoff score from 70 to 65. Since the MMPI-2 was published five years ago, it has withstood most of the criticisms that have been leveled against it. The elimination of nonworking items, the substitution of new items dealing with suicide and alcohol and other drug abuse, the development of new Content scales, and the advent of the F-back, Variable Response Inconsistency (VRIN) and True Response Inconsistency (TRIN) scales have greatly enhanced the utility of the MMPI-2. For those individuals who are concerned about the comparability of the MMPI and MMPI-2 results, it has been recommended by many psychologists that the MMPI-2 should be administered and the raw scores plotted on both the MMPI and MMPI-2 profile sheets. As time goes on, the MMPI-2 research will continue to validate its usage in place of the MMPI, and it will not be long before it may be inappropriate to continue to use the MMPI instead of the MMPI-2.

The MMPI-2 should only be used with adults who have an eighth-grade or higher reading level. When an adult does not have an eighth-grade or higher reading level, the test can still be administered by having the subject either listen to a standardized tape administration or having the items read to the subject. It is also possible to administer the MMPI rather than MMPI-2 if the individual has at least a sixth-grade reading level.

Many components of the MMPI-2 provide useful information in child custody evaluations.

Validity Scales

The L, F, and K scales on the MMPI-2 still remain the primary sources of information regarding the validity of the tests. However, as research continues, the VRIN and TRIN scales will provide increasingly useful information. Parents with high L scales are likely to be either excessively religious and moralistic or attempting to portray themselves in a very positive, "I'm perfect" light. This is particularly true when the L scale is elevated in conjunction with the K scale. With both the L and K scales elevated and a suppressed F scale, the resulting "V" pattern is commonly referred to as a "fake good" profile. If L is above 60 and K above 65 on the MMPI-2, the clinical scales may not be an accurate representation of the individual's psychological functioning, as there has probably been an overt attempt on the part of the subject to portray himself or herself in a highly favorable light. When the K scale is elevated alone, it represents defensiveness on the part of the parent. However, this defensiveness should not be considered significant unless the K scale is above 70 on the MMPI or 65 on the MMPI-2.

Research has demonstrated that the average K scale of individuals involved in custody evaluations is 62 on the MMPI. This suggests that people involved in custody evaluations are more defensive than the general population, which is not surprising, given the legal battle being fought. When the F scale is elevated and the L and K scales are not, this suggests either confusion or "faking bad" on the part of the parent. Also, a difference between the F and the F-back scores suggests the individual was either more or less careful toward the end of the test or that there was an inconsistency in the individual's test-taking approach that may affect the overall validity of the results. When Scales F and 8 are both highly elevated, there is a strong suggestion of psychopathology. A very high F (90 or above) could be an indication of extreme psychopathology, extreme effort by the parents to make themselves look bad, poor reading ability, or random responding. It is necessary for the clinician to make this discrimination.

Clinical Scales

When Scale 1 ("Hypochondriasis") is elevated, it is not likely to interfere with parenting skills, unless the parent is involved in a significant preoccupation with physical symptomatology.

Scale 2 ("Depression") is the most frequently elevated scale, as a result of being the most sensitive scale to nuances in the individual's environment. As a result, interpretation of this scale must be done carefully. When Scale 2 is elevated in conjunction with Scale 7 ("Psychasthenia"), the parent is relatively unlikely to be able to support the child's self-esteem development.

An elevation on Scale 3 ("Hysteria") is likely to be found in a parent who overreacts to and overinterprets problem areas. Consequently, reports of incidents may be overstated and must be weighed against tendencies to overreact and overinterpret. Mothers with high 3 and 6 ("Paranoia") scales are likely to feel that "if he struck me, it is an unforgivable act, and I can't let him near my children." These individuals tend to have an unforgiving aspect to their personality.

Generally, little "good news" is associated with an elevation of Scale 4 ("Psychopathic Deviate"). Elevations on Scale 4 present a type of deviance in thinking. This can be acceptable in highly educated individuals who channel the deviant thinking in positive ways. The lower the educational level, the greater the concern about elevation on Scale 4. In addition, when a 4–9 profile is found, it represents individuals who are likely to demonstrate antisocial tendencies and transfer these tendencies to their children through teaching and modeling. The 4–9 profile individual typically does not do well with children who need structure. Their lack of ability to connect interpersonally with other individuals will also interfere with childrearing.

It is important to look at the 4–9 elevation in conjunction with the Anxiety (ANX) supplementary scale. The lower the Anxiety scale, the greater the likelihood the individuals are demonstrating antisocial tendencies. If the Anxiety scale is elevated in conjunction with the 4-9 scale, however, it is less likely that there will be concerns associated with it. Individuals with elevated 4-9 profiles also have considerable difficulty accepting responsibility for their own behavior; they tend to blame others. This is another behavior that could be problematic if modeled for children. When losing in custody litigation, the "elevated 4-9" individual will need to blame others, stating that it was the attorney's fault, the evaluator's fault, or the judge's incompetence that led to the conclusion and not the result of his or her own behavior.

When Scales 4 and 6 are elevated together, there should be concern about the amount of anger and hostility that may be present and how that may interfere with the individual's ability to function with the children and interact with his or her ex-partner. When Scales 4-6-8, 4-6-9, or 4-6-8-9 are elevated together, this represents some of the most dangerous types of personality profiles. In these cases, the examiner must carefully evaluate the safety of the child in the company of that parent to ensure that the child is not endangered by being with that parent.

Elevation on Scale 6 ("Paranoia") is not unusual in child custody cases. Many activities occur during divorce litigation that can engender feelings of paranoia. The other side may be hiring someone to follow the individual and may in fact plot against that individual, appropriately raising the individual's level of suspiciousness. However, the custody dispute alone is not sufficient to drive the 6 Scale into the pathological range (65+), unless there is already some underlying paranoid component to the individual's personality.

When Scale 7 ("Psychasthenia") is elevated, the evaluator should be concerned that the parent's style of worrying, lack of self-confidence, and feelings of insecurity and inferiority will interfere with the parent's ability to effectively interact with the child(ren).

An elevation on Scale 8 ("Schizophrenia") does not necessarily mean the parent is schizophrenic. It does suggest confusion in thinking on the part of the parent. These individuals are relatively unlikely to be able to organize and structure their own lives or the lives of their children. The higher the 8 Scale, the greater the level of confusion, and the greater the likelihood that this process involves some psychotic thought processes.

Elevations on Scale 9 ("Hypomania") suggest impulsivity, need for excitement, and the presentation of being "wired." These individuals tend to place their needs ahead of those of their children and may not recognize the consequences of their behavior until after the behavior has been performed. This is particularly dangerous when elevated with Scales 4, 6, and/or 8.

Supplementary Scales

The three main supplementary scales evaluated are the Anxiety (A), Repression (R), and MacAndrew Alcoholism-Revised (MAC-R) scales. An individual with an elevated Anxiety scale may suffer from debilitating anxiety. This would suggest that the parent's anxiety could interfere with the ability to adequately provide stability in the child's life. This can lead to children feeling overburdened, with resulting psychological problems on the part of the child.

Individuals with high Repression scales are probably not dealing with their problems adequately, and they may deny concerns that other people have about them. When the Repression scale is elevated in conjunction with the L and K scales, it further supports the notion that the individual may be downplaying those aspects of his or her personality that are viewed as being detrimental.

An individual with an elevated MacAndrew Alcoholism Scale-Revised is not necessarily an active alcoholic. This scale can be elevated in alcoholics or other drug abusers who have been "dry" for years. In addition, adult children of alcoholics often have elevated MacAndrew scales, even if they are not alcoholics or other drug abusers themselves. Nevertheless, anytime the MacAndrew Alcoholism scale is elevated, it is incumbent upon the clinician to adequately evaluate the reasons for the elevation and to consider the likelihood of an alcoholic or addictive personality.

Individuals with low Ego-Strength (ES) scales may not have the psychic energy necessary to deal with crises, problem solving, and childrearing. These individuals also show a relatively low likelihood that they will be able to take advantage of therapeutic intervention.

Individuals with low Control (CN) scales will not have adequate control over whatever psychopathology has been demonstrated on the clinical scales. Individuals with high Control scales have developed a greater ability to control those negative aspects of their personalities demonstrated by elevated clinical scales. Individuals with low Control scales are generally demonstrating all of their pathology on the test, and there is little left to clinical prediction.

When the Over-Controlled Hostility (O-H) scale is elevated, the parent may have a considerable amount of underlying, unresolved anger that has not been dealt with adequately. As a result, these individuals should be recommended for individual psychotherapy. It should also be noted that elevations on the Over-Controlled Hostility scale are not just present in individuals who are angry all of the time but are elevated in individuals who may infrequently show excessive anger. These people tend to lack self-confidence and find it difficult to accept compliments from others.

It would be expected that the Family Problem (FAM) scale would be elevated, because the individuals are going through a custody determination dispute and/or custody litigation. As a result, it does not necessarily mean that the family is abusive, lacking in affection, or otherwise inappropriate under these circumstances.

The Work Interference (WRK) scale provides the evaluator with an opportunity to determine if there are characteristics in the subject's personality that would contribute to poor work performance. These variables can include low self-esteem, difficulty with concentration, obsessiveness, difficulty making decisions, and problems with tension and pressure.

Therapy is often recommended for parents following child custody evaluations. As a result, the Negative Treatment Indicators (TRT) scale can help discern if the parent is likely to benefit from psychotherapy. High scorers on the Negative Treatment Indicators scale do not believe that anyone can understand them or help them. In addition, they may not feel that it is necessary to change anything in their lives.

Critical Items

A number of lists of "critical items" have been developed for the MMPI/MMPI-2. Although the critical items were originally selected as those that were "highly indicative of severe psychopathology," that is often not the case. It becomes the examiner's responsibility to review those critical items answered in the scoreable direction for each individual. The clinician then uses his or her clinical judgment to determine whether the explanation for the answer is reasonable or indeed represents serious psychopathology. In most cases, this requires that the clinician ask the individual why he or she answered each critical item as he or she did. When the explanation of the critical item answer is reasonable, negative interpretation of the elevated clinical scales should be reduced. On the other hand, if the explanation for the answers on the critical items indicates serious psychopathology, the scores on the clinical scales would be taken as accurately reflective of psychopathology. For example, an item like "I believe I'm being followed" is a critical item. If the individual's spouse has hired a private investigator to follow the individual, it would be a legitimate concern. On the other hand, if the subject responds to this item as "no matter where I go, there are people in bushes taking pictures of me, standing on rooftops drawing sketches of me, and hiding in my kitchen cupboards," it would be a representation of severe psychopathology. As a result, it is essential that the clinician identify the source of the concern resulting from each critical item answered in the scoreable direction.

Subtle-Obvious Scales

There has been little more widely disputed on the MMPI/MMPI-2 than use of the Weiner-Harmon Subtle-Obvious scales. Some individuals feel these scales have little utility at all. Others perceive the information garnered from the use of the Subtle-Obvious scales as being particularly valuable in helping determine the validity of the MMPI/MMPI-2 results. Greene (1991) utilizes the method of summing the Subtle scores and the Obvious scores in looking at the difference between the two. The results are then interpreted to assess whether the individual is trying to make himself or herself look better or worse than he or she really is. A more conservative approach to the use of the Subtle-Obvious scales suggests interpreting the Subtle/Obvious differences only when there is a 20-point T-score difference between the Subtle and Obvious scores for a given scale. This interpretation would suggest that if the Obvious score is 20 points higher than the Subtle score, the individual was probably attempting (consciously or unconsciously) to overstate the pathology. On the other hand, a Subtle score 20 or more points higher than the Obvious score would suggest the individual was attempting, consciously or unconsciously, to understate the psychopathology.

When using the MMPI or MMPI-2 in a child custody evaluation, it is essential to interpret the Validity scales, Clinical scales, Supplementary scales, Content scales, Subtle-Obvious scales, and Critical Items. As a result, those individuals who hand-score just the Validity and Clinical scales are not going to be able to obtain as complete an interpretation as those who utilize the computer-scoring services available. Some ethical considerations may be associated with failing to score all of the scales and identify all of the critical items in interpreting the MMPI/MMPI-2 in child custody evaluations.

Although no specific profile can be identified as a "good parent" or "bad parent" in a child custody case, a recent study examined the differences between groups of participants in child custody cases. Ackerman and Ackerman (1992) evaluated the MMPI scores of 262 parents and 73 significant others involved in child custody cases between 1987 and 1992. All participants received the MMPI. Comparisons were made at several different levels. Mean scores were obtained for all parents, all mothers, all fathers, all placement parents, and all nonplacement parents. Placement parents were similarly divided into placement mothers and placement fathers; nonplacement parents were further subdivided into nonplacement mothers and nonplacement fathers. In addition, significant others were divided into female significant others and male significant others. The typical L-F-K profile demonstrates some defensiveness on the part of most participants in these various categories. The mean K score ranged from 59.1 to 63.1, with male significant others showing the highest level of defensiveness. When comparing all mothers and all fathers, there was no significant difference between MMPI profiles. When comparing all placement parents with all nonplacement parents, the nonplacement parents demonstrated two- to three-point higher scores across all scales than placement parents. Although some were not significant differences, the clear tendency of nonplacement parents to score higher is of interest.

However, the most interesting results were obtained when comparing placement and nonplacement parents by gender. The group that generally had the highest mean scores were the nonplacement mothers. This was particularly true for the differences found on the 4, 6, 8, and 9 scales. There was as much as a five-point difference between the mean scores of placement mothers and nonplacement mothers on these scales. These differences did not hold up when comparing nonplacement fathers with placement fathers. This suggests that when mothers lose custody of their children, the decision is more likely to be based on psychopathology than when fathers lose custody of their children. Comparing significant others, generally the male significant others had significantly higher scores than the female significant others, particularly on Scales K, 1, 4, 7, and 8.

In looking at the Supplementary scales, mothers, in general, were more anxious than fathers, had less control over emotions, and had more unresolved anger. If anger is measured by the Over-Controlled Hostility scale, placement mothers had the highest mean score on this scale, five points higher than placement fathers. Nonplacement mothers showed the highest level of anxiety, eight points higher than nonplacement fathers. In addition, nonplacement mothers showed the lowest amount of ego strength and the highest MacAndrew Alcoholism scale scores.

The preceding results should serve as guidelines and are not intended to be prescriptive in nature. Certainly, the individual circumstances associated with each case should dictate how results would apply in each child custody evaluation.

MMPI-A

The MMPI-A was developed as a separate measure for adolescents between 14 and 18 years of age. The original MMPI did not have a separate adolescent scale but used separate norms for adolescents. Instead of utilizing an arbitrary cutoff score, the MMPI-A provides a gray band between T-scores of 61 and 65, indicating potential clinical significance. Since this instrument is used for adolescents and not parents in custody evaluations, the results of the MMPI-A would generally not be used in helping determine who would make the most appropriate placement parent. However, if pathology is demonstrated by the adolescent, it would be necessary to determine which parent would be better able to support the child during these periods of emotional instability.

Other Tests

Tests like the MCMI-2, PIC, and 16-PF are not as widely used in custody evaluations as the MMPI. In one study, they were used in less than 10% of the cases, and in another study, they were in the bottom half of tests frequently used in forensic cases. One of the drawbacks associated with the MCMI-2 is that it is a test that is designed to be used only in clinical settings, not in custody disputes or other circumstances where the individuals are not seeking psychological treatment.

The Personality Inventory for Children (PIC) is a parent-rating instrument. It can be useful when attempting to differentiate the perceptions of one parent versus the other. When the results of the two PICs are different, the psychologist must discuss these differences with the parents and try to identify which parent has the more accurate perception.

PROJECTIVE TESTS

Projective tests include such instruments as the Rorschach Psychodiagnostic Series, Thematic Apperception Test (TAT), Children's Apperception Test (CAT), Robert's Apperception Test, and similar techniques.

The Rorschach is a widely used technique and can be particularly valuable in child custody evaluations. Although it is possible for the subject to "fake" the responses on almost all other tests, it is virtually impossible for the subject to know what specific Rorschach responses are going to mean and how they would be interpreted. When individuals are particularly defensive, it is likely that a guarded Rorschach will result.

There is some discussion as to whether a Rorschach needs to be scored to be of value. If a Rorschach is to be scored, it should be scored according to the Exner Scoring System. No other scoring system is as complete or up-to-date. As a result, it may be considered a violation of ethical standards to use a scoring procedure other than the Exner System. However, it is not always necessary to either score a Rorschach or do a formal inquiry to have it be clinically useful. A clinician who is experienced at administering Rorschach can determine an anxious Rorschach, a depressed Rorschach, a Rorschach that represents primary thought disorder, a guarded Rorschach, or other categories without going through the rigor of scoring and determining ratios.

Thematic Apperception and Children's Apperception Tests

The CAT and TAT can be particularly useful in child custody evaluations. It is not possible for a child taking the CAT to be sophisticated enough to slant the story in the direction desired to produce a particular outcome. But parents and older adolescents, if interested in doing so, are certainly sophisticated enough to do that on the TAT. However, slanting stories is more obvious to the examiner than parents might realize. If every TAT story yields themes of positive parent-child interaction, positive conflict resolution between parents and children, and exaggerated bonding between parents and children, it is fairly obvious what the parent is attempting to accomplish.

The TAT can be useful in picking up themes of depression, victimization, interpersonal relationship concerns, and nurturance needs. Even when parents are attempting to portray a specific type of response pattern, these themes may come to the forefront.

The Robert's Apperception Test can also be useful in these types of cases. However, the stimulus cards have been criticized by some as drawing too strongly for certain types of themes. As a result, this author prefers to use the TAT or CAT rather than the Robert's Apperception Test.

INCOMPLETE SENTENCES TESTS

Some form of incomplete sentence test should be used with parents and adolescents in child custody evaluations. A formal incomplete sentences protocol like the Sacks or the Rotter is not essential. Any series of open-ended questions that provides an opportunity for the subject to project responses to the stimulus stems is useful. This author prefers to use a self-styled series of questions, referred to as the Projective Questions Test, as described in Chapter 4.

CUSTODY EVALUATION INSTRUMENTS

One of the most widely known instruments developed for use in custody evaluations is the Bricklin Perceptual Scales. It provides the evaluator with an opportunity to identify the children's perception of the parents' competency, supportiveness, follow-up consistency, and admirable traits. The results are particularly useful if a child rates one parent as substantially better than the other in the four areas, especially if the child scores one parent at one extreme and the other parent at another extreme. Bricklin refers to the latter result as "mind made up" profile. However, in such cases it is not possible for the parent rated low by the child to be as bad as suggested or the parent rated high by the child to be as good as suggested. As a result, it could be interpreted that the child is not a reliable reporter of information. The Bricklin is a highly subjective measure that has some, but not a great deal of, reliability and validity data associated with it.

Bricklin (1990) has developed other instruments such as the Perception of Relationships Test (PORT). This instrument consists of seven subjective tasks designed to identify the parent of choice. Bricklin himself notes that the PORT does not have great reliability due to the continuing change of circumstances in a child's life.

The Custody Quotient is a questionnaire and not a validated instrument. However, it can still provide useful information in custody decision making as a minor instrument.

The Ackerman-Schoendorf Scale for Parent Evaluation of Custody (AS-PECT) is the only instrument that has been developed to look at many different variables identified by professional literature to measure who makes the more appropriate custodial or placement parent. The results of the Bricklin would represent only one of 56 different measures that the ASPECT utilizes. A thorough discussion of the ASPECT is found in Chapter 6.

Other Minor Instruments

Hundreds, if not thousands, of other minor instruments have been developed to measure many different components of functioning. Some of them are quite useful, but most are so narrow, with such poor standardization samples and such low reliability and validity as to render them largely useless or even confusing in child custody evaluations. When the examiner comes across a minor instrument, the criteria for using tests, identified earlier in this chapter, should be utilized to determine the appropriateness of including a particular test in a child custody evaluation test battery.

Projective Drawings

There are probably as many different projective drawings available to the clinician as the clinician's creativity allows. Traditional projective drawings, like Draw-A-Person, Draw-A-Family, House-Tree-Person, and Kinetic Family Drawing, can be useful in child custody evaluations. Since these are projective drawings, the interpretations are as good as the quality of the interpretation by the evaluator. The family drawing can be of particular use. It is helpful to look at the family constellation, the relative size of the people drawn in the family, the proximity of family members to one another, and who is included in and excluded from the family constellation. The Kinetic Family Drawing can be useful to help the evaluator address the interactions between family members. It is generally not necessary to administer many projective drawings. However, in the case of children who are nonverbal, almost a complete evaluation can be performed through the use of projective drawings. Many of the drawings that Oaklander (1978) recommends can be useful in these situations. They would include: draw a ship in a storm, scribble drawings, representational family drawings, and draw a safe place.

Psychological testing is an important component of the evaluation process. Generally, a complete psychological evaluation will include not only the interview but also tests of cognitive functioning (intelligence and achievement tests); objective personality tests, such as the Minnesota Multiphasic Personality Inventory (MMPI or MMPI-2); and projective tests. It is not good practice to base recommendations on the results of one or two psychological tests. It is through the use of a battery of tests that the evaluator has the opportunity to identify themes that weave their way through a number of tests and are not just apparent on an individual test.

CHAPTER 6

Ackerman-Schoendorf Scales for Parent Evaluation of Custody (ASPECT)

GENERAL DESCRIPTION

Chapters 3, 4, and 5 of this book deal with all of the components of a custody evaluation. Prior to the publication of the ASPECT, there was no test that incorporated all of the components of a custody evaluation. The ASPECT can be utilized to provide a summary of appropriateness of parents for placement.

Although most psychological tests are designed to provide information for a psychological evaluation that may be used in a variety of contexts, tests also are designed specifically to provide information for custody evaluation. The Ackerman-Schoendorf Scale for Parent Evaluation of Custody (ASPECT) is designed to directly indicate appropriateness for custody. This test attempts to identify those characteristics that are reported in psychological literature as being determinative of fitness for custody.

The first step in developing the ASPECT was a review of the literature to determine what criteria were being used to make custody recommendations by mental health professionals and how custody evaluations were currently being conducted. Fifty-six variables were reported in the literature and incorporated into the ASPECT.

The ASPECT is a clinical tool designed to aid mental health professionals in making child custody recommendations. Consisting of a group of standardized scales devised to evaluate parent fitness for custody, the ASPECT incorporates several commonly used instruments, in conjunction with the clinicians' observations, to quantify characteristics related to effective custodial parenting.

The ASPECT is divided into three subscales: the Observational scale, the Social scale, and the Cognitive-Emotional scale. The Observational scale assesses the quality of the parent's self-presentation during the evaluation process. The Social scale reflects interpersonal relationships as well as societal and intrafamilial concerns. The Cognitive-Emotional scale measures the individual's affective and cognitive capabilities in relation to childrearing. The combination of the Observational and Social scales is a measure of the outermost impression conveyed by the individual of his or her parenting effectiveness. These two scales are therefore seen as "overt" measures of fitness. On the other hand, the Cognitive-Emotional scale is considered to be a measure of the underlying cognitive and affective capacities for parenting and is therefore seen as a "covert" measure.

The various factors and issues that are considered pertinent to custody evaluations were used to form the foundation of the ASPECT. The general questions "Who would be the better custodial parent?" and "What custody arrangement is in the best interests of the child?" were set aside in favor of a series of specific questions that were generated to reflect each of the issues deemed essential by researchers and other mental health professionals in determining appropriate custody recommendations. On the basis of these questions, which are answered by the examiner, the ASPECT assesses various characteristics of each parent as well as the relationship and interaction between each parent and the child or children. A quantitative measure of these significant characteristics, relationships, and interactions is provided in the form of the Parental Custody Index (PCI), a score that may be regarded as an indicator of overall parenting effectiveness.

Each of the parents completes a Parent Questionnaire, which is composed of questions regarding preferred custody arrangements, living and child care arrangements, the children's development and education, the relationship between the parent and the children, and the relationship between the parents. It also includes questions about the parent's background, including past and present psychiatric treatment, past and current substance abuse, and legal history.

The examiner then completes a separate questionnaire for each parent. The examiner's questionnaire contains 56 items that reflect the factors recognized as meaningful in custody evaluations. Twelve of these items have been designated as critical items because they are considered to be highly significant indicators of deficits in parenting. To complete each parent's form, the examiner utilizes information derived from (a) observations and interviews of the parent, both alone and with the children; (b) the data from several psychological tests administered to the parents and the children; and (c) the parent's responses to the Parent Questionnaire. There are two versions of the 56-item questionnaire: the AutoScore™ Answer Form, which is completed and scored by hand, and the computer-scannable WPS TEST REPORT Answer Sheet, which is completed in pencil and then mailed to the publisher of the test, Western Psychological Services (WPS), for computerized scoring and interpretation.

ASPECT SUBSCALES

A weighted average of all three ASPECT subscales, the PCI is a global score that can be used to compare one parent to the other. Analysis of the differences between the parents' scores on individual subscales clarifies the specific ways in which the parents differ. Although the subscale scores are used to explain PCI differences, it is the PCI that is used to guide custody recommendations, which are not made based on subscale differences alone. A brief description of each of the subscales follows.

Observational Scale

The Observational scale assesses the self-presentation and appearance of the parent. Information used to score the items on the Observational scale is obtained primarily from observation of the parent and, to a lesser degree, from the parent's responses to specific items on the Parent Questionnaire. Items on the Observational scale reflect (a) the parent's physical appearance; (b) the manner in which the parent interacts with the examiner, the child, and the other parent; (c) the parent's initial understanding and articulation of the effects of the divorce on the child; and (d) the parent's own perception of his or her parenting abilities.

Social Scale

The Social scale addresses the parent's social conduct and interaction with others, including the child, the other parent, and the community. The parent-child relationship is a major factor in the social environment of the child, and it is therefore afforded the most items. This relationship can be further divided into the direct interaction between parent and child, the child's perception of the parent, and the social environment that the parent provides for the child. Direct interaction between parent and child is assessed by examining the quality of their observed interaction (e.g., warm, positive) and the manner in which they communicate (e.g., open, easy, honest). Items that more indirectly assess the parent-child relationship include the parent's ability to recognize present and future needs of the child, the parent's ability to provide discipline and self-care training, and the parent's motivation for seeking custody. The parent's ability to provide a healthy home environment and his or her capacity to understand and become involved with the child's education and school environment are indications of the extent to which the child's social needs are being (or will be) met.

An attempt was made to include items on the Social scale that represent a wide range of variables cited as being relevant to custody determinations. Many of the questions refer to very basic conformance to societal standards of adequate parenting. These items inquire about the parent's arrest history as well as any possible problems with alcoholism, physical abuse, sexual abuse, and other legal difficulties.

Cognitive-Emotional Scale

The psychological health and emotional maturity of parents are assessed by this subscale. The Cognitive-Emotional scale of the ASPECT includes items that reflect current psychological functioning, past psychiatric history, current stress, and overall cognitive functioning. To quantify and specify each parent's cognitive and affective functioning, the ASPECT utilizes specific elements of several psychological tests that are already frequently used in custody evaluations. By using measures from these established and widely accepted instruments and by weighting them equally, the ASPECT facilitates an evenhanded assessment and reduces examiner bias. This method also simplifies comparisons between the two parents.

PRINCIPLES OF USE

Respondent Population

The ASPECT is intended for use with parents engaged in a dispute over custody of their children. Because the ASPECT employs a self-report format, it should not be administered to individuals who are either unable or unwilling to cooperate in responding to the Parent Questionnaire or to testing in general. This would include hostile, uncooperative, or malingering subjects. Individuals with poor reading ability may have the questions read to them.

Clinicians should be cautious when examining subjects who have had prior exposure to the questions on the Parent Questionnaire. These individuals may be able to present themselves in a falsely positive light and therefore may not be suitable candidates for the ASPECT.

The ASPECT has not been used to determine placement with relatives or in cases involving either same-sex couples or couples who are cohabiting but are not married. Additionally, more than 10% of the items on the ASPECT do not apply to parents whose children are all under the age of two. Users who employ the ASPECT with respondents in any of these excluded groups will find that the results are not valid or cannot be scored.

Limitations

The assessment of fitness for custody is a complex process that requires a thorough understanding of current custody laws, in addition to clinical sensitivity and judgment. Although the ASPECT has been shown to predict individual court orders of custody, additional validity studies on the relationship of the PCI score to the satisfaction and health of the child have yet to be conducted. The ASPECT scales are intended to provide normative data for a wealth of information gained through the course of a thorough custody assessment. The PCI score provided by the ASPECT can be a useful anchor point for comparing one parent to the other on the basis of quantified results. In addition, the clinician may wish to give his or her own weighting to specific items, in accordance with the particular needs of the child or children in each individual case.

The ASPECT cannot completely counteract the effects of parents who present themselves in a falsely positive light. This must be considered when interpreting the results. The user should exercise clinical judgment in rendering a decision regarding placement based on the ASPECT.

Administration

The ASPECT should be administered to parents who are each seeking custody of their child or children. Each parent must be evaluated individually. Therefore, they should be tested and interviewed separately. The ASPECT should be administered only once to each subject, as multiple administrations may compromise its validity.

The ASPECT is intended for use with parents of children who are between 2 and 18 years of age. In cases where all of the children are under the age of 2, many of the items in the ASPECT will not be applicable, and they will therefore produce results that cannot be scored.

Administration of the ASPECT entails several assessment steps, which may be carried out in any order. Each parent is asked to complete a Parent Questionnaire and to take several psychological tests. In addition, each parent must be interviewed individually and observed during play with the child(ren), who are also individually tested and interviewed. When all of these tasks have been accomplished, the examiner then completes a 56-item questionnaire for each parent.

Test Materials

Along with the parent-child observations and the individual interviews of the parents and children, assessment data will be gathered from several tests and clinical instruments. To begin with, each parent completes a Parent Questionnaire. The parent's responses to these items are the principal scoring criteria discussed in the guidelines. Other item responses, though not specifically referenced in the guidelines, may be helpful in providing a more complete picture of the parent for use in formulating a final custody recommendation.

In addition to the Parent Questionnaire, each parent should be given the following psychological tests: (a) The Minnesota Multiphasic Personality Inventory (MMPI or MMPI-2) (Hathaway & McKinley, 1943, 1989); (b) the Rorschach test (Rorschach, 1942); (c) the Wechsler Adult Intelligence Scale, Revised (WAIS-R) (Wechsler, 1981); and (d) the Wide Range Achievement Test-Third Edition (WRAT3) (Jastak & Wilkinson, 1993).

Each child will need to receive (a) an age-appropriate IQ test; (b) the Draw-A-Family Test (Hulse, 1951, 1952); and (c) either the Thematic Apperception Test (TAT) (Murray, 1943) or the Children's Apperception Test (CAT) (Bellak & Bellak, 1949), depending upon the child's age.

INTERPRETATION

When interpreting the results of the ASPECT, clinical decisions should be based on consideration of the PCI, evaluation of individual scale patterns, examination of subscale scores, and analysis of the responses to individual items. In addition, clinicians should always incorporate their personal judgment and sensitivity to ensure appropriate recommendations. Test data and clinical impressions should be incorporated into a thoughtful custody evaluation that fits the demands of the specific situation.

The first step in interpreting ASPECT results is to determine each parent's approach to testing. As a result, positive scores for Cognitive-Emotional scale items 1 (elevated L scale on the MMPI or MMPI-2), 2 (elevated K scale on the MMPI or MMPI-2), and 11 (signs of having been guarded on the Rorschach) suggest a guarded approach. If all these items are scored positively, there is a strong likelihood that the parent has a guarded response to testing. If there is concern over the possibility of the parent "faking good," the examiner should look for other indications that this parent has excessive tendencies to strive for a positive self-presentation. Such indications might include low elevations on the MMPI, obvious signs of concealing information on the Parent Questionnaire, and discrepancies between the reports of the parents or between the reports of the parents and the child.

ASPECT Score Profile and T-Score Conversion

The score profile is a graphic presentation of both parents' ASPECT scores in relation to T-scores and percentiles. T-scores are derived by converting raw scores into standard scores with a mean of 50 and a standard deviation of 10, relative to the normative sample. ASPECT users can compare T-scores across scales and between parents, regardless of the number of items on each scale.

Parental Custody Index

The ASPECT assesses parent-child relationships and childrearing practices and beliefs as well as the overall psychological well-being of each parent. The Parental Custody Index (PCI), a weighted average of all three ASPECT subscales, is both an overall index of parenting effectiveness and a summary of all of the components of the ASPECT. The total PCI was constructed to assess the general appropriateness of the parent's self-presentation, the suitability of the social environment provided by the parent, and the extent of the parent's cognitive and emotional capacity to provide effective parenting. The results of an interrater reliability study indicate that the ASPECT is relatively insensitive to the scoring idiosyncrasies of examiners. The PCIs of both parents are compared. Any T-score difference of 10 points or more is interpretable. In general, T-score differences of 10 to 15 points are significant, differences of 16 to 20 points are very significant, and differences of more than 20 points are marked. When both parents have high PCI scores (i.e., above 60), it is likely that either will be an effective parent, and even marked differences in their PCI scores would be less critical in making custody recommendations.

As is true in any test that is part of a complete psychological evaluation, recommendation should not be based on the results of the ASPECT alone. The ASPECT is a compilation of many different components that have been reported in the professional literature to help identify who makes the best custodial parent. The PCI serves as a summary of all those components in the ASPECT. However, the results of the ASPECT should not be the single criterion used to determine who should be the custodial parent. In certain situations the results of the ASPECT would be irrelevant. For example, in a situation in which the father has been found guilty in court of sexually abusing his children, it is likely that the mother would be awarded custody regardless of the ASPECT scores. Because only two items on the Social scale of the ASPECT refer to sexual abuse, it is possible that the other areas would not indicate problems disqualifying the abusive parent as a custodial parent. It is likely, however, that a sexually abusing parent would have pathology that would show up in other areas of the ASPECT. In other circumstances, such as acute ongoing substance abuse, active psychoses, or other blatantly disqualifying situations, the results of the ASPECT would be more of interest than necessary to determine who the custodial parent should be.

Interpretation of the ASPECT, at this point, looks primarily at the PCI. At a later date, with a larger sample size, it may be possible to do more sophisticated interpretations on the subscales themselves. Interpretation begins by comparing the PCIs of the two individuals. With a standard deviation on the PCI of 10, a difference in scores of 10 points or more between the mother and the father is considered to be significant. When a significant difference occurs, the examiner can report "based on the results of the ASPECT, the mother/father would make a better custodial parent." However, before reaching this conclusion, the examiner must evaluate the significant difference based on cutoff score interpretation (scores above or below predetermined numbers).

It is assumed that the custody evaluation is performed in an effort not only to determine who would make the best custodial parent but also to make this determination based on what is in the best interests of the children. When no significant differences are reported on the PCI, the results of the ASPECT would suggest that neither parent would be a better custodial parent than the other. If the criterion of what is in the best interest of the child is being used, then it does not make a substantial difference which parent the child resides with if the ASPECT PCIs are relatively close. In these situations, it may be best not to make a recommendation for placement but instead to recommend that the parents try to mediate their differences. When mediation is successful, it saves the entire family the added financial and psychological burden of a custody dispute. Furthermore, the wounds heal much faster, there is less likelihood of relitigation, and the individuals have put the decision-making power into their own hands instead of the hands of a relative stranger—the judge. The results of the psychological evaluation and ASPECT can always be used to make a recommendation if the mediation process breaks down.

There are situations in which the scores can be significantly different but of no particular value. For example, if both scores fall above 85, which is the 80th percentile, both parents would make appropriate custodial parents, even if their scores are more than 10 points apart. When both scores fall below 65, which is the 12th percentile, it is likely that neither parent would make an appropriate custodial parent. As a result, interventions that include parenting classes, supervision, or even, in extreme cases, foster placement must be considered. When a significant difference occurs, it can be helpful to look at the actual items to determine which items are scored in the scoreable direction for each individual.

Although they occur infrequently, there are situations in which significant differences could occur in the PCI that do not result in practical differences for purposes of interpretation. For example, one parent could be one or two points above the cutoff scores for various measures on the Cognitive-Emotional scale, while the other parent is one or two points below the cutoff scores. A three- or four-point difference in the MMPI, WAIS-R, or WRAT3 does not constitute a clinical interpretable difference. For example, one parent scoring 69 and the other 71 or 72 on a scale of the MMPI would result in the difference between a yes or no score on the ASPECT. However, again, it would not be a clinically interpretable difference, even though one parent would score a yes and one a no on the ASPECT.

If the 10-point difference is the result of variables of lesser importance, then less weight would be given to the significant difference in PCIs.

The publishers (WPS) have developed a ChromaGraph (see Figure 6.1) on which the results can be directly plotted to facilitate interpretation. In addition, Figure 6.2 provides a sample of a computer-generated interpretive report.

Subscale Analysis

Subscale analysis serves to indicate areas of strength and weakness in parenting effectiveness and makes it possible to identify specific elements of

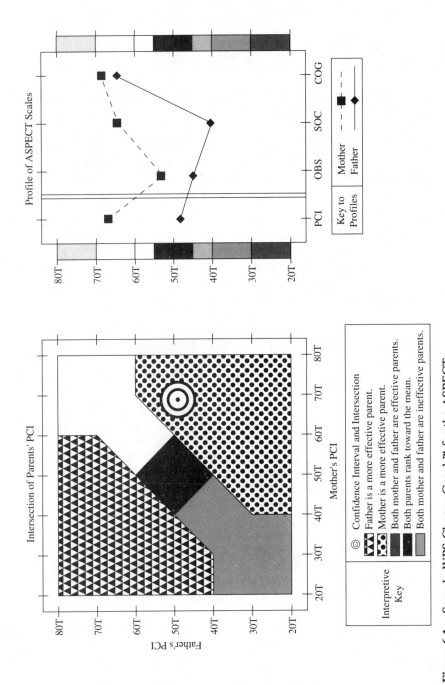

Figure 6.1. Sample WPS ChromoGraph™ for the ASPECT.
Copyright 1990 by Western Psychological Services. Reprinted by permission of the publisher: Western Psychological Services, 12031 Wilshire Boulevard, Los Angeles, California 90025.

the parents' skills. This information is useful when making recommendations for custody placement or further intervention. When the PCI scores
of the parents are equivalent, information about subscale differences can be
used to guide the court in planning arrangements.

As with the PCI, when comparing the two parents' subscale scores, any
difference of 10 T-score points is considered interpretable. This conservative
measure of differences among scales corresponds approximately to the standard error of the difference, a statistic that takes into account the reliability
of the scales. Again, T-score differences of 10 to 15 points are considered
significant; 16 to 20 points, very significant; and more than 20 points,
marked. Comparison of subscale scores provides a qualitative impression
of each parent's abilities in the areas addressed: however, the relationship
between the configuration of profiles and degrees of parenting effectiveness
has not been empirically explored.

Observational Scale

The Observational scale assesses the initial impression of parenting effectiveness created by each parent. High T-scores on this scale signify that the
parent presents a good initial impression of effective parenting. The item
with the highest item-to-total correlation is "Did the parent display angry
outbursts during the evaluation process?"

Social Scale

The Social scale gives an indication of the social environment provided by
the parent. Positive responses to items such as "Is there open communication between the parent and the child?" and "Does the parent provide
appropriate discipline?" reflect the provision of an adequate social environment. The examiner also makes a determination as to the extent of the
parent's involvement in the child's education and development. The three
questions with the highest item-to-total correlations are "Is there open communication between the parent and the child?" "Does the child's personality
testing suggest that he or she is threatened by the parent?" and "Does the
parent actively participate in the child's education?"

Cognitive-Emotional Scale

The Cognitive-Emotional scale assesses the parent's affective and cognitive
capacity for childrearing. A high score on this scale suggests that the parent
is appropriately open during testing and free from psychopathology, showing
adequate psychological adjustment, high ego strength, good social judgment,
and cognitive competence. The item that has the highest item-to-total correlation on this scale is "Was the Ego Strength scale on the MMPI above
45T?"

Item Analysis

In addition to examining differences between the parents' PCI and subscale
scores, the user can proceed to an analysis of the individual ASPECT items.

The Ackerman-Schoendorf Scales for Parent Evaluation of Custody (ASPECT)

A WPS TEST REPORT by Western Psychological Services
12031 Wilshire Boulevard
Los Angeles, California 90025
Copyright (c) 1990 by Western Psychological Services
A Computerized Interpretation System
by Leigh Silverton, Ph.D., Marc Ackerman, Ph.D., & Kathleen Schoendorf, Psy.D.
Version S800-001

```
FAMILY ID NUMBER:  0003              NUMBER OF CHILDREN:  02
ANSWER SHEET NUMBER:  97856412       AGE OF OLDEST OR ONLY CHILD:  07 years
PROCESSING DATE:  01/16/92           AGE OF YOUNGEST CHILD:  05 years

MOTHER'S INFORMATION
    AGE:  29
    EDUCATION:  18 years             EVALUATION DATE:  01/09/92
    ETHNICITY:  White                NUMBER OF PREVIOUS MARRIAGES:  0
    OCCUPATION:  Business Manager/Lower Professional/Teacher    LENGTH OF CURRENT MARRIAGE:  08 years

FATHER'S INFORMATION
    AGE:  33
    EDUCATION:  16 years             EVALUATION DATE:  01/13/92
    ETHNICITY:  White                NUMBER OF PREVIOUS MARRIAGES:  1
    OCCUPATION:  Administrative Personnel/Small Business Owner   LENGTH OF CURRENT MARRIAGE:  08 years
```

INTERPRETATION OF THE ASPECT ①

The Ackerman-Schoendorf Scales for Parent Evaluation of Custody (ASPECT) interpretive report is based on findings of research investigations with clinic families, relating Parental Custody Index scores to judges' final orders of custody. This report is intended to provide a description of the parenting effectiveness skills of custody applicants, according to theories surveyed in the ASPECT Manual. This report may also be useful for making a comparison of the parents on the basis of each one's interaction with their child or children, the impression each makes during separate interviews, and each one's cognitive and affective capacity for parenting.

This WPS TEST REPORT is a professional-to-professional consultation and should not be shown to the clients. It is intended to complement careful clinical assessment by a qualified mental health professional; it may also suggest further areas for evaluation. Guidelines for interpretation of this instrument, as well as a full discussion of its appropriate uses and limitations, can be found in the ASPECT Manual. (As used throughout this report, the word "child" may be interpreted as representing the majority of the children, when more than one child is involved in the custody evaluation.)

```
**********************************************************************
*    Users of this WPS TEST REPORT should be familiar with the      *
*    information (including interpretation guidelines, psychometric  *
*    properties, and test limitations) presented in the ASPECT Manual*
*    published by Western Psychological Services (Catalog No. W-273C).*
*    This WPS TEST REPORT should be used only in conjunction with the*
*    Manual.                                                         *
**********************************************************************
```

Western Psychological Services • 12031 Wilshire Boulevard • Los Angeles, California 90025-1251

WPS TEST REPORT.

Figure 6.2.   Sample WPS test report for the ASPECT.
Copyright 1990 by Western Psychological Services. Reprinted by permission of the publisher: Western Psychological Services, 12031 Wilshire Boulevard, Los Angeles, California 90025.

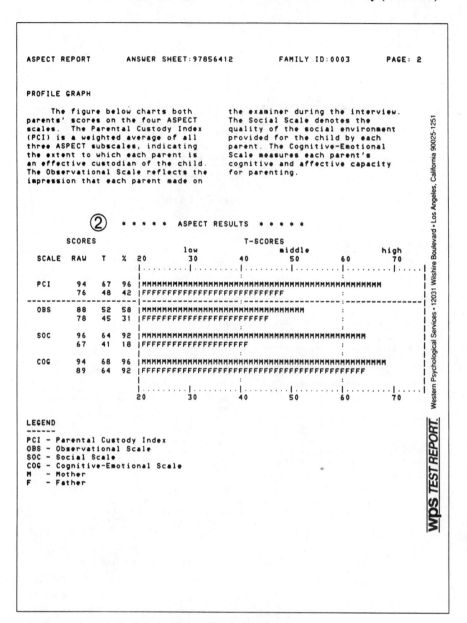

Figure 6.2. *Continued*

ASPECT REPORT   ANSWER SHEET:97856412   FAMILY ID:0003   PAGE: 3

```
******************************************
```
③   The Parental Custody Index
```
******************************************
```

    Mother received a markedly elevated PCI score compared to father. This pattern of results suggests that mother is apt to show a greater number of effective parenting behaviors and capacities than father.

    Father's PCI is in the average range. It ranks in the 42nd percentile of those in the normative sample.

    The mother's PCI is in the significantly high range, suggesting that her parenting effectiveness, as assessed by the ASPECT, is very good. It ranks in the 96th percentile of those in the normative sample.

```
******************************************
```
④   Observational Scale
```
******************************************
```

    The father's score on the Observational Scale is in the low average range and ranks in the 31st percentile of those in the normative sample. According to the examiner, his strengths are that he was able to state the effects of the divorce on his child, was cooperative with the evaluation process, and was appropriately contained during the interview. In addition, he was appropriately attired at the interview, showed adequate hygiene, and was positively engaged with the child during the interview. Also, he sets appropriate limits for the child.

    The mother's score on the Observational Scale is in the average range and ranks in the 58th percentile of those in the normative sample. According to the examiner, her strengths are that she was able to state the effects of the divorce on her child, was cooperative with the evaluation process, and was appropriately contained during the interview. Furthermore, she was appropriately attired during the interview, showed acceptable hygiene, and was positively engaged with the child during the interview. Likewise, she sets appropriate limits for the child and has a realistic perception of her own capacities as a parent.

Western Psychological Services • 12031 Wilshire Boulevard • Los Angeles, California 90025-1251

WPS TEST REPORT.

Figure 6.2. *Continued*

ASPECT REPORT   ANSWER SHEET:97856412   FAMILY ID:0003   PAGE: 4

⑤ **
                    Social Scale
    ****

The father's score on the Social Scale is in the low average range and ranks in the 18th percentile of those in the normative sample. According to the examiner, his strengths are that he provides an appropriate home environment for the child, is aware of developmental issues and can identify age-appropriate developmental milestones, and is sensitive to and able to identify the current and future needs of the child. Similarly, he is appropriately aware of information relevant to the child's education, provides appropriate general hygiene training, and actively participates in the child's education.

Moreover, the relationship between the father and the child appears to be close. Specifically, there appears to be open communication between the father and the child, a warm, positive feeling from the father to the child, and a warm, positive feeling from the child to the father.

In this regard, it is instructive to note that the child is able to identify valued attributes of the father. Likewise, personality testing suggests the child does not harbor angry feelings toward the father and the child does not feel threatened by the father. Father shows good indications of basic proper judgment. For example, he has never been arrested, does not show signs of serious alcohol abuse, and has never been charged with physical or sexual abuse.

The mother's score on the Social Scale is significantly elevated and ranks in the 92nd percentile of those in the normative group, suggesting that she has very effective social interaction with the child. According to the examiner, her strengths are that she provides an appropriate home environment for the child, can draw support from her own social networks, and is aware of the resources within the community upon which she can draw. Beyond that, she is sensitive to the child's need for time with father and does not sabotage the father's interaction with the child, is aware of developmental issues and can identify age-appropriate developmental milestones, and is sensitive to and able to identify the current and future needs of the child. In addition, she is appropriately aware of information relevant to the child's education, provides appropriate discipline for the child, and provides appropriate oral hygiene training. Also, she provides appropriate general hygiene training, has been cooperative with previous arrangements regarding custody, visitation, and placement, and actively participates in the child's education. Furthermore, she showed appropriate motivation for seeking custody.

Moreover, the relationship between the mother and the child appears to be close. Specifically, there appears to be open communication between the mother and the child, a warm, positive feeling from the mother to the child, and a warm, positive feeling from the child to the mother.

In this regard, it is instructive to note that the child is placed next to the mother in the Draw-A-Family Test and the child is able to identify valued attributes of the mother. Likewise, personality testing suggests the child does not harbor angry feelings toward the mother and the child does not feel threatened by the mother. Mother shows good indications of basic proper judgment. For example, she has never been arrested, does not show signs of serious alcohol abuse, and has never been charged with physical or sexual abuse.

Western Psychological Services • 12031 Wilshire Boulevard • Los Angeles, California 90025-1251

WPS TEST REPORT.

Figure 6.2. *Continued*

ASPECT REPORT   ANSWER SHEET:97856412   FAMILY ID:0003   PAGE: 5

⑥   **
         Cognitive-Emotional Scale
      ****

The father's score on the Cognitive-Emotional Scale ranks in the 92nd percentile of those in the normative group, suggesting that he shows very good cognitive and affective capacities for parenting. Specifically, he is not naively guarded in responding to objective personality tests, is not defensive on personality testing, and shows no manifest signs of psychopathology on the Minnesota Multiphasic Personality Inventory (MMPI). Likewise, he shows no extreme elevation of scores on the Minnesota Multiphasic Personality Inventory (MMPI), evidences good ego strength, and evidences good control. Similarly, he shows no signs of alcohol abuse, shows lucid thought processes and freedom from thought disorder, and shows a capacity for good reality testing on projectives. Beyond that, he is not guarded on projectives, has no history of psychiatric hospitalization, and is not currently taking psychiatric medications. In addition, he shows no history of substance abuse and does not depend upon the child to fulfill his own needs.

Father also shows many of the essential cognitive functions necessary for effective parenting. Specifically, his IQ is commensurate with that of the child's, his reading level is adequate, and his social judgment, as reflected in his Comprehension Score on the Wechsler Adult Intelligence Scale, Revised, is at least average.

The mother's score on the Cognitive-Emotional Scale ranks in the 96th percentile of those in the normative group, suggesting that she shows very good cognitive and affective capacities for parenting. Specifically, she is not naively guarded in responding to objective personality tests, is not defensive on personality testing, and shows no manifest signs of psychopathology on the Minnesota Multiphasic Personality Inventory (MMPI). Also, she shows no extreme elevation of scores on the Minnesota Multiphasic Personality Inventory (MMPI), evidences good ego strength, and evidences good control. Furthermore, she shows no signs of alcohol abuse, shows lucid thought processes and freedom from thought disorder, and shows a capacity for good reality testing on projectives. Likewise, she is not guarded on projectives, has no history of psychiatric hospitalization, and is not currently taking psychiatric medications. Similarly, she shows no history of substance abuse, does not depend upon the child to fulfill her own needs, and has resolved her own conflicts about the divorce.

Mother also shows many of the essential cognitive functions necessary for effective parenting. Specifically, her IQ is commensurate with that of the child's, her reading level is adequate, and her social judgment, as reflected in her Comprehension Score on the Wechsler Adult Intelligence Scale, Revised, is at least average.

Figure 6.2.   *Continued*

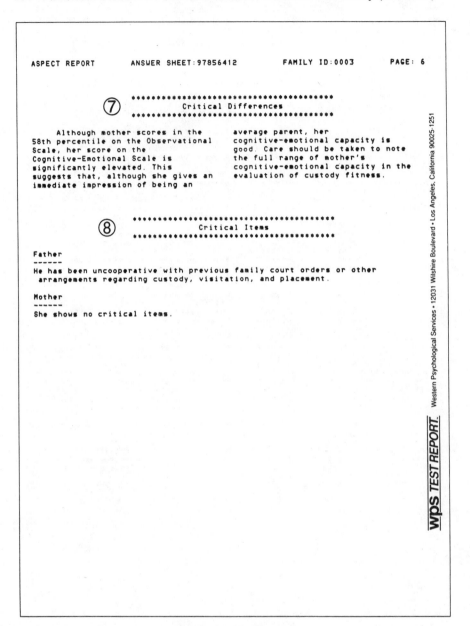

```
ASPECT REPORT        ANSWER SHEET:97856412        FAMILY ID:0003        PAGE: 6


              7   ************************************************
                                   Critical Differences
                  ************************************************

        Although mother scores in the     average parent, her
   58th percentile on the Observational   cognitive-emotional capacity is
   Scale, her score on the                good. Care should be taken to note
   Cognitive-Emotional Scale is           the full range of mother's
   significantly elevated. This           cognitive-emotional capacity in the
   suggests that, although she gives an   evaluation of custody fitness.
   immediate impression of being an



              8   ************************************************
                                     Critical Items
                  ************************************************

   Father
   ------
   He has been uncooperative with previous family court orders or other
    arrangements regarding custody, visitation, and placement.

   Mother
   ------
   She shows no critical items.
```

Western Psychological Services • 12031 Wilshire Boulevard • Los Angeles, California 90025-1251

WPS TEST REPORT.

Figure 6.2. *Continued*

ASPECT REPORT   ANSWER SHEET:97856412   FAMILY ID:0003   PAGE: 7

DISPLAY OF ITEM RESPONSES ⑨

The following table lists the actual item responses for these clients. These are the responses that were taken from the Answer Sheet by the WPS TEST REPORT scanner to generate this report.

Mother

OBS
1	2	3	4	5	6	7	8	9	
(Y)	(Y)	(N)	(Y)	(Y)	(Y)	(N)	(Y)	(Y)	

SOC
1	2	3	4	5	6	7	8	9	10
(Y)	(Y)	(Y)	(N)	(Y)	(Y)	(Y)	(Y)	(N)	(Y)
11	12	13	14	15	16	17	18	19	20
(Y)	(N)	(N)	(N)	(N)	(N)	(N)	(Y)	(Y)	(Y)
21	22	23	24	25	26	27	28		
(Y)	(Y)	(Y)	(N)	(N)	(Y)	(Y)	( )		

COG
1	2	3	4	5	6	7	8	9	10
(Y)	(Y)	(Y)	(Y)	(Y)	(Y)	(N)	(Y)	(N)	(Y)
11	12	13	14	15	16	17	18	19	
(N)	(N)	(N)	(N)	(N)	(Y)	(N)	(Y)	(Y)	

Father

OBS
1	2	3	4	5	6	7	8	9	
(Y)	(Y)	(N)	(Y)	(Y)	(Y)	(N)	(Y)	(N)	

SOC
1	2	3	4	5	6	7	8	9	10
(Y)	(N)	(N)	(Y)	(Y)	(Y)	(Y)	(N)	(N)	(N)
11	12	13	14	15	16	17	18	19	20
(Y)	(N)	(N)	(N)	(N)	(N)	(N)	(N)	(Y)	(Y)
21	22	23	24	25	26	27	28		
(Y)	(N)	(Y)	(N)	(N)	(Y)	(N)	( )		

COG
1	2	3	4	5	6	7	8	9	10
(Y)	(Y)	(Y)	(Y)	(Y)	(Y)	(N)	(Y)	(N)	(Y)
11	12	13	14	15	16	17	18	19	
(N)	(N)	(N)	(N)	(N)	(N)	(N)	(Y)	(Y)	

As shown in the table above, (_) indicates a missing response; (*) indicates a multiple response.

Western Psychological Services • 12031 Wilshire Boulevard • Los Angeles, California 90025-1251

WPS TEST REPORT

Figure 6.2. *Continued*

Item analysis establishes the basis for global differences among the scales of the ASPECT. This may prove essential when making custody recommendations, because all ASPECT items on each scale are weighted equally; the user may need to give more weight to particular items in some cases.

VALIDITY AND RELIABILITY OF ASPECT

The ASPECT is considered to be content valid, because the questions were derived from the literature on custody issues. The gender study as well as the intercorrelation matrix give evidence of construct validity. Predictive validity is measured in two separate ways. The first involves other psychologists administering the ASPECT but not tallying the results until after they have already formulated custody recommendations. Their recommendations are compared with the ASPECT predictions to gain a measure of predictive validity.

A second predictive validity study involves comparing judges' custody decisions with the prediction made by the ASPECT (Ackerman, 1992). An outcome study of 56 cases compared the results of the ASPECT with the eventual outcome of the case, whether the outcome was the result of a stipulation or a judge's order. In 59% of the cases, the outcome was the result of a judge's order, while in 41% of the cases it was a result of a stipulation. The study compared results in cases where there was a 10-point or greater difference in ASPECT scores between the parents and cases where there was less than a 10-point difference. As mentioned earlier, a 10-point or greater difference is considered a significant difference and should be viewed as being predictive. Less than a 10-point difference is not significant, and, as a result, the ASPECT does not predict who would make the best custodial parent. In 30 of the cases there was a 10-point or greater difference. In 28 of those 30 cases, or 93.3% of the time, the ASPECT results agreed with the judge's final order. In those 26 cases where there was less than a 10-point difference in the ASPECT scores, the ASPECT results agreed with the judge's decision 14 times and did not agree with the judge's decision 12 times. As a result, the 10-point difference cutoff was demonstrated as an accurate predictor of who would make the best custodial parent based on the judge's eventual recommendations after consideration of data from all relevant sources. Furthermore, the results substantiate the conclusion that a difference of less than 10 points is not interpretable in making a recommendation, as it represents close to an even split with the judge's ultimate decision. The preliminary research performed on the ASPECT demonstrates a high level of reliability and validity.

For interpretation, a T-score difference of 10 or more is considered to be moderate, 15 or more is substantial, and 20 or more is marked.

The research performed by Western Psychological Services indicated that the PCI summary score had an adequate internal consistency reliability of

.76. This was based on Alpha-coefficients with a KR-21 correction being computed on all 200 subjects. Overall interrater reliability on the PCI was .96. Many other accepted instruments report interrater reliabilities between .75 and .85, thus attesting to the excellent interrater reliability on the AS-PECT.

CASE HISTORIES

The ASPECT has been used clinically with a number of different types of subjects. The following case histories illustrate how clinical use of the AS-PECT PCI score, in conjunction with analysis of individual items, can aid in making recommendations to the court for custody decisions.

Case Study 1

Case Study 1 illustrates how family history and marked differences between the parents' ASPECT scores can support a custody decision. This case involved an upper-middle-class professional couple and their young daughter. The parents were separated, and the father had been accused by the mother of sexually abusing the child. However, because the child was young and had developmental disabilities, she could not substantiate or refute her mother's allegations. The father's PCI score was 27; the mother's, 56. The father's very low PCI score suggested major concerns beyond those raised by the accusation of sexual abuse.

Based on the sexual abuse allegations, the very low PCI score of the father, and the overall results of the ASPECT, the following rigidly structured reintroduction of the father to the daughter was recommended: Visitation between the father and daughter was to be contingent upon the father being involved in psychotherapy until the therapist deemed it no longer necessary. If the father terminated therapy prematurely, his visitation rights were to be suspended. Furthermore, initial visits were to be supervised by a mental health professional other than the father's therapist, in an effort to guarantee that the father would not be psychologically inappropriate with the child. When that mental health professional felt that his or her presence was no longer required, subsequent visits would be supervised by a disinterested third party. When the disinterested third party, in consultation with the guardian ad litem and the court-appointed psychologist, felt that this level of structure was no longer necessary, unsupervised visits would be allowed. It was understood that this process could take an unspecified number of months or years to accomplish.

Within a year and a half, the father's parenting skills had increased significantly, and the mother was no longer as concerned about the abuse-related issues. As a result, visitation became unsupervised by the time the child was nine. There have been no recurrent abuse allegations, and everybody appears to be comfortable with the current plan. This type of arrangement could be employed in any case in which there is serious concern about both parenting ability and physical or sexual abuse.

Case Study 2

Case Study 2 illustrates the use of the ASPECT in assessing underlying psychological problems that may impair the capacity for parenting. This was a case of a middle-class couple in their midthirties who had sons aged 11, 8, and 6. Both parents sought custody. The father alleged that the mother was unstable, and the mother claimed that the father spoiled the children. The father demonstrated some difficulty with decision making throughout the period of time preceding the divorce.

The father's PCI score was 53; the mother's, 37. Not only was the mother's PCI score 15 points lower than the father's, but examination of the individual scales also showed the mother to have particularly low scores on the Social and Cognitive-Emotional scales, and several items on the Social scale indicated that she had had psychiatric treatment. Furthermore, analysis of individual items on the Cognitive-Emotional scale revealed that the mother's Rorschach results indicated subtle signs of thought disorder, such as a low F+% and two Fabulized Combinations. There were also Rorschach indicators of an absence of emotional control, such as an emphasis on C and CF responses and a high number of FM responses.

The ASPECT thus tended to corroborate the father's view of the mother as being unstable. Differences between the parents' PCI scores, as well as subscale and item analyses, suggested that the father would make the best parent. It was therefore recommended that the father should be awarded primary custody of the children and that the mother should be given traditional visitation rights (i.e., every other weekend, alternating holidays, and half of each summer). The parents eventually agreed to this arrangement by stipulation. Two years after the agreement was reached, it was determined that the children were well adjusted and had stabilized in the father's environment.

Case Study 3

Case Study 3 illustrates the importance of item analysis in making custody recommendations based on the ASPECT. This case involved an upper-middle-class couple in their forties and their 12-year-old child. The mother had assumed custody of the child and was actively involved in the child's activities. An interview did not reveal substantial information to advocate this decision. The mother's PCI score was 50; the father's, 40. Although the father's PCI score was moderately lower than the mother's, analysis of individual items showed that placement with the father might be more appropriate. The father's overall history demonstrated greater stability than the mother's, and closer scrutiny of his answers to specific questions suggested that there was not a significant difference between the assessed capabilities of the two parents. Item analysis indicated that the depression in the father's score was partially artifactual. Specifically, some of the parents' score differences on the ASPECT were due to relatively minor discrepancies in their performance on personality tests. In examining each parent's MMPI results, for example, the mother had an L scale of 56, and the father's was 60; the mother had a K scale of 68, and the father's was 70; and the mother's Ego Strength scale score of 46 was also comparable to the father's 44. Although the father obtained an unfavorable response on one of the critical items—having been in trouble with the law—his legal difficulties had occurred when he was 13. In addition, although he was not aware of some of the child's important developmental and school-related information, this was because the mother had prohibited contact between the child and the father. When these factors were considered, the 10-point difference between the mother's and father's scores was reduced to less than a 5-point difference. Based on this information, the mother's and father's current living situations were compared, as they would be in a traditional custody evaluation, without using the ASPECT. After consideration of these determinants, it was recommended that custody of the child be granted to the father, with arrangements for the child to spend relatively equal time with the mother.

Case Study 4

Case Study 4 illustrates the use of mediation when both parents show relatively good parenting skills. The applicants were working-class parents in their late twenties who had three school-age children. The father's PCI score was 61; the mother's, 64. Because both parents had moderately high PCI scores, neither could be disqualified as an appropriate placement parent based on the PCI.

When both parents have high PCI scores that are close together, the examiner should not make a recommendation to the court. Instead, the parents should become involved in some type of mediation and/or negotiation. An arrangement allowing for relatively equal placement of the child might be considered in a situation of this nature. The "Ackerman Plan" (Ackerman & Kane, 1990), as it has been called by one judge, is such an arrangement. Under this plan, one parent receives primary placement, and the other parent alternates between having the children for an overnight visit one week and a four-day weekend visit the next. The four-day weekend visit is generally scheduled from Thursday night to Monday morning or from Friday night to Tuesday morning. This arrangement allows the secondary placement parent to do more than just visit briefly with the children; he or she remains actively involved with the duties of childrearing. Plans such as this also require ongoing communication between the parents.

Case Study 5

In Case Study 5, the mother and father both proved to be ineffective custodial parents, based on the PCI. The father received a PCI score of 27, and the mother's PCI score was 28. Both of these scores are more than two standard deviations below the mean on the PCI. For both parents, an analysis of individual items revealed that pathology was shown on the Rorschach, the clinical scales of the MMPI, the MacAndrew Alcoholism scale, the question about physical abuse, the questions about their children feeling threatened by them, and the question about their being in trouble with the law.

Although most states require that placement be with a natural parent unless it can be demonstrated that that parent would be harmful to the children, in this case it was deemed advisable to recommend foster placement. The extremely low PCI scores, in addition to the preponderance of critical items that contributed to those low scores, suggested that there were enough problems with each parent that both should be considered likely to have a negative influence on the overall development of their children.

When similar cases occur in states where the law allows placement in a foster home, such placement proceedings should be considered. However, before making that recommendation, the examiner must review those items that contributed to the low PCI scores to determine whether they are sufficiently critical.

In states that do not allow foster placement in such cases, safeguards must be recommended to guarantee as much as possible the well-being of the children. It is essential for the court to continue to review the case as frequently as once every six months but certainly not less than once a year. It is possible that, as time goes on and the review process continues, one parent will emerge as a more effective parent than the other. If this is the case, then that parent's time with the child should be increased. It is also possible that, during the ongoing review process, it may be demonstrated that either or both of the parents could indeed be harmful to the children, in which case consequent proceedings could result in foster placement.

In addition to the review process, parenting classes should be required and a mental health professional should be employed to oversee the entire visitation and parenting process. This does not mean that the visits have to be supervised, but the mental health professional's skills should be utilized to provide recommendations and guide the parents through difficult times as well as to report back to the court.

Based on all of the findings reported with the ASPECT, it is easy to see that it can be used to provide a summary of parents' effectiveness. It is the only broad-based quantifiable custody evaluation instrument available to psychologists at this time. Although the reliability and validity studies that have been performed yield very favorable results, more still needs to be done to assess the overall efficacy of this instrument. Even though the AS-

PECT summarizes 56 different variables appropriate for determining custody or placement, like all other tests, it should not be used as the sole recommendation in making a custody or placement determination. Generally, because of its summary characteristics, the ASPECT results can be weighed heavily in the evaluation process. However, there is always the possibility of situations that would overshadow the results of the ASPECT.

CHAPTER 7

Guidelines for Evaluating Parents' Behavior

INTRODUCTION

This chapter identifies and briefly discusses the recommendations for appropriate behaviors that parents should follow during separation and court proceedings and following divorce as well as the inappropriate behaviors they should avoid. As an evaluator, read through the questions in the following sections and subjectively determine how well parents are complying with the recommendations. A parent who is following most of the recommended positive, appropriate behaviors (the do's) and only a few or none of the identified negative, inappropriate behaviors (the don't's) is in a favorable position to obtain custody or placement; a parent who is performing only a few of the appropriate behaviors and most of the inappropriate behaviors is in an uncertain position to obtain custody or placement. All of the recommendations regarding behaviors (the do's versus the don't's) are based on research and the author's experience in more than 1,000 divorce cases.

EVALUATING APPROPRIATE BEHAVIORS (DO'S)

1. Do the parents understand that they should attempt mediation before litigation? The research clearly demonstrates that divorces that are mediated result in fewer adjustment problems for both children and parents, a shorter period of resolution of problems, and less likelihood of relitigation. It is generally a good idea to have an agreement among the parties and the attorneys that the mediator will be immune from testimony. As a result, each of the individuals can feel free to state concerns openly without fearing they will be used in future litigation.

2. Do the parents understand that two parents living apart will not see their child(ren) as often as two parents living together?

3. Do the parents understand that two individuals living apart will have more expenses than two individuals living together? In the author's experience, the issues addressed in questions number two and number three represent the most common problems in court during postjudgment hearings. The typical scenario involves the father who believes that the mother has too much time with the children and the mother who believes that the father has too much disposable income. Parents must realize that no matter how much time their ex-spouse spends with the children, that time with the children will no longer be available to them. In addition, one parent having more bills to pay than before does not indicate that the other parent has excessive disposable income.

Parents should realize that time with the child(ren) and financial support are two separate issues and that one has no legal effect on the other. Fathers may withhold support because they want more visitation, or the mother may withhold visitation because she does not receive support on a timely basis. In assessing placement time and support, the two should not become enmeshed with each other.

4. Have the parents considered a joint custody arrangement rather than a sole custody arrangement? Problems are associated with both joint and sole custody. Parents who are granted sole custody often present a feeling of "ownership" of the children. These feelings tend to lead summarily to the exclusion of the other parent. Even though two parents may not communicate effectively after the divorce, joint custody should be considered as the optimal choice. Joint custody implies that the parents will be able to cooperate well enough to make joint decisions about such issues as children's education, religious upbringing, and medical treatment. In most cases, by the time the divorce has taken place, most of these decisions will have already been made. The one exception is medical treatment for problems that are unforeseen at the time of the divorce. As a result, religious upbringing and education decisions tend not to become part of joint custody communications. Sole custody should be considered only when one parent is clearly harmful to the children, is an active substance abuser, is chronically mentally ill, is a habitual criminal, or has some other severe problem.

5. Are the parents willing to share holidays rather than alternating them? As we enter the 1990s, the concept of alternating holidays may be an archaic concept. If parents live in the same city, it is important for the children to retain contact with both sets of families during important holidays; there is no reason why the children should be prevented from seeing the father's relatives at Thanksgiving one year and the mother's relatives at Thanksgiving the next year. Important holidays such as Thanksgiving and Christmas can be shared so that the children have an opportunity to see both parents and their extended families for each of the holidays. These opportunities help provide children with lifelong positive memories of holiday times.

6. Have both parents together told the child(ren) in advance that the separation is going to take place? Unfortunately, all too often, children come home from school to find that one of the parents has moved out of the house without prior explanation or an opportunity to discuss the matter. It is vitally important to prepare the children before the actual separation takes place; this information should be communicated to the children by the parents together. This tells children that even though their parents are getting divorced, they will still have the capacity to work together in the children's best interests. Children under six should be given several days' notice; children over six should have a week's notice. The evaluator should note when one parent has refused to participate in this process.

7. Do parents understand that they should not move more often than necessary? Although several moves may be necessary because of the divorce, it is important to provide stability as soon as possible for the children. For example, it may be necessary for the parent to move first at the time of separation, then into temporary quarters after the divorce, and into a more permanent residence within a year or two of that. However, moving children five or six times within two years can have a detrimental effect on their psychological development.

8. Are the parents sensitive to the child(ren)'s needs as well as their own? Unfortunately, parents often become bogged down in meeting their own needs, to the detriment of recognizing their children's needs. Parents who cannot be sensitive to their children's needs may find them exhibiting maladaptive behavior.

9. Do the parents understand that they should plan and consult with the other parent in advance for time with the child(ren)? This recommendation applies to many factors in the overall development of children. When it comes to planning lessons, athletic activities, camp, recitals, extended medical treatment, out-of-town visits to relatives, or other routine activities, it is essential for the parents to communicate with one another prior to implementation of these plans. It serves only to increase the acrimony if one parent makes the plans without consulting the other and then attempts to follow through with the plans without the other parent's input. When a parent has not incorporated the other parent in these areas, the evaluator should raise this as a concern.

10. Do the parents observe time schedules with the child(ren) as strictly as possible? The tardy parent should phone, explaining the reason for being late and giving an estimated time of arrival. One way to reduce the likelihood of tardiness is to agree that the receiving parent will transport the children. For example, if the children are going to the mother's for a weekend visit, their mother would pick them up. When the visit is completed, their father would pick them up. As a result, there is less likelihood for tardiness. However, it is common courtesy to inform the other parent regarding tardiness.

11. Are the parents flexible with regard to visitation times for the other parent? No visitation schedule can take into account all the possible exceptions that may occur. As a result, flexibility is encouraged. It is important for parents not to count up the minutes, hours, or days that may be lost or gained as a result of this flexibility. The presumption is that, over the course of the children's childhood, the time will balance out. The author is reminded of a mediation session when a parent sat down and stated, "No mediation can take place until I get the three days' visitation time that my ex-wife owes me." The ex-wife responded that she had no knowledge of receiving three days of placement she was not entitled to. At that point the father pulled out a notebook covering three years of entries: the mother was 15 minutes late for a drop-off, an hour late in arriving home, took the children to a parent-child school function during the father's time, and so on. He pointed out that all of this time over the three years added up to approximately 72 hours, and he wanted his three days back before any mediation was going to take place. The author, as a mediator, was not able to convince the father that the amount of energy wasted in keeping track of these minutes could have been spent far more productively with the children. The father was also unable to recognize that he had been late occasionally and that his ex-wife could have docked him for those times but chose not to do so.

12. Have the parents done whatever is necessary to resolve the angry feelings toward the ex-spouse? As mentioned in Chapter 3, Wallerstein's research clearly demonstrates that there is a significant amount of depression in children whose parents are still fighting five years postjudgment. Ex-spouses do not have to love one another or even like one another. They must, however, be civil to one another in the presence of their children. Angry feelings will be conveyed to the children and can cause serious problems— in some cases, even clinical depression.

13. Do the parents present a united front when handling any problems with the child(ren)? Children should not be allowed to manipulate the parents by playing one against the other. If a problem arises and the mother and the father choose to respond to it in different ways, it presents an opportunity for the child to manipulate the situation. Discussions should take place and ground rules established for dealing with specific problems.

14. Do the parents permit their child(ren) to have too much decision-making power? This applies most frequently to allowing preadolescent children to decide whether they will or will not visit with a particular parent. When children of that age are allowed to have this kind of decision-making power, they might demand excessive and inappropriate power during their teenage years and perhaps even become uncontrollable. Older teenagers may reasonably have some say in how much time they spend with the parent and the timing of the placement.

15. Have the parents provided their children with therapeutic opportunities if the psychological adjustment appears too problematic? Parents should not be running to a therapist whenever a child has an adverse reaction to divorce. However, when adverse reactions last for months rather than weeks, they may have become habitual rather than transient. A difficult conflict results when one parent feels that psychotherapy is necessary and beneficial but the other parent says, "My kids aren't crazy and I'm not taking them to any shrink." In general, if either parent believes that therapy is warranted, a brief evaluation of the need for therapy should be available.

16. Have the parents told their children often that they are still loved and that they are not getting divorced from their parents? Parents all too often assume that their children understand this truth even though they are not frequently reminded. During the separation period and shortly after the divorce, children may need to be told often that they are loved. Their concern may be, "You stopped loving Mom. How do I know you won't stop loving me?" One way to reassure children is to tell them that the love between spouses is different from the love between parent and child. Although the love between spouses can fade away, there is a permanency to the love between parents and their children because parents love their children from the moment of birth, unlike the parents, who had to meet and fall in love and who therefore could fall out of love as well.

✓ *17. Have the parents provided their children with an emotional environment that allows them to continue to love the other parent and spend time with that parent?* Children often realize that their parents got divorced because they neither like nor love each other. They also recognize the acrimony between their parents. As a result, they can be fearful that one parent may see them being friendly with each other and become angry. Children must be made aware that it is perfectly acceptable and appropriate to show love and positive regard for the other parent.

✓ *18. Have the parents encouraged a good relationship between the child(ren) and the other parent's extended family?* The same thoughts apply to the children's feelings about aunts, uncles, and grandparents of the other parent. For one parent to criticize the other parent's extended family only puts pressure on the child and increases the problems between the divorced parents.

19. Have the parents encouraged children to remember the other parent on special occasions, allowing them to telephone on a reasonable basis (the time and length of the phone calls to be in accordance with family rules) and at special occasions? If children are unable to purchase birthday gifts or cards, Father's or Mother's Day gifts or cards, or cards for special occasions without help, the parents must encourage and aid them as necessary to make sure these occasions are recognized. Each parent needs to understand that the other would enjoy receiving recognition on appropriate occasions, just as much as they would.

20. Have parents used discretion as to the time and frequency of calls to the child(ren)? Parents must recognize that when their children are with the other parent, they will be involved in family time, quiet time, homework time, and other forms of interaction. Frequent, unnecessary phone calls become intrusive and serve to agitate. It is not necessary for the parent to have daily phone contact with the children during their placement with the other parent. Certainly, if the children desire this level of contact, it should occur. Otherwise, two or three phone calls per week are sufficient.

✓ *21. Do the parents recognize that their child(ren) will feel powerless and helpless?* Children are subject to decisions about where they will live, who they will live with, what school they will attend, what neighborhood they will live in, and who their friends will be, all with little or no direct consultation with them. Furthermore, if a judge is required to resolve conflicts, some decisions will be made by a complete stranger. As a result, they are likely to feel both powerless and helpless about the outcome of their lives.

22. Do the parents recognize that their child(ren) may feel insecure and exhibit regressive behavior? Insecurity in children may occur for the same reasons identified in the previous recommendation. In addition, insecurity can be associated with concerns like, "Mom already left. How do I know that Dad won't leave too?" It is not unusual for children to exhibit regressive behavior when under stress. This could include returning to thumb-sucking, bed-wetting, whining, tantrums, or other similar behaviors. If these behaviors continue for a relatively short time, psychotherapeutic intervention is not necessary. However, if they appear for more than two months, therapy may be warranted.

23. Have the parents provided an appropriate role model for the child(ren)? Parents should recognize that the behavior they exhibit serves as a model for their children and that they are actually teaching them how to respond. As a result, parents who are excessively angry, overreactive, or unduly depressed (or exhibit other extremes of behavior) may have children who are excessively angry, overreactive, or unduly depressed.

24. Are children allowed to see where the other parent is going to live after moving out of the house? Children need to know that the parent who is leaving the house is having his or her primary needs met. This is done by showing the children that the departing parent will have a place to sleep, a place to eat, and a bathroom. By seeing this dwelling as soon as possible, children are assured that their parent will have these amenities.

25. Have the parents put their differences aside long enough to attend school conferences together? When parents have a problem dealing with one another, it should not become the school's problem. Some school districts offer only one teacher conference, and the parents must decide whether to attend together or designate one parent to attend. When school systems are expected to provide two separate conferences for the parents, it makes the parents' problem the school's problem. Parents must also recognize that when their behavior is inappropriate in school, it will reflect negatively on their child(ren). Children and schools need the assurance that their parents are willing to put aside their differences to benefit their children.

26. Are the rights and responsibilities of both parents to consult with school officials concerning the child(ren)'s welfare and educational status and the right to inspect and receive student records if state law allows followed?

27. Are the rights of both parents to receive, or have forwarded promptly from the appropriate parent or school, copies of all school reports, calendar of school events, and notices of parent-teacher conferences followed?

28. Are the rights of both parents to be notified in the case of the child(ren)'s "serious illness" followed?

29. Are the parents able to exercise the right to authorize emergency medical, surgical, hospital, dental, institutional, and/or psychiatric care?

30. Do the parents recognize the right of both parents to inspect and receive the child(ren)'s medical and dental records and the right to consult with any treating physician, dentist, or mental health professional of the child(ren)? The previous five questions emphasize the recommendations that each parent must continue to be aware of all areas of information concerning his or her child. When this type of information is withheld or when parents are excluded from participating in these processes, postjudgment visitation or support conflicts are likely to appear. When parents are kept fully informed, they will feel more a part of the children's lives and are less likely to feel the necessity for postjudgment actions. When one parent does not inform the other, it will be weighed against them in a custody evaluation.

31. Do the parents recognize that their child(ren) need substantial contact with the same-gender parent during adolescence? Male children identify more closely with their fathers during adolescence, and female children identify more closely with their mothers during adolescence. As a result, it may be necessary to voluntarily alter placement time with the parents based on the increased needs of the children.

32. Have the parents allowed all grandparents to continue to have contact with the child(ren)? Many states currently have laws requiring that grandparent visitation be continued even after the divorce. By refusing to review cases from Wisconsin and Kentucky early in its 1992–1993 term, the U.S. Supreme Court has, in effect, endorsed grandparent visitation as well. Whether or not there is a state law, parents should recognize that the children are not getting divorced from the grandparents. There is a special place in children's memories for their grandparents. When one parent denies contact with the ex-spouse's parents because of animosity, it serves only to remove another important component of the childhood experience. Certainly, as part of this process, grandparents must be instructed not to criticize the other parent, because it can undermine the relationships and heighten the acrimony.

33. Do the parents communicate with each other openly, honestly, and regularly to avoid misunderstandings harmful to the child? Most of the child-rearing difficulties between divorced parents result from poor communication. When a child tells Mom what Dad said or tells Dad what Mom criticized, it is important for parents to be able to communicate about these concerns and "check it out." If the communication skills between parents are so poor that this is impossible, it allows children to continue manipulating their parents, increases the acrimony between parents, and teaches the children poor communication techniques.

34. Do the parents make plans directly with the other parent rather than through the child(ren)? Anytime the children are caught in the middle of communication, it becomes burdensome for them. It is unfair to expect children to assume the role of middleman.

35. Do the parents live as close to one another as practical, convenient, and reasonable? Children are more likely to feel that they have two homes if they can move conveniently between the houses, especially if they are old enough and the houses are near each other. Older children should be able to go to their "other house" to retrieve items they may have forgotten, discuss matters with the other parent, interact with pets, and so on. However, it should be made clear to the children that they will eat and sleep at the placement home, not the other home. This reduces the likelihood of them playing one parent against the other.

36. Are household routines maintained as much as possible? Many changes occur during a child's life at the time of separation and divorce. As much as possible, parents should maintain the basic structure of their lives. Chores, eating and sleeping routines, and regular schedules should be maintained as much as possible. Any changes should be discussed with the children in advance and kept to a minimum.

37. Do the parents maintain the same set of rules as much as possible in both homes? Although it may be a valuable lesson for children to learn that different rules can apply to different settings, if the basic routines are too different at each of the homes, it can increase the children's anxiety. As a result, it is beneficial to keep the rules for mealtime, bedtime, homework, and general situations as similar as possible between the two homes. At the same time, parents must realize that they cannot enforce rules or maintain discipline when the children are in the other parent's home. Unfortunately, this recommendation may be difficult to follow since many divorces occur because parents have different views of childrearing techniques; for example, one parent accuses the other of being too lax, and the other parent accuses the first of being too strict.

EVALUATING INAPPROPRIATE BEHAVIORS (DON'TS)

1. Have parents agreed to alternating, 50/50 arrangements? As family law has moved into the 1990s, it has been recognized that the traditional visitation/placement schedules do not allow both parents to have an extended, ongoing relationship with their child(ren). Consequently, many parents have attempted to develop equal placement schedules on a 50/50 basis, such as a Sunday-Wednesday/Wednesday-Sunday schedule, alternating weeks, or alternating two-week segments. The problem with this basic schedule is that it may not allow children to feel like they have a home. For example, a 12-

year-old girl was in therapy with this author. The court had ordered that she spend two weeks with her mother followed by two weeks with her father on an alternating basis throughout the entire calendar year. During the therapy process she talked about what she did at her mother's house and what she did at her father's house. The therapist asked her, "Where is *your* house?" The girl responded, "My mother has a house and my father has a house, but I don't have a house." When a child feels this way, it produces feelings of insecurity. When parents communicate effectively with one another, are flexible, and live within walking distance of one another, an alternating schedule may work because the children can move back and forth easily to pick up their belongings or elicit emotional support from the other parent. However, parents must recognize that giving the children too much mobility could allow them to play one parent off against the other.

In two recent cases, judges made decisions without recognition of how destructive these orders were to the children:

Case 1:

In an effort to not prejudice either parents' position, a judge made a temporary order at the beginning of the school year with a six-year-old special education student and his eight-year-old sister by placing them in alternating weeks with each parent. They were to attend the placement parents' neighborhood school during each parents' placement week. The schools were located in different counties.

Case 2:

After several days of testimony, a judge became frustrated with the acrimony between the parents, the attorneys, and the experts in a case where the mother wanted to move to California and the father wanted to remain in Wisconsin with their nine-year-old daughter. The judge ordered that this nine-year-old girl alternate school years between Wisconsin and California until high school.

2. Have parents avoided extended overnight visitation for infants (birth to 12 months)? This concept is supported by research, but it is also controversial. The thought is to permit nonplacement parents to have visits with children, but not overnight visits. Some believe it is essential for infants to sleep in the same crib every night, even when the nonplacement parent cared for the child during the day. Others may argue that it is not harmful when children spend overnights with grandparents. This may certainly be accurate, but overnight visits with grandparents generally do not occur several times a week. The nonplacement parent should be allowed to put the child to bed and go through the typical bedtime routine in the placement parent's home. Although this is an intrusion, children are not infants for long, and this temporary solution will provide the child with greater feelings of security.

3. Have parents fostered the child(ren)'s feelings of guilt over the divorce process? Young children often believe they have caused the divorce. Parents who encourage these feelings of guilt will also be promoting long-term psychological problems.

4. *Do parents let latency-aged child(ren) (especially 9 to 12 years of age) refuse visitation with the other parent?* Giving a child of this age the power to make an important decision of this nature is likely to produce further problems during adolescence. When allowed to make this type of decision, children may get the false impression that they will have the power to make other important decisions. Furthermore, a child who refuses visits at this age is often caught up in a loyalty issue and cannot be objective about the situation.

5. *Do parents allow teenage child(ren) to become too parental?* Teenaged children will often attempt to fill the role of the same-gender absent parent. The present parent will often feel good about being supported by this teenage child, who may assume false feelings of maturity.

6. *Do parents allow the child(ren) to exhibit too much acting-out behavior in response to the divorce process?* It is not unusual for children of divorced parents to engage in acting-out or regressive behavior. It becomes a greater problem if parents allow the acting-out behavior to become excessive because they feel sorrow and guilt over what the children are going through. Parents who think, "He's having such a hard time, let's not make him follow the bedtime rules," will face even greater acting-out behavior later. Children benefit when parents maintain consistent, fair structure in the home, including setting appropriate limits on the children's behavior.

7. *Have parents avoided taking sides or taking issue with decisions or actions made by the other parent, especially in front of the child(ren)?* When a child becomes involved in a dispute with one parent, it is important for the other parent to remain neutral if he or she was not part of the original problem or discussion. If one parent happens to disagree with what the other has done, this disagreement should be discussed privately. When a resolution is reached, the children should be informed. If a resolution cannot be reached, the children can be told how that lack of resolution will affect them.

8. *Have parents avoided putting the child(ren) in the middle of arranging visitations?* The visitations should be arranged with the other parent. To put this kind of responsibility on the child only adds to the child's burden.

9. *Do parents communicate with the other parent through the child(ren)?* Unfortunately, parents often look to the children to carry messages to the other parent. Because the parents are not communicating effectively with one another, they utilize their children to convey these messages. This puts the children in an awkward and inappropriate position.

10. *Do parents fight or argue with or degrade the other parent in the presence of the child(ren)?* It is too easy for angry parents to make derogatory comments about their ex-spouse in the presence of the children. This serves only to polarize the parties involved and put the children in a difficult position. Eventually, the children will grow tired of being caught in the

middle of these degrading remarks and will become angry with the parent making them.

11. Have parents avoided planning visitations with the child(ren) and then arrive late or not at all? An angry parent may arrive late for visitations to get back at the other parent. After all, it would certainly disrupt the other parent's plans to have to wait around for the ex-spouse to arrive. However, it is the children who are most hurt by this process. Many stories have been told about children sitting and looking out the living room window, waiting for the visiting parent, only to end up feeling more rejected when the parent is late or fails to arrive.

12. Have parents withheld time with the other parent as punishment for the child(ren) or the other parent? It is certainly important for parents to follow through on discipline that the other parent has invoked. However, for one parent to withhold visitation with the other to punish the child is grossly inappropriate. It is equally inappropriate for one parent to withhold visitation as a way of punishing the other.

13. Determine whether the parents discussed any of the financial aspects of the divorce process (support, maintenance, arrearages) with the child(ren). Two parents cannot live as cheaply apart as together. It can become very frustrating for parents to try to make budgets balance when their funds are so limited. As part of this frustration, they may express anger toward the other parent over financial issues. However, to discuss any financial issues with the children is inappropriate. It requires them to deal with an adult problem that they are not emotionally prepared to handle. Furthermore, it embroils children in the acrimony between the parents. When activities and purchases must be postponed or limited because of partial or late child support or maintenance payments, the parent should explain the circumstances to the child in a nonderogatory manner. For example, a parent should not say, "We won't be able to go to the movies tonight because your father is such an ass and we can never count on him to give us the money he should." Instead, a parent might say, "It's frustrating to me and I'm sure it's frustrating to you that we don't have enough money to go to the movies. I'll have to see what I can do to get your father to cooperate more."

14. Evaluate whether parents have accepted what the child(ren) says about the other parent without checking it out. When one parent automatically believes what a child has said about the other parent, it is often the beginning of further legal battles or other problems. Even in intact families, children may tell preposterous stories to the parents. If one parent hears something from the child about the other parent that sounds unreasonable, before getting all geared up for a battle, it is appropriate to verify the child's statement with the other parent. If the other parent cannot provide a reasonable explanation for what the child has said, it may become necessary to pursue the issue in other ways. In most cases, however, unnecessary complications can be avoided merely by checking with the other parent.

15. Evaluate whether parents have used the child(ren) as a pawn to express anger toward the other parent. Bringing a child late for visitation, scheduling activities during placement time with the other parent, or not allowing the child to come to the phone to talk to the other parent may be inappropriate expressions of anger by the placement parent. This is unfair not only to the other parent but to the child as well.

16. Have parents overburdened the child(ren) by requiring too much responsibility for growing up? When parents become overwhelmed by the circumstances of their divorce, it becomes too easy to ignore the needs of the children. Certainly, children need to learn to be responsible for their behavior and to carry their weight in maintaining the household. However, when children are put in the difficult position of assuming too much responsibility, they can easily become overburdened. For example, children should not be required to decide what school to attend or whether to have elective surgery.

17. Have parents overburdened the child(ren) by giving them the responsibility for maintaining the parent's psychological stability? This problem is illustrated by a role reversal: The child acts more like the parent and the parent acts more like the child (*parentification*). The child is put in the position of continually having to console the parent, provide psychological support for the parent, or provide solutions for the parent's problems. This is an excessive burden on the child.

18. Have parents overburdened the child(ren) by making the child(ren) the focus of arguments between the parents? Children can become overburdened by being "caught in the middle" when parents argue, especially about the child(ren).

Research clearly demonstrates that overburdened children have greater psychological problems and take longer to adjust to the difficulties associated with divorce. As a result, if your client is engaging in any of the three behaviors just described, they should desist for the good of the children.

19. Determine whether children have spent more time than necessary with a parent who exhibits severe mental illness. Research has also demonstrated that children who are required to spend a great deal of time with mentally ill parents feel less stable. An appropriate way to deal with this difficulty is to require the mentally ill parent to undergo individual psychotherapy for as long as the therapist deems necessary. Furthermore, the therapist should be allowed to report to the guardian ad litem or the court-appointed psychologist. When all three feel that visits with the mentally ill parent can be increased, it should be done gradually. By following this approach, the child's psychological need to maintain stability and the parental rights are both maintained.

20. Has either parent wanted to separate the children? Except in unusual circumstances, it is generally a bad idea to separate the children. When two children are involved in a divorce, parents may treat them as property and state that the mother and the father should each have one child. This may satisfy the needs of the parents but certainly not those of the children, because siblings generally need to remain together. For one thing, the sibling rivalry that occurs during childhood is a training ground for adulthood. It teaches children how to share, coexist, and deal with controversy. If the children are raised separately, as only children, they will not be exposed to these components of development.

Remaining together is also important because these children will probably survive their parents and need to maintain a relationship during adulthood. The relationship formed in childhood is likely to help the adult children work together to deal with their aging parents and to make necessary decisions about estates and other important family matters. On the other hand, it may not be as much of a problem to separate children when there are many siblings, and it is more economically feasible for three of them to live with the mother and three with the father. However, when children live separately, there should be periods of placement with all of the children together. An exception can also be made when the oldest minor child is nearing adulthood and would benefit from living apart from the other children. Because that child would be approximately 17 years old, the issue of sibling rivalry would no longer be relevant. In addition, the relationships among the children would already have been established by that time.

21. Has either parent introduced the child(ren) to every person they are dating? It is hard enough for children of divorce to deal with the termination of the marital relationship between their parents. Their burden increases if they are exposed to every new person the parent dates. When a child is introduced to every new date, it can also result in false hopes, unrealistic expectations, and further feelings of rejection. Once a relationship has progressed to the point of becoming a meaningful relationship, it can be advantageous to slowly introduce the children to that individual.

If possible, parents should date when the former spouse has the children. When this is not adequate or possible, parents should meet their dates outside the home. Lunch dates may be more desirable than evening dates because they do not involve the children. This is particularly important when the children are young (preteen) and when the divorce is recent (less than two years).

22. Has either parent allowed the child(ren) to observe sexually intimate behavior between them and a partner? This prohibition applies to both divorced parents and married parents. Although it may appear to be natural to expose children to intimate behavior, they are not psychologically ready to deal with these observations during childhood. Furthermore, divorced parents and their partners are more likely to be careless about preventing children from observing these behaviors because of the limitations imposed on the dating relationship.

23. Has either parent engaged in sexually intimate behavior when the child(ren) are sleeping in the same room, even if their beds are screened off from the adult's bed? Divorced or divorcing parents often live on severely limited budgets in housing that cannot accommodate everyone. Consequently, children and parents may be required to sleep in the same room. Parents may assume that the child(ren) are asleep and engage in sex only to find out that the child has observed their sexually intimate behavior. As a result, it is important to restrict sexually intimate behavior to times of complete privacy.

24. Has either parent slept in the same bed with children, except for occasional, unusual circumstances? Parents may think they should allow younger children to sleep with them to reduce the trauma associated with the separation or divorce. Allowing children to sleep with their parents under these circumstances can result in unrealistic fantasies, expectations, and feelings about the parents.

25. Has either parent asked their children to keep secrets from their ex-spouse? It is very disconcerting to a child to be told, "Whatever you do, don't tell your mother," or "Be sure not to let your father know." This places the child in the middle of the conflict, encourages the child to be deceptive, and will engender guilt feelings if they feel pressured to keep secrets from the other parent.

CHRIS'S SHATTERED EGO: THE AFTERMATH OF DIVORCE

This case describes how many of the "don'ts" just described can adversely affect a child.

In February 1993, Chris's parents came to the author with concerns about the behavior that they were seeing in Chris and Chris's sibling. Psychological testing was performed on Chris and it was determined, in large part, that the depressed-like symptoms that Chris was experiencing were related to the ongoing acrimony between Chris's mother and father.

An extensive meeting occurred with Chris's parents, in which it was explained that the research very clearly demonstrates that when parents continue to fight up to five years after the divorce has taken place, 37% of their children are clinically depressed. It was further pointed out that therapy with Chris was not the primary concern at that time. Instead, Chris's parents needed to be involved in family therapy to help them deal more effectively with each other. Chris's parents have been divorced for four and a half years. Each of them has since remarried, although they have no children from their subsequent marriages. Chris's father is a retired army officer, and Chris's mother does not work outside the home. The essence of the arguments between the parents have involved Chris's father's allegations that Mom is too lax and unstructured and Mom's allegations that Dad is too rigid, controlling, and structured.

Chris is a 14-year-old freshman in a public high school outside of the Milwaukee metropolitan area. In the early sessions of therapy, Chris reported great distress over the ongoing arguments between her parents about the behavior of the other parent. Chris indicated that every time she was with her father, he would continually badmouth her mother, and whenever spending time with her mother, she would continually badmouth the father. Each parent would present the message of "I'm okay and you're not" about the other parent. On a number of occasions, Chris was reduced to tears in my office when she witnessed her parents arguing about petty differences.

In September 1993, an emergency call was received from Chris's father who had her in a local hospital emergency room with what the emergency room's doctors described as an acute psychotic episode. During Chris's brief stay at the emergency room, a history was taken of her behavior during the previous weekend. Chris reported that there were periods where she "lost all memory." Chris's mother reported behavior that included seizurelike symptoms. The hospital performed a number of screening medical tests, including an electrocephalogram, to determine if there was any seizure disorder. All medical tests came back negative. As a result, it was immediately recommended that the parents take their child to Charter Hospital of Milwaukee, where Chris was admitted to the adolescent unit.

During the admission interview, it was quickly ascertained that Chris was indeed in a psychotic state. Chris was oriented times zero. Furthermore, Chris was not able to identify her parents or her therapist, who had worked with Chris for the past eight months.

Several days after the admission to the hospital, Chris was asked to describe what she recalled during the psychotic episode. Chris reported that she only recalled one thing. Chris stated that during the admission process, when the admissions coordinator was asking Chris's parents historical information, her parents were arguing about what was the correct answer to be given. Their child was in a psychotic state in front of them, and their response was to ignore the regressive decompensating psychotic behavior and instead choose to argue about historical events.

As the days went by, Chris disclosed that she had a large collection of knives and a single gun hidden in her bedroom, unbeknownst to her parents. Chris stated that it was necessary to have this cache of weapons for protection against whomever was trying to kill her. Furthermore, Chris stated experiencing both auditory and visual hallucinations. The auditory hallucinations were telling Chris "I will kill you . . . You can't hide from me . . . Why don't you just kill yourself? . . . Why don't you kill your parents?" In response to hearing these voices, Chris reported that she had thought of killing herself and, furthermore, had made more than simple gestures to do so. These gestures included cutting herself and scraping her skin with knives. In addition, Chris reported thoughts of killing her parents.

The hallucinations continued, and Chris was placed on antipsychotic medication. The fragility of Chris's ego was more apparent as time progressed. At any time that Chris's anxiety level elevated, even the slightest, she would easily slip into regressive, decompensating, and psychoticlike behavior. As a representative example, one day Chris's mother was supposed to bring an article of clothing to the hospital. Chris was so certain that her mother would not remember to bring the clothing that she began to cry hysterically and uncontrollably in group therapy and engaged in regressive-type behavior. When a staff member in the group presented Chris with the article of clothing that Chris's mother brought, Chris was unable to pull herself back together.

It was not unusual for Chris to deny that the hallucinations or delusions ever occurred two or three days after the fact. These experiences frightened Chris so much that it was necessary to deny that they had occurred, as opposed to admitting them and working through the process. As a result, it was more difficult to treat her, since so much energy was devoted to determining whether the original statements were true or the recantations were true. Unfortunately, this series of recantations only led Chris's father to further believe that there was nothing wrong with Chris and that whatever the problem was, was related to Chris's mother's behavior and not his own.

When family sessions took place and Chris's parents would argue with one another, Chris would sit on a chair in a fetal position sobbing. It should be noted that her parents largely ignored this behavior and continued to argue with one another. During family therapy it was pointed out to Chris's parents that if they did not find a way to coordinate their efforts, they would lose their child either to a permanent psychosis or suicide. Furthermore, Chris's parents reported that they recalled the therapist's message in February of how seriously all the arguing could affect Chris but did not believe that it could happen to their child.

During the night following each argumentative family therapy session, following weekend passes, and following those episodes where Chris's fragile ego had been tampered with, Chris would have auditory and/or visual hallucinations. She would report hearing voices that would keep her up most of the night. As stated earlier, these voices would threaten her life, instruct her to kill people, or warn her of impending danger.

Chris's parents finally started to recognize the impact of their behavior on their child, although there were indications that her father only paid lip-service to this understanding. Whenever Chris's father heard something that he perceived was a negative comment about Chris's mother, he would put his head back, roll his eyes, look at his ex-wife, and look at the therapist as if to say, "See, I told you so." Chris has still not been able to return to school on a full-time basis. It is not possible to determine how long it will be before that will occur. In addition, her ego is still very fragile, and she is only able to participate in whatever she does on a very tentative basis. Only time will tell how much Chris is able to reintegrate back into a more normalized type of life. Chris's discharge diagnosis was Acute Psychotic Depression, in remission. Her father's response at the time of discharge was frightening. He stated that he did not perceive that the seven weeks of hospitalization had done any good, that the staff did not know what they were talking about, and that he felt it necessary to seek a second opinion as the staff had clearly misinterpreted what had occurred with his child. Furthermore, he was very upset with the staff social worker for continually confronting him about how his behavior was negatively affecting his child. Instead of hearing the message, he would become defensive, argumentative, and attempt to deflect the concerns of his ex-wife.

Chris's mother was faced with the dilemma of recognizing Chris's father's attitude and the potential danger to Chris remaining in placement with her father. However, since the father would not voluntarily make any changes in Chris's placement schedule, Chris's mother was put in a "lose-lose" situation. She had the choice of either allowing Chris to stay with her father and be subjected to the potential for permanent ego damage or to take the matter to court and face the potential of regression that Chris may exhibit based on increased acrimony between her parents. Ultimately, Chris's father "fired" this author and took her to another therapist!

It could easily be stated that Chris's story is an isolated incident and does not reflect what children experience when their parents are not able to stop arguing with one another. Several months ago, an informal survey was taken of the seven children who were hospitalized at Charter Hospital, Milwaukee's child unit. As the Unit Service Director of that unit, this writer is directly or indirectly involved in all of the cases on that unit. During that particular week, the seven children who were hospitalized were between 7 and 11 years of age. All seven of the children came from nonintact families. Furthermore, in all seven cases, the parents were not able to deal effectively with one another. Four of the seven children were admitted to Charter Hospital following a bona fide suicide attempt. One had attempted to hang himself, one had put a plastic bag over her head, another had threatened her own life with a butcher knife, and the last had threatened his life with a hunting knife.

In surveying the admissions to Charter Hospital during 1993, well over 95% of the children admitted to the unit were from nonintact families, and a vast majority of these were cases where the parents were not able to effectively communicate with one another. It must be recognized, however, that there is an inherent problem in trying to resolve these types of concerns. Parents are being asked to communicate effectively with one another for the best interest of their children outside of the marriage, when they were not able to accomplish this task inside the marriage. Had they been able to communicate effectively with one another during the marriage, it is likely that the divorce would never have taken place. Parents mistakenly operate under the fallacy that when they get divorced they will be able to terminate their relationship with their ex-spouse. In fact, the relationship with their ex-spouse does not terminate as the result of divorce but continues until the youngest child reaches majority. Instead of the relationship terminating, the rules of the relationship change. Since many of these divorces are acrimonious, it becomes necessary for parents to seek professional help to facilitate the changing of the rules following the divorce.

In Chris's case, it was difficult for Chris to gain a strong ego identity by observing her parents. Chris's mother is a relatively unstructured, caring woman who loves Chris very much and who describes her household as being chaotic at times. Chris's father is a highly structured individual who is described by Chris's mother as being rigid. Chris's father also loves Chris very much. However, when Chris was with her mother, she would talk about Chris's father's approach as being inappropriate. Conversely, when Chris was with her father, he would talk about Chris's mother's approach as being inappropriate. As a result, Chris could not find a firm foundation upon which to develop her self-concept or her ego. Whatever there was of Chris's ego was attacked every time she would be in the presence of one parent or the other. Chris became so anxious about what was occurring, so depressed about the ongoing acrimony, that she had significant thoughts about killing herself accompanied by some self-endangering behavior. Her ego was under continual attack and eventually it shattered; then Chris became psychotic in an effort to prevent herself from committing suicide. The only way that Chris could escape suicide was by becoming psychotic.

After discharge from the hospital, Chris had three decompensating episodes within the first week, leading to rehospitalization. On these occasions, Chris was afraid her mother would kill herself; that she was not safe at her dad's house; and she was having suicidal thoughts. What were Chris's parents responses? Mom said, "I've got to go to court to get Chris out of her dad's house before he destroys Chris," and Dad presented a sequential series of "facts" in the form of a logical proof to demonstrate Mom's incompetence.

As professionals, we sometimes wonder what it takes for parents to understand the impact of their behavior on their children. Here, two seemingly intelligent parents were unable to put their differences aside for their child, even when Chris was sitting in front of them in a psychotic state. How do we get the message across to parents that winning isn't everything; that being right isn't everything? This author is not sure that Chris's parents will ever get the message. However, as professionals involved in these cases, both attorneys and psychologists have a moral and ethical obligation to not allow their clients to become like Chris's parents or their client's children to become like Chris. Winning must take a subordinate role to the best interests of the children.

CHAPTER 8

Abuse Allegations

INTRODUCTION

In the legal context, a psychological evaluation of the history presented frequently gives rise to specific concerns that must be addressed. The presence of any form of physical, sexual, or psychological abuse or victimization calls for a special emphasis during the evaluation.

Reports of physical abuse have shown a dramatic increase in the past two decades. "Each year since national statistics have been published on the number of child maltreatment reports, there has been the disturbing news that the number is greater than the year before. From 1983 to 1984 alone, there was an estimated 17% increase in reports involving 1,727,000 children in over one million families" (Eckenrode et al., 1988, p. 9). Between 1990 and 1991, the number of reports increased 6 percent, to 2.6 million (Brosig & Kalichman, 1991). This is partly a result of more cases being reported, due to increased public awareness, and not just an increase in incidence.

PHYSICAL ABUSE

The most recent national incidence studies have estimated that nearly 1 million children experienced harm as a result of physical maltreatment (including sexual abuse) in 1986. In addition, more than 1.5 million children experienced abuse or neglect. When comparing the 1986 incidence rate to the 1980 incidence rate, the number of children who experienced demonstrable harm increased 51%. In addition, the number of cases reported to Child Protective Services increased nearly 57% during that time. Furthermore, 53% of the cases that have been reported were substantiated in 1986. In 1986, 331,500 children, or 4.9 children per thousand, were physically abused in this country (U.S. Department of Health and Human Services, 1992).

One of the problems associated with reporting abuse is the difficulty in defining what constitutes "physical abuse." Most definitions of physical abuse include some behaviors that, in the past, were considered acceptable punishment. Basically, any type of physical intervention that causes injury or harm to the victim is considered physical abuse. Punishments involving the use of wooden spoons, paddles, switches, and belts that leave bruises or other marks are considered physical abuse today.

Abusiveness in the family does not only take place between parents and children. It also occurs among other family members, such as aunts, uncles, grandparents, and cousins.

The Children Abuse Prevention Treatment Act (Public Law 100–294) defines child abuse and neglect as:

physical or mental injury (sexual abuse or exploitation, negligent treatment or maltreatment) of a child (a person under the age of 18, unless the child protection law of that State in which the child resides specifies a younger age for cases not involving sexual abuse) by a person (including any employee of a residential facility or any staff personnel providing out-of-home care) who is responsible for the child's welfare under circumstances which indicate that the child's health or welfare is harmed or threatened thereby. . . .

Physical abuse is characterized by inflicting physical injury by punching, beating, kicking, biting, burning, or otherwise harming a child. Although the injury is not an accident, the parent or caretaker may not have intended to hurt the child. The injury may have resulted from overdiscipline or physical punishment that is inappropriate to the child's age. . . .

Child neglect is characterized by failure to provide the child's basic needs. Neglect can be physical, educational, or emotional. The latest incidence study defines these three types of neglect as follows: Physical neglect includes refusal of or delay in seeking health care, abandonment, expulsion from home, or not allowing a runaway to return, and inadequate supervision. Educational neglect is permission for chronic truancy, failure to enroll a child of mandatory school age, and inattention to a special educational need. (U.S. Department of Health and Human Services, 1992, pp. 3–4)

Characteristics

Although it can be difficult to predict who will be a child abuser, certain characteristics are present in many of these individuals.

Parents may be more likely to maltreat their children if they use drugs or alcohol (alcoholic mothers are three times more likely and alcoholic fathers eight times more likely to abuse or neglect their children than are nonalcoholic parents); are isolated, with no family or friends to depend on; were emotionally deprived, abused, or neglected as children; feel worthless and have never been loved or cared about; or are in poor health. Many abusive and neglectful parents do not intend to harm their children and often feel remorse about their maltreating behavior. However, their own problems may prevent them from stopping their harmful behavior and may result in resistance to outside intervention. It is important to remember that diligent and effective intervention efforts may overcome the parent's resistance and help them change their abusive and neglectful behavior.

Children are more likely to be at risk of maltreatment if they are unwanted, resemble someone the parents dislike, or have physical or behavioral traits which make them different or especially difficult to care for. (U.S. Department of Health and Human Service, 1992, p. 5)

Environmental conditions can affect the likelihood of an increase in the incidence of physical abuse. These include changes in financial condition, employment status, or family structure.

Milner and Chilamkurti (1991) identify several characteristics of physical abuse perpetrators. They found that the most frequently occurring characteristic is having been physically abused during the adult's own childhood. Research also demonstrates that physical abuse perpetrators show more physiological reactivity to child-related stimuli than nonperpetrators. Furthermore, abusive parents have more physical symptom-related complaints than nonabusive parents. In addition, abusing parents tend to have poorer self-concepts and lower ego-strengths than nonabusing parents. They have a greater external locus of control, which suggests that they look for control from outside themselves as opposed to from within. Abusing parents are more likely to see their children as being intentionally disruptive or disobedient. They have a greater expectation for the children to engage in appropriate behavior. Abusing parents also experience greater stress, greater depression, and greater levels of anxiety than nonabusing parents.

Milner and Chilamkurti report that though the relationship between physical abuse and alcohol consumption is complex, one does exist. Abusing parents feel more socially isolated and have lower rates of interaction with their children. These interactions tend to be more negative than positive. Abusing parents are more likely to rely on power as a form of discipline than nonabusing parents.

Substantiation

One of the problems with physical abuse allegations is the substantiation of child abuse and neglect reports. The percentage of those reports that have been substantiated following investigation has decreased (U.S. Department of Health and Human Services, 1992, p. 5). Eckenrode reports that more than half of the cases reported in 1974 were substantiated but only 25% of those reported in 1984 were substantiated. This study points out that one of the reasons for the lower rate of substantiation is that funding for social service agencies has not increased at the same rate as the number of reports. In addition, there is concern about the stress that families go through during the abuse investigation, only to have approximately two-thirds of the cases remain unsubstantiated. Eckenrode studied the factors related to substantiated reports and found that for physical abuse reports, those involving black and Hispanic children were much more likely to be substantiated than those involving white children. For sexual abuse reports with female victims, the size of the household and the number of adults and children in the family influenced substantiation. In child neglect cases, a higher substantiation rate among younger children may reflect the fact that neglect in the youngest age groups tends to be physical.

In general, a previous history of abuse or neglect in the accused family increases the probability of substantiation. Also when reports are made by professionals mandated by the law to report, the likelihood of substantiation is greater. Reports from nonprofessionals are least likely to be substantiated. Other significant factors include the number of contacts with the subjects of the report, the length of the investigation, and the effects of the court action.

Child Abuse Potential

Over the decades, research has demonstrated that the best single predictor of whether an individual will be abusive is if that individual was abused as a child. Many researchers have attempted to develop child abuse risk assessments. Much MMPI research has been performed, only to find investigators unable to replicate specific subscale patterns to distinguish abusers from nonabusers. Caldwell (1982) reports that the current methods used to assess maltreatment potential are encouraging but still limited. They point out that one of the difficulties in predicting child abuse is the varying definitions of what constitutes abuse. The author concludes, "Given that current risk assessment procedures provide a relatively small increase in program efficiency, the cost of using that must be evaluated carefully. . . . At the present, and most likely for the future, the assessment of child abuse potential is not a powerful aid to the efforts to prevent child abuse and neglect" (Caldwell, 1982, p. 21).

Milner (1989) developed the Child Abuse Potential (CAP) Inventory as a screening questionnaire for suspected adult perpetrators of physical child abuse. In a validation study that was performed using this particular instrument, 73.8% of the abusers and 99.1% of the nonabusers were correctly identified. A cutoff score has been developed with this instrument that helps categorize people as having a high or low level of child abuse potential. This instrument has been studied by Holden, Willis, and Foltz (1989) using both the CAP Inventory and the Parenting Stress Index, and the results of the study indicated that the CAP Inventory and the Parenting Stress Index appeared to measure relatively similar constructs.

Malinosky-Rummell and Hansen (1993) reviewed the literature on the long-term consequences on childhood physical abuse. This thorough work divides the research into seven basic topics.

The first area addressed is aggressive and violent behavior. When discussing adolescent violence, they note that "adolescents who exhibit aggressive and violent behaviors, including extrafamilial and dating violence, demonstrate higher rates of maltreatment than the general population. . . . Violent adolescent boys in residential facilities demonstrate higher rates of physical abuse than do less violent and nonviolent male comparison groups. . . . Among children who are receiving mental health treatment, those who have been physically abused exhibit more aggressive behavior than do their non-abused peers" (p. 70). When addressing adult violence toward nonfamilial persons, the authors state, "Overall, these findings imply that violent inmates and outpatients, particularly males, report higher rates of childhood physical abuse than do less violent comparison groups" (1993, p. 70). The authors next looked at adult violence toward children. They found "that approximately one-third (30% plus or minus 5%) of physically abused or neglected individuals abuse their own children" (p. 71). Adult violence toward dating partners was also addressed. The authors state, "Studies that use several different self-report methodologies demonstrate a relationship between childhood physical abuse and dating violence in college students. . . . Furthermore, approximately 5% of abusive subjects use the same form of violence on their dating partners as they had experienced or observed in childhood" (p. 71). Last, the authors addressed adult violence toward spouses. They report, "Of men whose parents did not hit each other, those who had been physically abused as teenagers had twice the rate of violence toward their wife than nonabused men. . . . Physically abused alcoholic men described significantly more marital violence toward their wife during treatment than did nonabused alcoholic comparison groups. . . . These findings imply that whereas childhood physical abuse relates to spouse abuse in men, it may not relate to women's involvement in abusive marital relationships. Furthermore, parental marital violence may also contribute to spouse abuse" (pp. 71–72).

The next major area reviewed involved nonviolent criminal behavior. The researchers conclude that "physically abused children demonstrate significantly more noncompliance, nonaggressive conduct disorders, and other externalizing behaviors than do nonabused comparison groups. . . . Present research has not shown a relationship between physical abuse and nonviolent criminal behavior" (p. 72).

When looking at substance abuse, Malinosky-Rummell and Hansen report "some evidence exists to support a relationship between childhood physical abuse and substance abuse in adolescents. . . . Thirty percent of the subjects had been physically or sexually abused, a higher rate than the general population. . . . The authors noted a high rate of parental substance abuse (75%) reported by the abused group, a finding supported by other research on adolescent inpatients. . . . Researchers describing the link between childhood physical abuse and adult substance abuse suggest that the stronger tendency to abuse substances is a result of abuse-related feelings and cognitions" (1993, pp. 72–73).

There is significant research to suggest that individuals who have been involved in physical abuse have higher suicidal and self-injurious behavior. "Maltreatment has been linked to adolescent self-injurious and suicidal behaviors in studies. . . . Thus, physical abuse appears to be related to self-injurious and suicidal behaviors in male and female inpatients, as well as female college students. Gender, form of maltreatment, and parental conflict may also affect this relationship" (p. 73).

The authors next address the issue of emotional problems, stating "physically abused youths who are six to sixteen years old, and children from violent or distressed families, display significantly more emotional problems, including anxiety and depression, than do nonabused community children. . . . In conclusion, physical abuse has been associated with a variety of emotional problems, including somatization, anxiety, depression, hostility, paranoid ideation, psychosis, and dissociation, in female inpatient and community samples" (p. 73).

Interpersonal relationships are also affected in individuals who have been physically abused as children. Research in this area, however, shows mixed findings. "Female inpatients who reported childhood physical abuse had significantly higher interpersonal sensitivity scores. . . . There is . . . a relationship between childhood physical abuse and negative findings about interpersonal relationship in adulthood" (p. 74). However, divorce rates do not appear to differ between abused and nonabused men.

Research also supports the notion that individuals' academic and vocational abilities are adversely affected by physical abuse during childhood.

The reviewers report that a number of moderator variables also affect abuse. These include individual factors such as the age, gender, form of maltreatment, and interaction with others. They also include family factors such as substance abuse and environmental factors, which would include socioeconomic status and outside influences. Socioeconomic status has been cited as a risk factor in physical abuse cases.

Family Violence

Family violence can take the form of spouse abuse and is sometimes referred to as domestic violence. It is defined as:

> the use or threat of physical violence by the abuser to gain control and power over the victim. It occurs in households of both married and cohabiting couples. Although either party may be the victim, most victims are women. The three types of spouse abuse (physical abuse, sexual violence, and psychological/emotional abuse) often occur in combination.
>
> . . . Physical abuse can take many forms including kicking, hitting, biting, choking, pushing, and assaults with weapons. Sometimes particular areas are

targeted, such as the abdomen of a pregnant woman. (U.S. Department of Health and Human Services, 1991, p. 3)

Victims stay in physically abusive relationships for many reasons. "Some victims stay because they blame themselves, believe the spouse will stop, are financially dependent, or fear that they or their children will be seriously injured or killed if they attempt to leave. Victims also stay because they have, or feel they have, no other place to go" (U.S. Department of Health and Human Services, 1991, p. 3).

When sexual violence occurs in a domestic situation, it is sometimes referred to as marital rape. These attacks can include assaults on the victim's breasts or genitals, sexual sadism, or forced sexual activity.

> Similar to rape occurring outside the family, marital rape appears to be mainly an act of violence and aggression in which sex is the method used to humiliate, hurt, degrade, and dominate the woman. The violence and brutality in the sexual relationship seem to escalate with time. The sexual violence is frequently accompanied by life-threatening acts or threats. (U.S. Department of Health and Human Services, 1991, p. 3)

Research has demonstrated that family violence has many different effects on the victim and the children.

Pageloe's research states, "Victims of all types of family violence share a common experience of denigration of self that results in diminished self-esteem. The shame and feeling of worthlessness, so often expressed by battered women, is shared by maltreated children as well as maltreated elderly parents" (1984, p. 81).

Finkelhor (1983) reports that depression, suicidal feelings, self-contempt, and an inability to trust and develop intimate relationships in later life are the fallout associated with living in a family where family abuse has occurred. Severely assaulted women had much higher rates of psychological distress, including four times the rate of depression and five and a half times the number of suicide attempts.

Crites and Coker (1988) report that children raised in abusive households learn that violence toward a loved one is acceptable behavior. In addition, they exhibit fear, emotional symptoms such as psychosomatic complaints, school phobias, enuresis (bed-wetting), and insomnia. Young children may put themselves at risk by attempting to stop the violence. In other cases they try to deny it by hiding. Very young children tend to identify with the aggressor and lose respect for the victim.

Crites and Coker additionally report that "the stress of avoiding, experiencing, and then (while in the relationship) recovering from psychological abuse and suffering from ongoing psychological trauma affects the ability of a mother to be a good parent" (1988, p. 11).

Goodman and Rosenberg (1991) report that memory for violent events witnessed in childhood may last a lifetime. They also indicate that, depending upon the age, gender, and extent of violence the children observed, the children themselves tend to feel worthless, mistrust intimate relationships, exhibit aggression, and may even be delayed intellectually.

One of the startling features of spousal abuse is that in 45% of the cases, the children were also being abused. Gelles and Strauss (198) report that child victims were two to three times more likely to have failing grades in school, difficulty forming friendships, disciplinary problems in school, physically assaultive behavior in school and the home, vandalism and theft, and alcohol and other drug-abuse-related problems. In addition, abused children had been arrested four times more often than nonabused children.

Veltkamp and Miller (1990) discuss the "spouse abuse accommodation syndrome" and suggest that this syndrome has several stages. Initially, the individual is likely to feel overwhelmed and intimidated during the acute stage of trauma. This is followed by a stage of cognitive disorganization and confusion. The third stage generally involves avoidance, which can be exhibited in two ways: conscious inhibitions or an avoidance resulting from unconscious denial. The perpetrator feeds into this cycle and reinforces the desire to continue the relationship. The men who perform this abuse generally do so as a result of their own lack of communication skills, fear of intimacy, and dependency upon the women they batter.

Veltkamp and Miller (1990) summarize by stating:

> the long-term effects of experiencing family violence suggest the following: (1) There tend to be self-destructive tendencies in victims, (2) Women who have been abused show significant adjustment difficulties and problems related to both interpersonal and sexual relationships with males and females, (3) Abuse victims tend to abuse their offspring, thus perpetuating abuse to the next generations, and (4) The most significant diagnostic profile for adults who are physically and sexually abused includes the following symptomatology: depression, self-destructive behavior, anxiety, and traumatic stress, feeling of isolation, poor self-esteem, and tendency towards re-victimization, substance abuse, difficulties in trusting others, and sexual maladjustment in adulthood. (p. 184)

Bolton and Bolton (1987) report many factors that contribute to the likelihood of family violence. They include repeated exposure to crises; poverty; reduced amount of support available; absence of the nuclear family working together in a crisis; a lower level of education; problematic employment patterns; overreliance on physical punishment; rigidity and inflexibility; and lack of involvement of extended family members.

Bolton and Bolton also identified those factors that contribute to appropriate family functioning. They include a willingness to nurture and protect family members; the ability to make needs known; absence of obvious mental illness; children's ability to elicit caregiving from parents; reciprocal relationships in the family; manageable levels of competition within the family; a supportive environment; lack of a totally dominant family member; and no nagging sense that something is wrong with the family interaction. Hershorn and Rosenbaum (1985) studied the effect of marital violence on children. They conclude:

> the results of . . . investigation are supportive of the hypothesis that parental marital discord and violence are associated with conduct problems in witnessing children. . . . The result supported the hypothesis that increased exposure to discord/violence and punitive maternal parenting were both associated with childhood problems. . . . These results suggest that exposure to marital discord/violence has a more generalized effect on the behavioral and emotional health of the child than does parenting style, which seems to relate more specifically to conduct disorder. . . . The results of the present investigations suggest that marital violence be added to the list of factors enumerated by Emery, which merit consideration in studying the relationship between marital turmoil and child problems. (pp. 264–265)

The Psychologically Battered Child

> A child is considered to be emotionally of psychologically abused when he or she is the subject of acts or omissions by the parents or other persons responsible for the child's care that have caused, or could cause a serious behavioral, cognitive, emotional, or mental disorder. In some cases of emotional/psychological abuse, the acts of the parents or other caretakers alone, without any harm to the child's behavior or condition, are sufficient to warrant Child Protective Services intervention. An example would be if the parents/caretakers use extreme or bizarre forms of punishment, such as torture or confinement of the child in a dark closet. For less severe acts, such as habitual scapegoating, belittling, or rejecting treatment, demonstrable harm to the child is often required for Child Protective Services to intervene. (U.S. Department of Health and Human Services, 1992, p. 3)

Emotional neglect includes "such actions as chronic or extreme spouse abuse in the child's presence, permission for drug or alcohol use by the child, and refusal of or failure to provide needed psychological care" (p. 2). Today the most frequently occurring form of abuse is that of emotional or psychological abuse. In 1986 it involved 180,100 children, or three per thousand.

Behaviors on the part of parents that "jeopardize the development of self-esteem, of social competency, of the capacity for intimacy, and positive healthy interpersonal relationship" are all aspects of psychological maltreatment (Garbarino, Guttmann, & Seely, 1987, p. 1). They give five examples of psychological maltreatment. They are:

1. Each morning a mother threatens her 4-year-old son with abandonment: "Maybe today is the day I go away and leave you alone. You better be good today, boy, or you'll never see me again."

2. A father restricts his 7-year-old daughter to her room every day after school: "I don't want you getting involved with any other kids; they're not good enough for you."
3. Each time a 10-year-old boy brings home his report card from school, his parents look it over with expressions of disgust: "No son of ours could be such a dummy; we wish you weren't around all the time reminding us of the mistake we made."
4. A 3-year-old boy's father suspects that he's not the boy's father, that the boy's mother had an affair while he was away on business. Now he refuses to speak to the boy: "He's not mine; I don't want anything to do with him."
5. A mother persuades her 13-year-old daughter to earn some money by having sex with the mother's "extra" boyfriends: "You're a little slut anyway, and I might as well get something out of being your mother." (p. 1)

The accepted definition of child maltreatment reported in Garbarino et al. came from the Interdisciplinary Glossary on Child Abuse and Neglect: "The definitions of emotional abuse include verbal or emotional assault, close confinement and threatened harm. The definitions of emotional neglect include inadequate nurturance/affection, knowingly permitting maladaptive behavior (for example, delinquency) and other refusal to provide essential care" (pp. 4–5).

Parental Factors Related to Maltreatment

Garbarino et al. (1987) identify several parental factors related to maltreatment. They include the following:

-   Parents' unavailability to respond to the children's needs. Such parents mainly ignore and reject their children. When they are unavailable to meet their children's physical needs, they fail to feed the children appropriately, to dress them as needed, or to enable them to get enough sleep or health care.
-   When parents give partial and inappropriate responses to the children's needs, mainly rejecting or corrupting the children. For example, the parents try to meet the child's physical and psychological needs, yet they lack sufficient resources, knowledge, and skills for doing so effectively.... Another inappropriate response is infantilization. Instead of placing excessively high demands on the children, the parents underestimate the children's physical abilities and mental capabilities and consistently prevent the children from actualizing their potentials.... A third type of inappropriate response, corrupting or missocializing, occurs when parents teach the children values that deviate from nor-

mative community values. In some instances, children are raised on values that differ markedly from those of the community—for example, values favoring drug abuse, sexual misconduct, or delinquent activity— and therefore place the child in jeopardy.

- Parents who make harsh and destructive responses to the needs of their children, mainly terrorizing, but also degrading, threatening, and exploiting their children. (pp. 54–56)

Garbarino et al. (1987) also examine four "personal characteristics" of the parents who psychologically maltreat their children:

1. The parent, himself or herself, has been psychologically maltreated as a child;
2. The parent is addicted to drugs or alcohol;
3. The parent creates an "interactional stress environment"; or
4. The parent is mentally ill or mentally retarded.

Garbarino et al. conclude:

the psychologically maltreated child is often identified by personal characteristics, perceptions, and behaviors that convey low self-esteem, a negative view of the world, and internalized or externalized anxieties and aggressions. Whether the child clings to adults or avoids them, his or her social behavior and responses are inappropriate and exceptional. (p. 64)

These authors state that infants are usually psychologically maltreated in the form of rejection, unavailability, malnourishment, or inconsistency. Children are psychologically maltreated by behavior suggesting they are unloved, unwanted, inferior, inadequate, and unrelated to any social system. Adolescents who are psychologically maltreated tend to exhibit patterns similar to those exhibited by children, except these patterns are often stronger and more elaborate and perhaps less linked to their parents.

Psychological or emotional abuse in domestic situations can take many forms. It is more than the typical verbal arguments that can occur in any family, and it results in a systematic destruction of the individual's self-esteem. It is not unusual for psychological or emotional abuse to occur in accompaniment with physical abuse or sexual violence.

Psychological or emotional abuse can take the form of economic domination, where "men who abuse attempted to control their partners by having complete power over the household finances. They try to keep the victim from working and therefore encourage the victim's economic dependence upon them" (U.S. Department of Health and Human Services, 1991, p. 3). They can:

use the children to maintain power and control over their partners. For example, they belittle or degrade the children as a means of harassing the victim.

Abusers may frighten their victims by using looks, actions, gestures, or loud voices; by smashing things; by destroying the victim's property. Abusers may threaten to take the children away from their spouse, to harm the children, or [to] commit suicide. Such threats add to the anxiety and fear experienced by victims and children. Men who [use this form of] abuse may control their partner's activities, companions, or whereabouts. [They] often control what their victims do, whom they see, and where they go. Many abusers feel threatened by anyone with whom their victims have contact. (U.S. Department of Health and Human Services, 1991, p. 4)

SEXUAL ABUSE

What Is Sexual Abuse?

One of the critical issues associated with proceeding with a sexual abuse allegation is trying to define sexual abuse. Wakefield and Underwager (1991), as part of their research in the area, ask, "Is it sexual abuse when a child catches a glimpse of an exhibitionist?" There is disagreement over this. Most people would not consider it abuse if a child is shown *Playboy* magazine by an older playmate. But what if a young child is shown hard-core pornography? Does a mother sleeping with her child constitute sexual abuse in the absence of sexual touching? What if the child is a teenager who becomes aroused by this? Most people would agree that it is sexual abuse if a 19-year-old woman has sexual contact with a six-year-old boy, but not if the boy is 16. However, what if the boy is 14? What if the 14-year-old boy initiates the experience with the woman and later views the experience as positive (p. 45)?

This is not to say that all sexual abuse allegations fit into a gray area of definition and are difficult to discern. The U.S. Department of Health and Human Services defines sexual abuse to include "fondling a child's genitals, intercourse, incest, rape, sodomy, exhibitionism, and sexual exploitation. To be considered child abuse, these have to be committed by a person responsible for the care of the child (e.g., a parent, a baby sitter, or a day care provider). If a stranger commits these acts, it would be considered sexual assault and handled solely by the police and criminal courts" (1992, pp. 2–3). Many experts believe that sexual abuse is the most underreported form of child maltreatment because of the secrecy or "conspiracy of silence" that so often characterizes these cases.

Finkelhor (1987) states that "child sexual abuse is most commonly used in reference to sexual activity involving a child that has at least one or two characteristics: It occurs within a relationship where it is deemed exploitive by virtue of an age difference or caretaking relationship that exists with the child; it occurs as a result of threat or force" (p. 233).

The number of cases of child sexual abuse has increased dramatically in the last decade. There were 133,600 cases (or 2.1 per thousand) of sexual abuse reported in 1986 as compared to 7,559 in 1976. This does not mean that there are more than 15 times as many incidences today as there were in 1976. Instead, it means that the public is more aware of sexual-abuse-related concerns and abuse is being reported more frequently.

Profile of Abuser and Abused

Finkelhor (1987) points out that:

> although good research is scarce, there is some reasonable empirical support for propositions that are consistent with some of these theories: (1) Some groups of abusers do have an unusual need for power and domination which may be related to their offender behavior; (2) most groups of offenders who have been tested using psychological monitors do show unusual levels of deviant sexual arousal to children; (3) many offenders have histories of being victims of sexual abuse themselves; (4) many offenders have conflict over adult heterosexual relationships or are experiencing disruption in normal adult heterosexual partnerships at the time of the offense; and (5) alcohol is connected to the commission of the acts in a large number of the offenses. (pp. 234–235)

He also states:

> according to recent community studies, the following factors are consistently associated with higher risk of abuse: (1) a child who is living without one of the biological parents; (2) a child whose mother is unavailable either as a result of employment outside of the home, disability or illness; (3) a child who reports that the parents' marriage is unhappy or conflictful; (4) a child who reports a poor relationship with the parents or being subject to extremely punitive discipline or child abuse; (5) a child who reports having a stepfather. (pp. 233–235)

Hanson, Steffy, and Gauthier (1993) examined the long-term recidivism rates of 197 child molesters who were released from prison between 1958 and 1974. They report, "Our results support previous research that child molesters are at risk for reoffending for many years. . . . The greatest risk appears to be the first five to ten years and that child molesters appear to be at significant risk for reoffending throughout their life. Forty-two percent of this sample were eventually reconvicted, with 23% of the recidivists being reconvicted more than 10 years after they were released" (p. 650). In conclusion, they state, "Our findings of substantial long-term recidivism suggest that any short-term treatment, no matter how well conceived and well delivered, is unlikely to effectively control any child molesters. Sexual offense recidivism is most likely to be prevented when interventions attempt to address the life-long potential for reoffenses and do not expect child molesters to be permanently "cured" following a single set of treatment sessions" (p. 651).

Wakefield and Underwager (1991) specifically addressed characteristics of women who sexually abused children. Although the vast majority of sexual abuse is perpetrated by men, approximately 14% of perpetration against boys and 6% of perpetration against girls was performed by females acting alone. There are several conclusions that they draw from the literature about female perpetrators. They are:

1. Awareness about women perpetrators of sexual abuse has greatly increased in recent years. However, sexual contact between children and women is a minority of child-adult sexual contact and the traditional view of child sexual abuse as a primarily male problem is correct.

2. Child sexual abuse by females does occur and may not be as rare as the earlier literature indicates.

3. There is a great range in the estimated frequency of sexual abuse by women from different studies and the definition of sexual abuse used, sample selected and methodology employed must be considered.

4. Some of the literature which discusses female perpetrators is likely to have included cases of false allegations, which gives a misleading picture of both the frequency with which females abuse children and the characteristics of such women.

5. Female child sexual abusers are less likely than men to fit the psychiatric definition of pedophile.

6. There are widely different circumstances in which females may engage in behavior that is defined as child sexual abuse and the circumstances that lead women to sexually abuse children can often be differentiated from those causing men to do so. One example of this is a sexual abuse which occurs in conjunction with a dominant male in which the woman plays a secondary role. Another is found by the retrospective surveys of college men in which many of the boys reported that they had engaged in incidents voluntarily and did not feel victimized.

7. Many studies depict women who sexually abuse children as being loners, socially isolated, alienated, likely to have had abusive childhoods, and apt to have emotional problems. However most are not psychotic. (pp. 63–64)

Rowan, Rowan, and Langelier (1990) studied the fact that because females tend to be more enmeshed in family systems, their abuse of children may be more difficult to detect. This may lead to some underreporting of female sexual abuse. Women also have more opportunities to touch than do men, and as a result, may not receive the same level of attention associated with inappropriate sexual contact. The authors conclude, "The most important factor seems to be disinhibition due to personality disorder and/or borderline intelligence and, perhaps more significantly, offending in the company of a dominant male" (p. 83).

Issues regarding the long-term effects of sexual victimization have been addressed in two studies. Herman, Russell, and Trocki (1986) studied 205 women who had histories of incest. They stated that patients frequently complained of chronic depression, anhedonia (an inability to experience pleasure), and inner deadness and may be driven periodically to seek relief in alcohol or other drug abuse, self-mutilation, and suicide attempts. They conclude:

> with the more severe degrees of sexual abuse, however, few women were able to escape without long-term sequelae. Victims who had experienced forceful and repeated, prolonged abuse or severe physical violation, and especially those abused by much older men, especially by their fathers or stepfathers, were very likely to report persistent difficulties in their adult lives." (p. 1296)

Gold (1986) studied the relationship between childhood sexual victimization and adult functioning. One hundred three women ranging in age from 18 to 57 were studied. Complete psychological evaluations were administered. Gold reports:

> For the first time, aspects of the woman's victimization experience, attributional style, and social support network were related to her adult functioning. . . . The victimized woman's present perception of the abusive experience and her perception of her mother's response to it were the only aspects of the victimization experience that were significantly related to her adult functioning. . . . The quality of the support reported by these women may reflect their ability to have close relationships with others, including sexual relationships. (p. 474)

This study gives support to the notion that the mother's response to the sexual abuse allegations can have a greater long-term negative effect on the child's resolution of the problems than the actual sexual abuse.

Scott and Stone (1986) examined the effects of father-daughter incest through use of the MMPI. They found that elevations on the 4 and 8 scales were most frequent with victims of father and daughter incest. Elevated 7–8 and 6–8 were the next most frequent scoring profiles. Scott and Stone state:

> These findings suggest that father-daughter incest victimization results in lower psychological adjustment for both age groups (adults and adolescents) and indicate the probability that the adjustment problems of child victims do, indeed, persist over time. . . . There is also evidence of "schizoid process" with deficits in ego strength (psychic energy) and serious identity confusion, as well as possible sexual preoccupation with concerns of vulnerability and inadequacy. (p. 257)

A summary of these striking similarities and differences between the two groups leads to the speculation that being sexually victimized by the father produces an arrestment of ego development and related identity confusion at the core of the personality. However, the variable (amount) of time since the molestation seems to determine how this core disturbance is expressed. Shorter time and less development is exemplified by the adolescent victim and seems to produce more of an identity crisis, while the long-term effects from living for years with the core damage may result in a more chronically depressed and "an at odds with the environment" resignation. (p. 258)

Another study concludes, "Perhaps the most significant new finding emerging from this study is the clear relationship between antisocial personality factors and child abuse potential. The significant differences between the (experimental group) and other women on the MMPI-2 content scale ASP (Antisocial Practices) suggest that this variable should be taken into consideration when assessing potential for child abuse" (Egeland, Erickson, Butcher, & Ben-Porath, 1991, p. 263).

Bona Fide Versus Fabricated Abuse Allegations

Recently, concern has increased about whether the sexual abuse allegations that are being made are bona fide or fabricated. The number of allegations of child sexual abuse is increasing at an alarming rate.

Unfortunately, when a custody/visitation dispute is in process, one parent only has to claim that the other parent has sexually abused one of the children, and the process comes to a dramatic halt. Generally, the accused parent is forbidden contact with the children until the issue is resolved.

In the past, evaluators relied on the amount of detail that the child was able to provide and the description of the abuse as indicators of whether the allegation was bona fide or fabricated. Gardner (1986) points out that this practice is unreliable. Children today have access to much more information about sex and sexuality than in the past. A child watching the six o'clock news can hear stories about day-care workers who have been charged with sexual abuse. Premium cable channels show explicit sexual behavior as early as seven o'clock in the evening. Even X-rated home videos are much more available to children, and soap operas have become sexual showcases during the daytime. Both general sex education and sexual abuse education occur in the schools starting as early as the preschool years. In the past, the only source of information that a child may have had about sexual abuse was when he or she had actually been abused. However, this information now could come from being abused or from any of the abuse-identified sources.

Gardner has developed criteria that he uses for differentiating fabricated from bona fide sexual abuse. He states that in bona fide sexual abuse, the mother will generally be upset, secretive, and embarrassed. However, in fabricated sexual abuse, the mother has the need to "tell the whole world" and does not express shame. In bona fide sexual abuse, the child will generally be fearful and timid in the presence of the abusing parent. On the other hand, in fabricated sexual abuse, the child will also want to "tell the whole world," will be comfortable in the presence of the accused, and may even scream the accusations in the face of the accused parent. The description of the abuse in bona fide situations will be consistent, real, and serious; however, in fabricated situations, the scenarios are often preposterous.

Case 1

A five-year-old girl accused her father of sexually abusing her. The girl at different times reported that the father, the mother, the mother's boyfriend, the father's therapist, and the mother's therapist had sexually abused her. Many of these accusations were made while sitting on the lap of her father. She appeared to be willing to tell anyone who would listen her story and added new details on each occasion. Furthermore, her mother was equally interested in telling the story of the alleged sexual abuse to any who would listen. In this particular situation, there was also reason to believe that the girl may have seen her mother masturbate on one occasion and have intercourse with her boyfriend on another occasion. This situation certainly suggested that sexual information may have been available to the child without sexual abuse. In this particular matter, the author of this text pointed out these criteria to the judge during testimony, and the father was eventually awarded custody.

Bresee, Stearns, Bess, and Pecker (1986) described five components that are found in mothers who are child-focused and are not fabricating or exaggerating the stories of sexual abuse. The components are as follows:

1. They expressed remorse for not protecting the child sufficiently to prevent the abuse;
2. They are willing to consider other possible explanations for the behavior or statements that arouse their suspicions;
3. They are willing to have the child interviewed without being present;
4. They are concerned about the impact on the child if he or she has to testify; and
5. If the allegations cannot be verified, they are willing to let go of the investigatory process as long as the child's well-being can be monitored through therapy or some other process. (p. 564)

Bresee et al. (1986) also point out that the mother who is primarily interested in attacking the father and whose reports are more suspect may:

1. Insist on being present when the child is interviewed and prompt him or her when he or she is questioned about the abuse;

2. Be unwilling to consider any other explanations for the child's statements, behavior, or symptoms;

3. Be eager for the child to testify at all costs;

4. Shop for other professionals who will verify her suspicions and involve the child in multiple examinations; and

5. Demand that the investigation continue, irrespective of the impact the process is having on the child. (p. 563)

In spite of this well-thought-out set of differentiating criteria, Bresee et al. identify four patterns that can complicate the diagnostic process. Children who demonstrate an underlying psychotic process may have sexual perceptions that could sound like sexual abuse. Children who have been sexually overstimulated in the manner identified by Gardner may show some of the same symptoms as victims of molestation. Children who name more than one adult perpetrator may get factual information perceptually confused. The last pattern concerns children who have been "coached" or otherwise influenced to describe the molestation. Bresee et al. found that, in an effort to deal with these four areas of concern, ongoing therapeutic sessions following the initial diagnostic period were very helpful in differentiating the bona fide from the fabricated abuse.

False Abuse Allegations

Over the past several years, research has been performed in an effort to help clinicians discriminate bona fide sexual abuse allegations from fabricated sexual abuse allegations. It has been the hope that this research would provide clinicians with a clearer understanding of these issues. Instead of the issues becoming more black and white, however, they have become more gray. Unfortunately, in almost all sexual abuse allegation cases when the alleged perpetrator has not admitted the offense, experts can be found to simultaneously testify that the allegations are bona fide and other experts to testify they are fabricated. As a result, at an increasing rate, the triers of fact are left with contradictory testimony from experts and are required to reach their own conclusions without the benefit of clear expert testimony.

The results of an Illinois case are important to consider when false sexual abuse allegations arise. In *Mullins v. Mullins*, the court's findings of:

evidence that the mother had refused to use father's surname as children's surname, had filed false sexual abuse complaints against father and had limited and/or denied him visitations were sufficient to support findings that the mother had engaged in a scheme to terminate father's parental rights and to destroy the children's relationship with him, warranting transfer of custody of the children to the father. (490 N.E. 2d, 1375)

The case was heard originally by Cook County Circuit Court Judge Ellen F. Rosin. The appellate court affirmed the original decision.

Mantel (1988) reviewed several hundred court cases involving child sexual abuse. He found that both children and adults made false reports. The false reports are grouped into several different categories. They include misunderstanding, misreporting, distortion through illness, distortion by design, professional error, and misrepresentation.

Simple misunderstanding was often a function of the adult misunderstanding the language that the child was using. Simple misreporting was often a result of an individual exaggerating reports. Mantel felt that distortion through illness may be a function of preoccupation with sexually bizarre content that may even represent a prepsychotic state. Distortion by design involves such areas as revenge, alienation, and divorce-related circumstances. Professional error can include suggestive questioning, inappropriate use of sexually anatomically correct dolls, and impassioned statements on the part of the professional. Misrepresentation can come from individuals who are opportunistic, have hidden agendas, or are looking for secondary gain associated with sexual abuse allegations. They can also adversely affect the presentations of suggestible children.

Mikkelsen, Guthiel, and Emens (1992) reviewed the literature on false abuse allegations by children and adolescents. They found four basic subtypes of false allegations. Subtype I were allegations found in the context of custody disputes. This subtype yielded the highest percentage of false allegations. Subtype II were false allegations resulting from the accuser's psychological disturbance, and Subtype III involved false allegations made by children or adolescents as a conscious manipulation of the system. Subtype IV is called *iatrogenic*. This refers to false allegations that result from contamination errors, inappropriate evaluation processes, and similar interfering variables.

Authors Yates and Musty (1988) report:

> Occasionally, a preschool child may erroneously accuse a parent of molestation. When this occurs, the child usually believes that his/her story is correct. A false accusation can be made when: an adult has persuaded a child that these sexual events actually occurred; when a child in the oedipal stage has misinterpreted care-giving ministrations; when a child's thought processes are confused by primary process material; or when a child is secondarily involved in the projective identifications of a dominant care giver. More than one of these mechanisms may operate in a given case. (p. 990)

The authors also point out that children often change their attitudes and stories about the accused parent when they are moved from the accusing parent and placed in the presence of the accused parent.

Case Examples

Two actual case examples will be presented to demonstrate bona fide and fabricated cases. Following the portion of the interview that provides information about the alleged sexual abuse incident, it can be helpful to ask more specific questions as part of the interview process in an effort to further substantiate the concerns about whether the allegations are bona fide or fabricated. In the bona fide case, the victim is generally able to answer all the additional detailed questions with reasonable responses. In the fabricated case, the child has generally been coached by someone. The coach cannot anticipate all the questions that are likely to be asked in the interview. As a result, when the child is asked additional detailed questions, there is no basis from which to answer. Therefore, responses are likely to be vague, preposterous, or lacking altogether. The following case examples represent these two situations.

Case 2

Nancy is a four-year-old girl who was brought to the therapist's office by her mother following visits with her father. The mother reported that the daughter claimed that her father, her aunt, and her sister, as well as Nancy herself, would take off their clothes and play kissing games. The therapist asked the child to describe the kissing games. The four-year-old girl said, "Daddy and auntie take off all their clothes and auntie kisses daddy's pee-pee and then daddy goes pee on auntie's face." The therapist followed up with additional questions, such as, "Where did this happen?" The child responded, "Auntie was lying on the floor when she kissed daddy's pee-pee. And you know what, when daddy went pee on auntie's face, it wasn't yellow, it was white and gooey." The therapist asked the child, "What did daddy's pee-pee look like when auntie was kissing it?" The child responded, "It was hard and about this long (holding her hands about six inches apart)." The examiner/therapist asked the child, "What did auntie look like with her clothes off?" The child stated, "It's funny cuz when auntie has her clothes on, her boobies are up here (pointing at nipple level) and when she has her clothes off, her boobies are way down here (pointing at navel level)." These are the types of detailed descriptions that make it very apparent that the child's report is bona fide. The detail was accurate, descriptive of actual sexual activity, and the child was able to respond to additional questions that a "coach" would probably not have anticipated.

Case 3

A five-year-old girl reported that her daddy "stuck his pee-pee in my bucky." In an effort to determine what the child meant by "bucky," the therapist/evaluator asked the child where her bucky was. She pointed to her vaginal area. In addition, through the use of SAC dolls, the child also pointed to the vaginal area. When the child was asked if her daddy had his clothes on or off when he put his pee-pee in her bucky, she stated, "On." When asked what her daddy's pee-pee looked like, she said, "It was this big" (stretching her arms as wide as they would go). When asked if her daddy's pee-pee was hard or soft when he put it in her bucky, she stated, "Soft." And last, when asked if it hurt when her daddy put his pee-pee in her bucky, she stated, "No." Certainly it is possible that something sexually inappropriate may have occurred between this father and child. However, by virtue of the child's responses to the specific detailed questions, it is unlikely that the father gained vaginal entry with his penis.

Generalizations About Sexual Abuse Allegations

Dillon (1987) examines 10 generalizations that have been made about child sexual abuse allegations. She points out that although they are not invariably false, they can be false.

Generalization 1. Nightmares, infantile behavior, excessive masturbation, and depression are signs of sexual abuse in children. Although these characteristics can be a sign of sexual abuse, they also can exist independently of sexual abuse in all children.

Generalization 2. When children say they were touched on their genitals, they mean sexual touching. Children under the age of five may describe acceptable hygiene in a manner that sounds like sexual abuse.

Generalization 3. If a child has presocial sexual knowledge, he or she gained that knowledge from direct sexual contact. This may certainly be the case, but the child "may have witnessed the parents during sexual activity, may have examined hidden pornographic magazines . . . may have watched explicit sexual acts on cable television, or may have been exposed to another child who educated him/her about sexual language and behavior" (p. 540).

Generalization 4. Children do not lie about sexual abuse. Research has been done that indicates that there are cases in which children have lied about sexual abuse.

Generalization 5. Children of any age can be tested reliably for sexual abuse. In fact, children under age five usually lack the verbal and conceptual abilities necessary for a full interview.

Generalization 6. The use of anatomically correct dolls is a valid procedure for sexual abuse assessment. Research was performed on 19 normal, nonabused children ranging in age from 2 to 4–9 (4 years, 9 months). "Three children fled the testing situation. Half of the remaining 16 exhibited unusual interactions with the doll's genitals, similar to interactions described by examiners in sexual abuse investigations" (p. 540).

Generalization 7. The more times the child is tested, the more reliable the results will be. In actuality, the opposite is more likely to be true.

Generalization 8. Knowing about the relationship between the parents is not necessary to ascertain whether sexual abuse has occurred. One research study reported that all seven false accusations examined were involved in family law litigation.

Generalization 9. Anyone with appropriate training in sexual abuse assessment can test accurately for sexual abuse of children. Being trained in sexual abuse assessment does not guarantee that the examiner has adequate knowledge of child development or child interview techniques or a lack of bias in sexual-abuse-related matters.

Generalization 10. It is better to err in falsely accusing someone of sexual abuse than to fail to confirm that a child has been sexually abused. As stated in the context of the book itself, the human and civil rights of both the alleged victim and alleged perpetrator must be considered.

Sexual Abuse Allegations in Child Custody/Visitation Disputes

As custody and visitation disputes become more prevalent, parents are finding more ways of alleging that the other parent should not have placement of the children. Sexual abuse allegations as part of custody/visitation disputes have continued to increase over the years. Some of these allegations are substantiated, while others are not. Faller (1991) states, "Proportionately, more false accusations of sexual abuse may be made in the context of divorce than in other situations. Most false allegations are made by adults, not children" (p. 88). In her study, approximately 15% of the allegations were false, and another 10% were inconclusive. She also concludes:

Under the stress of divorce and its aftermath, parental perceptions may become distorted and the behavior of former partners perceived as pathological. Occasional drinking episodes may be redefined as alcoholism. A desire for sexual activities or frequent sex may be characterized as perversion. A single slap during an argument may lead to the label of batterer. Having developed a distorted view of the ex-partner, the parent may conclude that anyone who is an alcoholic, a pervert, or a batterer, would also sexually abuse a child. (p. 89)

In addition, Faller (1991) points out that:

the parent or others may observe behavior by the child that could indicate sexual abuse, but could just as well have other explanations. Typical examples are resistance to visit with the suspected abuser, having nightmares before or after the visit, wetting the bed, or masturbation. Such behavior could be precipitated by stress related to the divorce, by fear of losing the custodial parent if loyalty to the other parent is shown, or by an appreciation that the custodial parent would welcome negative reactions to or comments about the ex-partner. (p. 89)

Because masturbation is often used as a reason for making a sexual abuse allegation, Faller points out that it is a normal activity among children and adults and that "furthermore, self stimulation is pleasurable, and children may need to comfort themselves in a divorce situation, especially if their parents are too preoccupied to nurture properly" (1991, p. 89).

Faller also identifies that parents may correctly perceive that children have been sexually abused but incorrectly attribute it to their ex-partners.

In discussing these areas of concern that may lead to false allegations during divorce, Faller points out that conscious lying by parents in making these allegations seems to be rather rare. Instead, false allegations tend to be more a function of distortion, misperception, and a lack of understanding of children's behaviors.

Psychological Effect of Sexual Abuse

There is no doubt that sexual abuse adversely affects children and can have a lifelong negative impact on their psychological functioning. Kendall-Tackett, Williams, and Finkelhor (1993) provided an exhaustive review of 45 studies that had been performed to examine the psychological effects of sexual abuse. They reported that the most commonly studied symptom was sexualized behavior. This included sexual play with dolls, placing objects in anuses or vaginas, excessive or public masturbation, seductive behavior, requesting sexual stimulation from adults or other children, and age-inappropriate sexual knowledge.

The symptomatology most frequently presented in sexually abused children include PTSD, which was found in 32% of the cases, poor self-esteem (35%), promiscuity (38%), and general behavior disorders (37%).

The authors looked at the effects of sexual abuse by age groups. They concluded:

> For preschoolers, the most common symptoms were anxiety, nightmares, general PTSD, internalizing, externalizing, and inappropriate sexual behavior. For school-age children, the most common symptoms include fear, neurotic and general mental illness, aggression, nightmares, school problems, hyperactivity, and regressive behavior. For adolescents, the most common behaviors were depression; withdrawn, suicidal, or self-injurious behavior; somatic complaints, illegal acts; running away; and substance abuse.
>
> Among symptoms that appear prominently for more than one age group were nightmares, depression, withdrawn behavior, neurotic mental illness, aggressive and regressive behavior. (p. 167)

They further concluded that depression, school and learning problems, and behavior problems were most prevalent symptoms across ages. Of particular note was the finding that significant percentages of victims were asymptomatic. The studies reviewed concluded that from 21% to 49% of those studied were asymptomatic. Kendall-Tackett, Williams, and Finkelhor (1993) concluded that these individuals may have been asymptomatic in ways that were not measured, they may not have yet manifested symptoms, or they may simply have been asymptomatic.

The authors further address the issue of intervening variables. They stated:

> In summary, findings of the various studies reviewed indicated that molestations that included a close perpetrator; a high frequency of sexual contact; a long duration; the use of force; and sexual acts that included oral, anal, or vaginal penetration led to a greater number of symptoms for victims. Similarly, as all of the studies that concluded these variables indicated, the lack of maternal support at the time of disclosure and a victim's negative outlook or coping style also led to increased symptoms. The influence of age at the time of assessment, age at onset, number of perpetrators, and time elapsed between the end of abuse and assessment is somewhat unclear at the present time and should be examined in future studies on the impact of intervening variables. (p. 171)

Kendall-Tackett, Williams, and Finkelhor next address the issue of abatement of symptoms. They found that as time progressed, symptoms abated or improved in 55% to 65% of children. However, depending on the study, from 10% to 24% of the children appeared to have symptoms that worsened.

Court involvement was also found to influence the effects of sexual abuse on children. Children involved in court proceedings demonstrated less resolution and a longer time to reach resolution. It has long been felt that children required to testify in court suffer the adverse effects of these proceedings. Williams (1992) reported that testimony provided by children in protected settings can mitigate the trauma. Williams found that children who testified via closed circuit television, videotape testimony, or closed courtrooms demonstrated fewer symptoms than children who were required to testify in open court.

Courtroom situations can be very intimidating to children. Facing the accused and not understanding the procedures associated with court testimony cause intense anxiety in children. In addition, the cross-examination and feeling of loneliness can be traumatic. Children are often isolated from their support system during testimony, especially if witnesses are sequestered. As a result, it is the psychologist's obligation to protect children from additional trauma as much as possible. In doing so, it may be necessary to testify in court as to the damages associated with children testifying in open court. Videotape, closed circuit television, and in-camera (in the judge's chambers) testimony are reasonable alternatives.

Briere and Runtz (1993) identified six areas of concern in reviewing child sexual abuse cases. The first area of concern, as identified in other studies, is Posttraumatic Stress Disorder. These individuals also suffer from "cognitive distortions" as a result of their abuse. Their perceptions tend to reflect an overestimation of danger or adversity. Briere and Runtz also identify "altered emotionality," with depression being the most common symptom. Furthermore, "disturbed relatedness" is found with survivors of sexual abuse. They tend to have fewer friends and less closeness and satisfaction from their friends, report poor social adjustment, and see themselves as being unworthy of healthy relationships. They also demonstrate difficulties with sexual intimacy. Avoidance through dissociative reactions is also common, as is a relationship between childhood sexual abuse and later substance abuse and an increase in suicidal ideation. Briere and Runtz also report that sexually abused individuals are often involved in tension-reducing activities such as sexual promiscuity, binging and purging, and self-mutilation. Last, they identify "impaired self-reference" as a problem area. This is accompanied by an inability to sooth or comfort one's self.

De Young (1986) points out that several traumagenic factors are present in children who have been sexually abused. The first traumagenic factor is traumatic sexualization. Because of the trauma of being sexually abused, these individuals often become sexually aggressive, engage in repetitious sexual play, or demonstrate age-inappropriate sexual knowledge or interest. Betrayal of the child's trust and dependency by the offending adult is a second traumagenic factor. This betrayal often leads to grief, depression, and dependency. A third traumagenic factor is the feeling of disempowerment. This feeling leads to symptoms of anxiety, fears, and hypervigilance. The final traumagenic factor is stigmatization. A child may often receive message of shame, guilt, or blame for the activity. These feelings can lead to low self-esteem, suicidal ideation, and self-destructive behavior.

De Young also points out that a young child who is being pressured to lie experiences stress just as does a child who is being coerced into secrecy by a sexual abuser. She points out, however, that a young child coerced into lying is probably unable to give elaborate details of the abuse or demonstrate the kinds of vulnerabilities documented about abused individuals.

Weston, Ludolph, Misile, Ruffins, and Block (1990) studied the effects of abuse on adolescents who had Borderline Personality Disorders. Their study concluded that histories of physical and especially sexual abuse are associated with severe psychological disturbances, in particular, Borderline Personality Disorder. This impacts a patient's ability to gain from therapeutic interventions. Borderline Personality Disorder patients who have also been abused tend to have intense savior fantasies about the therapist. This places unrealistic expectations on the therapy process and also leads to the likelihood of failure in therapy.

Sexton, Grant, and Nash (1990) studied the differences in body image between women who had been abused and those who had not. Not surprisingly, abused women had lower ratings on measures of body satisfaction than nonabused women. The researchers also found that women who were abused by relatives had significantly lower body ratings than those who were abused by nonrelatives.

Wyatt, Guthrie, and Notgrass (1992) studied the effects of sexual abuse of ethnic minority children. The authors concluded, because of racial discrimination, it is important for the assessor of sexual abuse in minority children to be able to discriminate true sexual abuse symptomatology from prejudicial stereotypes of minority behavior, to ensure that prejudicial misconceptions do not interfere with conclusions drawn.

Tharinger (1990) studied the impact of child sexual abuse on a child's ability to develop his or her own sexuality. Tharinger found that 16% to 41% of children who had been sexually abused manifest overt sexual behavior problems. The nature of the problems varied according to the age of the child. However, it should be pointed out that sexually abused children display more sexual problems than "comparison groups of normal children, nonabused clinic children, nonabused hospitalized children, diagnosed externalizing children, physically abused children, and physically abused hospitalized children" (p.335).

Leifer, Shapiro, Martone, and Kassem (1991) studied the Rorschach responses of sexually abused girls. They found that:

> in relation to the comparison group, the Rorschach protocols of the sexually abused girls indicated marked problems in ego-functioning. The abused girls showed more disturbances in their thinking, producing more responses related to unrealistic or illogical patterns of thoughts. These difficulties may be related to the high level of stress that the sexually abused girls were experiencing relative to their adaptive coping abilities. (p. 23)

Kluft (1988) reports:

> one fifth to one third of all women have experienced some form of childhood sexual encounter with an adult male, that between 4% and 12% have had some sort of sexual experience with a male relative, and that 1 in 100 have had a sexual experience with her father or stepfather.... A high incidence of incest victims among psychiatric patients ranging from 8% to 33% is reported. (p. 3)

This group of individuals demonstrates an ongoing vulnerability to exploitation and inappropriate relationships. They learn to be victims during childhood and look for continued relationships that will perpetuate their victimization. Kluft refers to this as the "sitting duck syndrome."

Based on this research, when involved in a custody evaluation that involves father-daughter incest, it is essential that therapeutic intervention address the victimization issue in an effort to prevent the child from continuing to live out the role of the victim in her adult life. Unfortunately, individuals who suffer from the sitting duck syndrome have learned to be victims during their childhood. As a result, there is a greater likelihood that they will seek out victimizing relationships. These are the individuals who become involved in relationships with people who will victimize them, marry individuals who will victimize them, and may even seek out therapists who will engage in therapist's sexual misconduct, thus victimizing them. Therefore, it becomes both the psychologist's and attorney's moral obligation to ensure that part of the resolution of any child sexual abuse case involves treatment for the child in an effort to break the victimization cycle.

Wyatt et al. (1992) studied the effects that child sexual abuse has on subsequent sexual revictimization. They report:

> survivors of sexual revictimization need to be aware that, without an understanding of the effects of these past experiences on their current behavior, they are at risk of being victimized again. In the process of examining past practices, it is often not surprising that women with patterns of frequent sexual activity may not appear to themselves and others as oversexed. Their sexual activity may, however, be more a function of not knowing how to select partners who require non-sexual relationships. Given that they have been survivors of child sexual abuse, they may need to relearn strategies for expressing their needs in relationships and for selecting partners with whom they can share sexual decision making. In these instances, learning how to perceive themselves as sexual beings and not sexual objects, to communicate their needs, to anticipate when contraceptive use is needed, and to negotiate with partners about the type and frequency of behaviors in which to participate may be essential to efforts to prevent revictimization. (p. 171)

They further conclude:

> One of the most critical goals of women who have been sexually revictimized is to understand how further sexual decision making can affect their lives and relationships. The effort of surviving is to assume control over sexual experiences that are essential to their healing. This specific type of counseling extends beyond traditional psychotherapy for abuse survivors. However, it can help to diminish the likelihood that women will encounter other traumatic sex-related life experiences that can jeopardize their health and well-being. (p. 172)

Validation of Child Sexual Abuse

Risin and MacNamara (1989) suggest "because psychologists are capable of performing complex evaluations, it is recommended that they be involved earlier in the investigation of sexual abuse allegations, either by performing the initial evaluation or by training other mental health workers to gather relevant information" (p. 182).

As an outgrowth of sexual abuse allegation concerns and additional concerns raised about the validity of repeated interviews, a recent interview technique has been developed to meet the needs of all the investigatory agencies. It is disadvantageous to interview a child repeatedly about abuse allegations. However, psychologists, attorneys, parents, social service agencies, district attorneys, and other interested professionals all require the information gathered from these interviews. The most appropriate way to approach this involves interviewing the child only one time by a mental health professional trained in child sexual abuse assessments. All of the other interested parties are on the other side of a one-way mirror observing the interview. The other interested parties have the capacity to communicate with the interviewer to guarantee that the questions that they desire to ask are asked, if appropriate. This can be accomplished through the use of an intercom-type system or a remote earphone-type system. In addition, the interview is videotaped as possible evidence and to allow professionals who enter the case at a later date to view it.

Psychologist's Role

Hall (1989) points out that the psychologist is familiar with developmental issues, knows how to interview the child, has objective information available through testing, and can serve as an effective consultant. She also points out that the psychologist's role should be limited to the extent that the psychologist is not pressured into declaring guilt or innocence of the alleged offender or declaring whether the abuse actually occurred.

Melton and Limber (1989) examined the appropriate roles for psychologists in child maltreatment cases. They referred to physical, sexual, and psychological abuse cases. They raise concerns about psychologists overstepping their bounds by becoming involved in the investigatory process. This was particularly true in cases investigating sexual abuse They state, "Whether the defendant shares characteristics of abusers or the victim shares characteristics of abused children tells little about whether the defendant perpetrated the specific offense of which he or she is accused" (p. 1225). The authors also point out that psychologists must be ever cognizant of the American Psychological Association's *Ethical Principles of Psychologists and Code of Conduct* in pursuing these matters, stating that psychologists should not overstep the bounds of their professional role, must be careful to avoid intrusions upon the due process rights of defendants, and should be sensitive to the ethical interests of victims. As an example, the authors state, "Intrusions on the privacy of victims should be no greater than necessary to meet the demands of justice" (p. 1226).

Melton and Limber also feel that it is important to continue to inform children about the progress of a case. They perceive that this increases the child's trust in the legal process and tends to make the child a more credible witness. In dealing with children, the authors also feel that psychologists must be honest about their limits of roles and expertise. They specifically state that the particular violation in mixing roles involves using the psychotherapy process as a "prosecutorial investigative tool."

In further investigating psychologists' overstepping their bounds, Melton and Limber believe that "under no circumstances should a court admit the opinion of an expert about whether the particular child has been abused or has told the truth" (p. 1230). They believe that whenever experts are asked to render opinions on the ultimate issue, experts are imposing their expertise in an area that should be left to the trier of fact.

Even though tests like the Child Abuse Potential (CAP) inventory have been developed and demonstrated a high hit rate in discriminating abusers from nonabusers, psychologists should take care not to use such tests exclusively in attempting to substantiate abuse allegations.

The authors conclude by saying, "No matter what the role, though, psychologists must keep in mind the compelling purposes of the legal process. They must show respect for the participants in the process and the authorities charged with decision making. Doing so is fully consistent with the high professional and personal duties of psychologists to promote human dignity" (p. 1232).

Sexually Anatomically Correct Dolls

The use of sexually anatomically correct (SAC) dolls in forensic evaluation has raised quite a controversy. As a result, the American Psychological Association Council of Representatives adopted a statement on February 8, 1991, with regard to the use of anatomically detailed dolls. The statement adopted is as follows:

In Forensic Evaluations.

Anatomically detailed dolls are widely used in conducting assessments in cases of alleged child sexual abuse. In general, such dolls may be useful in helping children to communicate when their language skills or emotional concerns include direct verbal responses. These dolls may also be useful communication props to help older children who may have difficulty expressing themselves verbally on sexual topics.

These dolls are available from a variety of vendors and are readily sold to anyone who wishes to purchase. The design, detail, and the nature of the dolls vary considerably across manufacturers. Neither the dolls, or their use are standardized or accompanied by normative data. There are currently no uniform standards for conducting interviews with the dolls.

We urge continued research in quest of more and better data regarding the stimulus properties of such dolls and normative behavior of abused and nonabused children. Nevertheless, doll-centered assessment of children, when used as part of a psychological evaluation, and interpreted by experienced and competent examiners, may be the best available practical solution for a pressing and frequent clinical problem (i.e., investigation of the possible presence of sexual abuse of a child).

Therefore, in conformity with the *Ethical Principles of Psychologists and Code of Conduct*, psychologists who undertake the doll-centered assessment of sexual abuse should be competent to use these techniques. We recommend that psychologists document by videotape (whenever possible), audiotape, or in writing the procedures used for each administration. Psychologists should be prepared to provide clinical and empirical rationale (i.e., published studies, clinical experiences, etc.) for procedures employed and for interpretation of results derived from using ADDs [anatomically detailed dolls]. (APA, 1991)

Melton and Limber (1989) also discuss the use of SAC dolls in sexual abuse allegation investigations. They state:

> use of SAC dolls has been mischaracterized as a "test" for sexual abuse, rather than a means for children to clarify their verbalizations through demonstration. The former conceptualization, which is based on a misunderstanding of the proper role of the clinicians in the fact-finding process, leads to exclusion of interview material altogether because of reliance on a scientifically unproven technique. (p. 1231)

The authors quote research that has been performed by Goodman and Aman (1987) that points out that "in an interview using dolls, young children frequently do explore the doll's genitalia visually and manually. However, young children not known to have been sexually abused infrequently engage in simulations of sexual activity with the dolls, although such play does occur occasionally, especially among the older preschoolers" (p. 1231). In addition, Melton and Limber state that the dolls can actually interfere with the child's ability to recall and describe the incident of maltreatment by distracting the child or eliciting distorted accounts of the events.

McIver, Wakefield, and Underwager (1990) compared the response of abused and nonabused children to SAC dolls. Their study demonstrated "that non-abused and abused children did not differ in their comments about the dolls or their behaviors and play with them. . . . Children frequently demonstrated aggressive and sexual acts that had occurred; this was particularly marked when the interviewer asked leading questions and cued and encouraged the child." These authors suggest that the use of SAC dolls may provide misleading information. Furthermore, they support what Melton and Limber reported when suggesting that psychologists be careful when using these dolls, as inappropriate use of them may constitute unethical conduct on the part of the psychologist.

Finally, Dawson (1992) studied the use of SAC dolls with nonabused children. The author reports:

> There were no instances in which the children acted out or described sexual intercourse or sexual fondling. . . . Additionally, there were very few instances of sexual aggression displayed by the children when exposed to SAD (Sexually Anatomically Detailed) dolls. . . . In contrast to the low incidence of sexual aggression that was displayed, there was a high incidence of sexual exploratory play. . . . Aggressive, non-sexual responses to the SAD dolls also occurred frequently. (pp. 148–149)

The authors of this study noticed that there were gender differences in the responses to the dolls. They report:

Girls showed more behavioral affection and verbal sexual exploratory play than did boys, overall. . . . When the dolls were undressed, the girls exhibited more behavioral sexual exploration (touching, looking, and examining the dolls) and verbal sexual exploration (making statements concerning the breasts or penis on the dolls). . . . In contrast to the boys, playing with the dolls, particularly when the dolls were undressed, had a generally activating effect on the girls' behavior. (p. 149)

Schaefer and Guyer (1988) suggest that "use of anatomical dolls as diagnostic devices be curtailed until their efficacy has been demonstrated in clinical trials subject to guidelines similar to those for any reported new medical or diagnostic device" (p. 10). They also point to the importance of "maintaining or restoring the relationship between the child and the alleged perpetrator during the evaluation process" (p. 10). The authors generate concern about the situation in which all contact between the alleged perpetrator and alleged victim is terminated when the allegation occurs in the context of a custody dispute. They state, "Unfortunately whether unfounded or confirmed, the enforced parent/child separation and the exposure of the child to the angry perceptions and projections of the accusing parent create a rupture between the accused parent and the child so severe that a positive relationship may never be fully restored" (p. 10).

Recantation is often used by the alleged perpetrator as "evidence" that the abuse did not actually take place. Recantation is a typical component of sexual abuse allegations. In the case of a bona fide sexual abuse allegation, the allegation may have been made by the child for a number of reasons, including desiring the behavior to terminate. However, when the allegation was made, the child was not aware that her father may be prohibited from seeing her, may be sent to jail, may be handcuffed and carried away, or may be required to have a supervisor during visits. The child may recant the allegation, not because the abuse did not occur but in an effort to have the return of a more normalized relationship with her father.

Comparing Abused and Nonabused Children

Gordon, Schroeder, and Abrams (1990) expected that abused children would have more knowledge about adult sexual behavior than nonabused children. They conclude:

We were surprised to find that within the range of knowledge about sexuality thought to be appropriate for young children, sexually abused and non-abused children did not differ. . . . The data from this study that looked specifically at sexual knowledge appear to contradict the results of other studies which may have found differences in sexual behavior between sexually abused children and non-abused controls. We did not find evidence of precocious sexual knowledge in the abused children. (p. 250)

The authors did note that the abused children responded in "unusual" ways, reflecting their distress during the interview. They also surmised that it was possible that the abused children knew more about sexuality than they were revealing.

Geffner (1990) talked about general characteristics associated with credible allegations of child sexual abuse and child sexual abuse accommodation syndrome. He also addressed the issue of PTSD as a diagnosis in sexual abuse cases. He states that the diagnosis of PTSD is the most frequently given diagnosis in child sexual abuse cases. However, he felt that with true child sexual abuse cases, there will also be child dissociative disorders associated with the PTSD. Symptoms include not remembering the abuse, "spacing out," denying obvious evidence, and doing self-mutilation.

Faller (1991) identified several areas that must be investigated in determining the likelihood of sexual abuse occurrence. They include:

1. The child's ability to describe the sexual behavior.
2. The child's ability to describe the context of the sexual abuse.
3. The child's affect when recounting the sexual abuse.
4. Medical evidence.
5. Confession of the offender. (1990, pp. 128–131)

Faller also makes the following points:

1. When a child describes sexually explicit behavior such as "Snot came out of my daddy's dinky," or "He put his ding-dong in my mouth and I choked," it is unlikely that this type of description would have occurred in a false allegation.
2. The child's ability to identify where the abuse occurred, what the offender said to obtain the child's involvement, where other family members were, what the victim and offender were wearing, what, if any, clothing was removed, and whether the offender said anything about telling or not telling is evidence that is likely to increasingly support the likelihood that the abuse occurred. A child merely stating "He stuck his finger in my butt," without being able to voluntarily provide any of the above information, is more likely to be a false allegation than if all the above information is available. However, in preschool children, the lack of this information may be a function of immature cognitive abilities, and not false allegations.
3. Reluctance to disclose, embarrassment, anger, anxiety, disgust, and fear are all functions of affect that is seen in children during descriptions of bona fide sexual abuse. It is common for very young children to engage in self-sexual arousal while describing these events.
4. In only about 10% to 20% of the cases are medical findings available.

5. In only about 10% of the cases does the offender confess. (1990, p. 131)

Incest Families

The effects of father-daughter incest were studied by researchers Swanson and Baiggio (1985). They report that the oldest daughter in the family is more likely to be the first victim of incestuous assault. The pressure for secrecy is generally a component of the incestuous relationship and adds to the burden placed on the child, resulting in fear and guilt on the part of the child. When the child reports the incest, the delicate balance in the family is generally disrupted. In a treatment setting, the first job of the therapist is to listen to the child in a believing manner and reassure her that she will be protected from the perpetrator. Once the victim has disclosed the incest, she generally feels a deep sense of having betrayed her parents and feels increasing ambivalence about her father. Swanson and Baiggio report:

> The incest victim often expresses a desire to confront her parents, hoping that they will accept the responsibility for the incest and acknowledge that they have harmed her. . . . The incest secret is not fully laid to rest until the victim is able to talk about the incest with someone other than her therapist. (1985, p. 673)

Samek (1991) provides significant information regarding the effects of sexual abuse allegations on incest families. Several issues need to be addressed as a part of the evaluation process, including questions on the sanity of the alleged victim, witness credibility, visitation and custody, and treatment needs, and whether the family should be reunited or kept apart. As stated in earlier research, Samek also opposes using SAC dolls on a regular basis. He states they are too distracting, add to the confusion of the child, and create ideas that may not have been present.

Incest Fathers

Samek points out that incest fathers typically have a close relationship with their children and lack psychological intimacy with their wives. They tend to be controlling in their interpersonal relationships and often come from dysfunctional families. Incest fathers have a greater than average problem with substance abuse, approaching 20% to 25% in research samples. Although these fathers present themselves as being honest, they are generally smooth and dishonest. They generally will make an extreme effort to convince the listener that the mother is hysterical. These fathers lack insight and empathy and focus on how they are being hurt—not on how their behavior is affecting others. They generally present themselves as good father figures when disciplining and handling children in general. Problems presented by these fathers include their inability to verbalize their feelings, portrayal of themselves as victims, and psychological naïveté.

Incest Mothers

The mothers of incest victims are generally either inadequate in their roles as mothers or attempt to care for everybody's needs by taking the posture of a "super mom." They tend to be highly dramatic and appear to have Hysterical Personality Disorders. They are also overprotective of others and overprotective of themselves. Like incest fathers, incest mothers often come from dysfunctional, abusive families. Initially they are reluctant to believe the allegations. These mothers have trouble disciplining their children and feel weak and powerless. In addition, they present themselves as being naïve and easy to manipulate and as having a low self-esteem.

Incest Victims

Generally, incest victims are slow to report the abuse. When they do report the abuse, they tend to underreport it in an effort to test the waters to determine how much they will be believed. Attorneys are likely to conclude, as a result, that the allegations are false. However, attorneys must understand that this is fairly typical of abuse victims. The victims themselves often feel responsible for the abuse and will not want to show that the behavior that occurred was abusive. Along with low self-esteem, they present sexual knowledge and behavior inappropriate for their chronological age. Incest victims as teenagers tend to be promiscuous and/or drug users and to act out in other ways (for example, opposition, truancy, or vandalism).

Family Dynamics

In the incest family, the mother is often distant while the father and daughter are enmeshed with one another. Secrecy is a significant component of the relationship, suggesting that the issues cannot be shared with anyone else. Many types of family secrets are kept. As a result, the boundaries with the community are high while the boundaries within the families themselves are low. The family, as a result of its feelings toward the accuser, will often attempt to reintegrate without the child who "told the secret." Family members are likely to blame that child for the problems. The mother presents herself as knowing nothing, while the father knows whether he did or did not perpetrate. It is possible that the child may or may not know whether the abuse took place, depending upon the age of the child. Even when abuse takes place, the incest mother will often overreact and present herself poorly. The father's response will be to say, "There's nothing wrong with me. It's all her fault." Initially, the daughter will present the information reluctantly and understate it. When she finally does disclose the information, she is likely to assume responsibility for the acts that have occurred.

False Memory Syndrome

An ongoing controversy has developed within the arena of sexual abuse allegations. As time goes on, the two sides of this controversy have become more polarized and, unfortunately, the real victims often get lost in the process.

A group has formed the "False Memory Syndrome Foundation." It is their position that a large number of the sexual abuse allegations are the result of therapeutic suggestibility, inappropriate hypnosis, and therapeutic manipulations. Research by reputable people demonstrates that individuals can be subject to suggestibility.

The other side of the controversy states that individuals *do* repress portions or all of traumatic memories with some frequency and that these repressed memories can be recalled through legitimate therapeutic processes. Proponents of this view also report reputable research that supports these positions.

It is important to point out that, to date, there is no diagnostic manual that identifies a concept called "False Memory Syndrome." However, and more important, the evaluator must understand that the polarization of this issue serves as a disservice to the client/patient. There are certainly cases where suggestibility adds to, or interferes with, the memory process, just as there are cases of legitimate repressed memories that later surface. It is not reasonable or accurate to take the stand that all of these cases are "false memory syndrome" or that all of these cases are legitimate repressed memories brought to the surface. This is probably best summarized by Johnson and Howell (1993). They state:

> Allegations of child sexual abuse naturally raise the ire of the populace at large as well as the fears and apprehension of those who may be falsely accused as perpetrators. Within this emotionally charged and litigious climate, the memory functions of children have become a matter of acute interest for those professionals involved in the ensuing investigations and legal proceedings. This is especially true, given that the child witness, approaching a court of law, is likely to encounter numerous circumstances that will invite memory distortion. These circumstances include interviews by concerned adults and protective service workers, as well as cross-examination by a defense attorney. Well-intentioned efforts may be replete with leading questions or subtle inferences that may distort episodic memory. (p. 213)

It must be kept in mind that the use of hypnosis increases the suggestibility of the client. As a result, many states will not allow information obtained under hypnosis as evidence in courts of law. Perry (1993) identifies a number of factors that psychologists must be aware of when approaching a case when a client/patient alleges childhood sexual abuse.

1. Obtain informed consent regarding the therapeutic process at the beginning of therapy.
2. Use a second opinion when appropriate.
3. Use hypnosis only if you have well-documented and recognized training.
4. Obtain informed consent before using hypnosis.
5. Avoid suggestion and leading.
6. Consider the alleged perpetrator.
7. Make it clear by progress notes and communication to the patient that the *patient* is responsible for the determination of abuse, *not* the therapist.
8. Routinely attempt to obtain pediatric, medical, and school records.
9. Never encourage or suggest a lawsuit.
10. Use caution in the recommendations of self-help books.
11. When group therapy is appropriate, refer to group at some level of treatment (e.g., do not refer someone to an incest group who has not yet retrieved incest memories).
12. Keep strict boundaries.
13. Use case consultation and staffings routinely.
14. Keep good records.
15. Refer patient for physical assessment if appropriate.
16. Use team approach when possible.
17. Have medical backup if the therapist is not a physician.

CHAPTER 9

Reporting the Results

COMMUNICATING THE RESULTS

After the evaluation has been completed, the psychologist should meet with the guardian ad litem. This is considered an information-sharing meeting and should be conducted prior to writing a report. At this meeting, the guardian ad litem and the psychologist share information and discuss their tentative conclusions. In the eventuality that there is a disagreement between the guardian ad litem and the psychologist, it should be noted that it is not necessary for the two to have a unified recommendation, though that is, of course, desirable. Each should understand the other's position, however, and why the disagreement has occurred.

Subsequent to the meeting between the guardian ad litem and the psychologist, it can be helpful to have another meeting with the attorney for each of the parents, the guardian ad litem, and the psychologist. It can be embarrassing for the psychologist to have written a report and have an attorney point out to the psychologist that a major area was not explored or an allegation not pursued. This may occur, for example, if one of the parents is somewhat anxious during the evaluation and forgets to mention an important area. The psychologist has an opportunity to pursue these additional areas and include them in the report as a result of this additional meeting.

It is only at the point that consultation with all three attorneys has occurred that the psychologist should consider reducing the material to written format—if the attorneys so desire. Generally speaking, there are a few reasons why attorneys would not want a report to be written.

One of these reasons is that, in some cases, the psychologist has recommended that the parties go to mediation as opposed to litigation. In this situation, it can be detrimental to the mediation process for each of the parents to have been provided with ammunition that may come from having received the report.

Report Writing: Results, Conclusions, and Opinions

The most crucial component of the custody evaluation is the report. Consideration must be given to whom will receive the report, how the information will be disseminated, and the format within which the report will be written.

Preparing the Report

Ondrovik and Hamilton (1992)* recommend the following structure:

> A written forensic report should initially name the source of the referral, detailing the circumstances and setting forth the legal issue to be addressed. It may also be important to present any circumstances which may be relevant to this particular evaluation, such as ongoing involvement with social service agencies in a custody/termination evaluation. If the referral is court ordered, the circumstances of the referral should be succinctly stated. Frequently, the judge has reduced the objectives of such an evaluation to a written order and the practitioner should quote or refer to this order. It is important to remember that orders for judges are generally prepared by attorneys representing parties in the case. Typically therefore, the orders will be either loosely worded and open ended or extremely specific, again requiring practitioner interpolation.
>
> A chronological listing of the dates and all of the contacts, including missed appointments, should be included. This is most easily handled by merely listing the dates and the individuals contacted chronologically.
>
> The written report should refer to data which was acquired in addition to information elicited in the patient interview. The source of this data, as well as the nature and date of the information, should be indexed appropriately.
>
> An extensive social history and background information concerning the client should be included as is relevant to the legal question to be addressed. This may include family of origin information, history of criminal or antisocial behaviors or physical disabilities which may be present.
>
> The report should detail all of the special assessment techniques, including all psychometric testing. Video or audio taping should be noted and the recording preserved for evidence. The results or conclusions of each psychometric technique should be detailed in the report, as well as validity, reliability and standardization statistics.
>
> Finally, the forensic practitioner should present clinical findings, summarizing significant observations and providing a DSM-III-R and an ICD-9 diagnosis as well as other statements concerning mental functioning, global functioning and stressors. . . .
>
> In addition, remaining within the scope of the referral question is of paramount importance. . . . Avoid offering gratuitous opinions on unpresented

---

* This material is reprinted from the American Journal of Forensic Psychology, Volume 10, issue 1, 1992. The Journal is a publication of the American College of Forensic Psychology, P.O. Box 5870, Balboa Island, CA 92662.

issues. . . . Limiting the amount of information included in a written report is an important goal. . . . Conclusions and opinions should be substantiated and supported through observation and information; however, the report should not contain a detailing of all of the facts or all observations. Rather, only those observations essential to the theories advanced should be included. . . . A forensic report should limit the use of clinical terms and phrases. . . . Importantly, the practitioner must be able to explain phrases, diagnoses and scale interpretations in court. (pp. 21–23)

In the written report, the expert presents the major data and conclusions that can be drawn from the data. Careful differentiation must be made between those conclusions that are made tentatively and those made "to a reasonable degree of medical/psychological/scientific certainty." Although the expert will have amassed a great deal of information, only the most salient information should be included in the report. Although the expert must provide support for her conclusions, only data that are essential to that task should be included.

It is important to realize that a report is a summary of the findings. In a recent court case, a psychologist had to review approximately 600 pages of materials generated from previous reports and the six evaluations performed for the case. The report for the evaluation was approximately 25 to 30 pages long. However, when the psychologist testified in court, the cross-examining attorney kept asking why specific minor pieces of information were left out of the report. It is not possible to distill 600 pages of materials down to 30 pages and include every piece of potentially relevant information. As a result, much information from the evaluation process is not included in the report.

In most psychological evaluations, the information will include both positive and negative information about an individual. If a report appears to be slanted in one direction or the other, a thorough attorney will attempt to uncover information not included in the report during cross-examination. The report, however, should not be written to include only information that supports the examiner's conclusions. It should also include nonsupporting material and the rationale for why the supporting material was weighed more heavily than the nonsupporting material. When a psychologist has not done this, the attorney is likely to bring this to the court's or jury's attention on cross-examination.

There is some difference of opinion as to how much background information should be included in the report. Some psychologists feel that it is important to include all of the developmental history from birth until the time of the report. Others, including this author, feel that it is only necessary to include specifically relevant background information. As a result, the background information section could be relatively short.

It is very important that the report is readable—that is, that it flows smoothly and that it is clear what one is addressing in each section. It is up to the psychologist's discretion whether each of the areas identified in the report should be entitled with subheadings, or if the report should just move from topic to topic without headings. It is not necessary to include headings when the introduction sentence of a paragraph identifies what that section of the report will discuss, as, for example, when a paragraph starts, "In summary . . . " or "The following recommendations. . . ."

Consensus among attorneys is that they prefer shorter reports, feeling that if they need more information, they can obtain it through questioning the psychologist informally or through testimony. When asked, most attorneys will admit that they immediately turn to the summary, conclusions, and recommendations section, often not reading the entire report unless the matter goes to court.

Sharing the Report

Clients have a right to receive information about the tests they have taken. However, it is the psychologist's responsibility to communicate the information so that it is not misunderstood, misused, or misrepresented by the clients. As a result, actual scores and raw data should not be provided to the clients.

Because it is essential that psychologists not do anything to compromise the integrity of the tests administered, they also cannot share raw test data with attorneys. It is not unethical for the attorney to receive a copy of information-gathering forms. The American Psychological Association's *Guidelines for Providers of Psychological Services* states, "Raw psychological data (e.g., test protocols, therapy or interview notes, or questionnaire returns), in which a user is identified are ordinarily released only with the written consent of the user or of the user's legal representative, and are released only to a person recognized by the psychologist as competent to interpret data" (APA, 1987, p. 7). Attorneys are generally not in the position to be able to fully understand the materials received and, consequently, the information could be inappropriately used. It is far more appropriate to share the raw data with another psychologist of the attorney's choice. Then the information is likely to be used accurately and with discretion. It can be very disconcerting for a psychologist to go into a deposition or trial and find that the raw data from an evaluation have been shared with an attorney by another psychologist, potentially requiring one psychologist to consider filing an ethics complaint against that psychologist. Furthermore, it is equally disconcerting to have an attorney reading from a test manual that is supposed to be protected by the psychologist, given the ethical and contractual responsibility of the psychologist to protect the integrity of the tests.

Each psychologist signs an agreement with the major test-publishing companies not to share test materials with nonpsychologists. An example comes from the Psychological Corporation's 1994 Catalog, the major suppliers of test materials: "Test materials and scores may be released only to persons qualified to interpret and use them properly" (p. 133). If the psychologist is put in the position of divulging specific test items or specific interpretations of various responses, the tests could be rendered invalid. Anyone in the court or reading the transcript of the case could know what types of answers to give and what types to avoid. As a result, none of those individuals could ever take the tests and obtain valid results. With all the civil and criminal cases in the country that utilize psychologists, the test would quickly become useless and would not be available to provide the necessary information to the courts. A dilemma arises when the psychologist's need to protect the data conflicts with the attorney's need to discover. However, in the experience of the author of this text, courts tend to uphold the psychologist's position. Any psychologist who faces a demand to violate the ethical and contractual requirements to maintain test security should consult the state psychological association or American Psychological Association attorneys.

Attorneys have an ethical responsibility upon receiving reports of psychological evaluations on their clients and their opponent's clients. It is inappropriate and potentially dangerous to share the reports with clients, if clients are likely to disseminate the information or may misinterpret the information given. Too many times, clients have taken the psychological evaluations and shown them to friends, neighbors, or relatives. They use the reports as a way to substantiate their positions and demonstrate their concerns about the other parent. The best way to handle this situation may be for the attorney to have a conference with a client and provide a summary of the results and recommendations, as opposed to giving a copy of the actual report to the client. If the individual is in psychotherapy, it may be appropriate and helpful to send a copy of the report to the treating therapist, who can go over it with the individual.

This author chooses to use a format where a complete evaluation report is separately written for each individual, followed by a separate summary report, with recommendations, addressed to either the guardian ad litem or the court. As a result, when a request is made for information on a party at a future date, that individual's report can be sent without having to extricate it from the body of a larger report. The summary report is generally two to three pages long, with a relatively brief summary paragraph about the findings for each individual followed by a recommendation section. This summary report generally commences with the statement, "As a psychologist duly licensed to practice in the state of . . . I do hereby certify that I evaluated the above-named individuals at the request of. . . . Furthermore, the recommendations made in this report are made to a reasonable degree of psychological certainty." As a result, the reader knows that recommendations are put into a legal framework and recognizes that they are made to a reasonable degree of psychological certainty (or "psychological probability" or "scientific certainty"—check your state's statutes for required or permitted language). The "recommendations" section of the report begins with: "Based on these evaluations, consultation with the attorneys, review of the above-listed materials, collateral interviews ... (add any other materials that were reviewed or sources of information), the following recommendations are being made:."

REPORT OUTLINE

Tests Administered

List the names and dates of all tests administered to all individuals.

Reason for Referral

Identify the referral source and the questions to be answered by the evaluation.

Background Information

Include all relevant information from the family of origin, the current family, and social history.

Collateral Contacts

Discuss significant others spoken to and information derived from the significant others.

Behavioral Observations

How did the parties interact with one another, interact with the testing materials, and interact with the examiner?

Cognitive Tests

This includes the results of all tests of cognitive functioning, such as intelligence tests, achievement tests, and learning-related tests.

Personality Tests

This section includes the results of all personality tests, such as MMPI-2, Rorschach, TAT.

ASPECT

This section reports the results of the ASPECT.

Summary and Recommendations

Summarize the findings in a paragraph and list the recommendations numerically.

Signature

Relevant credentials such as "licensed psychologist," "clinical psychologist," "ABPP."

JUDGES' CUSTODY DECISION CRITERIA

One hundred fifty-six judges were surveyed by Reidy, Silver, and Carlson (1989) in an effort to determine what factors were important in making their custody decisions. A number of factors were measured on a nine-point scale, with one equaling "not at all important" and nine equaling "extremely important." In weighing the evidence, the researchers found the following sources of evidence to be most important in the judges' decision-making process:

1. Desires of 15-year-old children
2. Custody investigation report
3. Testimony of the parties
4. Court-appointed psychologist's recommendations

The next factors, ranked in decreasing order of importance, were the testimony of school personnel, the desires of 10-year-olds, the psychologist retained by one of the attorneys, the testimony of extended family, the recommendations of attorneys, and the testimony of friends. Worthy of note is the view of judges surveyed that the desires of five-year-olds were by far the least important source of evidence in making custody decisions.

The researchers also obtained the mean ratings of criteria for deciding between joint custody and single-parent custody. In joint custody decisions, both judges and mental health practitioners rated the following criteria highest:

1. Parents' willingness to enter the joint custody arrangement
2. Quality of the relationship the child has with the parent
3. Wishes of 15-year-old children
4. Parents' inability to separate their interpersonal difficulties from parenting
5. Amount of anger and bitterness between parents
6. Psychological stability of the parents

The judges looked at the following, ranking them in descending order of importance:

1. Geographic proximity of the parents' homes

2. Behavioral problems exhibited by the child at home or at school
3. Ages of the children
4. Each parent's previous caretaking involvement.

The influence exerted by extended family members, the differences between parent discipline styles, the homosexual relationship of either parent, and the flexibility in parental work schedules followed next, with judges and mental health practitioners rating the criteria similarly. However, when the wishes of 10-year-olds were considered, mental health practitioners rated that evidence higher than did judges. Ratings for parental economic stability and placement of a child in day care while a parent works did not differ significantly between judges and mental health practitioners.

Neither judges nor mental health practitioners placed great significance on the following factors when making decisions regarding joint custody:

1. Number of children in the family
2. Marital status of the parents
3. Differences between parents' religious beliefs
4. Economic and physical similarities and differences between parental homes
5. Age of the parents
6. Wishes of the child at age five
7. Gender of the child

Of these final criteria, however, mental health practitioners placed a notably higher rating on the wishes of five-year-old children than did judges.

In conclusion, the authors state, "Several distinct trends can be drawn from our judicial sampling. First, in deciding custody disputes, judges attach greater significance to evidence from impartial sources, the parents themselves, and desires of older children than to evidence from sources aligned toward one parent or desires of younger children. . . . The majority of judges surveyed believe that joint physical and legal custody has not worked well for disputed cases" (Reidy et al., 1989, p. 86).

RECOMMENDATIONS

Joint Custody/Sole Custody

As discussed earlier in this book, some states do not allow psychologists to testify to the "ultimate issue." This section assumes that the psychologist *will* be allowed to testify to the ultimate question. Joint custody should be the initial issue addressed in making recommendations. When joint custody is not a viable alternative, sole custody should be recommended.

Joint custody keeps both parents involved in the parenting process much more effectively. It presupposes that both parents will be able to communicate effectively enough with each other to serve the best interest of their child(ren). The psychologist must be aware that this is asking people to do something outside the marriage they were not able to do within the marriage. Generally speaking, in a joint custody arrangement, parents are expected to be able to make joint decisions about such major areas as religion, education, nonemergency medical treatment, early enlistment in the armed forces, and underage marriages. Although this is the expectation, in many divorces the religious, educational, and medical decisions have already been made. As a result, it technically will not make a difference in these areas whether there is joint custody or sole custody.

Some state laws allow for joint custody with one parent having all the decision-making authority when parents cannot communicate as effectively as would be desired. This approach avoids the pitfalls associated with sole custody yet does not require optimal parental communication.

The problem with sole custody is that it suggests "ownership" to the sole custodial parent. In a sole custody relationship, the noncustodial parent is more likely to withdraw from the child(ren), be out of compliance with support payments, and be more litigious. However, sole custody is essential in some situations. When parents have gone through lengthy problems associated with joint custody and the process has clearly and irreparably broken down, sole custody remains the only option. Furthermore, in situations where one parent has significant mental health, substance abuse, or criminal problems, it is generally best to recommend sole custody to the other parent.

Based on these considerations, this author recommends joint custody in 90% to 95% of cases. Although the reasons to recommend sole custody in some cases may be good, joint custody more often serves the best interest of the child.

Abuse Allegations

Unfortunately, the majority of cases currently reaching the level of evaluation include physical and/or sexual abuse allegations. These concerns are discussed in detail in Chapter 8.

The recommendations that the evaluator makes will be based in part on the biases that the evaluator brings to the process. Some evaluators believe that parents have a right to spend time with their children regardless of their past behavior. Others believe that, at some point, parents pass the reasonable boundary of behavior and, as a result, the evaluator will recommend "no contact." This author generally believes that it should not be a question of whether the parent will or will not have contact time with his/her child(ren); it should be a question of the format within which this contact will take place.

When there has been a finding that abuse has taken place, precautions must be taken to protect the child(ren). This finding could occur in Children's Court, Family Court, and/or Criminal Court. The absence of a finding of sexual abuse in Criminal Court does not necessarily mean the abuse did not take place. Generally speaking, district attorneys will only prosecute when they feel they have an "airtight" case. Many times, prosecutors will indicate that charges will not be issued, *but this should not be construed as to mean that it is not felt that the abuse took place. This only means that there is not sufficient evidence to warrant taking this case to trial.*

When there has been an abuse finding, supervision must be a component of the visitation process. This supervision generally follows a five-step procedure. The steps are:

1. Therapeutic supervised visits. These visits take place in the confines of a therapeutic session with a psychotherapist. Initially, these contacts would only occur in the therapist's office. Prior to moving to the next step, the therapist may take the visits outside the office into the community. Parks, restaurants, and shopping malls are possible locations for these visits. At the end of the visit, the therapist provides feedback to the participants to address problem areas. The therapist can also be utilized to facilitate the reintroduction of family members to one another. The therapist is also able to terminate or suspend a given session when a problem arises and discuss that problem with the various family members. Once a sufficient comfort level has been achieved, the parties are ready for the next step of supervision.

2. Supervised visits by a disinterested third party. This disinterested third party would be an individual who does not have a relationship with either of the parties and who is generally paid for the service of providing supervision. This supervision can take place on-site or in a neutral location.

3. Supervision by an interested third party. An interested third party would be described as somebody who has a relationship with one or both of the parties. This individual must be approved by the parents, the guardian ad litem, and/or the court-appointed evaluator.

4. Unsupervised monitored visits. An unsupervised monitored visit is one in which the parties are continuing to meet with an outside individual, for example, a therapist, to evaluate the effectiveness of the visits, with that individual having the power to report back to the guardian ad litem and/or the court-appointed psychologist. The visit may take place with just the parent and child(ren), with the monitoring occurring in a weekly therapy session with the parent and child(ren).

5. Completely unsupervised, unmonitored visits.

The interested and disinterested supervisors should have the power to terminate the visit at any time that it is felt that inappropriate interaction is taking place between the parent and the child(ren) Furthermore, that supervisor should report back to the guardian ad litem and/or the court-appointed psychologist as soon as possible to discuss the concerns that were generated during that visit. In making this recommendation, the evaluator must be aware that finding supervisors in these cases is often not easy. Many cities, however, now have agencies that will provide these services at a relatively nominal cost. Even if the cost is only 10 to 15 dollars per hour, however, it can add up to thousands of dollars over the course of a year.

Therapy is also an important component in abuse-related cases. This author always recommends therapy for the perpetrator and ties visitation with the children to participation in the therapeutic process. The recommendation should always read, "The parents should be involved in individual psychotherapy until the therapist deems that it is no longer necessary." Furthermore, the guardian ad litem and/or the court-appointed psychologist should have access to the therapist to evaluate the progress being made. Many times therapists will refuse to perform therapy if they will be required to divulge the content of therapy, as it will interfere with the ability of the client/patient to be forthright and open. A compromise approach is to agree in advance that the therapist will report about therapeutic compliance (missed appointments, frequency of visits, motivation to participate) but will not be required to divulge any content of the therapy that may interfere with the therapeutic process. This does not result in any danger to the child(ren), since there are laws in all states about children's protective services and the mandated reporting of child abuse.

It can be frustrating for a therapist to be assigned to a case by the court and/or guardian ad litem where the parameters of therapy are already set forth by the court. As an example, this author was recently involved in a case where the judge ordered weekly contact for two months, biweekly contact for two months, and monthly contact for two months following the court date. This put the individual in the position of only paying lip service to the therapeutic process, since he knew that it would be time limited and the structure had already been set forth by the court. As a result, as indicated previously, it is always more appropriate to have the duration of therapy subject to the discretion of the therapist.

In those cases where a parent refuses to participate in therapy as a condition of visitation, there should be no visitation. This makes visitation a matter of the parent's choice, and not the court imposing a no-contact order.

The process of moving from supervised to unsupervised visitation is one that can take years to complete. In those cases where very young children have been abused, it may be necessary to continue supervision until such time as the child is old enough to be able to protect himself/herself by leaving, dialing 911, or accurately reporting to others.

When there are sexual abuse allegations, it is also important that the victim be involved in individual therapy. In addition, it may be necessary to have the nonperpetrating parent involved in therapy because of the unresolved feelings of anger or guilt or because the parent is engaging in inappropriate communication with the child(ren) about the victimization.

Alcohol or Other Drug Abuse

The first assumption is that children who are in the company of a parent who is under the influence of alcohol or other drugs is potentially in danger. As a result, any parent who is chronically under the influence of alcohol or other drugs during visitation runs the risk of losing the opportunity to visit with his/her child(ren). In cases where an individual continues to be involved in substance abuse, random drug screens should be part of the recommendation process. If an individual repeatedly comes up with "dirty" screens, it may be necessary to either temporarily suspend visits or move to supervised visits. A problem can be associated with giving one parent the power to refuse to allow a visit to take place when he/she believes that the other parent is under the influence of alcohol or other drugs. This, unfortunately, sets up a power play between two parents who are likely to be acrimonious anyway and can lead to more problems. That dilemma has no easy solution.

Criminal History

When a parent has been involved in repeated episodes of criminal behavior, it is unlikely that that parent will receive placement and/or sole custody of the child(ren). However, it is up to the evaluator to recommend what type of visitation should be allowed. One of the factors that must be addressed is whether the crimes were crimes against property or crimes against persons.

In some cases, a parent may be incarcerated at the time that the decision is being made regarding visitation. Some psychologists believe that a child should never be required to visit a parent in prison, whereas others believe that there is nothing wrong with this approach. It is this author's belief that a middle school–age child or younger should not be required to go to a maximum security prison to visit a parent. If a high school–age child wishes to do so, arrangements can be made. Maximum security prisons are scary places and can be very traumatic to young children. When a parent is serving out the remainder of a sentence in a minimum security setting, it is not inappropriate for young children to visit. Generally, those settings are less foreboding and look less like a prison environment.

Acrimonious Parents

There are times when the parents' need to win, to denigrate the other parent, and to continue the fighting supersedes the parents' ability to recognize the detriment of the behavior to the child(ren). Unfortunately, judges may be slow to level sanctions against these parents. They will give the parents too many last chances to demonstrate that they will terminate this type of behavior.

When only one parent continues with the above-mentioned behaviors, recommendations should be made that include individual therapy for that parent and reduced visitation/periods of placement time until the therapy is successfully completed. It should be the therapist who determines when therapy is terminated. Therapy should focus on helping the parent recognize the detrimental effects of those behaviors on the child(ren). If the offending parent does not cooperate with these recommendations, judges should be encouraged to enter contempt findings. In addition, time with children should be dramatically reduced and may need to be supervised.

When both parents engage in these types of behaviors, the approach should be somewhat different. Both parents should be required to be in individual therapy and joint therapy with a different therapist. This may appear to be therapeutic "overkill." However, it is the parents who have put themselves in this position, and it is the parents who must be accountable for their behavior.

Although judges may be reluctant to make drastic orders and mental health practitioners may be reluctant to make drastic recommendations, it may be necessary to put children in foster placement when the parents' acrimonious behavior results in severe psychological reactions. It may actually be in children's best interests to be in a nurturing foster placement rather than to subject them to the ego-destructive environment offered by parents whose personal needs outweigh the best interests of their child(ren).

Placement Schedules

A psychologist should avoid the temptation of providing an exacting placement schedule for weeks during school time, nonschool time, vacation time, and holiday time, unless the psychologist is fully aware of all of the factors involved in this decision-making process. These factors include knowing each of the parent's work schedules, the amount of vacation time they each have each year, what the family traditions are on both sides of the family during holiday times, what each parent's wishes are, where extended family lives, and other related issues. It is much better for the psychologist to recommend a general schedule than to go through each specific holiday, including specifying times for pick up and drop off. The various placement schedule possibilities are discussed in Chapter 3.

Other Recommendations

Psychologists can be called upon to make a variety of other recommendations that would be directly or indirectly related to the placement status.

These recommendations can include educational settings, necessity for special education programming, religious affiliations, and the like. The evaluator must be careful not to make recommendations outside his or her area of expertise. In cases where a psychologist is requested to make a recommendation outside his or her area of expertise, names of other professionals who can provide specific services should be included in the recommendations section.

No Recommendations

When a custody evaluation is performed by a psychologist, there is an assumption that the psychologist's expertise is being sought to aid the trier of fact (judge or jury) with mental health and related issues. What if the psychologist concludes that both parents are not only without pathology but also present themselves as psychologically healthy individuals? It is this author's belief that rendering an opinion favoring either parent under these circumstances moves the psychologist from being a mental health expert to acting like a trier of fact. When no conclusions can be drawn by the psychologist, based on the judgment that both parents are equally appropriate, it becomes the psychologist's obligation to so inform the court, leaving the ultimate conclusion to that trier of fact.

Perhaps the most important component of the evaluation process is reporting the results. The report must include all relevant data and should be disseminated in a thoughtful way so as to not add to the acrimony in the process. It is the recommendations section upon which the parents' futures will be based. The issue of joint versus sole custody and periods of placement are addressed in this section. In addition, the evaluator must respond to abuse, substance abuse, parental unreasonableness, criminal history, and other relevant areas in the recommendations section.

CHAPTER 10

Surviving Your Day in Court

One of the most significant trends in litigation has been the increased reliance on testimony by expert witnesses. Family law is no exception. Mental health professionals now appear routinely to express opinions in custody, visitation/placement, and sexual abuse allegation cases. Thus, the selection, preparation, and presentation of an expert witness is frequently crucial to the outcome.

BEFORE TESTIMONY

Preparation for Court

"The ultimate goal of forensic assessment is the collection, organization and communication of information in a manner that makes the information and conclusions useful to lawyers, judges and jurors. Therefore, a forensic practitioner must develop skills in consultation, report writing and oral testimony" (Ondrovik & Hamilton, 1992, p. 17).

> Because of [the] premium on the accuracy of information provided to the fact finder, the results of psychological tests should not be used in isolation from history, medical findings, and observations of behavior made by others. . . . Impressions from psychological testing in the forensic context should most appropriately be treated as hypotheses subject to verification through history, medical tests, and third-party observations. This "verification step" is crucial in forensic assessment for two reasons. First, psychological testing typically does not provide data that are directly relevant to the immediate legal issue. . . . Second, data obtained through psychological testing may, for a variety of reasons, provide an inaccurate representation of the individual. (Heilbrun, 1992, p. 257)

In some circumstances, expert testimony *must* be presented; in others, it *may* be presented. The first instance applies when "psychiatric or psychological issues are material in a case and lay people are incapable of reaching rationally based conclusions on these issues without specialized assistance" (Shuman, 1986, p. 174).

> In almost every case of medical malpractice, expert testimony is mandatory, not permissive. With few exceptions, the law traditionally has allowed the medical profession to establish its own liability standards; that is to say, the plaintiff must prove through expert testimony that the care or skill exercised by a defendant physician was inferior to that exercised by comparable professionals in the community. (Slovenko, 1988, p. 333)

Expert testimony *may* be presented when the judge determines that it would be helpful to her and/or the jury. Federal Rule of Evidence 702 permits the introduction of expert testimony when "scientific, technical, or other specialized knowledge will assist the trier of fact to understand the evidence or to determine a fact in issue" (Shuman, 1986, p. 175). Judges and juries expect expert witnesses to be unbiased educators, helping them to understand technical information necessary for their deliberations. As with other witnesses, the expert is required to swear to tell "the truth, the whole truth, and nothing but the truth." This is very different from the role of the attorney, whose job is to advocate for her client, not to ensure that all information potentially relevant to the decision-making process is presented to the trier of fact. "The law's theory is that witnesses keep the advocates honest. And the law has a secret weapon for keeping expert witnesses honest: the court's power to appoint its own expert witnesses" (Saks, 1990, p. 291). Seventeen states have adopted Rule 702 verbatim, and four other states have adopted modified versions of the rule.

Bottoms and David (1993) state, "Few would argue the wisdom of allowing judges the option of ignoring a consensus of 'experts' in favor of the individual integrity of evidence, or the prudence of asking questions about the sample, procedures or statistics behind a relevant finding. However, that legal experts, not scientists, will answer such questions should be of concern. Although this ruling opens the door for 'well-grounded and innovative' but unpublished evidence, it also potentially opens it for testimony based on questionable techniques that are unrecognized by the scientific community for good reason—reason not necessarily discernable by facto-finders untrained in scientific methodology" (p. 14).

The expert must have both the ability to do a high-quality assessment and the ability to understand what the assessment means in the context of the legal questions. The former involves:

> technical expertise which consists of the expert's having specialized skills in the areas of eliciting and clarifying the communications of persons who either have something to conceal (e.g., sexually abusive parents), or who are impaired or otherwise limited . . . in their capacity to provide information about themselves and the significant events of their development and current circum-

stances. The principal tools of technical expertise are an array of psychological and other specialized "tests." (Horner, Guyer, & Kalter, 1992, p. 143)

The latter form of expertise "consists of an expert's putative knowledge of the various content domains affecting relevant questions, as well as that expert's putative specialized skill in interpreting the manifest content of the subjects' behaviors and communications" (Horner, Guyer, & Kalter, 1992, p. 143). This means that the expert must possess substantial knowledge in each area she will investigate and communicate about. "It also means that the expert possesses recognized abilities to draw correct inferences from information yielded by her or his evaluations and review of documents. . . . These principle tools of cognate expertise comprise the ability to see or understand what the ordinary mind fails to see or understand" (Horner, Guyer, & Kalter, 1992, pp. 143–144).

According to Garb (1992):

> there is general agreement that, depending on the type of judgment that is to be made by a judge or jury, expert witnesses should be allowed to (a) describe a person's history and mental status, (b) make diagnoses, (c) evaluate whether a person is malingering, (d) make predictions of behavior (or at least describe difficulties in predicting behavior), and (e) evaluate psychological processes related to competence (e.g., competency to stand trial). . . . Mental health professionals can assist judges and juries by describing a person's history . . . and mental status. Clinicians are consistent and focused in their gathering information . . . and they are able to make reliable ratings of mental status. . . . Mental health professionals are more consistent than lay-persons in collecting information.
>
> With regard to neuropsychological assessment, there is empirical evidence that well-qualified neuropsychologists can make reliable diagnoses of the presence or absence of brain damage. . . . With regard to the diagnosis of mental disorders. . . , research on the reliability of psychodiagnoses made in everyday clinical practice indicates that acceptable levels of reliability have been obtained for many diagnostic categories but not for all categories. . . . Reliability has been low for personality disorders, and serious questions have been raised about the reliability of psychodiagnoses made for children. . . . A reason why reliability may be low for some diagnostic categories is that clinicians may not be adhering to the diagnostic criteria. . . . There is evidence that neuropsychologists are good at classifying patients as brain damaged or non-brain damaged, [with accuracy rates from 82% to 95% for the Luria-Nebraska Neuropsychological Battery or the Halstead-Reitan Battery]. (pp. 453–456)

Garb concludes:

> empirical research indicates that (a) judgments made by mental health professionals are frequently more valid than judgments made by lay persons and (b) forensically trained mental health professionals possess a body of specialized knowledge, not shared by other mental health professionals, that can be used

to assist judges and juries. . . . As long as clinicians are aware of the limitations of their expertise, they can provide valuable expert testimony. (1992, p. 462)

The quality of expert testimony depends on a number of factors. First, psychology and psychiatry are not exact sciences. "Facts" in both fields are those data which the present state of knowledge indicates are accurate, but they are always subject to displacement by information that becomes available at a later time. Many conclusions are based on the data a given expert accepts as factual, although another expert may draw conclusions from a different database. The weight of scientific opinion may fall on one side or the other, but on a given issue there may be two or more legitimate opinions, each based on a significant database. Each position may be widely enough held to be considered as having gained general acceptance in the field.

Second, research has shown that psychologists and psychiatrists are no better at predicting the future (except for making short-range predictions), whether with regard to dangerousness or to quality of parenting, than laypeople. In spite of this, they are frequently called upon to make long-range predictions; for example, which parent in a custody matter should be awarded custody of the children until they reach majority. Experts are likely to be asked to predict how long it will take someone to recover from a psychological injury.

Third, the quality of the expert's opinions depends on a number of factors. Different experts will display different levels of familiarity with the professional literature, and their personal experience in the area being testified about will vary. Some experts will work much harder than others to gather data on which to base an opinion in a particular case. Up to a point, the more data the expert collects, and the more diverse the sources of information (for example, the divorcing couple, the children, teachers, and other professionals), the better.

> Corroboration of information gathered in a forensic assessment is often vitally important. Thus, the practitioner should consider requests that certain information be subpoenaed or discovered. . . . The practitioner should document all efforts of collecting information, that is, who provides which information and refusals to provide information. . . . If the assessment is for the benefit of the attorney or the party, and thus protected by the attorney/client privilege, then the gathering of information may put the opposing counsel, or the court, on notice. Should this be the case, the attorney and the practitioner should have this understanding, and the attorney should certainly be informed that forensic assessments based upon self-report are often subject to extreme criticism in court. (Ondrovik & Hamilton, 1992, p. 19)

Thus, the attorney has the advantage of surprise if the consulting expert does not openly gather information but the disadvantage that the quality of the data presented by the expert will suffer significantly if all essential sources of information and corroboration cannot be addressed.

Fourth, a number of factors make the interface of psychology and the law a difficult one for the mental health professional.

First, legal decision making often is bedeviling to psychologists because it seems to require testimony that either is artificially certain or is made to seem unreliable. As scientists, psychologists are accustomed to regarding truth as established through an objective, impersonal inquiry, yielding fully disclosed results. . . . Second, truth in science is reached only probabilistically, rests on educated hypotheses about what works, and is always subject to change. . . . Third, scientists seek consistency. But, while courts try to adhere to established principles of law, achieving consistency is not itself a paramount virtue. . . . Fourth, in the courtroom each participant's personality is shaped by the role he or she is forced to play. . . . Fifth, psychologists must always be aware of the difference between being asked to testify in a "micro" or experimental context, and a "macro" or policy context. . . . Sixth, the all too frequent image is of a rational scientific psychologist seeking to enlighten, but often being rebuffed by traditional, archaic and irrational law. However, much of the psychology that is applied to legal issues has little in common with the natural sciences. . . . Seventh, psychologists themselves enter court with a prejudice against the adversary process. (Stromberg et al., 1988, pp. 591–592)

However, the fact that there are difficulties in translating psychological answers into legal answers does not mean that the attempt should not be made. These difficulties are "inherent in the adversarial process and can be found any time a legal question requires non-legal information from experts. . . . Clinicians have tended to be the ones who have pointed out the limitations on predicting behavior. But in *Barefoot v. Estell,* the U.S. Supreme Court reasoned that the fact-finding and adversary system would make up for the shortcomings of the predictions" (Bales, 1988, p. 17).

Preparing the Expert

The expert can also benefit the attorney by developing both general and specific questions for lay and expert witnesses, including helping to anticipate the arguments and theories of the opposition. It is also part of the expert's responsibilities to apprise the attorney of research, testing, and trends in professional areas that may affect the attorney's theories and plan of action. Ingenuity, creativity, and perseverance are important qualities in an expert.

If the expert is to be effective, she must be well prepared by the attorney. The following list is adapted from Goldzband (1980, pp. 18–21, 36, 37).

1. The expert should have access to all of the attorney's files, thus lessening the possibility that the expert might learn about some problem or data for the first time while on the stand.

2. The attorney should advise the expert to be candid about her findings, positive and negative. This increases the expert's credibility and appearance of objectivity.

3. The expert should be aware that she must make all of her files accessible to the attorney(s), and that her statements in court must be consistent with the information in the files.

4. The attorney and the expert should review the expert's credentials and determine how to present them in court.

5. The attorney and the expert should discuss the data to be presented by the expert, concentrating on how to cover all the important points without overwhelming the listener.

   The attorney should advise the expert whether to volunteer information that goes beyond the direct questions posed in a deposition or in court. Although the expert must give a full response to any questions asked, whether or not to present information that exceeds the precise question asked requires a judgment call. Do you want adverse counsel to know at the deposition how strong a case you have, so that settlement is more likely? Or do you want to save your strongest arguments for the courtroom?

   In considering her litigation strategy, the attorney may want to select an expert who comes across as either a strong advocate, a very gentle person with whom the jury can identify, or a professorial type who is carefully teaching the judge and/or jury about the technical aspects of the case.

   The expert should understand exactly which aspects of the trial the attorney wishes her to address. For example, when an attorney believes that joint custody is out of the question in a divorce case, but that liberal visitation might be achievable, the attorney may request that the expert emphasize the positive aspects of liberal visitation. In all cases, of course, the expert is ethically required to tell the truth and to present all the important data she possesses.

6. The attorney should caution the expert to answer the questions succinctly, not exceeding the scope of the question in her response. She should also be sure not to lose the listeners through excess use of technical terminology.

7. The expert should be prepared to discuss her fees and, if asked, to emphasize that she is being paid for professional services rather than for testimony. It should be noted that the expert is not asking to be paid fees in advance solely for fiscal reasons. Attorneys will often attempt to imply under cross-examination that mental health experts are "bought" by the individual paying the fee. As a result, attorneys are at times reluctant to pay experts in advance for fear that it will appear that the witness has been bought. However, just the opposite is true: It is less likely that the witness will appear as a bought witness

or hired gun if the fee is paid in advance, leaving the expert unencumbered in her testimony. In this way, the expert feels minimal pressure to provide testimony that will please the retaining attorney or fear she may receive no fee. It is unethical for experts to work on a contingency basis because they must be accepted by the court as largely (if not entirely) objective and unbiased. Even if there is no contingency payment agreement, not paying the expert in advance for her work gives the appearance of a contingency arrangement, thereby reducing the impact of the expert's conclusions on the judge and/or jury. Even if the expert is willing to wait for payment, it benefits the attorney and her client to insist on paying in advance. Unfortunately, a few states do not require or allow fees to be paid in advance. The expert must be aware of relevant state laws before demanding fees in advance.

8. The attorney should prepare the expert regarding what to expect on cross-examination. The cross-examination of an expert generally addresses five areas of testimony: lack of qualifications, bias, error in the observed or assumed facts, error in conclusion or opinion, and specific impeachments, that is, previous contradictory or inconsistent statements, writings, or general lack of credibility. The attorney should remind the expert that the shortcomings of the mental health field may be used as a means of discrediting expert testimony. The expert should also be aware that because "well-recognized publications" or "learned treatises" may be used to discredit testimony, she should avoid lending credibility to them by accepting them as authoritative. Rather, she should state, "I accept that book as authoritative in the field with certain reservations," thereby permitting disagreement when necessary.

9. Smith (1986) offers several specific suggestions regarding testimony-related behavior that an attorney should convey to the expert:

    a. Answer truthfully to the best of your knowledge ("I don't know" is perfectly acceptable).

    b. Keep responses simple, comprehensible to a lay jury.

    c. Keep responses on point regarding the questions asked.

    d. Reflect objectivity rather than mere subjective opinion in all responses.

    e. Respond accordingly to questions requiring description; reserve interpretations and conclusions for later.

    f. Do not respond immediately, but gather thoughts and weigh the answer.

    g. Maintain awareness of the flow and implications of the questions.

    h. Remain calm and answer directly and confidently.

In addition, the attorney should make certain that the expert is familiar with applicable case law, and should, if necessary, provide the expert with copies of court decisions with which the expert must be familiar.

The expert's notes should be organized in one or more tabulated notebooks, with an index to facilitate finding particular sections. This thorough preparation for court will demonstrate to the trier of fact that the expert prepared well for the evaluation. It will also suggest that the expert is interested in helping the court with its difficult job. The expert should bring a good photocopy of her notes and anything anticipated being introduced into evidence or that the other attorney(s) is expected to introduce. Most courts will allow the introduction of a good photocopy rather than the original, thus allowing the expert to keep her originals.

The expert needs to address the judge and/or jury when answering questions, particularly when long answers are given. It is easy to forget this and to face and address all answers to the attorney asking the question.

Further, the expert should pay attention to what the judge and/or jury are doing. If it appears that the trier of fact is losing attention, or if the judge stops writing down the expert's salient points, the expert needs to stop talking, shorten the presentation, or make the presentation more interesting.

It is important for the psychologist prior to testimony to realize who all of the parties are in the courtroom and what it is likely they will testify about. This information should be obtained from the attorney prior to going to court. Contrary to what is portrayed in movies, it is unlikely that the opposing side will present a "surprise" witness. Not only should the psychologist be aware of who the parties are but also what significant others are likely to testify and what other experts are likely to testify. The psychologist should work with the attorney to help provide questions for examination or cross-examination that may be relevant to the testimony of these other parties.

Helpful Hints

As the courts become more backlogged with cases, it is not unusual for court testimony to occur a year or more after the initial evaluation has been performed. It is essential for the psychologist to perform an evaluation (or the last updated evaluation) update in cases where there is greater than a six-month lapse between the original evaluation and court testimony. It is not necessary to repeat the entire evaluation; for example, one does not expect IQ to change significantly, so IQ tests need not be updated. However, it is very disconcerting to be on the witness stand and have an attorney on cross-examination ask, for example, "Well, Dr. Ackerman, how do you know that Mrs. Smith is still the same as she was when you evaluated her

15 months ago?" The performance of an updated evaluation reduces the likelihood of these kinds of questions being asked.

In the event that a deposition has been taken prior to court testimony, it is essential that the expert witness reread the deposition prior to going into court. One of the favorite ploys of attorneys on cross-examination is to attempt to catch the expert witness in a contradiction between testimony given at the deposition and testimony given in court. This is not to say that the expert cannot change an opinion between the time of the deposition and court testimony. There may be a change in circumstances that would necessitate a change of opinion. In those cases where the expert opinion is changed or modified in any way, it is important to be able to substantiate the reason for the change with objective data. When changes in opinion are made based on subjective impression, the witness's credibility is likely to be reduced.

Reasonable people can disagree. Judges know that, attorneys know that, and psychologists must keep that in mind. It is not unusual for psychologists in forensic settings to be faced with an expert who disagrees with one's original opinion. These disagreements should be presented in a professional, data based, and objective manner. Judges do not want to hear psychologists "bad-mouth" one another in court. When a psychologist gets on the witness stand and portrays another psychologist's behavior as "reprehensible" or states that "all of the APA principles of ethics were violated," instead of bolstering that psychologist's testimony, it tends to reduce the credibility of the psychologist. The judge is generally willing to listen to anything that an expert has to say but will weigh the testimony based on the judge's impression of the credibility of the witness. "Bad-mouthing" other experts reduces that credibility.

Having an appropriate support network is essential for an expert witness. There are many facets to this support network that should be in place to aid the expert witness. One or two colleagues should be available to "bounce ideas off of" and discuss various aspects of one's tentative conclusions. This, of course, is conducted without identifying the names of the parties. An attorney who functions as a personal consultant for the expert witness is another important member of the support team. Psychologists are not expected to know all of the subtleties of law. As a result, it can be beneficial to have an attorney to consult with when presented with situations that transcend the boundary of psychological expertise and enter into the legal arena. In addition, most state psychological associations have a component of their ethics committees that can provide brief consultation and opinion as to what a psychologist's behavior should be in particular circumstances. Whenever a colleague, attorney, or representative of a state association ethics committee is consulted in a case, it is important to document the content of that consultation, in the eventuality that the position the expert has taken is ever contested before a regulatory board or in a court of law. People listed in the National Register of Health Service Providers in Psychology may also, for a fee, obtain consultation from their consultant law firms.

ON THE WITNESS STAND

Demeanor

The psychologist should present herself/himself in an articulate, free-flowing manner. When the expert witness utilizes "ums," long gaps in testimony, and speaks with a quivering voice, the credibility of the testimony is likely to be reduced, even though the content may be both appropriate and essential.

On the other end of the continuum, the expert witness should not come across as being arrogant, flippant, or too rigid. Experts who present their positions as being the *only* correct approach are also less likely to be viewed as credible witnesses.

The best approach to testimony is to be confident and to present testimony in a professorial, yet noncondescending, manner. Listen carefully to the complete question from the attorney, pause a moment to construct your response and allow time for the other attorney(s) to make an objection, and then respond.

Credentials

When an expert witness has not previously testified before a particular judge, one of the attorneys may attempt to have the court stipulate to the expert's credentials in an effort to prevent the judge from hearing all of the credentials. A psychologist should advise the attorney for whom she/he is testifying that in the event that this occurs, the attorney should argue for the expert to at least provide a summary of the credentials. In that case, three or four high points of the individual's career will generally suffice.

It is necessary for the psychologist to have an updated vita available for each of the attorneys and the judge. For the psychologist who does a significant amount of forensic work, the vita should be updated at least yearly and preferably every time there is a significant change. The categories to be included in the vita are Academic Training, Academic Experience, Employment Experience, Teaching Experience, Membership in professional organizations and on professional committees, Publications, and Workshops led and Presentations made.

It is not unusual for an attorney, in qualifying an expert, to go through the expert witness's vita, line by line and page by page. As part of the preparation prior to trial, it can be advantageous to help the attorney highlight those portions of the vita that are most important for presentation in court. Too much detail is boring and a poor lead-in to testimony.

The psychologist should not be alarmed when an opposing attorney attempts to disqualify the expert witness's testimony. This is another strategy used by the opposing attorney to prevent testimony that may be detrimental to his/her case. It is very unusual for a judge to disqualify an expert. Generally, judges want to hear what the expert has to say. Instead of disqualifying the expert, they are more likely to weigh the testimony of the expert differently if there have been strong objections that are potentially valid to the expert testifying at all. It is also possible, in rare situations, that the judge would allow the expert witness to continue but treat the testimony as if it came from a lay witness rather than an expert witness, in which case the weight of the testimony would be dramatically reduced.

Testifying

There are generally two formats for testimony. One is "narrative" and the other is "question and answer." It is not unusual in Family Court for the judge to allow narrative testimony. This may simply involve the attorney on direct examination asking only a few questions, the answers to which can last a considerable length of time. For example, questions like, "Dr. Ackerman, please tell the court the results of your evaluation of the parties in this case." This could be followed with the question, "What are your conclusions and recommendations?" In other situations, attorneys or judges may object to this format and request that a separate question be asked for every piece of information to be shared with the court. This latter format can be both cumbersome and time consuming.

When a question is asked by an attorney, it is essential to wait for the other attorney to have an opportunity to object prior to commencing the answer. When an objection is made and sustained by the judge, the witness cannot answer the question even if the witness wishes to do so. Since the objection has been sustained, at that point there is no longer a question before the witness.

The witness's files should be organized to allow for easy access during testimony. The credibility of the witness who spends lengthy periods of time flipping through files looking for pieces of information may also be questioned. In a case where much information has been gathered, it is beneficial to break the information out into separate file folders. These could include files for each of the parties, reports from each of the other experts, transcripts of testimony by other experts, depositions that have been taken, and other relevant information.

The expert witness must be aware that any information that is taken to the witness stand can be viewed by the attorney and may be entered into evidence. It is disconcerting for a psychologist to be on the witness stand and have the attorney doing cross-examination request to see one's files. This would also be true in depositions. In this regard, the psychologist may have in his/her file what he/she considers "personal notes." There has been debate over what constitutes personal notes that are not "discoverable" (available to the other attorney or to the court) and those notes that are discoverable. Although "scribblings," marginal notes, and notations made on scraps of paper to remind the evaluator about certain things are generally considered personal notes and not discoverable notes, the conservative approach is to assume that *everything* in your file is discoverable and be prepared to respond accordingly.

Testimony can be made more effective when charts and graphs are available to the court. In cases that have been protracted over a long period of time, it is likely that a number of MMPIs have been administered. If there is a change in the MMPI profiles over time, plotting all of these profiles on one profile sheet and graphically demonstrating the results to the fact-finder may be easier for the court and attorneys to understand than narrative testimony. These graphic representations can also be helpful when portraying differences before and after hospitalizations, accidents, divorce, or other major life events.

OTHER ISSUES

The Ultimate Issue

In some jurisdictions the expert witness is not allowed to present opinions about the "ultimate issue." In most jurisdictions, however, the judge relies upon the expert witness to recommend custody or placement or offer an opinion as to whether the expert believes that sexual abuse did or did not occur. The expert is more likely to be permitted to offer an opinion on the ultimate issue in civil court than in criminal court.

> Traditionally an expert was not permitted to give an opinion on the ultimate issue or issues to be decided by a jury, on the theory that it would invade the province of the jury.... However, in complex cases involving issues beyond the ken of laymen, a judge or jury may need an expert's opinion on the ultimate issue in order to reach a fair verdict.... Indeed, more often than not an expert would not be considered "helpful" if he did not have or would not give an opinion on the ultimate issue. (Slovenko, 1988, pp. 355–356)

Grisso would not have the expert give an opinion on the ultimate legal issue, because "the final question has no answer that can be supported by scientific and clinical evidence alone. It requires applying legal and social values to make a choice, which is the domain of the judge or jury, not of the expert" (1990, p. 40). Grisso acknowledges, however, "many—perhaps most—mental health professionals who perform divorce custody evaluations for courts" would disagree.

> They argue—and many judges agree—the judge is in no better position than the clinician to decide what is best for the child.... Moreover, one can argue

that the judge is not at all required to conclude the case in the way that the clinician recommends. . . . From this perspective, asking the clinician to make a specific recommendation does no harm. (Grisso, 1990, p. 40)

He concludes that "currently this issue is unresolved." Martindale notes that "none of the major mental health professional organizations has formulated a position regarding whether an evaluator should make a recommendation regarding the ultimate issues" (1991, p. 485).

The rules of evidence governing expert testimony are based on the assumption that there is a distinction between facts and opinions. Because the judge and jury are often not chosen for their expertise in any particular area, if they are to understand the facts presented to them, they require assistance in some areas. Thus, people with expertise in areas such as human development, personality, psychopathology, and assessment are called on to go beyond the facts and to state opinions that may be helpful to the judge and/or jury in drawing conclusions.

Hearsay

As a general rule, hearsay evidence is not permitted in any court. However, since almost all of the information that an expert witness testifies to comes from other individuals, a hearsay exception is granted to the expert witness for any information that is obtained that forms a complete or partial basis for the opinion rendered by the expert.

The Specialty Guidelines for Forensic Psychologists address this issue:

When hearsay or otherwise inadmissible evidence may form the basis of their opinion, evidence or professional product, [psychologists] seek to minimize sole reliance upon such evidence. Where circumstances reasonably permit, forensic psychologists seek to obtain independent and personal verification of data relied upon as part of their professional services to the court or to a party to a legal proceeding. . . . When data . . . have not been corroborated, but are nevertheless utilized, forensic psychologists have an affirmative responsibility to acknowledge the uncorroborated status of those data and the reasons for relying upon such data. (Committee on Ethical Guidelines for Forensic Psychologists, 1991)

Depositions

There is a difference between testimony taken in a deposition and in a live courtroom setting. Generally, the deposition is used as a discovery method for the opposing attorney to obtain information as to what the expert's testimony will be in court. As a result, the vast majority of testimony provided in a deposition is in the form of cross-examination. Generally, the only direct questions will come in the form of clarification of questions by the opposing attorney. Objections can be made during a deposition. However, no judge is present to rule on the objection. As a result, the witness will usually be instructed to answer the question, even if an objection is raised. At a later date, if necessary, the attorneys will ask the judge to rule on the objection. When the objection is sustained, that portion of the deposition transcript that contains the response to the sustained objection will be stricken from the record. Testimony taken in deposition is sworn testimony, just as it is in court. It would be a mistake for the psychologist to assume that just because this testimony is not taking place in a courtroom setting that it is in some way less important and, as a result, they can be less well prepared and careful.

DIRECT EXAMINATION

The first rule of thumb in court testimony is that the expert should answer only the question that is asked. When the answer is insufficient, the attorney will follow up with additional questions. Since attorneys are often asking experts questions in an area that is unfamiliar, it can be appropriate for the witness to try to restate the question in a meaningful way—for example, "If by your question you mean..., then I can answer the question." Do not be afraid to ask the attorney to restate a question or to reformulate a question that is not understood. Since decisions may be rendered based on the content of your testimony, make sure that you understand the question being asked. In those circumstances where the expert does not know the answer to a question, it is not only acceptable but expected that the expert will state, "I don't know." It is not only acceptable to respond in that manner, but it also increases the credibility of the witness.

The expert witness's testimony should be same regardless of who is asking the questions. Since the expert is sworn to "tell the truth," the answer would be the same if asked by an attorney in either direct or cross-examination. Even though the answer to the question may not help the position of the attorney who retained the expert, the answer must still be the same.

One of the greatest dangers the psychologist faces in direct examination is going outside one's area of expertise. The attorney who is performing the direct examination wants to obtain as much useful information from the expert as possible. The attorney may not be aware of where a limit exists in the area of one's expertise. As a result, it becomes the expert witness's responsibility to respond appropriately when questions are asked that are outside one's area of expertise. For example, if asked, "Do you feel that Prozac was the appropriate medication to be used in this case?", it would be inappropriate for the psychologist to respond in any way other than "That is a question that should be asked of a medical doctor" or "That is outside my area of expertise." It may be necessary in court preparation to alert an attorney if a number of questions need to be asked that are outside the area of one's expertise and that it may be beneficial to retain an additional expert to address those areas.

It can be both boring and cumbersome to go through the psychological evaluation report sentence by sentence and test by test. This approach can literally put judges and jurors to sleep. This author has actually seen an attorney fall asleep during a lengthy, tedious answer. It is preferable for the witness to make the point as quickly as possible and proceed with the testimony. In the event further clarification is needed following cross-examination, the attorney always has the opportunity to clarify issues during redirect examination.

It is not unusual for there to be weak points in testimony. Since people do not present themselves in a black or white manner, there are always gray areas that require interpretation. It is beneficial to address these potential areas of weakness in direct testimony and defuse them as much as possible, rather than allowing the opposing attorney to make an issue out of them in cross-examination. When the weakness can be adequately addressed during direct examination, it reduces the likelihood that weak points will be exploited by the opposing counsel.

One of the more effective methods of providing direct testimony is to use information gathered from reports of experts used by the opposing attorney. When making a point in direct testimony, quoting citations from disagreeing experts that support your position can be beneficial. In addition, information gathered from professional materials such as journal articles, textbooks, and other professional sources should be cited whenever possible to support testimony. Attorneys refer to these as "learned treatises." When quoting learned treatises, it is beneficial to use those that represent recognized authorities in a particular field. If the other expert(s) in the case are familiar with prominent authors in the field, the attorney who retained you should also be encouraged to ask the other expert(s) if he/she recognizes these individuals as authorities. When another expert recognizes these individuals as authorities, the weight of one's testimony increases dramatically.

Since psychology and other mental health professions are not exact sciences, it is not necessary for the expert to reserve an opinion only for situations when one feels that something will absolutely occur. Instead, opinions are generally asked to a "reasonable degree of psychological certainty" or some comparable phrase. An expert is not stating that this will occur all the time but only that there is a reasonable degree of certainty that it will occur. Translated into statistical concepts, psychologists generally consider results to be significant when the p value is .05 or less. As a result, it would be fair to say that research that demonstrates this level of significance or better would also be demonstrating a reasonable degree of certainty.

CROSS-EXAMINATION

Nature of Cross-Examination

It is the opposing attorney's job to attempt to discredit the psychologist's testimony, reduce the weight of the testimony, uncover contradictions in testimony, and generally attack the expert witness's work product. This does not mean that the attorney does not like the expert, does not respect the expert, or necessarily thinks the expert did a bad job. If an attorney does not attempt to attack the expert's work product, the attorney would not be doing his job.

There is a major difference, however, between an attorney who attacks the expert as opposed to attacking the expert's work product. The attorney on cross-examination will often begin by asking a question that attempts to throw the expert off-guard. At times these questions can even be absurd and irrelevant. On one occasion, an attorney asked: "Dr. Ackerman, would you please tell the court why your name is listed first under psychologists," or "When was the last time a complaint was filed against you?" A good response to this sort of question includes smiling while responding, thus acknowledging you understand the game the attorney is playing.

One of the ways of preparing oneself for cross-examination is to remember that the expert knows more about the field of psychology than does the attorney. The attorney may be well read in several components of psychological theory but cannot possibly have the broad-based knowledge of a doctorally trained psychologist. The one exception is the rare occasion when the attorney is also a doctoral level psychologist.

Perhaps the most frustrating component of cross-examination is being required to answer questions "yes" or "no" when further explanation is necessary. The attorney does not want to hear the further explanation on cross-examination. A cross-examining attorney will often object when a lengthy answer is given to a question where a simple yes or no is desired. The court is likely to sustain these objections. Therefore, the other attorney should be encouraged to pursue these areas on redirect examination to provide the expert with the opportunity to render more lengthy answers.

Demeanor

It is not unusual for the expert witness to change his demeanor between examination and cross-examination. Under direct examination it is much less likely that the psychologist will have to defend himself than under cross-examination. An attorney may attempt to elicit anger from the expert witness as a means of reducing the effectiveness of the expert witness's testimony. Under all circumstances, the expert witness should remember not to take these assaults personally. On the other hand, an attorney may attempt to lull the expert witness into a false sense of security by beginning the cross-examination in a very friendly manner, only to attempt to catch the psychologist off-guard later in testimony. Remember to listen to every question carefully, make sure you understand what is being asked, and only then respond.

Attorney Ploys

When a psychologist brings a professional reference learned treatise into court for testimony, not only does it allow that psychologist to substantiate testimony, it also opens the door for the other attorney, on cross-examination, to take *other* components of that learned treatise out of context and utilize them as part of cross-examination. As a result, the psychologist must not only recognize the benefits from the learned treatise but, also, recognize those components that could be used against the psychologist in cross-examination and prepare responses for those possibilities. To avoid this problem, (1) do not bring professional books to depositions or trials; (2) if a reference is needed, for example, the specific diagnostic criteria from DSM-IV for some disorder, bring *only* a copy of those essential pages; and (3) *always* qualify a statement of approval of a reference, for example, "I accept that source as authoritative—but with some reservations" or "That is one of a number of important sources on this particular topic."

Since psychologists may not always have the opportunity to meet with everyone involved in the case or to examine all documents, hypothetical questions are often used as a means of eliciting additional information or attempting to force the psychologist to go beyond the data. For example, "Hypothetically, Dr. Ackerman, if you knew that Mr. Jones did ... how would it affect your opinion?" or "Would your opinion change if. . . ?" A crafty attorney can ask so many hypothetical questions on cross-examination so as to cloud the impact of the expert witness's testimony under direct examination. It then becomes the retaining attorney's responsibility to rehabilitate the expert's testimony under redirect.

Another component of this ploy is the probable/possible dichotomy. An attorney on cross-examination will often ask, "Isn't it possible, Dr. Ackerman, that. . . ?" It is hard to disagree with questions that use the word "possible," since almost anything is "possible." However, a judge or a jury hearing that there are multiple possibilities other than the hypothesis or conclusion that the expert has drawn may reduce the weight of the psychologist's testimony. As a result, it becomes imperative for the testifying psychologist to discriminate for the judge or jury the difference between those things that are *possible* and those things that are *probable*. Attorneys generally recognize this distinction but may need the help of the psychologist to point it out. The attorney who retained you should know to ask on redirect whether anything opposing counsel asked changed any major opinions—and to restate those opinions.

One may also defuse questions about possibilities by responding, for example, "Possible . . . is it *POSSIBLE*. . . " or "You're asking if it's *possible, not probable*. . . ?"

There are times when an attorney recognizes that he or she will not be able to win the case based on merits. On occasion, the attorney will attempt to put the profession of psychology on trial rather than the facts of the case. The following scenario represents an example of this type of process.

Two and a half hours into cross-examination, the attorney asks this author about the results of the Rorschach administered. The exchange follows:

Q. Dr. Ackerman, isn't it true that the Rorschach is 47% reliable?
A. No.
Q. Dr. Ackerman, if I was to read to you from this book that states that the Rorschach is 47% reliable, would you agree with it?
A. No.
Q. Let me quote, "The Rorschach is only considered to have 47% reliability." Would you agree with that?
A. Does it say 47% reliability or does it say .47 reliability?
Q. It says .47 reliability.
A. That is a reliability coefficient and not a percentage.
Q. What is a reliability coefficient?
A. There are well over a dozen types of reliability coefficients. Which one would you like me to describe?
Q. All of them.
A. (Looking at the judge) I am not sure that the court wants me to waste its valuable time going through a description of all the various correlation coefficients.
Court: Please move on, Attorney Jones.

Ordinarily, when an attorney attempts to put the profession of psychology on trial in cross-examination, the other attorney will object. However, when this does not occur, the expert witness must answer the questions objectively, unless it reaches the point of absurdity, at which point one may appeal to the judge.

A good attorney will not only cross-examine the expert on what is included in the report but also on what has been left out of the report. As mentioned earlier in this book, a psychologist cannot include every piece of information in a report and still have it be short enough to be readable. As a result, the evaluator must select what should and should not be included in the report. The evaluator must be certain that no major relevant pieces of information have been left out of the report. It is not only upsetting but perhaps represents bias to sit on the witness stand and have an attorney point out to the expert, on cross-examination, that the expert neglected to include the fact that the person whom he recommended as primary placement parent had been arrested on three separate occasions for driving under the influence of alcohol. When the evaluator chooses to leave major pieces of information out of the report, it is essential that a rationale for leaving that information out is available in the event of a challenge during a cross-examination.

It is not unusual for an attorney to leave discussions of the fees for the last part of cross-examination in an effort to make it look like the expert has been "bought." The most reasonable response to any direct or indirect inference that the psychologist's testimony has been bought is to state, "I am paid for my time and not for my opinion." In addition, reference can be made to the fact that the psychologist worked very hard at establishing a reputation in the community, and a few hundred dollars one way or the other is not worth ruining all the years of reputation-building that have occurred. It is particularly helpful to be able to state, "I was paid in advance for my time in court, so there is no financial incentive to my testifying in any direction other than the truth."

Like all other people, psychologists are human beings and are subject to making errors. Even the most diligent psychologist will occasionally make an error. Every effort should be made to check and double-check test scores to ensure that errors are not made. In the eventuality that an error is identified while the expert is on the witness stand, one of two approaches needs to occur. If the error is minor in nature, such as a wrong address, misrecording an MMPI score by one T-score, or similar inconsequential errors, the examiner should point out that indeed an error was made but it will not significantly affect the results. However, if there is any possibility whatsoever that the error may affect the results, and potentially the recommendations, the psychologist must so state to the court and indicate that testimony cannot continue until such time as the psychologist has been able to determine the effect that the error will have on the overall conclusions.

POTENTIAL TROUBLE SPOTS

Subpoenaed Records

Since psychologists are obligated to maintain test integrity, both by ethical requirements and contractual agreements with publishers who hold the copyrights for tests, it would be a violation of ethical standards and contractual requirements for psychologists to submit to attorneys or courts their raw data, test booklets, or test materials. This area is addressed in more detail in Chapter 2 of this book. (p. 14)

It is possible that the judge may still order the psychologist to release this information to either the attorneys or the court. If that occurs, the testifying psychologist can request that, prior to releasing the information, the psychologist would like an opportunity to contact his or her own attorney to help resolve this ethical/legal dilemma. Psychological Corporation requests that if litigation reaches the stage where the court orders release of "proprietary test materials" to nonprofessionals, such as counsel, that the court issue a protective order prohibiting parties from making copies of the materials, requiring that the materials be returned to the professional at the conclusion of the proceedings and requiring the materials not be publicly available as part of the record of the case, where this is done by sealing part of the record or not including the materials in the record at all.

Psychologist's Legal Responsibility for Testimony

Many cases have been heard in trial courts, appellate courts, and the U.S. Supreme Court that have upheld quasi-judicial immunity for psychologists who have been court appointed.

In *Howard v. Drapkin,* 271 Cal. Rptr. 893 (Cal. App. 2, Dist. 1990), the court held that absolute quasi-judicial immunity is extended through neutral third parties for their conduct in performing dispute resolution services in connection with the judicial process. In this case, a parent who was upset with the recommendation of a psychologist hired by both parties to evaluate allegations of sexual abuse sued the psychologist. Both the trial and appellate court agreed that the psychologist was entitled to "common law immunity as a quasi-judicial officer" participating in a judicial process.

In *Gootee v. Lichtner,* 274 Cal. Rptr. 679 (Cal. App. 4, Dist 1990), the father who was subject to a custody evaluation alleged that the psychologist negligently administered and interpreted psychological tests. The court found that allowing the father to pursue court action would defeat the purpose behind the privilege—to ensure a witness complete and truthful testimony, eliminating any fear of costly litigation resulting from that testimony.

In *Guity v. Kandilakis,* 821 S.W. 2d 595 (Tenn. Ct. App. 1991), a father sued a psychologist for disclosing information from previous counseling sessions even though the psychologist was ordered by the court to do so. The trial court granted summary judgment, since the court had ordered the psychologist to disclose the information. However, the appeals court stated that the trial court had erred in allowing the psychologist to testify but concluded that the psychologist was immune from the suit because he would have been found in contempt of court if he had refused to testify.

In *Snow v. Koeppl,* 159 Wis. 2d 77, 464 N.W. 215 (Ct. App. 1990), a psychologist included information from previous counseling records (with a different therapist) as part of a court-ordered custody evaluation. The psychologist was sued for invasion of privacy and breach of confidentiality based on these disclosures. Both the trial and appellate court found that the psychologist was entitled to absolute immunity.

In *Deed v. Condrell,* 568 N.Y.S. 2d, 679 (Sup. 1991), a mother who had received joint custody of her daughter submitted to court-ordered counseling with a court-appointed psychologist. The psychologist subsequently recommended that the court award sole custody to the girl's father. The mother sued the psychologist, claiming that the psychologist exceeded the bounds of his professional role as the court-appointed evaluator. The court held that the psychologist could not be subject to civil action since he rendered his opinions pursuant to a judicial directive in the course of a judicial proceeding.

In *Zim v. Benezra,* 545 N.Y.S. 2d 893 (Sup. 1989), a mother was treated by a psychiatrist who also treated her son. She sued the psychiatrist for disclosing privileged information that resulted in her losing custody of her son. A summary judgment was granted because the psychiatrist was ordered to testify by Family Court and any refusal would have resulted in contempt of court findings.

In *Myers v. Price,* 463 N.W. 2d 773 (Minn. Ct. App. 1990), the parents who were suspected of sexually abusing their children were evaluated by the court-appointed therapist. They brought a malpractice action against the therapist, his supervisor, and his clinic. The Court of Appeals affirmed that the defendants were entitled to quasi-judicial immunity.

The husband in *Lavit v. Superior Court of Arizona,* 839 P. 2d 1141 (Ariz. Ct. App. 1992), brought action against a psychologist who conducted child custody evaluations. The psychologist requested summary judgment on the grounds of absolute judicial immunity. The lower court denied his motion for summary judgment. However, the Court of Appeals held that the psychologist was entitled to absolute judicial immunity.

In *Dolan v. Von Zweck,* 477 N.E. 2d 200 (Mass. Ct. App. 1985), a father commenced a defamation action against a psychiatrist for sending a letter to an attorney in a child custody case. The lower court entered a summary judgment in favor of the psychiatrist. After the father appealed, the Appeals Court held that the psychiatrist was not liable for the letter that contained otherwise defamatory matter about the father.

Again, in *Williams v. Congdon,* 257 S.E. 2d 667 (N.C. Ct. App. 1979), a father brought suit against a psychiatrist, contending that information that the psychiatrist shared caused custody of the father's child to be awarded to his ex-wife. The Appeals Court found that the defendant's report, which was made at the judge's request with the agreement of the parties, was absolutely privileged and could not be made the basis of a cause of action for either medical malpractice or liability.

Blinka (1993) reports that the Supreme Court has declared that the Frye "standard, absent from and incompatible with the Federal Rules of Evidence, should not be applied in federal trials. The reliability or trustworthiness of scientific knowledge depended upon the fealty of the theory or technique to the scientific method, which involves repeated testing and refinement as a way of establishing the validity of the procedure or idea. In short, scientific validity ultimately turns on the purpose for which the evidence is offered" (p. 12). The Court majority offered several bases for assessing the validity and fit of the expert testimony by the trial judge. Among them, the general acceptance standard of Frye is considered an important factor. ". . . It would be a mistake to dismiss the general acceptance test as dead or no longer worth worrying about" (p. 12).

"Daubert is a vote of confidence for trial judges but leaves them with precious little instruction on how to decide in a particular case between contending scientists. . . . The proponent must convince the trial judge that it is more likely than not that the evidence is reliable and fits the facts of the case. If the judge just does not know which expert to believe, the evidence must be excluded because the proponent failed to meet the burden of proof" (Blinka, 1993, p. 13).

Biases

When a psychologist has been involved in a number of custody evaluations, biases of that psychologist become apparent. For example, it is unusual for this author to recommend the children be split between two parents, which would be identified as a bias. There are times when psychologists will make recommendations that are exceptions to their own biases. When this occurs, the psychologist must be prepared to explain to the attorney who retained the psychologist, and the court, what exceptions occurred resulting in the psychologist making a recommendation outside of their general bias. Certainly, exceptions to any rule of thumb occur, but information to support those exceptions must be available and identifiable.

Maintaining Mental Well-Being

It is the ethical obligation of the psychologist to attempt to maintain the mental well-being of all individuals who are involved in the process. It can be very detrimental for an individual to listen to a psychologist provide testimony in a courtroom that would be psychologically damaging to hear. For example, when the psychologist is asked if he or she believes that the plaintiff or defendant is suicidal, the psychologist is under oath to tell the truth. It is possible that the psychologist believes that the individual is suicidal but has not shared those thoughts with the patient/client. How damaging it would be for the patient/client to hear for the first time in an open courtroom that his or her therapist believes that he or she is suicidal! As a result, it has always been this author's practice to ask the patient/client's attorney to have the individual about whom testimony is being given excused from the courtroom, to protect the person from the potential adverse affects of the testimony. This always holds true in cases when the expert testifying is the therapist. However, it may or may not hold true when a custody evaluation is being performed.

There are times when one of the parents in a custody case is extremely emotionally unstable. Hearing testimony that describes the instability, perception of prognosis, and adverse recommendations can reduce the stability and actually precipitate an emotional outburst or even an acute psychotic episode. In such cases, it is necessary to request that the attorney for this individual ask the person not to remain in the courtroom during testimony. In the event that the attorney and/or the client insist on being present for the testimony, the psychologist must begin testimony with a statement identifying the concerns about having the client present, the request made to have the client leave the courtroom, and, last, the refusal of the client to leave.

Altering Data

Although it may seem obvious that under no circumstances should a psychologist alter data, requests are made on occasion by attorneys to have psychologists do so. When the attorney asks for data to be altered in any way, the psychologist must flatly refuse and explain to the attorney that data will have to be used as is or not at all.

Case 1

A number of years ago this author evaluated a family in a custody dispute. When the nine-year-old boy was interviewed, he reported that his mother would partake in simulated breast feeding with him several times a week with both of them being unclothed. When this matter was discussed with the mother, she acknowledged that this activity occurred and that she perceived it as being harmless. This psychologist reported to the mother's attorney the findings and indicated that it would be inadvisable to have the attorney call the psychologist for testimony, as it would be necessary to report this information to the court. The attorney's response was to suggest that I just not bring up the material. When informed that this was not a possibility, the attorney suggested that she would declare that information her work product and, as a result, this author could not testify to that information. Again, it was indicated that this was not possible. The attorney concluded that this psychologist's testimony was not required.

Case 2

Recently, this author was meeting with an attorney to review testimony. Upon providing some information, the attorney stated, "That is a case breaker. You need to take that out of your file." This author asked, "How can I do that?", implying from an ethical point of view. However, the attorney perceived the question as a mechanical question and stated, "That's easy, just rewrite that page and leave that information out." The attorney was informed that he either had to accept the information as recorded or not call this psychologist as an expert witness.

While the psychologist may not alter or hide any data and must report all important data, one should also explain any data that may be misperceived if taken out of context or that requires additional information to be properly understood. For example, a parent taking a bath or shower with a 3-year-old of the same or opposite gender need have no pejorative implications, while the same could not be said if the child were 13.

Making Predictions

Psychologists can paint themselves into a corner by making long-term predictions and stating them to be a reasonable degree of psychological certainty. With all of our expertise, psychologists are generally little or no better at making long-term predictions than anybody else. As a result, it is safest to only make short-term predictions (whether about child custody or dangerousness) and explain what research has shown.

Dual Relationships

It is inappropriate for a psychologist to perform therapy, mediation, or a custody evaluation of someone whom he or she has had a previous relationship with. This constitutes a dual relationship. These include familial, social, sexual, emotional, financial, supervisory, political, administrative, or legal relationships. It can be very difficult to avoid these circumstances in small towns or rural areas. However, when it becomes absolutely necessary under those circumstances, the psychologist must fully disclose the relationship information prior to performing the evaluations, include the information in the written report, and identify the information in testimony, so there is no perception that one is attempting to cover up this material.

Test Security

Under no circumstances should the psychologist bring projective test cards, cognitive or achievement test questions, or materials from tests into courtrooms to demonstrate to the judge, jury, or attorneys how these tests function. One may invent a similar question or show a similar inkblot or drawing to offer some idea of what the test consists of.

Therapists Testifying

The therapist will be called upon at times to testify in a custody case. It is always appropriate to request that the patient/client be asked to leave the courtroom at the time of testimony. When the therapist is performing therapy with children, it is also essential that the children *not* be notified that the therapist will be testifying. This can interfere not only with the trust in the therapist but also in the therapeutic relationship as a whole. There are times where the attorneys will agree that a therapist assigned to a child will not be required to testify in court. This allows the therapist to perform her duties without each of the parents attempting to pressure the psychologist to be on one side or the other. In the event that the attorneys later agree that the therapist should testify, it should be over the therapist's strong objection. Once therapy has been commenced with the understanding that testimony will not be required, it will be handled differently from the way it would if the therapist knew that testimony would be required. As a result, it is not fair to either the therapist or the client to change the rules part way through the process. This should be explained to the judge, who should be asked to decide whether the testimony should be required, and not left up to the attorney's discretion.

Sequestering Witnesses

Sometimes witnesses are sequestered to prevent them from hearing the testimony of other witnesses. Generally, this will only apply to witnesses who are going to testify at a later date. Once a witness is finished testifying, the court will generally allow that witness to remain in the courtroom for other witnesses' testimony. In addition, an expert serving as a consultant to an attorney may remain in the courtroom to aid the attorney in the questioning process, so long as that expert is never called upon to testify. Many judges will also allow an expert witness to remain, while excluding fact witnesses, recognizing that the expert—and the fact-finder—may gain important data to add to his or her database for later testimony.

Limited Recommendations

When a psychologist sees only one of the parents, with or without the children, it is not appropriate to make a custody recommendation. Furthermore, it is unethical and violates the guidelines for custody evaluations put forth by the American Psychological Association. An attorney for a state psychology licensing board recently stated that it was his perception that this would be an actionable offense based on gross negligence. This would also apply in such cases where a psychologist rendered an opinion about whether sexual abuse had occurred based on interviewing only the alleged perpetrator father and not interviewing the children and/or the mother of the children. What follows is an example of recommendations drawn from a recent report of a psychologist that illustrates this problem. "The following recommendation is made with the awareness that the mother was evaluated without evaluating the father. Nevertheless, I am quite confident and comfortable in stating that the mother has the intellectual and emotional resources to be a competent parent to her two young sons. . . . Therefore, it is my recommendation that the mother be granted primary placement, although in joint custody, with the father of her two young sons. Thank you for this referral. I.M. Forhyre, Ph.D., Consulting Psychologist."

SUMMARY OF TIPS FOR SURVIVING YOUR DAY IN COURT

Mechanics

- Arrive on time.
- Dress conservatively.
- Bring your notes.
- Be organized.
- Remain calm.
- Remember, you know more than the attorney.

Substantive

- Answer truthfully.
- Admit when you do not know the answer.
- Do not volunteer additional information.
- Answer only the question asked.
- Know your state laws regarding the ultimate issue, professional certainty.
- Stay within your area of expertise.
- Use "learned treatises" wisely.
- Know your code of ethics.

Other Concerns

- Have an adequate support network.
- Avoid dual relationships.

Glossary of Legal Terms

Adjourn To postpone a court action to a later date.

Adjudicate Have the court determine, such as, paternity was *adjudicated* by the court.

Admissible evidence Evidence that the judge allows to be included in the trial.

Affidavit A sworn notarized statement used instead of live testimony.

Alimony/maintenance Payments received by a spouse or ex-spouse to support them for a period of time.

Appearance Coming to court to testify.

Bifurcated trial When two issues are tried at different times, such as, placement and support.

Calendar The legal system's word for schedule or appointment book.

Case law When law is developed as the result of appellate court decisions.

Contempt A person can be found in contempt for misbehaving in court or disobeying court orders.

Continuance When the court postpones the trial at its request or the request of an attorney.

Cross examination Questioning by the attorney on the other side of the case. Sometimes referred to as "cross."

Defendant The individual who defends himself or herself against actions brought by plaintiffs.

Deponent An individual who is deposed in a deposition.

Deposition When an individual testifies, not in open court. Used to discover what the witness will say when the case goes to court.

Direct examination Questioning by the attorney who has requested the witness testify. Sometimes referred to as "direct."

Discovery The process by which attorneys gain information prior to trial in an effort to determine what testimony will be at trial.

Ex parte There is a communication with the court or proceeding in court without the other side being present or having been given notice.

Finding   The decision made by the judge or the jury.

Guardian ad litem   A guardian appointed by the court to represent the best interest of the child(ren). In most states, it is required that the guardian ad litem be an attorney. However, in some states, that is not necessary. Furthermore, a guardian ad litem can be appointed for one of the parents in the event that it is felt that that parent is incompetent to represent his or her best interests.

Hearsay   Information obtained from a source other than the witness testifying. Generally, expert witnesses are allowed to testify to hearsay if the information was used as a basis for the conclusions reached by the expert witness.

In camera   Testimony given before the judge in the judge's chambers. It can also refer to testimony when the courtroom has been cleared of spectators and witnesses.

In re   With regard to or in reference to. For example, In re *Smith v. Jones.*

Interrogatories   Questions provided by an attorney to gain information from parties or witnesses in a case.

Learned treatise   A document, research article, or book that experts within a profession would rely upon to provide reliable information.

Objection overruled   When the court does not uphold the objection and allows the question or testimony to stand.

Objection sustained   When the court upholds the objection that was raised and disallows the question or testimony.

Party   The individual filing or responding to court actions.

Petitioner   The person who commences or files the divorce action.

Plaintiff   The individual who "complains" or brings the action to court.

Postjudment   After the case is over. A postjudgment dispute would occur after the parties were divorced and a court action is commenced. Such as communication between an attorney and client or a therapist and client.

Pro se   Literally means for one's self. This is when an individual represents himself or herself in a trial.

Quash   To make void or to eliminate, such as, *quash* a subpoena.

Recidivist   Person who repeats the same crime that has been committed previously.

Respondent   The individual who responds to the divorce action of the petitioner.

Restraining order   An order given to protect one party from the actions of another party. This is often given when one party has already physically harmed another party. Sometimes referred to as a "TRO" (temporary restraining order).

Retainer   Funds that are requested in advance of work performed, against which charges will be made.

Sequester   When witnesses are asked to not be present in the courtroom during the testimony of other witnesses prior to their own testimony.

Stipulation   An agreement that is reached between the parties and/or attorneys that takes the place of a trial.

Subpoena   A document that "commands" that a witness appear to testify at a given time and place.

Subpoena duces tecum   This subpoena requires not only appearing to testify but also bringing documents requested.

Support   The amount of money that is designated to be paid for the provision of children's needs.

Temporary orders   Orders made by the court between the time the divorce is filed and when it is final. Sometimes called "interlocutory."

Termination of parental rights (TPR)   When the court orders that the parent no longer has any rights or responsibilities for the child.

Trier of fact   The judge in a trial without a jury, or the jury.

Ultimate issue   In divorce cases this refers to who would make the most appropriate placement or custodial parent.

Voir dire   When a witness is subject to voir dire, questions of competency or expertise will be asked to determine if the witness is qualified.

Weight of evidence   The amount of emphasis that is given to a piece of evidence or a person's testimony.

APPENDIX B

*Ethical Principles of Psychologists and Code of Conduct**

CONTENTS

INTRODUCTION

PREAMBLE

GENERAL PRINCIPLES
Principle A: Competence
Principle B: Integrity
Principle C: Professional and Scientific Responsibility
Principle D: Respect for People's Rights and Dignity
Principle E: Concern for Others' Welfare
Principle F: Social Responsibility

ETHICAL STANDARDS
1. General Standards
1.01 Applicability of the Ethics Code
1.02 Relationship of Ethics and Law
1.03 Professional and Scientific Relationship
1.04 Boundaries of Competence
1.05 Maintaining Expertise
1.06 Basis for Scientific and Professional Judgments
1.07 Describing the Nature and Results of Psychological Services
1.08 Human Differences
1.09 Respecting Others
1.10 Nondiscrimination
1.11 Sexual Harassment
1.12 Other Harassment
1.13 Personal Problems and Conflicts
1.14 Avoiding Harm
1.15 Misuse of Psychologists' Influence
1.16 Misuse of Psychologists' Work
1.17 Multiple Relationships
1.18 Barter (With Patients or Clients)
1.19 Exploitative Relationships
1.20 Consultations and Referrals
1.21 Third-Party Requests for Services
1.22 Delegation to and Supervision of Subordinates
1.23 Documentation of Professional and Scientific Work
1.24 Records and Data
1.25 Fees and Financial Arrangements
1.26 Accuracy in Reports to Payors and Funding Sources
1.27 Referrals and Fees

2. Evaluation, Assessment, or Intervention
2.01 Evaluation, Diagnosis, and Interventions in Professional Context

2.02 Competence and Appropriate Use of Assessments and Interventions
2.03 Test Construction
2.04 Use of Assessment in General and With Special Populations
2.05 Interpreting Assessment Results
2.06 Unqualified Persons
2.07 Obsolete Tests and Outdated Test Results
2.08 Test Scoring and Interpretation Services
2.09 Explaining Assessment Results
2.10 Maintaining Test Security

3. Advertising and Other Public Statements
3.01 Definition of Public Statements
3.02 Statements by Others
3.03 Avoidance of False or Deceptive Statements
3.04 Media Presentations
3.05 Testimonials
3.06 In-Person Solicitation

4. Therapy
4.01 Structuring the Relationship
4.02 Informed Consent to Therapy
4.03 Couple and Family Relationships
4.04 Providing Mental Health Services to Those Served by Others
4.05 Sexual Intimacies With Current Patients or Clients
4.06 Therapy With Former Sexual Partners
4.07 Sexual Intimacies With Former Therapy Patients
4.08 Interruption of Services
4.09 Terminating the Professional Relationship

5. Privacy and Confidentiality
5.01 Discussing the Limits of Confidentiality
5.02 Maintaining Confidentiality
5.03 Minimizing Intrusions on Privacy
5.04 Maintenance of Records
5.05 Disclosures
5.06 Consultations
5.07 Confidential Information in Databases
5.08 Use of Confidential Information for Didactic or Other Purposes
5.09 Preserving Records and Data
5.10 Ownership of Records and Data
5.11 Withholding Records for Nonpayment

6. Teaching, Training Supervision, Research, and Publishing
6.01 Design of Education and Training Programs
6.02 Descriptions of Education and Training Programs
6.03 Accuracy and Objectivity in Teaching
6.04 Limitation on Teaching
6.05 Assessing Student and Supervisee Performance
6.06 Planning Research
6.07 Responsibility
6.08 Compliance With Law and Standards
6.09 Institutional Approval
6.10 Research Responsibilities
6.11 Informed Consent to Research
6.12 Dispensing With Informed Consent
6.13 Informed Consent in Research Filming or Recording
6.14 Offering Inducements for Research Participants
6.15 Deception in Research
6.16 Sharing and Utilizing Data
6.17 Minimizing Invasiveness
6.18 Providing Participants With Information About the Study
6.19 Honoring Commitments
6.20 Care and Use of Animals in Research
6.21 Reporting of Results
6.22 Plagiarism
6.23 Publication Credit
6.24 Duplicate Publication of Data
6.25 Sharing Data
6.26 Professional Reviewers

7. Forensic Activities
7.01 Professionalism
7.02 Forensic Assessments
7.03 Clarification of Role
7.04 Truthfulness and Candor
7.05 Prior Relationships
7.06 Compliance With Law and Rules

8. Resolving Ethical Issues
8.01 Familiarity With Ethics Code
8.02 Confronting Ethical Issues
8.03 Conflicts Between Ethics and Organizational Demands
8.04 Informal Resolution of Ethical Violations
8.05 Reporting Ethical Violations
8.06 Cooperating With Ethics Committees
8.07 Improper Complaints

**Ethical Principles of Psychologists and Code of Conduct,* 47 American Psychologist 1597–1611 (1992). Copyright 1992 by the American Psychological Association. Reprinted by permission.

240

INTRODUCTION

The American Psychological Association's (APA's) Ethical Principles of Psychologists and Code of Conduct (hereinafter referred to as the Ethics Code) consists of an Introduction, a Preamble, six General Principles (A–F), and specific Ethical Standards. The Introduction discusses the intent, organization, procedural considerations, and scope of application of the Ethics Code. The Preamble and General Principles are *aspirational* goals to guide psychologists toward the highest ideals of psychology. Although the Preamble and General Principles are not themselves enforceable rules, they should be considered by psychologists in arriving at an ethical course of action and may be considered by ethics bodies in interpreting the Ethical Standards. The Ethical Standards set forth *enforceable* rules for conduct as psychologists. Most of the Ethical Standards are written broadly, in order to apply to psychologists in varied roles, although the application of an Ethical Standard may vary depending on the context. The Ethical Standards are not exhaustive. The fact that a given conduct is not specifically addressed by the Ethics Code does not mean that it is necessarily either ethical or unethical.

Membership in the APA commits members to adhere to the APA Ethics Code and to the rules and procedures used to implement it. Psychologists and students, whether or not they are APA members, should be aware that the Ethics Code may be applied to them by state psychology boards, courts, or other public bodies.

This Ethics Code applies only to psychologists' work-related activities, that is, activities that are part of the psychologists' scientific and professional functions or that are psychological in nature. It includes the clinical or counseling practice of psychology, research, teaching, supervision of trainees, development of assessment instruments, conducting assessments, educational counseling, organizational consulting, social intervention, administration, and other activities as well. These work-related activities can be distinguished from the purely private conduct of a psychologist, which ordinarily is not within the purview of the Ethics Code.

The Ethics Code is intended to provide standards of professional conduct that can be applied by the APA and by other bodies that choose to adopt them. Whether or not a psychologist has violated the Ethics Code does not by itself determine whether he or she is legally liable in a court action, whether a contract is enforceable, or whether other legal consequences occur. These results are based on legal rather than ethical rules. However, compliance with or violation of the Ethics Code may be admissible as evidence in some legal proceedings, depending on the circumstances.

In the process of making decisions regarding their professional behavior, psychologists must consider this Ethics Code, in addition to applicable laws and psychology board regulations. If the Ethics Code establishes a higher standard of conduct than is required by law, psychologists must meet the higher ethical standard. If the Ethics Code standard appears to conflict with the requirements of law, then psychologists make known their commitment to the Ethics Code and take steps to resolve the conflict in a responsible manner. If neither law nor the Ethics Code resolves an issue, psychologists should consider other professional materials[1] and the dictates of their own conscience, as well as seek consultation with others within the field when this is practical.

The procedures for filing, investigating, and resolving complaints of unethical conduct are described in the current Rules and Procedures of the APA Ethics Committee. The actions that APA may take for violations of the Ethics Code include actions such as reprimand, censure, termination of

---

This version of the APA Ethics Code was adopted by the American Psychological Association's Council of Representatives during its meeting, August 13 and 16, 1992, and is effective beginning December 1, 1992. Inquiries concerning the substance or interpretation of the APA Ethics Code should be addressed to the Director, Office of Ethics, American Psychological Association, 750 First Street, NE, Washington, DC 20002-4242.

This Code will be used to adjudicate complaints brought concerning alleged conduct occurring on or after the effective date. Complaints regarding conduct occurring prior to the effective date will be adjudicated on the basis of the version of the Code that was in effect at the time the conduct occurred, except that no provisions repealed in June 1989, will be enforced even if an earlier version contains the provision. The Ethics Code will undergo continuing review and study for future revisions; comments on the Code may be sent to the above address.

The APA has previously published its Ethical Standards as follows:

American Psychological Association. (1953). *Ethical standards of psychologists.* Washington, DC: Author.
American Psychological Association. (1958). Standards of ethical behavior for psychologists. *American Psychologist, 13,* 268–271.
American Psychological Association. (1963). Ethical standards of psychologists. *American Psychologist, 18,* 56–60.
American Psychological Association. (1968). Ethical standards of psychologists. *American Psychologist, 23,* 357–361.
American Psychological Association. (1977, March). Ethical standards of psychologists. *APA Monitor,* pp. 22–23.
American Psychological Association. (1979). *Ethical standards of psychologists.* Washington, DC: Author.
American Psychological Association. (1981). Ethical principles of psychologists. *American Psychologist, 36,* 633–638.
American Psychological Association. (1990). Ethical principles of psychologists (Amended June 2, 1989). *American Psychologist, 45,* 390–395.

Request copies of the APA's Ethical Principles of Psychologists and Code of Conduct from the APA Order Department, 750 First Street, NE, Washington, DC 20002-4242, or phone (202) 336-5510.

---

[1]Professional materials that are most helpful in this regard are guidelines and standards that have been adopted or endorsed by professional psychological organizations. Such guidelines and standards, whether adopted by the American Psychological Association (APA) or its Divisions, are not enforceable as such by this Ethics Code, but are of educative value to psychologists, courts, and professional bodies. Such materials include, but are not limited to, the APA's *General Guidelines for Providers of Psychological Services* (1987), *Specialty Guidelines for the Delivery of Services by Clinical Psychologists, Counseling Psychologists, Industrial/ Organizational Psychologists, and School Psychologists* (1981), *Guidelines for Computer Based Tests and Interpretations* (1987), *Standards for Educational and Psychological Testing* (1985), *Ethical Principles in the Conduct of Research With Human Participants* (1982), *Guidelines for Ethical Conduct in the Care and Use of Animals* (1986), *Guidelines for Providers of Psychological Services to Ethnic, Linguistic, and Culturally Diverse Populations* (1990), and *Publication Manual of the American Psychological Association* (3rd ed., 1983). Materials not adopted by APA as a whole include the APA Division 41 (Forensic Psychology)/American Psychology–Law Society's *Specialty Guidelines for Forensic Psychologists* (1991).

APA membership, and referral of the matter to other bodies. Complainants who seek remedies such as monetary damages in alleging ethical violations by a psychologist must resort to private negotiation, administrative bodies, or the courts. Actions that violate the Ethics Code may lead to the imposition of sanctions on a psychologist by bodies other than APA, including state psychological associations, other professional groups, psychology boards, other state or federal agencies, and payors for health services. In addition to actions for violation of the Ethics Code, the APA Bylaws provide that APA may take action against a member after his or her conviction of a felony, expulsion or suspension from an affiliated state psychological association, or suspension or loss of licensure.

PREAMBLE

Psychologists work to develop a valid and reliable body of scientific knowledge based on research. They may apply that knowledge to human behavior in a variety of contexts. In doing so, they perform many roles, such as researcher, educator, diagnostician, therapist, supervisor, consultant, administrator, social interventionist, and expert witness. Their goal is to broaden knowledge of behavior and, where appropriate, to apply it pragmatically to improve the condition of both the individual and society. Psychologists respect the central importance of freedom of inquiry and expression in research, teaching, and publication. They also strive to help the public in developing informed judgments and choices concerning human behavior. This Ethics Code provides a common set of values upon which psychologists build their professional and scientific work.

This Code is intended to provide both the general principles and the decision rules to cover most situations encountered by psychologists. It has as its primary goal the welfare and protection of the individuals and groups with whom psychologists work. It is the individual responsibility of each psychologist to aspire to the highest possible standards of conduct. Psychologists respect and protect human and civil rights, and do not knowingly participate in or condone unfair discriminatory practices.

The development of a dynamic set of ethical standards for a psychologist's work-related conduct requires a personal commitment to a lifelong effort to act ethically; to encourage ethical behavior by students, supervisees, employees, and colleagues, as appropriate; and to consult with others, as needed, concerning ethical problems. Each psychologist supplements, but does not violate, the Ethics Code's values and rules on the basis of guidance drawn from personal values, culture, and experience.

GENERAL PRINCIPLES

Principle A: Competence

Psychologists strive to maintain high standards of competence in their work. They recognize the boundaries of their particular competencies and the limitations of their expertise. They provide only those services and use only those techniques for which they are qualified by education,

training, or experience. Psychologists are cognizant of the fact that the competencies required in serving, teaching, and/or studying groups of people vary with the distinctive characteristics of those groups. In those areas in which recognized professional standards do not yet exist, psychologists exercise careful judgment and take appropriate precautions to protect the welfare of those with whom they work. They maintain knowledge of relevant scientific and professional information related to the services they render, and they recognize the need for ongoing education. Psychologists make appropriate use of scientific, professional, technical, and administrative resources.

Principle B: Integrity

Psychologists seek to promote integrity in the science, teaching, and practice of psychology. In these activities psychologists are honest, fair, and respectful of others. In describing or reporting their qualifications, services, products, fees, research, or teaching, they do not make statements that are false, misleading, or deceptive. Psychologists strive to be aware of their own belief systems, values, needs, and limitations and the effect of these on their work. To the extent feasible, they attempt to clarify for relevant parties the roles they are performing and to function appropriately in accordance with those roles. Psychologists avoid improper and potentially harmful dual relationships.

Principle C: Professional and Scientific Responsibility

Psychologists uphold professional standards of conduct, clarify their professional roles and obligations, accept appropriate responsibility for their behavior, and adapt their methods to the needs of different populations. Psychologists consult with, refer to, or cooperate with other professionals and institutions to the extent needed to serve the best interests of their patients, clients, or other recipients of their services. Psychologists' moral standards and conduct are personal matters to the same degree as is true for any other person, except as psychologists' conduct may compromise their professional responsibilities or reduce the public's trust in psychology and psychologists. Psychologists are concerned about the ethical compliance of their colleagues' scientific and professional conduct. When appropriate, they consult with colleagues in order to prevent or avoid unethical conduct.

Principle D: Respect for People's Rights and Dignity

Psychologists accord appropriate respect to the fundamental rights, dignity, and worth of all people. They respect the rights of individuals to privacy, confidentiality, self-determination, and autonomy, mindful that legal and other obligations may lead to inconsistency and conflict with the exercise of these rights. Psychologists are aware of cultural, individual, and role differences, including those due to age, gender, race, ethnicity, national origin, religion, sexual orientation, disability, language, and socioeconomic status.

Psychologists try to eliminate the effect on their work of biases based on those factors, and they do not knowingly participate in or condone unfair discriminatory practices.

Principle E: Concern for Others' Welfare

Psychologists seek to contribute to the welfare of those with whom they interact professionally. In their professional actions, psychologists weigh the welfare and rights of their patients or clients, students, supervisees, human research participants, and other affected persons, and the welfare of animal subjects of research. When conflicts occur among psychologists' obligations or concerns, they attempt to resolve these conflicts and to perform their roles in a responsible fashion that avoids or minimizes harm. Psychologists are sensitive to real and ascribed differences in power between themselves and others, and they do not exploit or mislead other people during or after professional relationships.

Principle F: Social Responsibility

Psychologists are aware of their professional and scientific responsibilities to the community and the society in which they work and live. They apply and make public their knowledge of psychology in order to contribute to human welfare. Psychologists are concerned about and work to mitigate the causes of human suffering. When undertaking research, they strive to advance human welfare and the science of psychology. Psychologists try to avoid misuse of their work. Psychologists comply with the law and encourage the development of law and social policy that serve the interests of their patients and clients and the public. They are encouraged to contribute a portion of their professional time for little or no personal advantage.

ETHICAL STANDARDS

1. General Standards

These General Standards are potentially applicable to the professional and scientific activities of all psychologists.

1.01 Applicability of the Ethics Code

The activity of a psychologist subject to the Ethics Code may be reviewed under these Ethical Standards only if the activity is part of his or her work-related functions or the activity is psychological in nature. Personal activities having no connection to or effect on psychological roles are not subject to the Ethics Code.

1.02 Relationship of Ethics and Law

If psychologists' ethical responsibilities conflict with law, psychologists make known their commitment to the Ethics Code and take steps to resolve the conflict in a responsible manner.

1.03 Professional and Scientific Relationship

Psychologists provide diagnostic, therapeutic, teaching, research, supervisory, consultative, or other psychological services only in the context of a defined professional or scientific relationship or role. (See also Standards 2.01, Evaluation, Diagnosis, and Interventions in Professional Context, and 7.02, Forensic Assessments.)

1.04 Boundaries of Competence

(a) Psychologists provide services, teach, and conduct research only within the boundaries of their competence, based on their education, training, supervised experience, or appropriate professional experience.

(b) Psychologists provide services, teach, or conduct research in new areas or involving new techniques only after first undertaking appropriate study, training, supervision, and/or consultation from persons who are competent in those areas or techniques.

(c) In those emerging areas in which generally recognized standards for preparatory training do not yet exist, psychologists nevertheless take reasonable steps to ensure the competence of their work and to protect patients, clients, students, research participants, and others from harm.

1.05 Maintaining Expertise

Psychologists who engage in assessment, therapy, teaching, research, organizational consulting, or other professional activities maintain a reasonable level of awareness of current scientific and professional information in their fields of activity, and undertake ongoing efforts to maintain competence in the skills they use.

1.06 Basis for Scientific and Professional Judgments

Psychologists rely on scientifically and professionally derived knowledge when making scientific or professional judgments or when engaging in scholarly or professional endeavors.

1.07 Describing the Nature and Results of Psychological Services

(a) When psychologists provide assessment, evaluation, treatment, counseling, supervision, teaching, consultation, research, or other psychological services to an individual, a group, or an organization, they provide, using language that is reasonably understandable to the recipient of those services, appropriate information beforehand about the nature of such services and appropriate information later about results and conclusions. (See also Standard 2.09, Explaining Assessment Results.)

(b) If psychologists will be precluded by law or by organizational roles from providing such information to particular individuals or groups, they so inform those individuals or groups at the outset of the service.

1.08 Human Differences

Where differences of age, gender, race, ethnicity, national origin, religion, sexual orientation, disability, language, or socioeconomic status significantly affect psychologists' work concerning particular individuals or groups, psychologists obtain the training, experience, consultation, or supervision necessary to ensure the competence of their services, or they make appropriate referrals.

1.09 Respecting Others

In their work-related activities, psychologists respect the rights of others to hold values, attitudes, and opinions that differ from their own.

1.10 Nondiscrimination

In their work-related activities, psychologists do not engage in unfair discrimination based on age, gender, race, ethnicity, national origin, religion, sexual orientation, disability, socioeconomic status, or any basis proscribed by law.

1.11 Sexual Harassment

(a) Psychologists do not engage in sexual harassment. Sexual harassment is sexual solicitation, physical advances, or verbal or nonverbal conduct that is sexual in nature, that occurs in connection with the psychologist's activities or roles as a psychologist, and that either: (1) is unwelcome, is offensive, or creates a hostile workplace environment, and the psychologist knows or is told this; or (2) is sufficiently severe or intense to be abusive to a reasonable person in the context. Sexual harassment can consist of a single intense or severe act or of multiple persistent or pervasive acts.

(b) Psychologists accord sexual-harassment complainants and respondents dignity and respect. Psychologists do not participate in denying a person academic admittance or advancement, employment, tenure, or promotion, based solely upon their having made, or their being the subject of, sexual-harassment charges. This does not preclude taking action based upon the outcome of such proceedings or consideration of other appropriate information.

1.12 Other Harassment

Psychologists do not knowingly engage in behavior that is harassing or demeaning to persons with whom they interact in their work based on factors such as those persons' age, gender, race, ethnicity, national origin, religion, sexual orientation, disability, language, or socioeconomic status.

1.13 Personal Problems and Conflicts

(a) Psychologists recognize that their personal problems and conflicts may interfere with their effectiveness. Accordingly, they refrain from undertaking an activity when they know or should know that their personal problems are likely to lead to harm to a patient, client, colleague, student, research participant, or other person to whom they may owe a professional or scientific obligation.

(b) In addition, psychologists have an obligation to be alert to signs of, and to obtain assistance for, their personal problems at an early stage, in order to prevent significantly impaired performance.

(c) When psychologists become aware of personal problems that may interfere with their performing work-related duties adequately, they take appropriate measures, such as obtaining professional consultation or assistance, and determine whether they should limit, suspend, or terminate their work-related duties.

1.14 Avoiding Harm

Psychologists take reasonable steps to avoid harming their patients or clients, research participants, students, and others with whom they work, and to minimize harm where it is foreseeable and unavoidable.

1.15 Misuse of Psychologists' Influence

Because psychologists' scientific and professional judgments and actions may affect the lives of others, they are alert to and guard against personal, financial, social, organizational, or political factors that might lead to misuse of their influence.

1.16 Misuse of Psychologists' Work

(a) Psychologists do not participate in activities in which it appears likely that their skills or data will be misused by others, unless corrective mechanisms are available. (See also Standard 7.04, Truthfulness and Candor.)

(b) If psychologists learn of misuse or misrepresentation of their work, they take reasonable steps to correct or minimize the misuse or misrepresentation.

1.17 Multiple Relationships

(a) In many communities and situations, it may not be feasible or reasonable for psychologists to avoid social or other nonprofessional contacts with persons such as patients, clients, students, supervisees, or research participants. Psychologists must always be sensitive to the potential harmful effects of other contacts on their work and on those persons with whom they deal. A psychologist refrains from entering into or promising another personal, scientific, professional, financial, or other relationship with such persons if it appears likely that such a relationship reasonably might impair the psychologist's objectivity or otherwise interfere with the psychologist's effectively performing his or her functions as a psychologist, or might harm or exploit the other party.

(b) Likewise, whenever feasible, a psychologist refrains from taking on professional or scientific obligations when preexisting relationships would create a risk of such harm.

(c) If a psychologist finds that, due to unforeseen factors, a potentially harmful multiple relationship has arisen, the psychologist attempts to resolve it with due regard for the best interests of the affected person and maximal compliance with the Ethics Code.

1.18 Barter (With Patients or Clients)

Psychologists ordinarily refrain from accepting goods, services, or other nonmonetary remuneration from patients or clients in return for psychological services because such arrangements create inherent potential for conflicts, exploitation, and distortion of the professional relationship. A psychologist may participate in bartering only if (1) it is not clinically contraindicated, and (2) the relationship is not exploitative. (See also Standards 1.17, Multiple Relationships, and 1.25, Fees and Financial Arrangements.)

1.19 Exploitative Relationships

(a) Psychologists do not exploit persons over whom they have supervisory, evaluative, or other authority such as students, supervisees, employees, research participants, and clients or patients. (See also Standards 4.05–4.07 regarding sexual involvement with clients or patients.)

(b) Psychologists do not engage in sexual relationships with students or supervisees in training over whom the psychologist has evaluative or direct authority, because such relationships are so likely to impair judgment or be exploitative.

1.20 Consultations and Referrals

(a) Psychologists arrange for appropriate consultations and referrals based principally on the best interests of their patients or clients, with appropriate consent, and subject to other relevant considerations, including applicable law and contractual obligations. (See also Standards 5.01, Discussing the Limits of Confidentiality, and 5.06, Consultations.)

(b) When indicated and professionally appropriate, psychologists cooperate with other professionals in order to serve their patients or clients effectively and appropriately.

(c) Psychologists' referral practices are consistent with law.

1.21 Third-Party Requests for Services

(a) When a psychologist agrees to provide services to a person or entity at the request of a third party, the psychologist clarifies to the extent feasible, at the outset of the service, the nature of the relationship with each party. This clarification includes the role of the psychologist (such as therapist, organizational consultant, diagnostician, or expert witness), the probable uses of the services provided or the information obtained, and the fact that there may be limits to confidentiality.

(b) If there is a foreseeable risk of the psychologist's being called upon to perform conflicting roles because of the involvement of a third party, the psychologist clarifies the nature and direction of his or her responsibilities, keeps all parties appropriately informed as matters develop, and resolves the situation in accordance with this Ethics Code.

1.22 Delegation to and Supervision of Subordinates

(a) Psychologists delegate to their employees, supervisees, and research assistants only those responsibilities that such persons can reasonably be expected to perform competently, on the basis of their education, training, or experience, either independently or with the level of supervision being provided.

(b) Psychologists provide proper training and supervision to their employees or supervisees and take reasonable steps to see that such persons perform services responsibly, competently, and ethically.

(c) If institutional policies, procedures, or practices prevent fulfillment of this obligation, psychologists attempt to modify their role or to correct the situation to the extent feasible.

1.23 Documentation of Professional and Scientific Work

(a) Psychologists appropriately document their professional and scientific work in order to facilitate provision of services later by them or by other professionals, to ensure accountability, and to meet other requirements of institutions or the law.

(b) When psychologists have reason to believe that records of their professional services will be used in legal proceedings involving recipients of or participants in their work, they have a responsibility to create and maintain documentation in the kind of detail and quality that would be consistent with reasonable scrutiny in an adjudicative forum. (See also Standard 7.01, Professionalism, under Forensic Activities.)

1.24 Records and Data

Psychologists create, maintain, disseminate, store, retain, and dispose of records and data relating to their research, practice, and other work in accordance with law and in a manner that permits compliance with the requirements of this Ethics Code. (See also Standard 5.04, Maintenance of Records.)

1.25 Fees and Financial Arrangements

(a) As early as is feasible in a professional or scientific relationship, the psychologist and the patient, client, or other appropriate recipient of psychological services reach an agreement specifying the compensation and the billing arrangements.

(b) Psychologists do not exploit recipients of services or payors with respect to fees.

(c) Psychologists' fee practices are consistent with law.

(d) Psychologists do not misrepresent their fees.

(e) If limitations to services can be anticipated because of limitations in financing, this is discussed with the patient, client, or other appropriate recipient of services as early as is feasible. (See also Standard 4.08, Interruption of Services.)

(f) If the patient, client, or other recipient of services does not pay for services as agreed, and if the psychologist wishes to use collection agencies or legal measures to collect the fees, the psychologist first informs the person that such measures will be taken and provides that person an opportunity to make prompt payment. (See also Standard 5.11, Withholding Records for Nonpayment.)

1.26 Accuracy in Reports to Payors and Funding Sources

In their reports to payors for services or sources of research funding, psychologists accurately state the nature of the research or service provided, the fees or charges, and where applicable, the identity of the provider, the findings, and the diagnosis. (See also Standard 5.05, Disclosures.)

1.27 Referrals and Fees

When a psychologist pays, receives payment from, or divides fees with another professional other than in an employer–employee relationship, the payment to each is based on the services (clinical, consultative, administrative, or other) provided and is not based on the referral itself.

2.   Evaluation, Assessment, or Intervention

2.01 Evaluation, Diagnosis, and Interventions in Professional Context

(a) Psychologists perform evaluations, diagnostic services, or interventions only within the context of a defined professional relationship. (See also Standard 1.03, Professional and Scientific Relationship.)

(b) Psychologists' assessments, recommendations, reports, and psychological diagnostic or evaluative statements are based on information and techniques (including personal interviews of the individual when appropriate) sufficient to provide appropriate substantiation for their findings. (See also Standard 7.02, Forensic Assessments.)

2.02 Competence and Appropriate Use of Assessments and Interventions

(a) Psychologists who develop, administer, score, interpret, or use psychological assessment techniques, interviews, tests, or instruments do so in a manner and for purposes that are appropriate in light of the research on or evidence of the usefulness and proper application of the techniques.

(b) Psychologists refrain from misuse of assessment techniques, interventions, results, and interpretations and take reasonable steps to prevent others from misusing the information these techniques provide. This includes refraining from releasing raw test results or raw data to persons, other than to patients or clients as appropriate, who are not qualified to use such information. (See also Standards 1.02, Relationship of Ethics and Law, and 1.04, Boundaries of Competence.)

2.03 Test Construction

Psychologists who develop and conduct research with tests and other assessment techniques use scientific procedures and current professional knowledge for test design, standardization, validation, reduction or elimination of bias, and recommendations for use.

2.04 Use of Assessment in General and With Special Populations

(a) Psychologists who perform interventions or administer, score, interpret, or use assessment techniques are familiar with the reliability, validation, and related standardization or outcome studies of, and proper applications and uses of, the techniques they use.

(b) Psychologists recognize limits to the certainty with which diagnoses, judgments, or predictions can be made about individuals.

(c) Psychologists attempt to identify situations in which particular interventions or assessment techniques or norms may not be applicable or may require adjustment in administration or interpretation because of factors such as individuals' gender, age, race, ethnicity, national origin, religion, sexual orientation, disability, language, or socioeconomic status.

2.05 Interpreting Assessment Results

When interpreting assessment results, including automated interpretations, psychologists take into account the various test factors and characteristics of the person being assessed that might affect psychologists' judgments or reduce the accuracy of their interpretations. They indicate any significant reservations they have about the accuracy or limitations of their interpretations.

2.06 Unqualified Persons

Psychologists do not promote the use of psychological assessment techniques by unqualified persons. (See also Standard 1.22, Delegation to and Supervision of Subordinates.)

2.07 Obsolete Tests and Outdated Test Results

(a) Psychologists do not base their assessment or intervention decisions or recommendations on data or test results that are outdated for the current purpose.

(b) Similarly, psychologists do not base such decisions or recommendations on tests and measures that are obsolete and not useful for the current purpose.

2.08 Test Scoring and Interpretation Services

(a) Psychologists who offer assessment or scoring procedures to other professionals accurately describe the purpose, norms, validity, reliability, and applications of the procedures and any special qualifications applicable to their use.

(b) Psychologists select scoring and interpretation services (including automated services) on the basis of evidence of the validity of the program and procedures as well as on other appropriate considerations.

(c) Psychologists retain appropriate responsibility for the appropriate application, interpretation, and use of assessment instruments, whether they score and interpret such tests themselves or use automated or other services.

2.09 Explaining Assessment Results

Unless the nature of the relationship is clearly explained to the person being assessed in advance and precludes provision of an explanation of results (such as in some organizational consulting, preemployment or security screenings, and forensic evaluations), psychologists ensure that an explanation of the results is provided using language that is reasonably understandable to the person assessed or to another legally authorized person on behalf of the client. Regardless of whether the scoring and interpretation are done by the psychologist, by assistants, or by automated or other outside services, psychologists take reasonable steps to ensure that appropriate explanations of results are given.

2.10 Maintaining Test Security

Psychologists make reasonable efforts to maintain the integrity and security of tests and other assessment techniques consistent with law, contractual obligations, and in a manner that permits compliance with the requirements of this Ethics Code. (See also Standard 1.02, Relationship of Ethics and Law.)

3. Advertising and Other Public Statements

3.01 Definition of Public Statements

Psychologists comply with this Ethics Code in public statements relating to their professional services, products, or publications or to the field of psychology. Public statements include but are not limited to paid or unpaid advertising, brochures, printed matter, directory listings, personal resumes or curricula vitae, interviews or comments for use in media, statements in legal proceedings, lectures and public oral presentations, and published materials.

3.02 Statements by Others

(a) Psychologists who engage others to create or place public statements that promote their professional practice, products, or activities retain professional responsibility for such statements.

(b) In addition, psychologists make reasonable efforts to prevent others whom they do not control (such as employers, publishers, sponsors, organizational clients, and representatives of the print or broadcast media) from making deceptive statements concerning psychologists' practice or professional or scientific activities.

(c) If psychologists learn of deceptive statements about their work made by others, psychologists make reasonable efforts to correct such statements.

(d) Psychologists do not compensate employees of press, radio, television, or other communication media in return for publicity in a news item.

(e) A paid advertisement relating to the psychologist's activities must be identified as such, unless it is already apparent from the context.

3.03 Avoidance of False or Deceptive Statements

(a) Psychologists do not make public statements that are false, deceptive, misleading, or fraudulent, either because of what they state, convey, or suggest or because of what they omit, concerning their research, practice, or other work activities or those of persons or organizations with which they are affiliated. As examples (and not in limitation) of this standard, psychologists do not make false or deceptive statements concerning (1) their training, experience, or competence; (2) their academic degrees; (3) their credentials; (4) their institutional or association affiliations; (5) their services; (6) the scientific or clinical basis for, or results or degree of success of, their services; (7) their fees; or (8) their publications or research findings. (See also Standards 6.15, Deception in Research, and 6.18, Providing Participants With Information About the Study.)

(b) Psychologists claim as credentials for their psychological work, only degrees that (1) were earned from a regionally accredited educational institution or (2) were the basis for psychology licensure by the state in which they practice.

3.04 Media Presentations

When psychologists provide advice or comment by means of public lectures, demonstrations, radio or television programs, prerecorded tapes, printed articles, mailed material, or other media, they take reasonable precautions to ensure that (1) the statements are based on appropriate psychological literature and practice, (2) the statements are otherwise consistent with this Ethics Code, and (3) the recipients of the information are not encouraged to infer that a relationship has been established with them personally.

3.05 Testimonials

Psychologists do not solicit testimonials from current psychotherapy clients or patients or other persons who because of their particular circumstances are vulnerable to undue influence.

3.06 In-Person Solicitation

Psychologists do not engage, directly or through agents, in uninvited in-person solicitation of business from actual or potential psychotherapy patients or clients or other persons who because of their particular circumstances are vulnerable to undue influence. However, this does not preclude attempting to implement appropriate collateral contacts with significant others for the purpose of benefiting an already engaged therapy patient.

4. Therapy

4.01 Structuring the Relationship

(a) Psychologists discuss with clients or patients as early as is feasible in the therapeutic relationship appropriate issues, such as the nature and anticipated course of therapy, fees, and confidentiality. (See also Standards 1.25, Fees and Financial Arrangements, and 5.01, Discussing the Limits of Confidentiality.)

(b) When the psychologist's work with clients or patients will be supervised, the above discussion includes that fact, and the name of the supervisor, when the supervisor has legal responsibility for the case.

(c) When the therapist is a student intern, the client or patient is informed of that fact.

(d) Psychologists make reasonable efforts to answer patients' questions and to avoid apparent misunderstandings about therapy. Whenever possible, psychologists provide oral and/or written information, using language that is reasonably understandable to the patient or client.

4.02 Informed Consent to Therapy

(a) Psychologists obtain appropriate informed consent to therapy or related procedures, using language that is reasonably understandable to participants. The content of informed consent will vary depending on many circumstances; however, informed consent generally implies that the person (1) has the capacity to consent, (2) has been informed of significant information concerning the procedure, (3) has freely and without undue influence expressed consent, and (4) consent has been appropriately recorded.

(b) When persons are legally incapable of giving informed consent, psychologists obtain informed permission from a legally authorized person, if such substitute consent is permitted by law.

(c) In addition, psychologists (1) inform those persons who are legally incapable of giving informed consent about the proposed interventions in a manner commensurate with the persons' psychological capacities, (2) seek their assent to those interventions, and (3) consider such persons' preferences and best interests.

4.03 Couple and Family Relationships

(a) When a psychologist agrees to provide services to several persons who have a relationship (such as husband and wife or parents and children), the psychologist attempts to clarify at the outset (1) which of the individuals are patients or clients and (2) the relationship the psychologist will have with each person. This clarification includes the role of the psychologist and the probable uses of the services provided or the information obtained. (See also Standard 5.01, Discussing the Limits of Confidentiality.)

(b) As soon as it becomes apparent that the psychologist may be called on to perform potentially conflicting roles (such as marital counselor to husband and wife, and then witness for one party in a divorce proceeding), the psychologist attempts to clarify and adjust, or withdraw from, roles appropriately. (See also Standard 7.03, Clarification of Role, under Forensic Activities.)

4.04 Providing Mental Health Services to Those Served by Others

In deciding whether to offer or provide services to those already receiving mental health services elsewhere, psychologists carefully consider the treatment issues and the potential patient's or client's welfare. The psychologist discusses these issues with the patient or client, or another legally authorized person on behalf of the client, in order to minimize the risk of confusion and conflict, consults with the other service providers when appropriate, and proceeds with caution and sensitivity to the therapeutic issues.

4.05 Sexual Intimacies With Current Patients or Clients

Psychologists do not engage in sexual intimacies with current patients or clients.

4.06 Therapy With Former Sexual Partners

Psychologists do not accept as therapy patients or clients persons with whom they have engaged in sexual intimacies.

4.07 Sexual Intimacies With Former Therapy Patients

(a) Psychologists do not engage in sexual intimacies with a former therapy patient or client for at least two years after cessation or termination of professional services.

(b) Because sexual intimacies with a former therapy patient or client are so frequently harmful to the patient or client, and because such intimacies undermine public confidence in the psychology profession and thereby deter the public's use of needed services, psychologists do not engage in sexual intimacies with former therapy patients and clients even after a two-year interval except in the most unusual circumstances. The psychologist who engages in such activity after the two years following cessation or termination of treatment bears the burden of demonstrating that there has been no exploitation, in light of all relevant factors, including (1) the amount of time that has passed since therapy terminated, (2) the nature and duration of the therapy, (3) the circumstances of termination, (4) the patient's or client's personal history, (5) the patient's or client's current mental status, (6) the likelihood of adverse impact on the patient or client and others, and (7) any statements or actions made by the therapist during the course of therapy suggesting or inviting the possibility of a posttermination sexual or romantic relationship with the patient or client. (See also Standard 1.17, Multiple Relationships.)

4.08 Interruption of Services

(a) Psychologists make reasonable efforts to plan for facilitating care in the event that psychological services are interrupted by factors such as the psychologist's illness, death, unavailability, or relocation or by the client's relocation or financial limitations. (See also Standard 5.09, Preserving Records and Data.)

(b) When entering into employment or contractual relationships, psychologists provide for orderly and appropriate resolution of responsibility for patient or client care in the event that the employment or contractual relationship ends, with paramount consideration given to the welfare of the patient or client.

4.09 Terminating the Professional Relationship

(a) Psychologists do not abandon patients or clients. (See also Standard 1.25e, under Fees and Financial Arrangements.)

(b) Psychologists terminate a professional relationship when it becomes reasonably clear that the patient or client no longer needs the service, is not benefiting, or is being harmed by continued service.

(c) Prior to termination for whatever reason, except where precluded by the patient's or client's conduct, the psychologist discusses the patient's or client's views and needs, provides appropriate pretermination counseling, suggests alternative service providers as appropriate, and takes other reasonable steps to facilitate transfer of responsibility to another provider if the patient or client needs one immediately.

5.   Privacy and Confidentiality

These Standards are potentially applicable to the professional and scientific activities of all psychologists.

5.01 Discussing the Limits of Confidentiality

(a) Psychologists discuss with persons and organizations with whom they establish a scientific or professional relationship (including, to the extent feasible, minors and their legal representatives) (1) the relevant limitations on confidentiality, including limitations where applicable in group, marital, and family therapy or in organizational consulting, and (2) the foreseeable uses of the information generated through their services.

(b) Unless it is not feasible or is contraindicated, the discussion of confidentiality occurs at the outset of the relationship and thereafter as new circumstances may warrant.

(c) Permission for electronic recording of interviews is secured from clients and patients.

5.02 Maintaining Confidentiality

Psychologists have a primary obligation and take reasonable precautions to respect the confidentiality rights of those with whom they work or consult, recognizing that confidentiality may be established by law, institutional rules, or professional or scientific relationships. (See also Standard 6.26, Professional Reviewers.)

5.03 Minimizing Intrusions on Privacy

(a) In order to minimize intrusions on privacy, psychologists include in written and oral reports, consultations, and the like, only information germane to the purpose for which the communication is made.

(b) Psychologists discuss confidential information obtained in clinical or consulting relationships, or evaluative data concerning patients, individual or organizational clients, students, research participants, supervisees, and employees, only for appropriate scientific or professional purposes and only with persons clearly concerned with such matters.

5.04 Maintenance of Records

Psychologists maintain appropriate confidentiality in creating, storing, accessing, transferring, and disposing of records under their control, whether these are written, automated, or in any other medium. Psychologists maintain and dispose of records in accordance with law and in a manner that permits compliance with the requirements of this Ethics Code.

5.05 Disclosures

(a) Psychologists disclose confidential information without the consent of the individual only as mandated by law, or where permitted by law for a valid purpose, such as (1) to provide needed professional services to the patient or the individual or organizational client, (2) to obtain appropriate professional consultations, (3) to protect the patient or client or others from harm, or (4) to obtain payment for services, in which instance disclosure is limited to the minimum that is necessary to achieve the purpose.

(b) Psychologists also may disclose confidential information with the appropriate consent of the patient or the individual or organizational client (or of another legally authorized person on behalf of the patient or client), unless prohibited by law.

5.06 Consultations

When consulting with colleagues, (1) psychologists do not share confidential information that reasonably could lead to the identification of a patient, client, research participant, or other person or organization with whom they have a confidential relationship unless they have obtained the prior consent of the person or organization or the disclosure cannot be avoided, and (2) they share information only to the extent necessary to achieve the purposes of the consultation. (See also Standard 5.02, Maintaining Confidentiality.)

5.07 Confidential Information in Databases

(a) If confidential information concerning recipients of psychological services is to be entered into databases or systems of records available to persons whose access has not been consented to by the recipient, then psychologists use coding or other techniques to avoid the inclusion of personal identifiers.

(b) If a research protocol approved by an institutional review board or similar body requires the inclusion of personal identifiers, such identifiers are deleted before the information is made accessible to persons other than those of whom the subject was advised.

(c) If such deletion is not feasible, then before psychologists transfer such data to others or review such data collected by others, they take reasonable steps to determine that appropriate consent of personally identifiable individuals has been obtained.

5.08 Use of Confidential Information for Didactic or Other Purposes

(a) Psychologists do not disclose in their writings, lectures, or other public media, confidential, personally identifiable information concerning their patients, individual or organizational clients, students, research participants, or other recipients of their services that they obtained during the course of their work, unless the person or organization has consented in writing or unless there is other ethical or legal authorization for doing so.

(b) Ordinarily, in such scientific and professional presentations, psychologists disguise confidential information concerning such persons or organizations so that they are not individually identifiable to others and so that discussions do not cause harm to subjects who might identify themselves.

5.09 Preserving Records and Data

A psychologist makes plans in advance so that confidentiality of records and data is protected in the event of the psychologist's death, incapacity, or withdrawal from the position or practice.

5.10 Ownership of Records and Data

Recognizing that ownership of records and data is governed by legal principles, psychologists take reasonable and lawful steps so that records and data remain available to the extent needed to serve the best interests of patients, individual or organizational clients, research participants, or appropriate others.

5.11 Withholding Records for Nonpayment

Psychologists may not withhold records under their control that are requested and imminently needed for a patient's or client's treatment solely because payment has not been received, except as otherwise provided by law.

6.   Teaching, Training Supervision, Research, and Publishing

6.01 Design of Education and Training Programs

Psychologists who are responsible for education and training programs seek to ensure that the programs are competently designed, provide the proper experiences, and meet the requirements for licensure, certification, or other goals for which claims are made by the program.

6.02 Descriptions of Education and Training Programs

(a) Psychologists responsible for education and training programs seek to ensure that there is a current and accurate description of the program content, training goals and objectives, and   requirements that must be met for satisfactory completion of the program. This information must be made readily available to all interested parties.

(b) Psychologists seek to ensure that statements concerning their course outlines are accurate and not misleading, particularly regarding the subject matter to be covered, bases for evaluating progress, and the nature of course experiences. (See also Standard 3.03, Avoidance of False or Deceptive Statements.)

(c) To the degree to which they exercise control, psychologists responsible for announcements, catalogs, brochures, or advertisements describing workshops, seminars, or other non-degree-granting educational programs ensure that they accurately describe the audience for which the program is intended, the educational objectives, the presenters, and the fees involved.

6.03 Accuracy and Objectivity in Teaching

(a) When engaged in teaching or training, psychologists present psychological information accurately and with a reasonable degree of objectivity.

(b) When engaged in teaching or training, psychologists recognize the power they hold over students or supervisees and therefore make reasonable efforts to avoid engaging in conduct that is personally demeaning to students or supervisees. (See also Standards 1.09, Respecting Others, and 1.12, Other Harassment.)

6.04 Limitation on Teaching

Psychologists do not teach the use of techniques or procedures that require specialized training, licensure, or expertise, including but not limited to hypnosis, biofeedback, and projective techniques, to individuals who lack the prerequisite training, legal scope of practice, or expertise.

6.05 Assessing Student and Supervisee Performance

(a) In academic and supervisory relationships, psychologists establish an appropriate process for providing feedback to students and supervisees.

(b) Psychologists evaluate students and supervisees on the basis of their actual performance on relevant and established program requirements.

6.06 Planning Research

(a) Psychologists design, conduct, and report research in accordance with recognized standards of scientific competence and ethical research.

(b) Psychologists plan their research so as to minimize the possibility that results will be misleading.

(c) In planning research, psychologists consider its ethical acceptability under the Ethics Code. If an ethical issue is unclear, psychologists seek to resolve the issue through consultation with institutional review boards, animal care and use committees, peer consultations, or other proper mechanisms.

(d) Psychologists take reasonable steps to implement appropriate protections for the rights and welfare of human participants, other persons affected by the research, and the welfare of animal subjects.

6.07 Responsibility

(a) Psychologists conduct research competently and with due concern for the dignity and welfare of the participants.

(b) Psychologists are responsible for the ethical conduct of research conducted by them or by others under their supervision or control.

(c) Researchers and assistants are permitted to perform only those tasks for which they are appropriately trained and prepared.

(d) As part of the process of development and implementation of research projects, psychologists consult those with expertise concerning any special population under investigation or most likely to be affected.

6.08 Compliance With Law and Standards

Psychologists plan and conduct research in a manner consistent with federal and state law and regulations, as well as professional standards governing the conduct of research, and particularly those standards governing research with human participants and animal subjects.

6.09 Institutional Approval

Psychologists obtain from host institutions or organizations appropriate approval prior to conducting research, and they provide accurate information about their research proposals. They conduct the research in accordance with the approved research protocol.

6.10 Research Responsibilities

Prior to conducting research (except research involving only anonymous surveys, naturalistic observations, or similar research), psychologists enter into an agreement with participants that clarifies the nature of the research and the responsibilities of each party.

6.11 Informed Consent to Research

(a) Psychologists use language that is reasonably understandable to research participants in obtaining their appropriate informed consent (except as provided in Standard 6.12, Dispensing With Informed Consent). Such informed consent is appropriately documented.

(b) Using language that is reasonably understandable to participants, psychologists inform participants of the nature of the research; they inform participants that they are free to participate or to decline to participate or to withdraw from the research; they explain the foreseeable consequences of declining or withdrawing; they inform participants of significant factors that may be expected to influence their willingness to participate (such as risks, discomfort, adverse effects, or limitations on confidentiality, except as provided in Standard 6.15, Deception in Research); and they explain other aspects about which the prospective participants inquire.

(c) When psychologists conduct research with individuals such as students or subordinates, psychologists take special care to protect the prospective participants from adverse consequences of declining or withdrawing from participation.

(d) When research participation is a course requirement or opportunity for extra credit, the prospective participant is given the choice of equitable alternative activities.

(e) For persons who are legally incapable of giving informed consent, psychologists nevertheless (1) provide an appropriate explanation, (2) obtain the participant's assent, and (3) obtain appropriate permission from a legally authorized person, if such substitute consent is permitted by law.

6.12 Dispensing With Informed Consent

Before determining that planned research (such as research involving only anonymous questionnaires, naturalistic observations, or certain kinds of archival research) does not require the informed consent of research participants, psychologists consider applicable regulations and institutional review board requirements, and they consult with colleagues as appropriate.

6.13 Informed Consent in Research Filming or Recording

Psychologists obtain informed consent from research participants prior to filming or recording them in any form, unless the research involves simply naturalistic observations in public places and it is not anticipated that the recording will be used in a manner that could cause personal identification or harm.

6.14 Offering Inducements for Research Participants

(a) In offering professional services as an inducement to obtain research participants, psychologists make clear the nature of the services, as well as the risks, obligations, and limitations. (See also Standard 1.18, Barter [With Patients or Clients].)

(b) Psychologists do not offer excessive or inappropriate financial or other inducements to obtain research participants, particularly when it might tend to coerce participation.

6.15 Deception in Research

(a) Psychologists do not conduct a study involving deception unless they have determined that the use of deceptive techniques is justified by the study's prospective scientific, educational, or applied value and that equally effective alternative procedures that do not use deception are not feasible.

(b) Psychologists never deceive research participants about significant aspects that would affect their willingness to participate, such as physical risks, discomfort, or unpleasant emotional experiences.

(c) Any other deception that is an integral feature of the design and conduct of an experiment must be explained to participants as early as is feasible, preferably at the conclusion of their participation, but no later than at the conclusion of the research. (See also Standard 6.18, Providing Participants With Information About the Study.)

6.16 Sharing and Utilizing Data

Psychologists inform research participants of their anticipated sharing or further use of personally identifiable research data and of the possibility of unanticipated future uses.

6.17 Minimizing Invasiveness

In conducting research, psychologists interfere with the participants or milieu from which data are collected only in a manner that is warranted by an appropriate research design and that is consistent with psychologists' roles as scientific investigators.

6.18 Providing Participants With Information About the Study

(a) Psychologists provide a prompt opportunity for participants to obtain appropriate information about the nature, results, and conclusions of the research, and psychologists attempt to correct any misconceptions that participants may have.

(b) If scientific or humane values justify delaying or withholding this information, psychologists take reasonable measures to reduce the risk of harm.

6.19 Honoring Commitments

Psychologists take reasonable measures to honor all commitments they have made to research participants.

6.20 Care and Use of Animals in Research

(a) Psychologists who conduct research involving animals treat them humanely.

(b) Psychologists acquire, care for, use, and dispose of animals in compliance with current federal, state, and local laws and regulations, and with professional standards.

(c) Psychologists trained in research methods and experienced in the care of laboratory animals supervise all procedures involving animals and are responsible for ensuring appropriate consideration of their comfort, health, and humane treatment.

(d) Psychologists ensure that all individuals using animals under their supervision have received instruction in research methods and in the care, maintenance, and handling of the species being used, to the extent appropriate to their role.

(e) Responsibilities and activities of individuals assisting in a research project are consistent with their respective competencies.

(f) Psychologists make reasonable efforts to minimize the discomfort, infection, illness, and pain of animal subjects.

(g) A procedure subjecting animals to pain, stress, or privation is used only when an alternative procedure is unavailable and the goal is justified by its prospective scientific, educational, or applied value.

(h) Surgical procedures are performed under appropriate anesthesia; techniques to avoid infection and minimize pain are followed during and after surgery.

(i) When it is appropriate that the animal's life be terminated, it is done rapidly, with an effort to minimize pain, and in accordance with accepted procedures.

6.21 Reporting of Results

(a) Psychologists do not fabricate data or falsify results in their publications.

(b) If psychologists discover significant errors in their published data, they take reasonable steps to correct such errors in a correction, retraction, erratum, or other appropriate publication means.

6.22 Plagiarism

Psychologists do not present substantial portions or elements of another's work or data as their own, even if the other work or data source is cited occasionally.

6.23 Publication Credit

(a) Psychologists take responsibility and credit, including authorship credit, only for work they have actually performed or to which they have contributed.

(b) Principal authorship and other publication credits accurately reflect the relative scientific or professional contributions of the individuals involved, regardless of their relative status. Mere possession of an institutional position, such as Department Chair, does not justify authorship credit. Minor contributions to the research or to the writing for publications are appropriately acknowledged, such as in footnotes or in an introductory statement.

(c) A student is usually listed as principal author on any multiple-authored article that is substantially based on the student's dissertation or thesis.

6.24 Duplicate Publication of Data

Psychologists do not publish, as original data, data that have been previously published. This does not preclude republishing data when they are accompanied by proper acknowledgment.

6.25 Sharing Data

After research results are published, psychologists do not withhold the data on which their conclusions are based from other competent professionals who seek to verify the substantive claims through reanalysis and who intend to use such data only for that purpose, provided that the confidentiality of the participants can be protected and unless legal rights concerning proprietary data preclude their release.

6.26 Professional Reviewers

Psychologists who review material submitted for publication, grant, or other research proposal review respect the confidentiality of and the proprietary rights in such information of those who submitted it.

7.   Forensic Activities

7.01 Professionalism

Psychologists who perform forensic functions, such as assessments, interviews, consultations, reports, or expert testimony, must comply with all other provisions of this Ethics Code to the extent that they apply to such activities. In addition, psychologists base their forensic work on appropriate knowledge of and competence in the areas underlying such work, including specialized knowledge concerning special populations. (See also Standards 1.06, Basis for Scientific and Professional Judgments; 1.08, Human Differences; 1.15, Misuse of Psychologists' Influence; and 1.23, Documentation of Professional and Scientific Work.)

7.02 Forensic Assessments

(a) Psychologists' forensic assessments, recommendations, and reports are based on information and techniques (including personal interviews of the individual, when appropriate) sufficient to provide appropriate substantiation for their findings. (See also Standards 1.03, Professional and Scientific Relationship; 1.23, Documentation of Professional and Scientific Work; 2.01, Evaluation, Diagnosis, and Interventions in Professional Context; and 2.05, Interpreting Assessment Results.)

(b) Except as noted in (c), below, psychologists provide written or oral forensic reports or testimony of the psychological characteristics of an individual only after they have conducted an examination of the individual adequate to support their statements or conclusions.

(c) When, despite reasonable efforts, such an examination is not feasible, psychologists clarify the impact of their limited information on the reliability and validity of their reports and testimony, and they appropriately limit the nature and extent of their conclusions or recommendations.

7.03 Clarification of Role

In most circumstances, psychologists avoid performing multiple and potentially conflicting roles in forensic matters. When psychologists may be called on to serve in more than one role in a legal proceeding—for example, as consultant or expert for one party or for the court and as a fact witness—they clarify role expectations and the extent of confidentiality in advance to the extent feasible, and thereafter as changes occur, in order to avoid compromising their professional judgment and objectivity and in order to avoid misleading others regarding their role.

7.04 Truthfulness and Candor

(a) In forensic testimony and reports, psychologists testify truthfully, honestly, and candidly and, consistent with applicable legal procedures, describe fairly the bases for their testimony and conclusions.

(b) Whenever necessary to avoid misleading, psychologists acknowledge the limits of their data or conclusions.

7.05 Prior Relationships

A prior professional relationship with a party does not preclude psychologists from testifying as fact witnesses or from testifying to their services to the extent permitted by applicable law. Psychologists appropriately take into account ways in which the prior relationship might affect their professional objectivity or opinions and disclose the potential conflict to the relevant parties.

7.06 Compliance With Law and Rules

In performing forensic roles, psychologists are reasonably familiar with the rules governing their roles. Psychologists are aware of the occasionally competing demands placed upon them by these principles and the requirements of the court system, and attempt to resolve these conflicts by making known their commitment to this Ethics Code and taking steps to resolve the conflict in a responsible manner. (See also Standard 1.02, Relationship of Ethics and Law.)

8.   Resolving Ethical Issues

8.01 Familiarity With Ethics Code

Psychologists have an obligation to be familiar with this Ethics Code, other applicable ethics codes, and their application to psychologists' work. Lack of awareness or misunderstanding of an ethical standard is not itself a defense to a charge of unethical conduct.

8.02 Confronting Ethical Issues

When a psychologist is uncertain whether a particular situation or course of action would violate this Ethics Code, the psychologist ordinarily consults with other psychologists knowledgeable about ethical issues, with state or national psychology ethics committees, or with other appropriate authorities in order to choose a proper response.

8.03 Conflicts Between Ethics and Organizational Demands

If the demands of an organization with which psychologists are affiliated conflict with this Ethics Code, psychologists clarify the nature of the conflict, make known their commitment to the Ethics Code, and to the extent feasible, seek to resolve the conflict in a way that permits the fullest adherence to the Ethics Code.

8.04 Informal Resolution of Ethical Violations

When psychologists believe that there may have been an ethical violation by another psychologist, they attempt to resolve the issue by bringing it to the attention of that individual if an informal resolution appears appropriate and the intervention does not violate any confidentiality rights that may be involved.

8.05 Reporting Ethical Violations

If an apparent ethical violation is not appropriate for informal resolution under Standard 8.04 or is not resolved properly in that fashion, psychologists take further action appropriate to the situation, unless such action conflicts with confidentiality rights in ways that cannot be resolved. Such action might include referral to state or national committees on professional ethics or to state licensing boards.

8.06 Cooperating With Ethics Committees

Psychologists cooperate in ethics investigations, proceedings, and resulting requirements of the APA or any affiliated state psychological association to which they belong. In doing so, they make reasonable efforts to resolve any issues as to confidentiality. Failure to cooperate is itself an ethics violation.

8.07 Improper Complaints

Psychologists do not file or encourage the filing of ethics complaints that are frivolous and are intended to harm the respondent rather than to protect the public.

This is the new APA *Ethical Principles of Psychologists and Code of Conduct*, adopted by the Council of Representatives in August. The Code took effect on December 1, 1992.

APPENDIX C

Specialty Guidelines for Forensic Psychologists[1]

COMMITTEE ON ETHICAL GUIDELINES FOR FORENSIC PSYCHOLOGISTS[2]

The *Specialty Guidelines for Forensic Psychologists,* while informed by the *Ethical Principles of Psychologists* (APA, 1990) and meant to be consistent with them, are designed to provide more specific guidance to forensic psychologists in monitoring their professional conduct when acting in assistance to courts, parties to legal proceedings, correctional and forensic mental health facilities, and legislative agencies. The primary goal of the *Guidelines* is to improve the quality of forensic psychological services offered to individual clients and the legal system and thereby to enhance forensic psy-

---

[1] The *Specialty Guidelines for Forensic Psychologists* were adopted by majority vote of the members of Division 41 and the American Psychology-Law Society. They have also been endorsed by majority vote by the American Academy of Forensic Psychology. The Executive Committee of Division 41 and the American Psychology Law Society formally approved these *Guidelines* on March 9, 1991. The Executive Committee also voted to continue the Committee on Ethical Guidelines in order to disseminate the *Guidelines* and to monitor their implementation and suggestions for revision. Individuals wishing to reprint these *Guidelines* or who have queries about them should contact either Stephen L. Golding, Ph.D., Department of Psychology, University of Utah, Salt Lake City, UT 84112, 801–581–8028 (voice) or 801–581–5841 (FAX) or other members of the Committee listed below. Reprint requests should be sent to Cathy Osizly, Department of Psychology, University of Nebraska-Lincoln, Lincoln, NE 68588–0308.

[2] These Guidelines were prepared and principally authored by a joint Committee on Ethical Guidelines of Division 41 and the American Academy of Forensic Psychology (Stephen L. Golding, [Chair], Thomas Grisso, David Shapiro, and Herbert Weissman [Co-chairs]). Other members of the Committee included Robert Fein, Kirk Heilbrun, Judith McKenna, Norman Poythress, and Daniel Schuman. Their hard work and willingness to tackle difficult conceptual and pragmatic issues is gratefully acknowledged. The Committee would also like to acknowledge specifically the assistance and guidance provided by Dort Bigg, Larry Cowan, Eric Harris, Arthur Lerner, Michael Miller, Russell Newman, Melvin Rudov, and Ray Fowler. Many other individuals also contributed by their thoughtful critique and suggestions for improvement of earlier drafts which were widely circulated.

chology as a discipline and profession. The *Specialty Guidelines for Forensic Psychologists* represent a joint statement of the American Psychology-Law Society and Division 41 of the American Psychological Association and are endorsed by the American Academy of Forensic Psychology. The *Guidelines* do not represent an official statement of the American Psychological Association.

The *Guidelines* provide an aspirational model of desirable professional practice by psychologists, within any subdiscipline of psychology (e.g., clinical, developmental, social, experimental), when they are engaged regularly as experts and represent themselves as such, in an activity primarily intended to provide professional psychological expertise to the judicial system. This would include, for example, clinical forensic examiners; psychologists employed by correctional or forensic mental health systems; researchers who offer direct testimony about the relevance of scientific data to a psycholegal issue; trial behavior consultants; psychologists engaged in preparation of *amicus* briefs; or psychologists, appearing as forensic experts, who consult with, or testify before, judicial, legislative, or administrative agencies acting in an adjudicative capacity. Individuals who provide only occasional service to the legal system and who do so without representing themselves as *forensic experts* may find these *Guidelines* helpful, particularly in conjunction with consultation with colleagues who are forensic experts.

While the *Guidelines* are concerned with a model of desirable professional practice, to the extent that they may be construed as being applicable to the advertisement of services or the solicitation of clients, they are intended to prevent false or deceptive advertisement or solicitation, and should be construed in a manner consistent with that intent.

I. PURPOSE AND SCOPE
A. Purpose
1. While the professional standards for the ethical practice of psychology, as a general discipline, are addressed in the American Psychological Association's *Ethical Principles of Psychologists,* these ethical principles do not relate, in sufficient detail, to current aspirations of desirable professional conduct for forensic psychologists. By design, none of the *Guidelines* contradicts any of the *Ethical Principles of Psychologists;* rather, they amplify those *Principles* in the context of the practice of forensic psychology, as herein defined.
2. The *Guidelines* have been designed to be national in scope and are intended to conform with state and Federal law. In situations where the forensic psychologist believes that the requirements of law are in conflict with the *Guidelines,* attempts to resolve the conflict should be made in accordance with the procedures set forth in these *Guidelines* [IV(G)] and in the *Ethical Principles of Psychologists.*

B. Scope
1. The *Guidelines* specify the nature of desirable professional practice by forensic psychologists, within any subdiscipline of psychology (e.g., clinical, developmental, social, experimental), when engaged regularly as forensic psychologists.
   a. "Psychologist" means any individual whose professional activities are defined by the American Psychological Association or by regulation of title by state registration or licensure, as the practice of psychology.
   b. "Forensic psychology" means all forms of professional psychological conduct when acting, with definable foreknowledge, as a psychological expert on explicitly psycholegal issues, in direct assistance to courts, parties to legal proceedings, correctional and forensic mental health facilities, and administrative, judicial, and legislative agencies acting in an adjudicative capacity.
   c. "Forensic psychologist" means psychologists who regularly engage in the practice of forensic psychology as defined in I(B)(1)(b).
2. The *Guidelines* do not apply to a psychologist who is asked to provide professional psychological services when the psychologist was not informed at the time of delivery of the services that they were to be used as forensic psychological services as defined above. The *Guidelines* may be helpful, however, in preparing the psychologist for the experience of communicating psychological data in a forensic context.
3. Psychologists who are not forensic psychologists as defined in I(B)(1)(c), but occasionally provide limited forensic psychological services, may find the *Guidelines* useful in the preparation and presentation of their professional services.
C. Related Standards
1. Forensic psychologists also conduct their professional activities in accord with the *Ethical Principles of Psychologists* and the various other statements of the American Psychological Association that may apply to particular subdisciplines or areas of practice that are relevant to their professional activities.
2. The standards of practice and ethical guidelines of other relevant "expert professional organizations" contain useful guidance and should be consulted even though the present *Guidelines* take precedence for forensic psychologists.

II. **RESPONSIBILITY**
A. Forensic psychologists have an obligation to provide services in a manner consistent with the highest standards of their profession. They are responsible for their own conduct and the conduct of those individuals under their direct supervision.

B. Forensic psychologists make a reasonable effort to ensure that their services and the products of their services are used in a forthright and responsible manner.

III. COMPETENCE

A. Forensic psychologists provide services only in areas of psychology in which they have specialized knowledge, skill, experience, and education.

B. Forensic psychologists have an obligation to present to the court, regarding the specific matters to which they will testify, the boundaries of their competence, the factual bases (knowledge, skill, experience, training, and education) for their qualification as an expert, and the relevance of those factual bases to their qualification as an expert on the specific matters at issue.

C. Forensic psychologists are responsible for a fundamental and reasonable level of knowledge and understanding of the legal and professional standards that govern their participation as experts in legal proceedings.

D. Forensic psychologists have an obligation to understand the civil rights of parties in legal proceedings in which they participate, and manage their professional conduct in a manner that does not diminish or threaten those rights.

E. Forensic psychologists recognize that their own personal values, moral beliefs, or personal and professional relationships with parties to a legal proceeding may interfere with their ability to practice competently. Under such circumstances, forensic psychologists are obligated to decline participation or to limit their assistance in a manner consistent with professional obligations.

IV. RELATIONSHIPS

A. During initial consultation with the legal representative of the party seeking services, forensic psychologists have an obligation to inform the party of factors that might reasonably affect the decision to contract with the forensic psychologist. These factors include, but are not limited to
1. the fee structure for anticipated professional services;
2. prior and current personal or professional activities, obligations, and relationships that might produce a conflict of interests;
3. their areas of competence and the limits of their competence; and
4. the known scientific bases and limitations of the methods and procedures that they employ and their qualifications to employ such methods and procedures.

B. Forensic psychologists do not provide professional services to parties to a legal proceeding on the basis of "contingent fees," when those services involve the offering of expert testimony to a court or administrative body, or when they call upon the psychologist to make affirmations or representations intended to be relied upon by third parties.

C. Forensic psychologists who derive a substantial portion of their income from fee-for-service arrangements should offer some portion of their professional services on a *pro bono* or reduced fee basis where the public interest or the welfare of clients may be inhibited by insufficient financial resources.

D. Forensic psychologists recognize potential conflicts of interest in dual relationships with parties to a legal proceeding, and they seek to minimize their effects.

   1. Forensic psychologists avoid providing professional services to parties in a legal proceeding with whom they have personal or professional relationships that are inconsistent with the anticipated relationship.

   2. When it is necessary to provide both evaluation and treatment services to a party in a legal proceeding (as may be the case in small forensic hospital settings or small communities), the forensic psychologist takes reasonable steps to minimize the potential negative effects of these circumstances on the rights of the party, confidentiality, and the process of treatment and evaluation.

E. Forensic psychologists have an obligation to ensure that prospective clients are informed of their legal rights with respect to the anticipated forensic service, of the purposes of any evaluation, of the nature of procedures to be employed, of the intended uses of any product of their services, and of the party who has employed the forensic psychologist.

   1. Unless court ordered, forensic psychologists obtain the informed consent of the client or party, or their legal representative, before proceeding with such evaluations and procedures. If the client appears unwilling to proceed after receiving a thorough notification of the purposes, methods, and intended uses of the forensic evaluation, the evaluation should be postponed and the psychologist should take steps to place the client in contact with his/her attorney for the purpose of legal advice on the issue of participation.

   2. In situations where the client or party may not have the capacity to provide informed consent to services or the evaluation is pursuant to court order, the forensic psychologist provides reasonable notice to the client's legal representative of the nature of the anticipated forensic service before proceeding. If the client's legal representative objects to the evaluation, the forensic psychologist notifies the court issuing the order and responds as directed.

3. After a psychologist has advised the subject of a clinical forensic evaluation of the intended uses of the evaluation and its work product, the psychologist may not use the evaluation work product for other purposes without explicit waiver to do so by the client or the client's legal representative.

F. When forensic psychologists engage in research or scholarly activities that are compensated financially by a client or party to a legal proceeding, or when the psychologist provides those services on a *pro bono* basis, the psychologist clarifies any anticipated further use of such research or scholarly product, discloses the psychologist's role in the resulting research or scholarly products, and obtains whatever consent or agreement is required by law or professional standards.

G. When conflicts arise between the forensic psychologist's professional standards and the requirements of legal standards, a particular court, or a directive by an officer of the court or legal authorities, the forensic psychologist has an obligation to make those legal authorities aware of the source of the conflict and to take reasonable steps to resolve it. Such steps may include, but are not limited to, obtaining the consultation of fellow forensic professionals, obtaining the advice of independent counsel, and conferring directly with the legal representatives involved.

V. **CONFIDENTIALITY AND PRIVILEGE**

A. Forensic psychologists have an obligation to be aware of the legal standards that may affect or limit the confidentiality or privilege that may attach to their services or their products, and they conduct their professional activities in a manner that respects those known rights and privileges.

1. Forensic psychologists establish and maintain a system of record keeping and professional communication that safeguards a client's privilege.

2. Forensic psychologists maintain active control over records and information. They only release information pursuant to statutory requirements, court order, or the consent of the client.

B. Forensic psychologists inform their clients of the limitations to the confidentiality of their services and their products (see also Guideline IV E) by providing them with an understandable statement of their rights, privileges, and the limitations of confidentiality.

C. In situations where the right of the client or party to confidentiality is limited, the forensic psychologist makes every effort to maintain confidentiality with regard to any information that does not bear directly upon the legal purpose of the evaluation.

D. Forensic psychologists provide clients or their authorized legal representatives with access to the information in their records and a meaningful explanation of that information, consistent with existing Federal and state statutes, the *Ethical Principles of Psychologists,* the *Standards for Educational and Psychological Testing,* and institutional rules and regulations.

VI. METHODS AND PROCEDURES

A. Because of their special status as persons qualified as experts to the court, forensic psychologists have an obligation to maintain current knowledge of scientific, professional and legal developments within their area of claimed competence. They are obligated also to use that knowledge, consistent with accepted clinical and scientific standards, in selecting data collection methods and procedures for an evaluation, treatment, consultation or scholarly/empirical investigation.

B. Forensic psychologists have an obligation to document and be prepared to make available, subject to court order or the rules of evidence, all data that form the basis for their evidence or services. The standard to be applied to such documentation or recording *anticipates* that the detail and quality of such documentation will be subject to reasonable judicial scrutiny; this standard is higher than the normative standard for general clinical practice. When forensic psychologists conduct an examination or engage in the treatment of a party to a legal proceeding, with foreknowledge that their professional services will be used in an adjudicative forum, they incur a special responsibility to provide the best documentation possible under the circumstances.

1. Documentation of the data upon which one's evidence is based is subject to the normal rules of discovery, disclosure, confidentiality, and privilege that operate in the jurisdiction in which the data were obtained. Forensic psychologists have an obligation to be aware of those rules and to regulate their conduct in accordance with them.

2. The duties and obligations of forensic psychologists with respect to documentation of data that form the basis for their evidence apply from the moment they know or have a reasonable basis for knowing that their data and evidence derived from it are likely to enter into legally relevant decisions.

C. In providing forensic psychological services, forensic psychologists take special care to avoid undue influence upon their methods, procedures, and products, such as might emanate from the party to a legal proceeding by financial compensation or other gains. As an expert conducting an evaluation, treatment, consultation, or scholarly/empirical investigation, the forensic psychologist maintains professional integrity by examining the issue at hand from all reasonable perspectives, actively seeking information that will differentially test plausible rival hypotheses.

D. Forensic psychologists do not provide professional forensic services to a defendant or to any party in, or in contemplation of, a legal proceeding prior to that individual's representation by counsel, except for persons judicially determined, where appropriate, to be handling their representation *pro se*. When the forensic services are pursuant to court order and the client is not represented by counsel, the forensic psychologist makes reasonable efforts to inform the court prior to providing the services.

1. A forensic psychologist may provide emergency mental health services to a pretrial defendant prior to court order or the appointment of counsel where there are reasonable grounds to believe that such emergency services are needed for the protection and improvement of the defendant's mental health and where failure to provide such mental health services would constitute a substantial risk of imminent harm to the defendant or to others. In providing such services the forensic psychologist nevertheless seeks to inform the defendant's counsel in a manner consistent with the requirements of the emergency situation.

2. Forensic psychologists who provide such emergency mental health services should attempt to avoid providing further professional forensic services to that defendant unless that relationship is reasonably unavoidable [see IV(D)(2)].

E. When forensic psychologists seek data from third parties, prior records, or other sources, they do so only with the prior approval of the relevant legal party or as a consequence of an order of a court to conduct the forensic evaluation.

F. Forensic psychologists are aware that hearsay exceptions and other rules governing expert testimony place a special ethical burden upon them. When hearsay or otherwise inadmissible evidence forms the basis of their opinion, evidence, or professional product, they seek to minimize sole reliance upon such evidence. Where circumstances reasonably permit, forensic psychologists seek to obtain independent and personal verification of data relied upon as part of their professional services to the court or to a party to a legal proceeding.

1. While many forms of data used by forensic psychologists are hearsay, forensic psychologists attempt to corroborate critical data that form the basis for their professional product. When using hearsay data that have not been corroborated, but are nevertheless utilized, forensic psychologists have an affirmative responsibility to acknowledge the uncorroborated status of those data and the reasons for relying upon such data.

2. With respect to evidence of any type, forensic psychologists avoid offering information from their investigations or evaluations that does not bear directly upon the legal purpose of their

professional services and that is not critical as support for their product, evidence or testimony, except where such disclosure is required by law.

3. When a forensic psychologist relies upon data or information gathered by others, the origins of those data are clarified in any professional product. In addition, the forensic psychologist bears a special responsibility to ensure that such data, if relied upon, were gathered in a manner standard for the profession.

G. Unless otherwise stipulated by the parties, forensic psychologists are aware that no statements made by a defendant, in the course of any (forensic) examination, no testimony by the expert based upon such statements, nor any other fruits of the statements can be admitted into evidence against the defendant in any criminal proceeding, except on an issue respecting mental condition on which the defendant has introduced testimony. Forensic psychologists have an affirmative duty to ensure that their written products and oral testimony conform to this Federal Rule of Procedure (12.2[c]), or its state equivalent.

1. Because forensic psychologists are often not in a position to know what evidence, documentation, or element of a written product may be or may lend to a "fruit of the statement," they exercise extreme caution in preparing reports or offering testimony prior to the defendant's assertion of a mental state claim or the defendant's introduction of testimony regarding a mental condition. Consistent with the reporting requirements of state or federal law, forensic psychologists avoid including statements from the defendant relating to the time period of the alleged offense.

2. Once a defendant has proceeded to the trial stage, and all pretrial mental health issues such as competency have been resolved, forensic psychologists may include in their reports or testimony any statements made by the defendant that are directly relevant to supporting their expert evidence, providing that the defendant has "introduced" mental state evidence or testimony within the meaning of Federal Rule of Procedure 12.2(c), or its state equivalent.

H. Forensic psychologists avoid giving written or oral evidence about the psychological characteristics of particular individuals when they have not had an opportunity to conduct an examination of the individual adequate to the scope of the statements, opinions, or conclusions to be issued. Forensic psychologists make every reasonable effort to conduct such examinations. When it is not possible or feasible to do so, they make clear the impact of such limitations on the reliability and validity of their professional products, evidence, or testimony.

VII. PUBLIC AND PROFESSIONAL COMMUNICATIONS

A. Forensic psychologists make reasonable efforts to ensure that the products of their services, as well as their own public statements and professional testimony, are communicated in ways that will promote understanding and avoid deception, given the particular characteristics, roles, and abilities of various recipients of the communications.

1. Forensic psychologists take reasonable steps to correct misuse or misrepresentation of their professional products, evidence, and testimony.

2. Forensic psychologists provide information about professional work to clients in a manner consistent with professional and legal standards for the disclosure of test results, interpretations of data, and the factual bases for conclusions. A full explanation of the results of tests and the bases for conclusions should be given in language that the client can understand.

   a. When disclosing information about a client to third parties who are not qualified to interpret test results and data, the forensic psychologist complies with Principle 16 of the *Standards for Educational and Psychological Testing.* When required to disclose results to a nonpsychologist, every attempt is made to ensure that test security is maintained and access to information is restricted to individuals with a legitimate and professional interest in the data. Other qualified mental health professionals who make a request for information pursuant to a lawful order are, by definition, "individuals with a legitimate and professional interest."

   b. In providing records and raw data, the forensic psychologist takes reasonable steps to ensure that the receiving party is informed that raw scores must be interpreted by a qualified professional in order to provide reliable and valid information.

B. Forensic psychologists realize that their public role as "expert to the court" or as "expert representing the profession" confers upon them a special responsibility for fairness and accuracy in their public statements. When evaluating or commenting upon the professional work product or qualifications of another expert or party to a legal proceeding, forensic psychologists represent their professional disagreements with reference to a fair and accurate evaluation of the data, theories, standards, and opinions of the other expert or party.

C. Ordinarily, forensic psychologists avoid making detailed public (out-of-court) statements about particular legal proceedings in which they have been involved. When there is a strong justification to do so, such public statements are designed to assure accurate representation of their role or their evidence, not to advocate the positions of parties in the legal proceeding. Forensic psychologists address particular legal proceedings in publications or communications only to the extent that the information relied upon is part of a public record, or consent for that use has been properly obtained from the party holding any privilege.

D. When testifying, forensic psychologists have an obligation to all parties to a legal proceeding to present their findings, conclusions, evidence, or other professional products in a fair manner. This principle does not preclude forceful representation of the data and reasoning upon which a conclusion or professional product is based. It does, however, preclude an attempt, whether active or passive, to engage in partisan distortion or misrepresentation. Forensic psychologists do not, by either commission or omission, participate in a misrepresentation of their evidence, nor do they participate in partisan attempts to avoid, deny, or subvert the presentation of evidence contrary to their own position.

E. Forensic psychologists, by virtue of their competence and rules of discovery, actively disclose all sources of information obtained in the course of their professional services; they actively disclose which information from which source was used in formulating a particular written product or oral testimony.

F. Forensic psychologists are aware that their essential role as expert to the court is to assist the trier of fact to understand the evidence or to determine a fact in issue. In offering expert evidence, they are aware that their own professional observations, inferences, and conclusions must be distinguished from legal facts, opinions, and conclusions. Forensic psychologists are prepared to explain the relationship between their expert testimony and the legal issues and facts of an instant case.

APPENDIX D

Guidelines for Child Custody Evaluations in Divorce Proceedings[1]

DRAFTED BY THE COMMITTEE ON PROFESSIONAL PRACTICE AND
STANDARDS,
A COMMITTEE OF THE BOARD OF PROFESSIONAL AFFAIRS
WITH INPUT FROM THE COMMITTEE ON CHILDREN, YOUTH, AND FAMILIES
ADOPTED BY THE COUNCIL OF REPRESENTATIVES
OF THE AMERICAN PSYCHOLOGICAL ASSOCIATION,
FEBRUARY 1994

INTRODUCTION

Decisions regarding child custody and other parenting arrangements occur within several different legal contexts, including parental divorce, guardianship, neglect or abuse proceedings, and termination of parental rights. The following guidelines were developed for psychologists conducting child custody evaluations, specifically within the context of parental divorce. These guidelines build upon the APA Ethical Principles of Psychologists and Code of Conduct (APA, 1992) and are aspirational in intent. *As guidelines, they are not intended to be either mandatory or exhaustive. The goal of the guidelines is to promote proficiency in using psychological expertise in conducting child custody evaluations.*

Parental divorce requires a restructuring of parental rights and responsibilities in relation to children. If the parents can agree to a restructuring arrangement, which they do in the overwhelming proportion (90%) of divorce custody cases (Melton, Petrila, Poythress, & Slobogin, 1987), there is no dispute for the court to decide. However, if the parents are unable to reach such an agreement, the court must help to determine the relative

[1] Acknowledgements: COPPS 1991–1993 members, Richard Cohen, Alex Carballo Dieguez, Kathleen Dockett, Sam Friedman, Colette Ingraham, John Northman, John Robinson, Deborah Tharinger, Susana Urbina, Phil Witt, and James Wulach; BPA Liaisons 1991–1993, Richard Cohen, Joseph Kobos, and Rodney Lowman; and CYF members, Don Routh and Carolyn Swift.

allocation of decision making authority and physical contact each parent will have with the child. The courts typically apply a "best interest of the child" standard in determining this restructuring of rights and responsibilities.

Psychologists provide an important service to children and the courts by providing competent, objective, impartial information in assessing the best interests of the child, by demonstrating a clear sense of direction and purpose in conducting a child custody evaluation, by performing their roles ethically, and by clarifying to all involved the nature and scope of the evaluation. The Ethics Committee of the American Psychological Association has noted that psychologists' involvement in custody disputes has at times raised questions in regard to the misuse of psychologists' influence, sometimes resulting in complaints against psychologists being brought to the attention of the APA Ethics Committee (APA Ethics Committee, 1985; Hall & Hare-Mustin, 1983; Keith-Spiegel & Koocher, 1985; Mills, 1984) and raising questions in the legal and forensic literature (Grisso, 1986; Melton, Petrila, Poythress, & Slobogin, 1987; Mnookin, 1975; Ochroch, 1982; Okpaku, 1976; Weithorn, 1987).

Particular competencies and knowledge are required for child custody evaluations to provide adequate and appropriate psychological services to the court. Child custody evaluation in the context of parental divorce can be an extremely demanding task. For competing parents the stakes are high as they participate in a process fraught with tension and anxiety. The stress on the psychologist/evaluator can become great. Tension surrounding child custody evaluation can become further heightened when there are accusations of child abuse, neglect, and/or family violence.

Psychology is in a position to make significant contributions to child custody decisions. Psychological data and expertise, gained through a child custody evaluation, can provide an additional source of information and an additional perspective not otherwise readily available to the court on what appears to be in a child's best interest, and thus can increase the fairness of the determination the court must make.

GUIDELINES FOR CHILD CUSTODY EVALUATIONS IN DIVORCE PROCEEDINGS

I.   ORIENTING GUIDELINES: PURPOSE OF A CHILD CUSTODY EVALUATION

1.   The Primary Purpose of the Evaluation Is to Assess the Best Psychological Interests of the Child.

The primary consideration in a child custody evaluation is to assess the individual and family factors that affect the best psychological interests of the child. More specific questions may be raised by the court.

2. The Child's Interests and Well-Being Are Paramount.

In a child custody evaluation, the child's interests and well-being are paramount. Parents competing for custody, as well as others, may have legitimate concerns, but the child's best interests must prevail.

3. The Focus of the Evaluation Is on Parenting Capacity, the Psychological and Developmental Needs of the Child, and the Resulting Fit.

In considering psychological factors affecting the best interests of the child, the psychologist focuses on the parenting capacity of the prospective custodians in conjunction with the psychological and developmental needs of each involved child. This involves: 1) an assessment of the adults' capacity for parenting, including whatever knowledge, attributes, skills, and abilities, or lack thereof, are present; 2) an assessment of the psychological functioning and developmental needs of each child, and the wishes of each child, where appropriate; and 3) the functional ability of each parent to meet these needs, which includes an evaluation of the interaction between each adult and child.

The values of the parents relevant to parenting, ability to plan for the child's future needs, capacity to provide a stable and loving home, and any potential for inappropriate behavior or misconduct that might negatively influence the child also are considered. Psychopathology may be relevant to such an assessment, in so far as it has impact on the child or the ability to parent, but it is not the primary focus.

II. **GENERAL GUIDELINES: PREPARING FOR A CHILD CUSTODY EVALUATION**

4. The Role of the Psychologist Is a Professional Expert, Who Strives to Maintain an Objective, Impartial Stance.

The role of the psychologist is as a professional expert. The psychologist does not act as a judge, who makes the ultimate decision applying the law to all relevant evidence. Neither does the psychologist act as an advocating attorney, who strives to present his or her client's best possible case. The psychologist, in a balanced, impartial manner, informs and advises the court and the prospective custodians of the child of the relevant psychological factors pertaining to the custody issue. The psychologist should be impartial regardless of whether he or she is retained by the court or by a party to the proceedings. If either the psychologist or the client cannot accept this neutral role, the psychologist should consider withdrawing from the case. If not permitted to withdraw, in such circumstances, the psychologist acknowledges past roles and other factors which could affect impartiality.

5. The Psychologist Gains Specialized Competence.

A. A psychologist contemplating performing child custody evaluations is aware that special competencies and knowledge are required for the undertaking of such evaluations. Competence in performing psychological assessments of children, adults, and families is necessary but not sufficient. Education, training, experience and/or supervision in the areas of child and family development, child and family psychopathology, and the impact of divorce on children, help to prepare the psychologist to participate competently in child custody evaluations. The psychologist also strives to become familiar with applicable legal standards and procedures, including laws governing divorce and custody adjudications in his or her state or jurisdiction.

B. The psychologist uses current knowledge of scientific and professional developments, consistent with accepted clinical and scientific standards, in selecting data collection methods and procedures. The Standards for Educational and Psychological Testing (APA, 1985) are adhered to in the use of psychological tests and other assessment tools.

C. In the course of conducting child custody evaluations, allegations of child abuse, neglect, family violence, or other issues may occur that are not necessarily within the scope of a particular evaluator's expertise. If this is so, the psychologist seeks additional consultation, supervision, and/or specialized knowledge, training or experience in child abuse, neglect, and family violence to address these complex issues. The psychologist is familiar with the laws of his or her state addressing child abuse, neglect, and family violence, and acts accordingly.

6. The Psychologist Is Aware of Personal and Societal Biases and Engages in Nondiscriminatory Practice.

The psychologist engaging in child custody evaluations is aware of how biases regarding age, gender, race, ethnicity, national origin, religion, sexual orientation, disability, language, culture and socioeconomic status may interfere with an objective evaluation and recommendations. The psychologist recognizes and strives to overcome any such biases, or withdraws from the evaluation.

7. The Psychologist Avoids Multiple Relationships.

Psychologists generally avoid conducting a child custody evaluation in a case in which the psychologist served in a therapeutic role for the child or his or her immediate family or has had other involvement which may compromise the psychologist's objectivity. This should not, however, preclude the psychologist from testifying in the case as a fact witness concerning treatment of the child. In addition, during the course of a child custody evaluation, a psychologist does not accept any of the involved participants in the evaluation as a therapy client. Therapeutic contact with the child or involved participants following a child custody evaluation is undertaken with caution.

A psychologist asked to testify regarding a therapy client who is involved in a child custody case is aware of the limitations and possible biases inherent in such a role, and possible impact on the ongoing therapeutic relationship. While the court may require the psychologist to testify as a fact witness regarding factual information he or she became aware of in a professional relationship with a client, that psychologist should generally decline the role of an expert witness who gives a professional opinion regarding custody and visitation issues (see Ethical Standard 7.03), unless so ordered by the court.

III. PROCEDURAL GUIDELINES: CONDUCTING A CHILD CUSTODY EVALUATION

8. The Scope of the Evaluation Is Determined by the Evaluator, Based on the Nature of the Referral Question.

The scope of the custody-related evaluation is determined by the nature of the question or issue raised by the referring person or the court, or is inherent in the situation. While comprehensive child custody evaluations generally require an evaluation of all parents or guardians and children, as well as observations of interactions between them, the scope of the assessment in a particular case may be limited to evaluating the parental capacity of one parent, without attempting to compare the parents or to make recommendations. Likewise, the scope may be limited to evaluating the child. Or a psychologist may be asked to critique the assumptions and methodology of the assessment of another mental health professional. A psychologist also might serve as an expert witness in the area of child development, providing expertise to the court without relating it specifically to the parties involved in a case.

9. The Psychologist Obtains Informed Consent from All Adult Participants and, as Appropriate, Informs Child Participants.

In undertaking child custody evaluations, the psychologist ensures that each adult participant is aware of: 1) the purpose, nature, and method of the evaluation; 2) who has requested the psychologist's services; and 3) who will be paying the fees. The psychologist informs adult participants about the nature of the assessment instruments and techniques and informs those participants about the possible disposition of the data collected. The psychologist provides this information, as appropriate, to children, to the extent that they are able to understand.

10. The Psychologist Informs Participants about the Limits of Confidentiality and the Disclosure of Information.

A psychologist conducting a child custody evaluation ensures that the participants, including children to the extent feasible, are aware of the limits of confidentiality characterizing the professional relationship with the psychologist. The psychologist informs participants that in consenting to the evaluation, they are consenting to disclosure of the evaluation's findings in the context of the forthcoming litigation, and any other proceedings deemed necessary by the courts. A psychologist obtains a waiver of confidentiality from all adult participants, or from their authorized legal representatives.

11. The Psychologist Uses Multiple Methods of Data Gathering.

The psychologist strives to use the most appropriate methods available for addressing the questions raised in a specific child custody evaluation, and generally uses multiple methods of data gathering, including, but not limited to, clinical interviews, observation and/or psychological assessments. Important facts and opinions are documented from at least two sources whenever their reliability is questionable. The psychologist, for example, may review potentially relevant reports, e.g., from schools, health care providers, child care providers, agencies, and institutions. Psychologists may also interview extended family, friends, and other individuals on occasions when the information is likely to be useful. If information is gathered from third parties that is significant and may be used as a basis for conclusions, psychologists corroborate it by at least one other source wherever possible and appropriate, and document this in the report.

12. The Psychologist Neither Overinterprets Nor Inappropriately Interprets Clinical or Assessment Data.

The psychologist refrains from drawing conclusions not adequately supported by the data. The psychologist interprets any data from interviews or tests, as well as any questions of data reliability and validity, cautiously and conservatively, seeking convergent validity. The psychologist strives to acknowledge to the court any limitations in methods or data used.

13. The Psychologist Does Not Give Any Opinion Regarding the Psychological Functioning of Any Individual Who Has Not Been Personally Evaluated.

This guideline, however, does not preclude the psychologist from reporting what an evaluated individual (such as the parent or child) has stated, or from addressing theoretical issues or hypothetical questions, so long as the limited basis of the information is noted.

14. Recommendations, If Any, Are Based Upon What Is in the Best Psychological Interests of the Child.

While the profession has not reached consensus about whether psychologists ought to make recommendations about the final custody determination to the courts, psychologists are obligated to be aware of the arguments on both sides of this issue, and to be able to explain the logic of their position concerning their own practice.

If the psychologist does choose to make custody recommendations, they should be derived from sound psychological data, and must be based upon the best interests of the child, in the particular case. Recommendations are based on articulated assumptions, data, interpretations, and inferences based upon established professional and scientific standards. Psychologists guard against relying upon their own biases or unsupported beliefs in rendering opinions in particular cases.

15. The Psychologist Clarifies Financial Arrangements.

Financial arrangements are clarified and agreed upon *prior* to commencing a child custody evaluation. When billing for a child custody evaluation, the psychologist does not misrepresent his or her services for reimbursement purposes.

16. The Psychologist Maintains Written Records.

All records obtained in the process of conducting a child custody evaluation are properly maintained and filed in accord with the APA Record Keeping Guidelines (APA, 1993) and relevant statutory guidelines.

All raw data and interview information are recorded with an eye towards their possible review by other psychologists or the court, where legally permitted. Upon request, appropriate reports are made available to the court.

BIBLIOGRAPHY

References

American Psychological Association. (1992). Ethical principles of psychologists and code of conduct. *American Psychologist, 47* (12), 1597–1611.

———. (1993). *Record keeping guidelines.* Washington, DC: Author.

———. (1985). *Standards for educational and psychological testing.* Washington, DC: Author.

American Psychological Association, Ethics Committee. (1985). *Annual report of the American Psychological Association Ethics Committee.* Washington, DC: American Psychological Association, Ethics Department.

Grisso, T. (1986). *Evaluating competencies: Forensic assessments and instruments.* New York: Plenum.

Hall, J. E., & Hare-Mustin, R. T. (1983). Sanctions and the diversity of ethical complaints against psychologists. *American Psychologist, 38,* 714–729.

Keith-Spiegel, P., & Koocher, G. P. (1985). *Ethics in psychology.* New York: Random House.

Melton, G. B., Petrila, J., Poythress, N. G., & Slobogin, C. (1987). *Psychological evaluations for the courts: A handbook for mental health professionals and lawyers.* New York: Guilford Press.

Mills, D. H. (1984). Ethics education and adjudication within psychology. *American Psychologist, 39,* 669–675.

Mnookin, R. H. (1975). Child-custody adjudication: Judicial functions in the face of indeterminacy. *Law and Contemporary Problems, 39,* 226–293.

Ochroch, R. (1982). *Ethical pitfalls in child custody evaluations.* Paper presented at the American Psychological Association, Washington, DC.

Okpaku, S. (1976). Psychology: Impediment or aid in child custody cases? *Rutgers Law Review, 29,* 1117–1153.

Weithorn, L. A. (Ed.). (1987). *Psychology and child custody determinations: Knowledge, roles, and expertise.* Lincoln, NE: University of Nebraska Press.

Other Resources: State Guidelines

Georgia Psychological Association. (1990). *Recommendations for psychologists' involvement in child custody cases.* Atlanta, GA: Author.

Metropolitan Denver Interdisciplinary Committee on Child Custody. (1989). *Guidelines for child custody evaluations.* Denver, CO: Author.

Nebraska Psychological Association. (1986). *Guidelines for child custody evaluations.* Lincoln, NE: Author.

New Jersey State Board of Psychological Examiners. (1993). *Specialty guidelines for psychologists in custody/visitation evaluations.* Newark, NJ: Author.

North Carolina Psychological Association. (draft, 1993). *Child custody guidelines.* Unpublished manuscript.

Oklahoma Psychological Association. (1988). *Ethical guidelines for child custody evaluations.* Oklahoma City, OK: Author.

Pennsylvania Psychological Association, Clinical Division/Task Force on Child Custody Evaluation. (1991). *Roles for psychologists in child custody disputes.* Unpublished manuscript.

Other Resources: Forensic Guidelines

Committee on Ethical Guidelines for Forensic Psychologists. (1991). Specialty guidelines for forensic psychologists. *Law and Human Behavior, 6,* 655–665.

Other Resources: Pertinent Literature

Ackerman, M. J., & Kane, A. W. (1993). *How to examine psychological experts in divorce and other civil actions* 2nd Edition. Colorado Springs, CO: Wiley Law Publications.

American Psychological Association, Board of Ethnic Minority Affairs. (1991). *Guidelines for providers of psychological services to ethnic, linguistic, and culturally diverse populations.* Washington, DC: American Psychological Association.

American Psychological Association, Committee on Women in Psychology and Committee on Lesbian and Gay Concerns. (1988). *Lesbian parents and their children: A resource paper for psychologists.* Washington, DC: American Psychological Association.

Beaber, R. J. (1982, Fall). Custody quagmire: Some psycholegal dilemmas. *The Journal of Psychiatry & Law,* 309–326.

Bennett, B. E., Bryant, B. K., VandenBos, G. R., & Greenwood, A. (1990). *Professional liability and risk management.* Washington, DC: American Psychological Association.

Bolocofsky, D. N. (1989). Use and abuse of mental health experts in child custody determinations. *Behavioral Sciences and the Law, 7*(2), 197–213.

Bozett, F. (1987). *Gay and lesbian parents.* New York: Praeger.

Bray, J. H. (1993). What's the best interest of the child? Children's adjustment issues in divorce. *The Independent Practitioner. 13,* 42–45.

Bricklin, B. (1992). Data-based tests in custody evaluations. *American Journal of Family Therapy, 20,* 254–265.

Cantor, D. W., & Drake, E. A. (1982). *Divorced parents and their children: A guide for mental health professionals.* New York: Springer.

Chesler, P. (1991). *Mothers on trial: The battle for children and custody.* New York: Harcourt Brace Jovanovich.

Deed, M. L. (1991). Court-ordered child custody evaluations: Helping or victimizing vulnerable families. *Psychotherapy, 28,* 76–84.

Falk, P. J. (1989). Lesbian mothers: Psychosocial assumptions in family law. *American Psychologist, 44,* 941–947.

Gardner, R. A. (1989). Family evaluation in child custody mediation, arbitration, and litigation. Cresskill, NJ: Creative Therapeutics.

———. (1992). *The parental alienation syndrome: A guide for mental health and legal professionals.* Cresskill, NJ: Creative Therapeutics.

———. (1992). *True and false accusations of child abuse.* Cresskill, N.J.: Creative Therapeutics.

Goldstein, J., Freud, A., & Solnit, A. J. (1980). *Before the best interests of the child.* New York: Free Press.

———. (1980). *Beyond the best interests of the child.* New York: Free Press.

Goldstein, J., Freud, A., Solnit, A. J., & Goldstein, S. (1986). *In the best interests of the child.* New York: Free Press.

Grisso, T. (1990). Evolving guidelines for divorce/custody evaluations. *Family and Conciliation Courts Review, 28*(1), 35–41.

Halon, R. L. The comprehensive child custody evaluation. *American Journal of Forensic Psychology, 8*(3), 19–46.

Hetherington, E. M. (1990). Coping with family transitions: Winners, losers, and survivors. *Child Development, 60,* 1–14.

Hetherington, E. M., Stanley-Hagen, M., & Anderson, E. R. (1988). Marital transitions: A child's perspective. *American Psychologist, 44,* 303–312.

Johnston, J., Kline, M. & Tschann, J. (1989). Ongoing postdivorce conflict: Effects on children of joint custody and frequent access. *Journal of Orthopsychiatry, 59,* 576–592.

Koocher, G. P., & Keith-Spiegel, P. C. (1990). *Children, ethics, and the law: Professional issues and cases.* Lincoln: University of Nebraska Press.

Kreindler, S. (1986). The role of mental health professions in custody and access disputes. In R. S. Parry, E. A. Broder, E. A. G. Schmitt, E. B. Saunders, & E. Hood (Eds.), *Custody disputes: Evaluation and intervention.* Lexington, MA: Lexington Books.

Martindale, D. A., Martindale, J. L., & Broderick, J. E. (1991). Providing expert testimony in child custody litigation. In P. A. Keller & S. R. Heyman (Eds.), *Innovations in clinical practice: A source book* (Vol. 10). Sarasota, FL: Professional Resource Exchange.

Patterson, C. J. (in press). Children of lesbian and gay parents. *Child Development.*

Saunders, T. R. (1991). An overview of some psycholegal issues in child physical and sexual abuse. *Psychotherapy in Private Practice, 9*(2), 61–78.

Schutz, B. M., Dixon, E. B., Lindenberger, J. C., & Ruther, N. J. (1989). *Solomon's sword: A practical guide to conducting child custody evaluations.* San Francisco: Jossey-Bass.

Stahly, G. B. (1989). *Testimony on child abuse policy to APA Board.* Paper presented at the American Psychological Association Board of Directors meeting, New Orleans, LA.

Thoennes, N., & Tjaden, P. G. (1991). The extent, nature, and validity of sexual abuse allegations in custody/visitation disputes. *Child Abuse & Neglect, 14,* 151–163.

Wallerstein, J. S., & Blakeslee, S. (1989). *Second chances: Men, women, and children a decade after divorce.* New York: Ticknor & Fields.

Wallerstein, J. S., & Kelly, J. B. (1980). *Surviving the breakup.* New York: Basic Books.

Weissman, H. N. (1991). Child custody evaluations: Fair and unfair professional practices. *Behavioral Sciences and the Law, 9,* 469–476.

Weithorn, L. A., & Grisso, T. (1987). Psychological evaluations in divorce custody: Problems, principles, and procedures. In L. A. Weithorn (Ed.), *Psychology and child custody determinations.* Lincoln, NE: University of Nebraska Press.

White, S. (1990). The contamination of children's interviews. *Child youth and family services quarterly, 13*(3).

Wyer, M. M., Gaylord, S. J. & Grove, E. T. The legal context of child custody evaluations. In L. A. Weithorn (Ed.), *Psychology and child custody determinations.* Lincoln, NE: University of Nebraska Press.

Academy of Family Mediators Standards of Practice for Family and Divorce Mediation*

PREAMBLE

Mediation is a family-centered conflict resolution process in which an impartial third party assists the participants to negotiate a consensual and informed settlement. In mediation, whether private or public, decision-making authority rests with the parties. The role of the mediator includes reducing the obstacles to communication, maximizing the exploration of alternatives, and addressing the needs of those it is agreed are involved or affected.

Mediation is based on principles of problem solving that focus on the needs and interests of the participants; fairness; privacy; self determination; and the best interest of all family members.

These standards are intended to assist and guide public, private, voluntary, and mandatory mediation. It is understood that the manner of implementation and mediator adherence to these standards may be influenced by local law or court rule.

INITIATING THE PROCESS

Definition and Description of Mediation

The mediator shall define mediation and describe the differences and similarities between mediation and other procedures for dispute resolution. In

---

*Used with permission of Academy of Family Mediators.

defining the process, the mediator shall delineate it from therapy, counseling, custody evaluation, arbitration, and advocacy.

Identification of Issues

The mediation shall elicit sufficient information from the participants so that they can mutually define and agree on the issues to be resolved in mediation.

Appropriateness of Mediation

The mediator shall help the participants evaluate the benefits, risks, and costs of mediation and the alternatives available to them.

Mediator's Duty of Disclosure

Biases

The mediator shall disclose to the participants any biases or strong views relating to the issues to be mediated.

Training and Experience

The mediator's education, training, and experience to mediate the issues should be accurately described to the participants.

PROCEDURES

The mediator shall reach an understanding with the participants regarding the procedures to be followed in mediation. This includes but is not limited to the practice as to separate meetings between a participant and the mediator, confidentiality, use of legal services, the involvement of additional parties, and conditions under which mediation may be terminated.

Mutual Duties and Responsibilities

The mediator and the participants shall agree upon the duties and responsibilities that each is accepting in the mediation process. This may be a written or verbal agreement.

IMPARTIALITY AND NEUTRALITY

Impartiality

The mediator is obligated to maintain impartiality toward all participants. Impartiality means freedom from favoritism or bias, either in word or action. Impartiality implies a commitment to aid all participants, as opposed to a single individual, in reaching a mutually satisfactory agreement. Impartiality means that a mediator will not play an adversarial role.

The mediator has a responsibility to maintain impartiality while raising questions for the parties to consider as to the fairness, equity, and feasibility of proposed options for settlement.

Neutrality

Neutrality refers to the relationship that the mediator has with the disputing parties. If the mediator feels, or any one of the participants states, that the mediator's background or personal experiences would prejudice the mediator's performance, the mediator should withdraw from mediation unless all agree to proceed.

Relationship to Participants

The mediator should be aware that post-mediation professional or social relationships may compromise the mediator's continued availability as a neutral third party.

Conflict of Interest

A mediator should disclose any circumstance to the participants that might cause a conflict of interest.

COSTS AND FEES

Explanation of Fees

The mediator shall explain the fees to be charged for mediation and any related costs and shall agree with the participants on how the fees will be shared and the manner of payment.

Reasonable Fees

When setting fees, the mediator shall ensure that they are explicit, fair, reasonable, and commensurate with the service to be performed. Unearned fees should be promptly returned to the clients.

Contingent Fees

It is inappropriate for a mediator to charge contingent fees or to base fees on the outcome of mediation.

Referrals and Commissions

No commissions, rebates, or similar forms of remuneration shall be given or received for referral of clients for mediation services.

CONFIDENTIALITY AND EXCHANGE OF INFORMATION

Confidentiality

Confidentiality relates to the full and open disclosure necessary for the mediation process. A mediator shall foster the confidentiality of the process.

Limits of Confidentiality

The mediator shall inform the parties at the initial meeting of limitations on confidentiality, such as statutorily or judicially mandated reporting.

Appearing in Court

The mediator shall inform the parties of circumstances under which mediators may be compelled to testify in court.

Consequences of Disclosure of Facts Between Parties

The mediator shall discuss with the participants the potential consequences of their disclosure of facts to each other during the mediation process.

Release of Information

The mediator shall obtain the consent of the participants prior to releasing information to others. The mediator shall maintain confidentiality and render anonymous all identifying information when materials are used for research or training purposes.

Caucus

The mediator shall discuss policy regarding confidentiality for individual caucuses. In the event that a mediator, on consent of the participants, speaks privately with any person not represented in mediation, including children, the mediator shall define how information received will be used.

Storage and Disposal of Records

The mediator shall maintain confidentiality in the storage and disposal of records.

Full Disclosure

The mediator shall require disclosure of all relevant information in the mediation process, as would reasonably occur in the judicial discovery process.

SELF-DETERMINATION

Responsibilities of the Participants and the Mediator

The primary responsibility for the resolution of a dispute rests with the participants. The mediator's obligation is to assist the disputants in reaching an informed and voluntary settlement. At no time shall a mediator coerce a participant into agreement or make a substantive decision for any participant.

Responsibility to Third Parties

The mediator has a responsibility to promote the participants' consideration of the interests of children and other persons affected by the agreement. The mediator also has a duty to assist parents to examine, apart from their own desires, the separate and individual needs of such people. The participants shall be encouraged to seek outside professional consultation when appropriate or when they are otherwise unable to agree on the needs of any individual affected by the agreement.

PROFESSIONAL ADVICE

Independent Advice and Information

The mediator shall encourage and assist the participants to obtain independent expert information and advice when such information is needed to reach an informed agreement or to protect the rights of a participant.

Providing Information

A mediator shall give information only in those areas where qualified by training or experience.

Independent Legal Counsel

When the mediation may affect legal rights or obligations, the mediator shall advise the participants to seek independent legal counsel prior to resolving the issues and in conjunction with formalizing an agreement.

PARTIES' ABILITY TO NEGOTIATE

The mediator shall ensure that each participant has had an opportunity to understand the implications and ramifications of available options. In the event a participant needs either additional information or assistance in order for the negotiations to proceed in a fair and orderly manner or for an agreement to be reached, the mediator shall refer the individual to appropriate resources.

Procedural Factors

The mediator has a duty to ensure balanced negotiations and should not permit manipulative or intimidating negotiation techniques.

Psychological Factors

The mediator shall explore whether the participants are capable of participating in informed negotiations. The mediator may postpone mediation and refer the parties to appropriate resources if necessary.

CONCLUDING MEDIATION

Full Agreement

The mediator shall discuss with the participants the process for formalization and implementation of the agreement.

Partial Agreement

When the participants reach a partial agreement, the mediator shall discuss with them procedures available to resolve the remaining issues.

Without Agreement

Termination by Participants

The mediator shall inform the participants of their right to withdraw from mediation at any time and for any reason.

Termination by Mediator

If the mediator believes that participants are unable or unwilling to participate meaningfully in the process or that a reasonable agreement is unlikely, the mediator may suspend or terminate mediation and should encourage the parties to seek appropriate professional help.

Impasse

If the participants reach a final impasse, the mediator should not prolong unproductive discussions that would result in emotional and monetary costs to the participants.

TRAINING AND EDUCATION

Training

A mediator shall acquire substantive knowledge and procedural skill in the specialized area of practice. This may include but is not limited to family and human development, family law, divorce procedures, family finances, community resources, the mediation process, and professional ethics.

Continuing Education

A mediator shall participate in continuing education and be personally responsible for ongoing professional growth. A mediator is encouraged to join with other mediators and members of related professions to promote mutual professional development.

ADVERTISING

A mediator shall make only accurate statements about the mediation process, its costs and benefits, and the mediator's qualifications.

RELATIONSHIP WITH OTHER PROFESSIONALS

THE RESPONSIBILITY OF THE MEDIATOR TOWARD OTHER MEDIATORS

Relationship with Other Mediators

A mediator should not mediate any dispute that is being mediated by another mediator without first endeavoring to consult with the person or persons conducting the mediation.

Co-mediation

In those situations where more than one mediator is participating in a particular case, each mediator has a responsibility to keep the others informed of developments essential to a cooperative effort.

RELATIONSHIPS WITH OTHER PROFESSIONALS

A mediator should respect the complementary relationship between mediation and legal, mental health, and other social services and should promote cooperation with other professionals.

ADVANCEMENT OF MEDIATION

Mediation Service

A mediator is encouraged to provide some mediation service in the community for nominal or no fee.

Promotion of Mediation

A mediator shall promote the advancement of mediation by encouraging and participating in research, publishing, or other forms of professional and public education.

PARTICIPATING ORGANIZATIONS

Academy of Family Mediators
American Academy of Matrimonial Lawyers
American Arbitration Association
American Association for Mediated Divorce
American Association of Pastoral Counselors
American Bar Association
   Family Law Section, Mediation and Arbitration Committee
   Special Committee on Alternative Dispute Resolution
American Psychological Association
Association of Family and Conciliation Courts
Association of Family and Conciliation Courts—California Chapter
British Columbia Judges Committee on Family Law
California State Bar, Family Law Section, Custody and Visitation
   Committee
Canadian Federal Government—Department of Justice
Policy and Planning Center for Dispute Resolution, Denver, Colorado
Children's Judicial Resource Council
Colorado Bar, Family Law Section
Council on Accreditation of Services for Families and Children
Family Mediation Association
Family Mediation Center, Scottsdale, Arizona
Family Mediation Service of Ontario

Hennepin County Court Services
Legal Aid of Quebec
Los Angeles Conciliation Court
Maricopa County Conciliation Court
Mediation Association of Southern Arizona
Mediation Consortium of Washington State
Mediation Council of Illinois
Mediation Institute of California
Minnesota Council of Family Mediation
Montreal Conciliation Court
National Association of Social Workers
National Council on Family Relations
National Institute for Dispute Resolution
Northwest Mediation Service
Ontario Association for Family Mediation
Pima County Superior Court
Pinal County Conciliation Court
San Diego County Superior Court Family Services
Society of Professionals in Dispute Resolution
South Florida Council on Divorce Mediation
Southern California Mediation Network
State Bar of California—Legal Specialization Committee
Wisconsin Association of Family and Divorce Mediators

APPENDIX F

American Professional Society on the Abuse of Children Guidelines for Psychosocial Evaluation of Suspected Sexual Abuse in Young Children*

STATEMENT OF PURPOSE

These Guidelines for mental health professionals reflect current knowledge and consensus about the psychosocial evaluation of suspected sexual abuse in young children. They are not intended as a standard of practice to which practitioners are expected to adhere in all cases. Evaluators must have the flexibility to exercise clinical judgment in individual cases. Laws and local customs may also influence the accepted method in a given community. Practitioners should be knowledgeable about various constraints on practice and prepared to justify their decisions about particular practices in specific cases. As experience and scientific knowledge expand, further refinement and revision of these Guidelines are expected.

These Guidelines are specific to psychosocial assessments. Sexual abuse is known to produce both acute and long-term negative psychological effects requiring therapeutic intervention. Psychosocial assessments are a systematic process of gathering information and forming professional opinions about the source of statements, behavior, and other evidence that form the basis of concern about possible sexual abuse. Psychosocial evaluations are broadly concerned with understanding developmental, familial, and historical factors and events that may be associated with psychological adjustment. The results of such evaluations may be used to assist in legal decision making and in directing treatment planning.

Interviews of children for possible sexual abuse are conducted by other professionals as well, including child protective service workers, law enforcement investigators, special "child interviewers," and medical practitioners. Such interviews are most often limited to a single, focused session which concentrates on eliciting reliable statements about possible sexual abuse; they are not designed to assess the child's general adjustment and functioning. Principles about interviewing contained in the Guidelines may be applied to investigatory or history-taking interviews. Some of the preferred practices, however (e.g., number of interviews), will not apply.

Psychosocial evaluators should first establish their role in the evaluation process. Evaluations performed at the request of a court may require a different stance and include additional components than those conducted for purely clinical reasons. The difference between the evaluation phase and a clinical phase must be clearly articulated if the same professional is to be involved. In all cases, evaluators should be aware that any interview with a child regarding possible sexual abuse may be subject to scrutiny and have significant implications for legal decision making and the child's safety and well-being.

GUIDELINES

I.   THE EVALUATOR
   A. Characteristics
   1. The evaluator should possess an advanced mental health degree in a recognized discipline (e.g., MD, or Masters or Ph.D. in psychology, social work, counseling, or psychiatric nursing).
   2. The evaluator should have experience evaluating and treating children and families. A minimum of two years of professional experience with children is expected, three to five years is preferred. The evaluator should also possess at least two years of professional experience with sexually abused children. If the evaluator does not possess such experience, supervision is essential.
   3. It is essential that the evaluator have specialized training in child development and child sexual abuse. This should be documented in terms of formal course work, supervision, or attendance at conferences, seminars, and workshops.
   4. The evaluator should be familiar with current professional literature on sexual abuse and be knowledgeable about the dynamics and the emotional and behavioral consequences of abuse experiences.
   5. The evaluator should have experience in conducting forensic evaluations and providing court testimony. If the evaluator does not possess such experience, supervision is essential.

      6. The evaluator should approach the evaluation with an open mind to all possible responses from the child and all possible explanations for the concern about possible sexual abuse.

II.   **COMPONENTS OF THE EVALUATION**

  A. Protocol

      1. A written protocol is not necessary; however evaluations should routinely involve reviewing all pertinent materials; conducting collateral interviews when necessary; establishing rapport; assessing the child's general functioning, developmental status; and memory capacity; and thoroughly evaluating the possibility of abuse. The evaluator may use discretion in the order of presentation and method of assessment.

  B. Employer of the Evaluator

      1. Evaluation of the child may be conducted at the request of a legal guardian prior to court involvement.

      2. If a court proceeding is involved, the preferred practice is a court-appointed or mutually agreed upon evaluation of the child.

      3. Discretion should be used in agreeing to conduct an evaluation of a child when the child has already been evaluated or when there is current court involvement. Minimizing the number of evaluations should be a consideration; additional evaluations should be conducted only if they clearly further the best interests of the child. When a second opinion is required, a review of the records may eliminate the need for reinterviewing the child.

  C. Number of Evaluators

      1. It is acceptable to have a single evaluator. However, when the evaluation will include the accused or suspected individual, a team approach is the preferred practice, with information concerning the progress of the evaluation readily available among team members. Consent should be obtained from all participants prior to releasing information.

  D. Collateral Information Gathered as Part of the Evaluation

      1. Review of all relevant background material as part of the evaluation is the preferred practice.

      2. The evaluation report should document all the materials used and demonstrate their objective review in the evaluation process.

  E. Interviewing the Accused or Suspected Individual

      1. It is not necessary to interview the accused or suspected individual in order to form an opinion about possible sexual abuse of the child.

      2. An interview with or review of the statements from a suspected or accused individual (when available) may provide additional

relevant information (e.g., alternative explanations, admissions, insight into relationship between child and accused individual).

3. If the accused or suspected individual is a parent, preferred practice is for the child evaluator to contact or interview that parent. If a full assessment of the accused or suspected parent is indicated, a team approach is the preferred practice.

F. Releasing Information

1. Suspected abuse should always be reported to authorities as dictated by state law.

2. Permission should be obtained from legal guardians for receipt of collateral materials and for release of information about the examination to relevant medical or mental health professionals, other professionals (e.g., schoolteachers), and involved legal systems (e.g., CPS, law enforcement). Discretion should be used in releasing sensitive individual and family history which does not directly relate to the purpose of the assessment.

3. When an evaluation is requested by the court, information should be released to all parties to the action after consent is obtained.

III. INTERVIEWING

A. Recording of Interviews

1. Audio or video recording may be preferred practice in some communities. Professional preference, logistics, or clinical consideration may contraindicate recording of interviews. Professional discretion is permitted in recording policies and practices.

2. Detailed written documentation is the minimum requirement, with specific attention to questions and responses (verbal and nonverbal) regarding possible sexual abuse. Verbatim quotes of significant questions and answers are desirable.

3. When audio and video recording are used, the child must be informed. It is desirable to obtain written agreement from the child and legal guardian(s).

B. Observation of the Interview

1. Observation of interviews by involved professionals (CPS, law enforcement, etc.) may be indicated if it reduces the need for additional interviews.

2. Observation by non-accused and non-suspected primary caregiver(s) may be indicated for particular clinical reasons; however, great care should be taken that the observation is clinically appropriate, does not unduly distress the child, and does not affect the validity of the evaluation process.

3. If interviews are observed, the child must be informed and it is desirable to obtain written agreement from the child and legal guardian(s).

C. Number of Interviews

1. Preferred practice is two to six sessions for directed assessment. This does not imply that all sessions must include specific questioning about possible sexual abuse. The evaluator may decide based on the individual case circumstances to adopt a less direct approach and reserve questioning. Repeated direct questioning of the child regarding sexual abuse when the child is not reporting or is denying abuse is contraindicated.

2. If the child does not report abuse within the two to six sessions of directed evaluation, but the evaluator has continuing concerns about the possibility of abuse, the child should be referred for extended evaluation or therapy which is less directive but diagnostically focused, and the child's protection from possible abuse should be recommended.

D. Format of Interview
1. Preferred practice is whenever possible, to interview first the primary caretaker to gather background information.
2. The child should be seen individually for initial interviews, except when the child refuses to separate. Discussion of possible abuse in the presence of the caretaker during initial interviews should be avoided except when necessary to elicit information from the child. In such cases, the interview setting should be structured to reduce the possibility of improper influence by the caretaker upon the child's behavior.
3. Joint sessions with the child and the non-accused caretaker or accused or suspected individual may be helpful to obtain information regarding the overall quality of the relationships. The sessions should not be conducted for the purpose of determining whether abuse occurred based on the child's reactions to the accused or suspected individual. Nor should joint sessions be conducted if they may cause significant additional trauma to the child. A child should never be asked to confirm the abuse statements in front of an accused individual.

IV. **CHILD INTERVIEW**
A. General Principles
1. The evaluator should create an atmosphere that enables the child to talk freely, including providing physical surroundings and a climate that facilitates the child's comfort and communication.
2. Language and interviewing approach should be developmentally appropriate.
3. The evaluator should take the time necessary to perform a complete evaluation and should avoid any coercive quality to the interview.
4. Interview procedures may be modified in cases involving very young, pre-verbal, or minimally verbal children or children with

special problems (e.g., developmentally delayed, electively mute).

B. Questioning

1. The child should be questioned directly about possible sexual abuse at some point in the evaluation.

2. Initial questioning should be as non-directive as possible to elicit spontaneous responses. If open-ended questions are not productive, more directive questioning should follow.

3. The evaluator may use the form of questioning deemed necessary to elicit information on which to base an opinion. Highly specific questioning should only be used when other methods of questioning have failed, when previous information warrants substantial concern, or when the child's developmental level precludes more non-directive approaches. However, responses to these questions should be carefully evaluated and weighed accordingly.

C. Use of Dolls and Other Devices

1. A variety of non-verbal tools should be available to assist the child in communication, including drawings, toys, doll-houses, dolls, puppets, etc.

2. Anatomically detailed dolls should be used with care and discretion. Preferred practice is to have them available for identification of body parts, clarification of previous statements, or demonstration by non- or low-verbal children after there is indication of abuse activity.

3. The anatomically detailed dolls should not be considered a diagnostic test. Unusual behavior with the dolls may suggest further lines of inquiry and should be noted in the evaluation report, but is not generally considered conclusive of a history of sexual abuse.

D. Psychological Testing

1. Formal psychological testing of the child is not indicated for the purpose of proving or disproving a history of sexual abuse.

2. Testing is useful when the clinician is concerned about the child's intellectual or developmental level, or about the possible presence of a thought disorder. Psychological tests can also provide helpful information regarding a child's emotional status.

3. Evaluation of non-accused and accused individuals often involves complete psychological testing to assess for significant psychopathology or sexual deviance.

V. CONCLUSIONS/REPORT

A. General Principles

1. The evaluator should take care to communicate that mental health professionals have no special ability to detect whether an individual is telling the truth.

2. The evaluator may directly state that abuse did or did not occur, or may say that a child's behavior and words are consistent or inconsistent with abuse, or with a history or absence of history of abuse.

3. Opinions about whether abuse occurred or did not occur should include supporting information (e.g., the child's and/or the accused individual's statements, behavior, psychological symptoms). Possible alternative explanations should be addressed and ruled out.

4. The evaluation may be inconclusive. If so, the evaluator should cite the information that causes continuing concern but does not enable confirmation or disconfirmation of abuse. If inconclusiveness is due to such problems as missing information or an untimely or poorly conducted investigation, these obstacles should be clearly noted in the report.

5. Recommendations should be made regarding therapeutic or environmental interventions to address the child's emotional and behavioral functioning and to ensure the child's safety.

ACKNOWLEDGMENTS

These Guidelines are the product of APSAC's Task Force on the Psychosocial Evaluation of Suspected Sexual Abuse in Young Children, chaired by Lucy Berliner, MSW. A group of experts who responded to a lengthy, open-ended, mailed survey provided the content for the first draft. That draft was revised based on comments from a large number of practitioners who responded to mailed requests for input and who participated in the open Task Force meeting held at the Fourth Annual Health Science Response to Child Maltreatment conference, held in San Diego, California, in January, 1990. The next draft was published for comment in APSAC's newsletter, The Advisor, in Spring, 1990. Revised according to suggestions made by APSAC members and Board, this is the final result.

Appreciation goes to all the practitioner/experts who contributed much of their time and expertise to make these Guidelines valuable. Special thanks goes to Richard Stille, Ph.D., who helped synthesize the first draft. The Guidelines will be updated periodically. Any comments or suggestions about them should be directed to Lucy Berliner through APSAC, 332 South Michigan Avenue, Suite 1600, Chicago, Illinois, 60604, (312) 554–0166.

References

Achenbach, Thomas M. (1991). *Manual for the youth-self report and 1991 profile.* Burlington, VT: University of Vermont.

Ackerman, M. J. (1984). Recent psychological research on the effect of divorce on children. *Wisconsin Journal of Family Law, 1,* 19–31.

———. (1987). Child sexual abuse: Bona fide or fabricated. *American Journal of Family Law, 1,* 181–185.

———. (1990). Child sexual abuse: Bona fide or fabricated-revisited. *American Journal of Family Law, 5,* 325–336.

———. (1992). Issues in child sexual abuse allegation: Incest families and child testimony *American Journal of Family Law, 6,* 29–32.

———. (1992). Predictive validity of the ASPECT. *Ackerman-Schoendorf Scales for Parent Evaluation of Custody (ASPECT).*

———. (1993). Surviving your day in court. *Register Report, 19*(4), 10–11.

———. (1994). A child's shattered ego: The aftermath of divorce. *American Journal of Family Law, 8,* 17–72.

Ackerman, M. J., & Ackerman, S. (1992). Comparison of different subgroups on the MMPI of parents involved in custody litigation. (unpublished).

Ackerman, M. J., & Kane, A. W. (1990). *How to examine psychological experts in divorce and other civil actions.* Colorado Springs: John Wiley & Sons.

———. (1993). *Psychological experts in divorce, personal injury, and other civil actions* (2nd ed.). Colorado Springs: John Wiley & Sons.

Ackerman, M. J., & Schoendorf, K. (1992). *The Ackerman-Schoendorf Parent Evaluation of Custody Test (ASPECT).* Los Angeles: Western Psychological Services.

Amato, P. R., & Bruce, K. (1991). Parents divorce and the well-being of children: A meta-analysis. *Psychological Bulletin, 110,* 26–46.

American Professional Society on the Abuse of Children. (1990). *Guidelines for psychosocial evaluation of suspected sexual abuse in young children.* Chicago, IL: Author.

American Psychological Association. (1981). Ethical principles of psychologists. *American Psychologist, 36,* 633–638.

———. (1981). Specialty guidelines for the delivery of services. *American Psychologist, 36,* 640–681.

———. (1984). Casebook for providers of psychological services. *American Psychologist, 39,* 663–668.

———. (1985). *Standards for educational and psychological testing.* Washington, DC: Author.

———. (1987). General guidelines for providers of psychological services. *American Psychologist, 42,* 1–12.

———. (1992). Ethical principles of psychologists and code of conduct. *American Psychologist, 47,* 1597–1611.

———. (1993). Record keeping guidelines. *American Psychologist, 48,* 640–681.

———. (1991). *APA Monitor, 22,* 22.

———. (1993). *APA Monitor, 24,* 41.

Arditti, J. (1992). Differences between fathers with joint custody and non-custodial fathers. *American Journal of Orthopsychiatry, 62,* 187–195.

Bales, J. (1988). APA rebuts criticism of clinician witnesses. *APA Monitor, 19,* 17.

Barber, B. L., & Eccles, J. S. (1992). Long-term influence of divorce in single parenting and adolescent families and work-related values, behaviors, and aspirations. *Psychological Bulletin, 111,* 108–126.

Bazelon, D. (1982). Veils, values and social responsibility. *American Psychologist, 37,* 115–121.

Bellak, L., & Bellak, S. (1949). *Children's Apperception Test.* Larchmont, NY: C.P.S.

Berman, A. (1986). The expert at trial: Personality persuades. *Family Advocate, 9,* 11–12.

Bisnair, L., Firestone, P., & Rynard, D. (1990). Factors associated with academic achievement in children following parental separation. *American Journal of Orthopsychiatry, 60,* 67–76.

Blau, T. (1984). *The psychologist as expert witness.* New York: John Wiley & Sons, Inc.

Blinka, D. (1993). Scientific evidence in Wisconsin after Daubert. *Wisconsin Lawyer, 10,* 12–61.

Bolton, F. G., & Bolton, S. R. (1987). *A guide for clinical and legal practitioners, working with the violent family.* Troy, NY: Sage Publications.

Bonkowski, S. E. (1989). Lingering sadness: Young adults' response to parental divorce. *Journal of Contemporary Social Work, 17,* 219–223.

Bottoms, B., & David, S. (1993). Scientific evidence no longer subject to "Frye test." *APA Monitor, 24,* 14.

Boyer, J. (1990). Assuming risk in child custody evaluations. *Register Report, 16,* 8–9.

Bresee, P., Stearns, J., Bess, B., & Pecker, L. (1986). Allegations of child sexual abuse in child custody disputes: A therapeutic assessment model. *American Journal of Orthopsychiatry, 56,* 550–559.

Bricklin, B. (1984). *Bricklin perceptual scales.* Furlong, PA: Village Publishing.

———. (1990). *Perception of relationships tests (PORT).* Furlong, PA: Village Publishing.

Briere, J., & Runtz, M. (1993). Child sexual abuse, long-term sequelae and implications for psychological assessment. *Journal of Interpersonal Violence, 3,* 312–330.

Brodsky, S. (1991). *Testifying in court: Guidelines and maxims for the expert witness.* Washington, DC: American Psychological Association.

Bronfenbrenner, U. (1979). *The ecology of human development: Experiments by nature and design.* Cambridge, MA: Harvard University Press.

Brosig, C. L., & Kalichman, S. C. (1991, August). *Child abuse reporting laws: Their effects on clinicians' reporting behavior.* Paper presented at the 99th Annual Convention of the American Psychological Association, San Francisco.

Cain, B. S. (1989). Parental divorce during the college years. *Psychiatry, 52,* 135–146.

Caldwell, A. (1982). *Families of MMPI code types.* Paper presented at the 12th Annual Symposium on the MMPI, Tampa, FL.

Caldwell, A., & O'Hare, C. (1986). *A handbook of MMPI personality types.* Santa Monica, CA: Clinical Psychology Services.

Carlson, B. E. (1990). Adolescent observers of marital violence. *Journal of Family Violence, 5,* 285–299.

Cohen, M. G. (1991). *The joint custody handbook.* Philadelphia: The Running Press.

Cohn, J. B. (1990). On the practicalities of being an expert witness. *American Journal of Forensic Psychiatry, 11,* 11–20.

Committee on Ethical Guidelines for Forensic Psychologists. (1991). Specialty guidelines for forensic psychologists. *Law and Human Behavior, 15,* 655–665.

Cooke, G., & Cooke, M. (1991). Dealing with sexual abuse allegations in the context of custody evaluations. *American Journal of Forensic Psychology, 9,* 55–67.

Crites, C., & Coker, D. (1988). What therapists see that judges miss. *The Judges Journal, 27,* 9–13, 40–41.

Dawson, B., Vaughan, A. R., & Wagner, W. G. (1992). Normal responses to sexually anatomical detailed dolls. *Journal of Family Violence, 7,* 135–152.

Deed, M. L. (1991). Court-ordered child custody evaluations: Helping or victimizing vulnerable families. *Psychotherapy, 28,* 76–84.

Demo, D., & Acock, A. (1988). The impact of divorce on children. *Journal of Marriage and Family, 50,* 619–688.

Denham, S. (1989). Maternal affect and toddlers' social-emotional competence. *American Journal of Orthopsychiatry, 59,* 368–376.

De Young, M. (1986). A conceptual model for judging the truthfulness of a young child's allegation of sexual abuse. *American Journal of Orthopsychiatry, 56,* 550–559.

Dillon, K. (1987). *False sexual abuse allegations; Causes and concerns.* Silver Spring, MD: National Association of Social Workers.

Early, E. (1990). Imagined, exaggerated, and malingered post-traumatic stress disorder. In C. Meek, *Post-Traumatic Stress Disorder: Assessment, differential diagnosis, and forensic evaluation,* (pp. 137–156). Sarasota, FL: Professional Resource Exchange.

Eckenrode, J., Powers, J., Doris, J., Munsch, J., & Bolger, N. (1988). Substantiation of child abuse and neglect reports. *Journal of Consulting and Clinical Psychology, 6,* 9–16.

Egeland, B., Erickson, M., Butcher, J. N., & Ben-Porath, Y. (1991). MMPI-2 profiles of women at risk for child abuse. *Journal of Personality Assessment, 57,* 254–263.

Ellison, E. (1983). Issues concerning parental harmony and children's psychosocial adjustment. *American Journal of Orthopsychiatry, 53,* 73–79.

Elterman, M. F., & Ehrenberg, M. F. (1991). Sexual abuse allegations in child custody disputes. *International Journal of Law and Psychiatry, 14,* 269–286.

Erikson, S. (1984). *Divorce mediation workshop.* Wisconsin Psychological Association.

Exner, J. E., Jr. (1990). *A Rorschach workbook for the comprehensive system.* (3d ed.) Asheville, NC: Rorschach Workshops.

Exner, J. E., Jr., & Clark, B. (1978). The Rorschach. In B. Wolman (Ed.), *Clinical diagnosis of mental disorders* (pp. 147–178). New York: Plenum Press.

Facchino, D., & Aron, A. (1990). Divorced fathers with custody: Method of obtaining custody in divorce adjustment. *Journal of Divorce, 13,* 45–56.

Faller, K. C. (1990). *Understanding child sexual maltreatment.* Newbury Park, CA: Sage Publications.

———. (1991). Possible explanations for child sexual abuse allegations in divorce. *American Journal of Orthopsychiatry, 61,* 86–91.

Faller, K., Froning, M., & Lipovsky, J. (1991). The parent-child interview: Use in evaluating child allegations of sexual abuse by the parent. *American Journal of Orthopsychiatry, 61,* 552–557.

Finkelhor, D. (1983). *The dark side of families: Current family violence research.* Beverly Hills, CA: Sage Publications.

———. (1987). The sexual abuse of children: Current research reviewed. *Psychiatric Annals, 17,* 233–241.

———. (1990). Early and long-term effects of child sexual abuse: An update. *Professional Psychology: Research and Practice, 21,* 325–330.

Forehand, R., Wierson, M., McCombs, A., Thomas, R., Fauber, L. A., Kempton, T., & Long, N. (1991). A short-term longitudinal examination of young adolescent functioning following divorce: The role of family factors. *Journal of Abnormal Psychology, 19,* 97–111.

Franke, L. (1983). *Growing up divorced.* New York: Linden Press/Simon & Schuster.

Franklin, K., Janoff-Bulman, R., & Roberts, J. E. (1990). Long-term impact of parental divorce on optimism and trust: Changes in general assumptions or narrow beliefs? *Journal of Personality and Social Psychology, 59,* 743–755.

Frost, A. K., & Pakiz, B. (1990). The effects of marital disruption on adolescence: Time as a dynamic. *American Journal of Orthopsychiatry, 60,* 544–550.

Garb, H. (1992). The trained psychologist as expert witness. *Clinical Psychology Review, 12,* 451–467.

Garbarino, J., Guttman, E., & Seeley, J. (1987). *The psychologically battered child.* San Francisco: Jossey-Bass.

Gardner, R. (1986). *Issues in child and adolescent therapy in divorce.* 5th Annual Intervention for the Child and Family at Risk Workshop, Milwaukee, WI.

———. (1989). *Family evaluation and child custody, mediation, arbitration, and litigation.* Cresskill, NJ: Creative Therapeutics.

———. (1991). Joint custody is not for everyone. In J. Folberg (Ed.), *Joint custody and shared parenting* (pp. 88–96). New York: Guilford Press.

Geffner, R. A. (1990). *Characteristics of victims of sexual abuse: Reference for child witnesses.* A symposium presented at the 98th Annual Convention of the American Psychological Association, Boston.

Gelles, R., & Strauss, M. (1988). *Intimate violence.* New York: Simon & Schuster.

Glenn, N. D., & Kramer, K. B. (1987). The marriages and children of children of divorce. *Journal of Marriage and Family, 49,* 811–825.

Gold, E. (1986). Long-term effects of sexual victimizing in childhood: An attributional approach. *Journal of Consulting and Clinical Psychology, 54,* 471–475.

Golding, S., Grisso, T., & Shapiro, D. (1989). *Working draft: Specialty guidelines for forensic psychologists (June 1989 revision).* Washington, DC: American Psychological Association.

Goldstein, J. (1991). In whose best interest? In J. Folberg (Ed.), *Joint custody and shared parenting* (pp. 11–25). New York: Guilford Press.

Goldstein, J. A., Freud, A., & Solnit, A. J. (1973). *Beyond the best interests of the child.* New York: Free Press.

———. (1980). *Beyond the best interests of the child.* London: Burnett Books.

Goldzband, M. (1980). *Custody cases and expert witnesses, a manual for attorneys.* New York: Harcourt Brace Jovanovich.

Goodenough, F. (1926). *Measurement of intelligence by drawings.* New York: Harcourt, Brace and World.

Goodman, G. S., & Aman, C. (1987). *Children's use of anatomically correct dolls to report an event.* Paper presented at the meeting of the Society for Research in Child Development, Baltimore. In Melton, G., & Limber, S., (1989) Psychologists' involvement in cases of maltreatment: Limits of role and expertise. *American Psychologist, 44,* 1225–1233.

Goodman, G., & Rosenberg, M. (1991). The child witness to family violence: Clinical and legal considerations. In D. J. Sonkin (Ed.), *Domestic violence on trial* (pp. 97–125). New York: Springer Publishing Co.

Gordon, B., Schroeder, C., & Abrams, M. (1990). Children's knowledge of sexuality: A comparison of sexually abused and nonabused children. *American Journal of Orthopsychiatry, 60,* 250–257.

Gordon, M. (1990). Males and females as victims of childhood sexual abuse: An examination of gender effect. *Journal of Family Violence, 5,* 321–332.

Gottman, J. M., & Fainsilber-Katz, L. (1989). Effects of marital discord on young children's peer interaction and health. *Developmental Psychology, 25,* 373–381.

Greene, R., (1991). *MMPI-2/MMPI—An interpretive manual.* Needham Heights, MA: Allyn and Bacon.

Greene, R., & Leslie, L. (1989). Mother's behavior and son's adjustment following divorce. *Journal of Divorce, 12,* 335–251.

Greif, G. (1987). Mothers without custody. *Social Work, 32,* 11–16.

Greif, G., & DeMaris, A. (1990). Single fathers with custody. *The Journal of Contemporary Services, 1,* 259–266.

———. (1992). Single custodial fathers in contested custody suits. *Journal of Psychiatry and Law, 20,* 223–239.

Grisso, T. (1990). Evolving guidelines for divorce/custody evaluations. *Family & Conciliation Courts Review, 28,* 35–41.

Guidubaldi, J., Cleminshaw, H., Perry, J., Nastasi, B., & Adams, B. (1984). *Longitudinal effects of divorce on children: A report from the NASPKSU nationwide study.* Paper presented to the 92nd Annual Convention of the American Psychological Association, Toronto, Canada.

Hall, G. C. (1989). WAIS-R and MMPI profiles of men who have sexually assaulted children: Evidence of limited utility. *Journal of Personality Assessment, 53,* 402–412.

Hall, G., Majuro, R., Vitaliano, P., & Proctor, W. (1986). The utility of the MMPI with men who have sexually assaulted children. *Journal of Consulting and Clinical Psychology, 54,* 493–496.

Hall, G. C., Sheperd, J. B., & Mundrak, P. (1992). MMPI taxonomies of child sexual and non-sexual offenders: A cross validation and extension. *Journal of Personal Assessment, 58,* 127–137.

Hall, M. (1989). The role of psychologists as experts in cases involving allegations of child sexual abuse. *Family Law Quarterly, 23,* 451–464.

Hanson, R. K., Steffy, R. A., & Gauthier, R. (1993). Long-term recidivism of child molesters. *Journal of Consulting and Clinical Psychology, 64,* 646–652.

Hathaway, S. R., & McKinley, J. C. (1943). *The Minnesota Multiphasic Personality Inventory.* Minneapolis: University of Minnesota Press.

———. (1989). *The Minnesota Multiphasic Personality Inventory-2: Manual for administration and scoring.* Minneapolis: University of Minnesota Press.

Healy, J., Malley, J., & Stewart, A. (1990). Children and their fathers after parental separation. *American Journal of Orthopsychiatry, 60,* 531–543.

Heilbrun, K. (1992). The role of psychological testing in forensic assessment. *Law & Human Behavior, 16,* 257–272.

Herman, J., Russell, D., & Trocki, K. (1986). Long-term effects of incestuous abuse in childhood. *American Journal of Psychiatry, 143,* 1293–1296.

Hershorn, M., & Rosenbaum, A. (1985). Children of marital violence: a closer look at the unintended victims. *American Journal of Orthopsychiatry, 52,* 260–266.

Hetherington, E. M. (1979). Divorce: a child's perspective. *American Psychologist, 34,* 851–858.

Hetherington, E. M., Cox, M., & Cox, R. (1978). The aftermath of divorce. In J. Stevens & M. Matthews (Eds.), *Mother-child, father-child relations.* Washington, DC: National Association for the Education of Young Children.

Hodges, W. F. (1991). *Interventions for children of divorce* (2nd ed.). New York: John Wiley & Sons, Inc.

Hoeffer, B. (1981). Children acquisition of sex-role behavior in lesbian-mother families. *American Journal of Orthopsychiatry, 51,* 536–543.

Holden, W. E., Willis, D. J., & Foltz, L. (1989). Child abuse potential and parenting stress: Relationships in maltreating parents. *Psychological Assessment: A Journal of Consulting and Clinical Psychology, 1,* 64–67.

Horner, T. M., Guyer, M. J., & Kalter, N. M. (1992). Prediction, prevention, and clinical expertise in child custody cases in which allegations of child sexual abuse have been made. *Family Law Quarterly, 26,* 141–170.

Howell, R. J., & Toepke, K. E. (1984). Summary of the child custody laws for the fifty states. *The American Journal of Family Therapy, 12,* 56–60.

Hulse, W. (1951). The emotionally disturbed child draws his family. *The Quarterly Journal of Child Behavior, 3,* 152–154.

———. (1952). Childhood conflict expressed through family drawings. *Journal of Projective Techniques, 16,* 66–79.

Ilfeld, F., Ilfeld, H., & Alexander, J. (1982). Does joint custody work? A first look at outcome data of relitigation. *American Journal of Psychiatry, 139,* 62–66.

Jastak, S., & Wilkinson, G. S. (1993). *Wide range achievement test, Revised.* Wilmington, DE: Jastak Associates.

Johnson, E. K., & Howell, R. (1993). Memory processes in children: Implications for investigations of alleged child sexual abuse. *Bulletin of the Academy of Psychiatry and the Law, 1,* 213–226.

Kalter, N., Kloner, A., Schreier, S., & Okla, K. (1989). Predictors of children's postdivorce adjustment. *American Journal of Orthopsychiatry, 59,* 605–618.

Kaufman, A., & Kaufman, N. (1983). *Kaufman assessment battery for children: Administration and scoring manual.* Circle Pines, MN: American Guidance Service.

———. (1983). *Kaufman assessment battery for children: Interpretative manual.* Circle Pines, MN: American Guidance Service.

———. (1990). *Administration and scoring manual for the Kaufman Brief Intelligence Test.* Circle Pines, MN: American Guidance Service.

Kaye, S. (1989). The impact of divorce on children's academic performance. In *Children of divorce: Development and clinical issues* (pp. 283–298). New York: Haworth Press.

Keilin, W. G., & Bloom, L. J. (1986). Child custody evaluation practices: A survey of experienced professionals. *Professional Psychology: Research and Practice, 17,* 338–346.

Keith-Spiegel, P., & Koocher, G. P. (1985). *Ethics in psychology: Professional standards and cases.* New York: Random House.

Kendall-Tackett, K., Williams, L., & Finkelhor, D. (1993). Impact of sexual abuse on children: A review and synthesis of recent empirical studies. *Psychological Bulletin, 113,* 164–180.

Kirkpatrick, M., Smith, C., & Roy, R. (1981). Lesbian mothers and their children: A comparative study. *American Journal of Orthopsychiatry, 51,* 545–551.

Kline, M., Tschann, J. M., Johnston, J. R., & Wallerstein, J. (1989). Children's adjustment in joint and sole physical custody families. *Developmental Psychology, 25,* 430–438.

Klopfer, B., Ainsworth, M., Klopfer, W., & Holt, R. (1954). *Developments in the Rorschach technique.* Vol. I. New York: Harcourt Brace and World.

Kluft, R. (1988). *Incest and adult psychopathology: An overview and a study of the 'sitting duck syndrome.'* Philadelphia: The Institute of the Pennsylvania Hospital.

Knapp, S., & Vandercreek, L. (1985). Psychotherapy and privileged communications in child custody cases. *Professional Psychology: Research and Practice, 16,* 398–407.

Kurdek, L. A., & Berg, B. (1983). Correlates of children's adjustment to their parents' divorces. In L. Kurdek (Ed.), *Children and divorce, new decisions for child development.* San Francisco: Jossey-Bass.

Lamb, S., & Cullinan, M. (1991, August). *Normal childhood sexual play and games. A survey of female undergraduates' memories.* Paper presented at the 99th Annual Convention of the American Psychological Association, San Francisco.

Leifer, M., Shapiro, J. P., Martone, M. W., & Kassem, L. (1991). Rorschach assessment of psychological functioning in sexually abused girls. *Journal of Personality Assessment, 56,* 14–28.

Lopez, F. G., Campbell, V. L., & Wadkins, C. E., Jr. (1988). The relation of parental divorce to college student development. *Journal of Divorce, 1,* 83–98.

Lundy, A. (1988). Instructional set and thematic apperception test validity. *Journal of Personality Assessment, 52,* 309–320.

Maccoby, E., Depner, C., & Mookin, R. (1990). Co-parenting in the second year after divorce. *Journal of Divorce and the Family, 52,* 141–155.

Malinosky-Rummell, R., & Hansen, D. J. (1993). Long-term consequences of childhood physical abuse. *Psychological Bulletin, 114,* 68–79.

Mantel, D. M. (1988). Clarifying erroneous child sexual abuse allegations. *American Journal of Orthopsychiatry, 58,* 618–621.

Martindale, D., Martindale, J., & Broderick, J. (1991). Providing expert testimony in child custody litigation. In P. Keller, & S. Heyman, *Innovations in Clinical Practice: A Source Book* (Vol 10, 481–497). Sarasota. FL: Professional Resource Exchange.

Masheter, C. (1990). Post-divorce relationships between ex-spouses: A literature review. *Journal of Divorce and Remarriage, 14,* 97–122.

———. (1991). Post-divorce relationships between ex-spouses: The roles of attachment and interpersonal conflict. *Journal of Marriage and Family, 53,* 103–110.

McIver W., II, Wakefield, H., & Underwager, R. (1990, August). *Behavior of abused and non-abused children in interviews with anatomically correct dolls.* Paper presented at the 98th Annual Convention of the American Psychological Association, Boston.

Melendez, F., & Marcus, E. H. (1990). Mental distress claims: Testing the psychological tests. *American Journal of Forensic Psychiatry, 11* (3), 19–22.

Melton, G. B., & Limber, S. (1989). Psychologists' involvement in cases of maltreatment: Limits of role and expertise. *American Psychologist, 44,* 1225–1233.

Mikkelsen, E., Gutheil, T., & Emens, M. (1992). False sexual abuse allegations by children and adolescents: Contextual factors and clinical subtypes. *American Journal of Psychotherapy, 55,* 556–570.

Miller, R. D. (1992). Professional versus personal ethics: Methods for system reform? *Bulletin of the American Academy of Psychiatry and Law, 20,* 163–177.

Miller-Perrin, C., & Wurtele, S. K. (1990). Reactions to childhood sexual abuse: Implications for post-traumatic stress disorder. In C. Meek, *Post traumatic stress disorder: Assessment differential diagnosis, and forensic evaluation* (pp. 91–135). Sarasota, FL: Professional Resources Exchange.

Millon, T. (1989). *Millon Clinical Multiaxial Inventory-II.* Minneapolis, MN: National Computer Systems.

Milner, J. S. (1989). Additional cross-validation of the child abuse potential inventory. *Psychological Assessment: A Journal of Consulting and Clinical Psychology, 1,* 219–223.

Milner, J. S., & Chilamkurti, C. (1991). Physical child abuse perpetrator characteristics. A review of the literature. *Journal of Interpersonal Violence, 6,* 345–366.

Mulholland, D. J., Watt, N. F., Philpott, A., & Sarlin, N. (1991). Academic performance of children of divorce: Psychological resilience and vulnerability. *Psychiatry, 54,* 268–280.

Mullins v. Mullins. (1986). 490 N. E. 2d 1375 (Ill. App. Ct.)

Murray, H. A., & Staff of the Harvard Psychology Clinic. (1943). *Thematic apperception test manual.* Cambridge, MA: Harvard University Press.

National Register of Health Service Providers in Psychology. (1992). Washington, DC: Council for the National Register of Health Service Providers in Psychology.

Neal, J. H. (1983). Children's understanding of their parents' divorces. In L. Kurdek (Ed.), *Children and divorce, new directions for child development.* San Francisco: Jossey-Bass.

Newsweek. (December 6, 1986).

Oaklander, V. (1978). *Windows to our children.* Moab, UT: Real People Press.

Ondrovik, J., & Hamilton, D. (1992). Forensic challenge: Expert testimony. *American Journal of Forensic Psychology, 10,* 15–24.

Pageloe, M. (1984). *Family violence.* New York: Praeger.

Pearson, J., & Thoennes, N. (1990). Custody after divorce: Demographic and attitudinal patterns. *American Journal of Orthopsychiatry, 60,* 233–249.

Perry, N. (1993). *False memory controversy and the treatment of trauma.* Paper presented at the Wisconsin Psychological Association, Fall Conference, Madison, Wisconsin.

Podboy, J., & Kastle, A. (1992). *The intentional misuse of standard psychological tests in complex trials.* Paper presented at the American College of Forensic Psychology's 8th Annual Symposium in Forensic Psychology, San Francisco.

Pope, K. S., & Vasquez, M. J. T. (1991). *Ethics in psychotherapy and counseling.* San Francisco: Jossey-Bass.

Psychological Corporation. (1987). *Catalog: Tests, products and services for psychological assessment.* New York: Harcourt Brace Jovanovich.

———. (1994). *Catalog: Tests, products and services for psychological assessment.* New York: Harcourt Brace Jovanovich.

Reidy, T., Silver, R., & Carlson, A. (1989). Child custody decisions: A survey of judges. *Family Law Quarterly, 23,* 75–87.

Richards, C., & Goldenberg, E. (1986). Fathers with joint physical custody of young children: A preliminary look. *The American Journal of Family Therapy, 14,* 154–161.

Risin, L., & MacNamara, R. (1989). Validation of child sexual abuse: The psychologist's role. *Journal of Clinical Psychiatry, 45,* 175–184.

Rogers, M. L. (1992). Delusional disorder and the evolution of mistaken sexual allegations in child custody cases. *American Journal of Psychology, 10,* 47–69.

Rorschach, H. (1942). *Psychodiagnostics: A diagnostic test based on perception* (P. Lemkau & B. Kronenberg, Trans.) Bern, Switzerland: Huber. (Original German ed. published 1921; U.S. distributor, Grune & Stratton.)

Roseby, V. (1984, August). *A custody evaluation model for preschool children.* Paper presented at the 92nd Annual Convention of the American Psychological Association, Toronto.

Rotter, J., & Rafferty, J. (1950). *Manual, the Rotter incomplete sentences blank.* Cleveland: The Psychological Corporation.

Rowan, E. L., Rowan, L. B., & Langelier, P. (1990). Women who molest children. *Bulletin of the American Academy of Psychiatry & Law, 18,* 79–83.

Saks, M. J. (1990). Expert witnesses, nonexpert witnesses, and nonwitness experts. *Law and Human Behavior, 148,* 291–313.

Samek, W. (1991, August). *Forensic assessment of incest families.* Paper presented at the 99th Annual Convention of the American Psychological Association, San Francisco.

Sandler, I., Wolchik, S., Braver, S., & Fogas, B., (1991). Stability and quality of life events and psychological symptomatology in children of divorce. *American Journal of Community Psychology, 19,* 501–520.

Schachere, K. (1990). Attachment between working mothers and their infants: The influence of family processes. *American Journal of Orthopsychiatry, 60,* 19–34.

Schaefer, M., & Guyer, M. (1988, August). *Allegations of sexual abuse in custody and visitation disputes: A legal and clinical challenge.* Paper presented at the 96th Annual Convention of the American Psychological Association, Atlanta.

Schetky, D. H. (1992). Ethical issues in forensic child and adolescent psychiatry. *Journal of the American Academy of Child and Adolescent Psychiatry, 31,* 403–407.

Schwartz, L. L. (1985). *The effects of divorce on children at different ages: A descriptive study* (ERIC, ED 261–267).

Scott, R., & Stone, D. (1986). MMPI profile constellations in incest families. *Journal of Consulting and Clinical Psychology, 54,* 364–368.

———. (1986). MMPI measures of psychological disturbance in adolescent and adult victims of father-daughter incest. *Journal of Clinical Psychology, 42,* 251–259.

Seltzer, J. A. (1991). Relationships between fathers and children who live apart: The father's role after separation. *Journal of Marriage and Family, 53,* 79–101.

Sexton, M. C., Grant, C. D., & Nash, M. R. (1990, August). *Sexual abuse and body image: A comparison of abused and non-abused women.* Paper presented at the 98th Annual Convention of the American Psychological Association, Boston.

Shiller, V. (1986). Joint versus maternal custody for families with latency age boys: Parent characteristics and child adjustment. *American Journal of Orthopsychiatry, 56,* 486–489.

Shuman, D. W. (1986). *Psychiatric and psychological evidence.* Colorado Springs: Shepard's/McGraw-Hill.

Shybunko, D. E. (1989). Effects of post-divorce relationship on child adjustment. In *Children of divorce: Developmental and clinical issues* (pp. 299–313). New York: Haworth Press, Inc.

Skafte, D. (1985). *Child custody evaluations: A practical guide.* Beverly Hills: Sage.

Slovenko, R. (1988). The role of the expert (with focus on psychiatry) in the adversarial system. *The Journal of Psychiatry and Law, 16,* 333–373.

Smith, J. (1986). *Medical malpractice psychiatric care.* Colorado Springs: Shepard's/McGraw-Hill.

Sorensen, E., & Goldman, J. (1989). Judicial perceptions in determining primary physical residence. *Journal of Divorce, 12,* 69–87.

Sparr, L. F., & Boehnlein, J. K. (1990). Posttraumatic stress disorder in tort actions: Forensic minefield. *Bulletin of the American Academy of Psychiatry and Law, 18,* 283–302.

Steinman, S. (1981). The experience of children in a joint custody arrangement: A report of a study. *American Journal of Orthopsychiatry, 51,* 403–414.

Stolberg, A. L., & Anker, J. M. (1984). Cognitive and behavioral changes in children resulting from parental divorce and consequent environmental changes. *Journal of Divorce, 7,* 23–40.

Stone, N. M., & Shear, L. E. (1988). The boundaries of mental health expertise in dependency and family law: A proposal for standards of practice. *Conciliation Courts Review, 26,* 49–67.

Stromberg, C. D., Haggarty, D. J., Leibenluft, R. F., McMillian, M. H., Mishkin, B., Robin, B. L., & Trilling, H. R. (1988). *The psychologist's legal handbook.* Washington, DC: Council for the National Register of Health Service Providers in Psychology.

Swanson, L., & Baiggio, M. K. (1985). Therapeutic perspectives on father-daughter incest. *American Journal of Psychiatry, 142,* 667–674.

Tharinger, D. (1990). Impact of child sexual abuse on developing sexuality. *Professional Psychology. Research and Practice, 21,* 331–337.

Thompson, R. A., Tinsley, B. R., Scalora, M. J., & Park, R. D. (1989). Grandparents; visitation rights: Legalizing the ties that bind. *American Psychologist, 49,* 1217–1282.

U.S. Department of Health and Human Services. (1991). *Family violence: An overview.* Washington, DC: National Center on Abuse and Neglect.

——. (1992). *Child abuse and neglect: A shared community concern.* Washington, DC: National Center on Abuse and Neglect.

Veltkamp, L. J., & Miller, T. (1990). Clinical strategies in recognizing spouse abuse. *Psychiatric Quarderly, 61,* 179–187.

Wakefield, H., & Underwager, R. (1991). Female child sexual abusers: A critical review of the literature. *American Journal of Forensic Psychology, 9,* 43–70.

Wallerstein, J. S. (1983). Children of divorce: The psychological tasks of the child. *American Journal of Orthopsychiatry, 53,* 230–245.

——. (1985). Children of divorce: Preliminary report of a ten-year follow-up of older children and adolescents. *Journal of the American Academy of Child Psychiatry, 24,* 545–553.

——. (1986). *Cape Cod Institute.* Greenwich, CT: Institute for Psychological Study.

——. (1987). Children of divorce: Report of a ten-year follow-up of early latency age children. *American Journal of Orthopsychiatry, 57,* 199–211.

——. (1991a). *Current research on long-term effects of divorce on children.* 15th Annual Child Custody Conference, Keystone, CO.

——. (1991b). The long-term effects of divorce on children: A review. *Journal of the American Academy of Child and Adolescent Psychiatry, 30,* 349–360.

Wallerstein, J., & Corbin, S. (1986). Father-child relationships after divorce: Child support and educational opportunity. *Family Law Quarterly, 20,* 109–128.

Wallerstein, J. S., & Kelley, J. B. (1980). *Surviving the break-up: How children and parents cope with divorce.* New York: Basic Books.

Ware, C. (1982). *Sharing parenthood after divorce.* New York: Viking Press.

Wechsler, D. (1974). *Manual for the Wechsler Intelligence Scale for Children-Revised.* New York: Psychological Corporation.

———. (1981). *Wechsler Adult Intelligence Scale-Revised.* New York: Psychological Corporation.

Weiner, I. B. (1989). On competence and ethicality in psychodiagnostic assessment. *Journal of Personality Assessment, 53,* 827–831.

Weithorn, L. (1987). Psychological consultation in divorce custody litigation: Ethical considerations. In L. Weithorn (Ed.), *Psychology and Child Custody Determinations.* Lincoln, NE: University of Nebraska Press.

Welch, K. (1991). *Gender differences and the impact of parental divorce on parent-child relationships and future plans.* Paper presented at the 99th Annual Convention of the American Psychological Association, San Francisco.

Weston, D., Ludolph, P., Misile, B., Ruffins, S., & Block, J. (1990). Physical and sexual abuse in adolescent girls with borderline personality disorder. *American Journal of Orthopsychiatry, 60,* 55–66.

Williams, A. D. (1992). Bias and debiasing techniques in forensic psychology. *American Journal of Forensic Psychology, 10,* 19–26.

Wyatt, G. E. (1990). Sexual abuse of ethnic minority children: Identifying dimensions of victimization. *Professional Psychology: Research and Practice, 21,* 338–343.

Wyatt, G. E., Guthrie, D., & Notgrass, C. M. (1992). Differential effects of women's child sexual abuse and subsequent sexual revictimization. *Journal of Consulting and Clinical Psychology, 60,* 167–173.

Yates, E., & Musty, T. (1988). Preschool children's erroneous allegations of sexual molestation. *American Journal of Psychiatry, 145,* 989–992.

Zaslow, M. J. (1988). Sex differences in children's response to parental divorce: 1. Research methodology and post-divorce family forms. *American Journal of Orthopsychiatry, 58,* 355–378.

———. (1989). Sex differences in children's response to parental divorce: 2. Samples, variables, ages, and sources. *American Journal of Orthopsychiatry, 59,* 118–141.

Ziskin, J. (1981). *Coping with psychiatric and psychological testimony* (3d ed.). Venice, CA: Law and Psychology Press.

Author Index

A

Academy of Family Mediators, 276
Ackerman, M. J., 48, 136, 139
Amato, P. R., 55
American Academy of Psychiatry and the Law, 28
American Professional Society on the Abuse of Children, 93, 285, 291
American Psychological Association, 11–13, 15, 17, 23–25, 27, 30–33, 100, 105–06, 188–89, 199, 235, 240, 255, 266–67, 269, 272
Arditti, J., 50

B

Bales, J., 214
Barber, B. L., 60
Bazelon, D., 17
Berman, A., 13
Bisnair, L., 61
Blau, T., 29–30
Blinka. O., 231
Bolton, F. G., 167
Bonkowski, S. E., 59
Bottoms, B., 211
Boyer, J., 12
Bresee, P., 176–77
Bricklin, B., 117, 183–84
Brodsky, S., 19
Bronfenbrenner, U., 48
Brosig, C. L., 160

C

Cain, B. S., 59
Caldwell, A., 163

Carlson, B. E., 59
Cohen, M. G., 46, 266
Committee on Ethical Guidelines for Forensic Psychologists, 28–29, 222
Crites, C., 166

D

Dawson, B., 189
Deed, M. L., 18, 21
Demo, D., 54
Denham, S., 50
De Young, M., 184
Dillon, K., 180

E

Eckenrode, J., 160, 162
Egeland, B., 175
Ellison, E., 36
Erikson, S., 36
Exner, J. E., 104

F

Facchino, D., 49
Faller, K. L., 181–82, 191
Finkelhor, D., 166, 171–72
Forehand, R., 59
Franke, L., 58
Franklin, K., 60
Frost, A. K., 59

G

Garb, H., 212
Garbarino, J., 168–70
Gardner, R., 39, 75–79, 175, 177
Geffner, R. A., 191

Gelles, R., 167
Glenn, N. D., 60
Gold, E., 174
Goldstein, J., 1, 38–39
Goldzband, M., 214
Goodman, G. S., 166, 189
Gordon, B., 190
Greene, R., 50, 113
Greif, G., 49–50
Grisso, T., 20, 25, 221–22, 267
Guidubaldi, J., 67

H
Hall, G. C., 187, 267
Hanson, R. K., 9, 172
Hanson, S., ix
Hathaway, S. R., 123
Healy, J., 50
Heilbrun, K., 11, 102–03, 210
Herman, J., 174
Hershorn, M., 168
Hetherington, E. M., 48, 54
Hodges, W. F., 40, 42–43, 51
Hoeffer, B., 51
Holden, W. E., 163
Horner, T. M., 212
Howell, R. J., 23
Hulse, W., 124

I
Ilfeld, F., 38

J
Jastak, S., 124
Johnson, E. K., 92, 194

K
Kalter, N., 54
Kaye, S., 60–61
Keilin, W. G., 82, 104–07
Keith-Spiegel, P., 10, 266

Kendall-Tackett, K., 182–83
Kirkpatrick, M., 51
Kline, M., 38
Kluft, R., 185
Knapp, S., 31
Kurdek, L. A., 48

L
Leifer, M., 185
Lopez, F. G., 59
Lundy, A., 104

M
Maccoby, E., 49
Malinosky-Rummell, R., 163–64
Mantel, D. M., 178
Martindale, D., 11, 221
Masheter, C., 48–49
McIver, W. II, 189
Melendez, F., 21
Melton, G. B., 187, 189, 266–67
Mikkelsen, E., 178
Miller, R. D., 23
Milner, J. S., 162–63
Mulholland, D. J., 61
Murray, H. A., 124

N
Neal, J. H., 48

O
Oaklander, V., 118
Ondrovik, J., 197, 210, 213

P
Pageloe, M., 166
Pearson, J., 38
Perry, N., 194
Podboy, J., 21
Pope, K. S., 10, 13

R

Reidy, J., 202–03
Richards, C., 50
Risin, L., 186
Rorschach, H., 124
Roseby, V., 48
Rowan, E. L., 173

S

Saks, M. J., 211
Samek, W., 192
Sandler, I., 58
Schachere, K., 50
Schaefer, M., 190
Schetky, D. H., 12
Schwartz, L. L., 34
Scott, R., 174
Seltzer, J. A., 50
Sexton, M. C., 184
Shiller, V., 38
Shuman, D. W., 211
Shybunko, D. E., 58
Skafte, D., 16
Slovenko, R., 211, 221
Smith, J., 216
Sorenson, E., 39–40
Steinman, S., 38
Stolberg, A. L., 48
Stone, N. M., 17, 23
Stromberg, C. D., 14–15, 17, 214
Swanson, L., 192

T

Tharinger, D., 185, 266
Thompson, R. A., 53

U

U.S. Department of Health and
    Human Services, 160–62,
    166, 168, 171

V

Veltkamp, L. J., 167

W

Wakefield, H., 171, 173
Wallerstein, J. S., 35, 48, 51,
    54–55, 65, 68, 70–75, 97,
    145
Wechsler, D., 124
Weiner, I. B., 17, 113
Weithorn, L., 15, 18–19, 25, 267
Welch, K., 61
Western Psychological Services,
    127, 129, 136
Weston, D., 184
Williams, A. D., 19–20, 183
Wyatt, G. E., 184, 186

Y

Yates, E., 178

Z

Zaslow, M. J., 61
Ziskin, J., 19
Zosel, M., xi

Subject Index

A

Abuse
  adolescents, 170, 182, 184
  allegations, 91, 175, 177–78,
    204, 206
    bona fide sexual abuse,
      175–77, 179, 190
    false abuse allegations,
      175–79, 191
  body image, 184
  child abuse, 100
  Child Abuse Potential (CAP),
    163, 188
  child abuser, 161
  coaching, 90
  emotional abuse, 170
  ethnic minority children, 184
  false memory syndrome, 194
  female perpetrators, 173
  masturbation, 182
  physical abuse, 122, 160–61
  psychological abuse, 41
  psychologically battered child,
    168
  psychologically maltreated, 170
  psychologist's role, 187
  recantation, 190
  recidivism, 172
  revictimization, 186
  Rorschach, 185
  sexual abuse, 41, 85, 92, 122,
    137, 171
  sexual abuse assessment, 181
  sexual assault, 85
  sexually anatomically correct
    dolls (SAC), 93, 178, 180,
    188, 190–92
  sitting duck syndrome, 185
  spouse abuse accommodation
    syndrome, 167
  substantiation, 162–63

Academic achievement, 61,
  79–80, 98
  grades, 60
Academy of Family Mediators, 36
Achievement Test, 60, 67, 108
Ackerman-Schoendorf Scales for
    Parent Evaluation of
    Custody (ASPECT), 3, 117,
    119–25
Acting Out, 151
Activities of Daily Living, 2
  outside activities, 86
Adjourn, 237
Adjudicate, 237
Admissible Evidence, 237
Adolescence, 70, 148, 151, 182,
  184
  age of false maturity, 58
  psychological maltreatment,
    170
Adult Children of Alcoholics, 112
Adversarial Divorce, 35–36
Affidavit, 237
Alcoholism, 122, 164, 181
Alcohol-Related Problems, 2, 84,
  90, 172
  alcohol or other drug abuse, 84,
    206
Alienate, 106, 178
  parental alienation syndrome,
    74–79
Alimony/Maintenance, 237
American Professional Society on
    the Abuse of Children
    Guidelines for Psychosocial
    Evaluation of Suspected
    Sexual Abuse in Young
    Children, 285
Appearance, 237
Arbitration, 37

Arrearages, 152

B
Best Interests of Children, 9, 16,
    18–19, 25, 31, 101, 38–39,
    75, 79, 126, 144, 159,
    203–04
Biases, 11, 17, 19–20, 100, 216,
    227, 231
Bifurcated Trial, 237
Bona fide Sexual Abuse, 175–77,
    179, 190
Borderline Personality Disorder,
    184
Brainwashing, 75–76, 78

C
Calendar, 237
Case Law, 237
Child
    acting-out behavior, 63, 66
    age of anger, 57
    age of guilt, 56
    age of sadness, 56
    attachment problems, 41
    birth order, 70
    body image, 184
    boys, 69
    child abuse, 100
    court testimony, 183
    dating, 154
    elementary school years, 56
    girls, 69
    incest, 192
        families, 192
        fathers, 192
        mothers, 193
        victims, 194
    interviews, 89
    middle school years, 57–58
    overburdened child, 70–71, 153
    parentification, 153
    preschool years, 55, 182

protective services, 90, 160,
    168, 206
psychological maltreatment,
    170
punishment, 161, 167
regressive behavior, 63, 147
repetitive behavior, 64
role reversal, 153
school records, 2, 98
secrets, 155, 192
sexually intimate behavior,
    154–55
sibling rivalry, 154
support, 52
Child Abuser, 161
Child Custody Evaluation
    Guidelines, 33, 100
Children Abuse Prevention
    Treatment Act, 161
Coaching, 90
Cognitive Functioning, 2
Collaborative Report, 3
College Years, 59
    education, 53
Confidentiality, 12, 25, 30
Consultation with Attorneys, 106
Contempt, 238
Continuance, 238
Cooperative Divorce, 35
Court-Appointed Psychologist, 40,
    153, 205–06
Court Records, 2
Court Testimony, 106, 183
Criminal Behavior, 164, 206
Cross-Examination, 215–18, 220,
    222–28, 237

D
Dangerousness, 17, 213
Data, 16–18, 20, 22, 213, 215,
    231–32
Defendant, 237
Deponent, 237
Deposition, 16, 27, 218, 222, 237

Development Milestones, 84
Diminished Capacity, 51–52
Direct Examination, 213, 225–26, 237
Discipline, 87
Discovery, 222, 237
Domestic Violence, 165–66
Drug-Related Problems, 2, 84
DSM-III-R/DSM-IV, 20, 22, 226
Dual Relationship, 7, 25–26, 233
Duty to Warn or Protect, 23
    Tarasoff, 23

E
Emotional Abuse, 169–70
Emotional Assault, 169
Emotional Neglect, 168
Employment, 85
Ethical Principles of Psychologists
    and Code of Conduct, 10,
    11, 13, 22, 23, 27, 30, 32,
    187–88, 240
Evaluation
  behavioral observations, 2, 94
  bias, 11, 17, 19–20
  collateral information, 2, 101
  educational history, 83
  employment history, 83, 85
  establish rapport, 101
  formal observations, 94
  home visits, 97, 104
  interviews, 2, 14, 82–83, 104
  medical records, 2
  observation, 95, 123
  outside activities, 86
  police records, 98
  report, 16, 106
  significant others, 2, 217
  updated evaluations, 217–18
Ex parte, 237
Experts
  consultants, 7
  court-appointed psychologist, 4,
    205–06

disqualifying the expert, 220
  expert witness, 219–20
  hired gun, 4–7, 9, 19–20, 27
  rebuttal witness, 6
  second opinion expert, 5–6

F
False Abuse Allegations, 175–79,
    191
False Memory Syndrome
    Foundation, 194
Family Violence, 165
Fees, 25–28, 31, 106, 215–16
  contingency fees, 28
  retainer, 27, 29
Finances, 152
  arrearages, 152
  maintenance, 152
  support, 152
Finding, 238

G
Gender Differences, 61
Grades and Achievement Test, 60
Grandparents, 148, 150
  roles, 54
  visitation, 53
Guardian ad litem, 4, 9, 12, 27,
    78–79, 92–93, 96, 98, 153,
    196, 200, 205–06, 238
Guidelines for Child Custody
    Evaluations, 33, 100, 234,
    266
Guidelines for Providers of
    Psychological Services, 23,
    199

H
Habitual Criminal, 143
Hearsay, 29, 222, 238
Hired Gun, 4–7, 9, 19–20, 27,
    216

Household Routines, 149

I
Iatrogenic Harm, 24
In camera, 238
Incest, 192
    families, 192
    family dynamics, 193
    fathers, 192
    mothers, 193
    secrecy, 192, 193
    victims, 193
Informed Consent, 5, 12, 25, 101
In re, 238
Insecurity, 62, 63
Interrogatories, 238
Interviews, 16, 82–83, 101, 104,
    106
Invoking Privilege, 97

J
Joint Custody, 18, 37–40, 49, 75,
    107, 143, 203–04
Judges' Custody Decision
    Criteria, 202

L
Learned Treatises, 6, 216, 224,
    226, 238
Legal Cases
    Barefoot v. Estell, 214
    Deed v. Condrell, 230
    Dolin v. Van Zweck, 229
    Gootee v. Lichtner, 229
    Guity v. Kandilakis, 229
    Howard v. Drapkin, 229
    *Lavit v. Superior Court of
        Arizona,* 230
    Myers v. Price, 230
    Snow v. Koeppl, 229
    Tarasoff, 23
    Williams v. Congdon, 230

Zim v. Benezra, 230
Loyalty Issue, 151

M
Maintenance, 152
Masturbation, 181–82
Mediation, 7, 26, 35–37, 126, 139,
    142, 145, 196, 233
Mental Measurements Yearbook,
    102–03
Multiple Relationships, 100

N
National Register of Health
    Service Providers in
    Psychology, 219
Neglect, 41, 100
Neuropsychological Testing, 11,
    21, 212
    neuropsychological assessment,
    212
No Contact Order, 93, 95
No-Fault Divorce, 34

O
Object Constancy, 43
Objections
    objection overruled, 238
    objection sustained, 238
Outside Activities, 86
Overnight Visitation for Infants,
    150

P
Parental Alienation Syndrome,
    75–79
Parents
    criminal history, 207
    diminished capacity, 51–52
    Disneyland parent, 43
    fit parent, 2, 22

Parents (*continued*)
  homosexual parents, 50–51
  joint custody, 18, 37–40, 49, 75,
    143
  parental alienation syndrome,
    74–79
  parental death, 55
  primary placement, 40
  secrets, 155
  sexually intimate behavior, 155
  shared placement, 40
  sole custody, 37–39, 41, 143
  stepparents, 96
Party, 238
Personality Functioning, 2
Personal Notes, 29, 220–21
Petitioner, 238
Physical Abuse Perpetrators, 162
Physical Punishment, 90
Placement, 149, 208
  Ackerman Plan, 45–46, 139
  alternating schedule, 150
  50/50 schedules, 43, 46, 56, 149
  foster placement, 208
  joint placement, 40
  primary placement, 40
  shared placement, 40
  visitation, 40
Plaintiff, 238
Postjudgment, 238
Posttraumatic Stress Disorder
    (PTSD), 21, 182–83, 191
Privilege, 30–31
Pro se, 5, 238
Problems of Divorce,
  abandonment/rejection, 60
  depression, 66
  guilt, 64
  helplessness, 62
  powerlessness, 62
  regressive behavior, 63
  unresolved anger, 65
Profile of Abuser, 172
Protective Services, 85, 90, 160,
    168, 206

Psychological Tests
  Ackerman-Schoendorf Scales
    for Parent Evaluation of
    Custody (ASPECT), 3, 117,
    119–26 136–41
  Cognitive-Emotional Scale,
    119, 120, 122, 124, 128
  Observational Scale, 119,
    121, 128
  Parental Custody Index
    (PCI), 120–21, 123–26,
    136, 138–40
  Social Scale, 119, 121, 125,
    128
    alcoholism, 122
    physical abuse, 122
    sexual abuse, 122
  Bender-Gestalt, 105–06
  Bricklin Perceptual Scales, 117
  California Personality
    Inventory (CPI), 108
  California Psychological
    Inventory, 105
  Child Abuse Potential
    Inventory (CAP), 163, 188
  Children's Apperception Test
    (CAT), 116
  Children's Sentence
    Completions, 106
  Clinical Analysis Questionnaire,
    105
  Clinical Interview, 107
  Custody Quotient, 117
  Draw-A-Family Test, 123
  Draw-A-Person Test, 105–06
  Exner Scoring System, 116
  Family Relations Test, 106
  Halstead-Reitan Battery, 212
  House-Tree Person Projective
    Technique, 105–06
  Intelligence Testing, 106–08
  IQ, 107–08
  Kaufman Assessment Battery
    for Children (K-ABC), 107

Kaufman Brief Intelligence
   Test (K-BIT), 108
McCarthy Scales of
   Children's Abilities
   (MSCA), 107
Rorschach Psychodiagnostic
   Series, 21
Sanford-Binet-4th Edition
   (SB:FE), 107
Shipley Hartford, 108
Slosson, 108
Wechsler Adult Intelligence
   Scale (WAIS, WAIS-R),
   11–16, 126
Wechsler Intelligence Scale
   for Children (WISC, WISC-
   R, and WISC-III), 11, 104,
   107
Incomplete Sentences Test, 107,
   116
Kinetic Family Drawings,
   105–06
Luria-Nebraska
   Neuropsychological
   Battery, 212
Millon Clinical Multiaxial
   Inventory-2nd Edition
   (MCMI-II), 108, 115
Minnesota Multiphasic
   Personality Inventory
   (MMPI, MMPI-2, MMPI-
   A), 4, 11, 13–14, 16, 19,
   103–04, 108–09, 113–15,
   118, 123–24, 126, 128, 140,
   163, 174–75, 221
   Clinical Scales, 110, 114
   Anxiety (ANX), 110
   Scale 1 (Hypochondriasis),
      110
   Scale 2 (Depression), 110
   Scale 3 (Hysteria), 110
   Scale 4 (Psychopathic
      Deviate), 110
   Scale 6 (Paranoia), 110–11

Scale 7 (Psychasthenia),
   110–11
Scale 8 (Schizophrenia),
   111
Scale 9 (Hypomania), 111
Content Scales, 114
Critical Items, 113–14
F-back, 109
Subtle Obvious Scales,
   113–14
Supplementary Scales, 111,
   114
   Anxiety (A), 110–11
   Ego Strength Scale, 128
   Family Problems (FAM),
      111
   L and K Scales, 112
   MacAndrews Alcoholism-
      Revised (MAC-R),
      111–12, 115, 140
   Negative Treatment
      Indicators (TRT), 113
   Repression (R), 111–12
   Work Interference, 112
True Response Inconsistency
   (TRIN), 109
Validity Scales, 109, 114
L, F, and K Scales, 109–10
Variable Response
   Inconsistency (VRIN), 109
Wiggins Content Scales, 109
Parental Stress Index, 163
Parent-Child Interaction Test,
   105, 123
Peabody Picture Vocabulary
   Test, 106
Perception of Relationships
   Test (PORT), 117
Personality Inventory for
   Children (PIC), 105, 108,
   111, 115
Projective Drawings, 105–06,
   118
   Draw-A-Person Test, 118
   Draw-A-Family Test, 118,
      124

Psychological Tests (*continued*)
  House-Tree-Person Test, 118
  Kinetic Family Drawing, 118
  Robert Apperception Test, 106,
    116
  Rorschach Psychodiagnostic
    Series, 21, 103–04, 107,
    116, 124, 185
  Rotter Incomplete Sentences
    Test, 117
  Sacks Incomplete Sentences
    Test, 117
  Sentence Completion Test, 105
  Sixteen Personality Factor
    Questionnaire (16-PF), 105,
    108, 115
  Strange Situation Test, 106
  Tasks of Emotional
    Development Test, 106
  Thematic Apperception Test
    (TAT), or Children's
    Apperception Test (CAT),
    103–04, 116, 124, 106, 124
  Wechsler Adult Intelligence
    Scale-Revised (WAIS-R),
    11, 16, 107, 124, 126
  Wechsler Intelligence Scale for
    Children (WISC, WISC-R,
    WISC-III), 11
  Wide Range Achievement Test
    (WRAT-R or WRAT3) or
    other achievement tests,
    106, 108, 124, 126
Psychologically Battered Child,
  168
Psychologically Maltreated, 170
Punishment, 161

Q
Quash, 238

R
Recidivist, 172, 238
Records, 16, 148

maintaining records, 31
written records, 101
Regressive Behavior, 63, 147, 151
Releases, 9, 30, 83
Respondent, 238
Restraining Order, 93, 95, 238
Retainer, 27, 238
Rules, 149

S
Schedules, 144, 149
School Conferences, 147
School Reports, 148
Separation, 144, 149
Sequestering Witnesses, 234, 238
Sexual Abuse Assessment, 181
Sexually Anatomically Correct
    Dolls, 93, 178, 180, 188,
    190–92
Significant Others, 2, 217
Sole Custody, 37–41, 203–04, 207
Specialty Guidelines for Forensic
    Psychologists, 28, 32, 255
Spousal Abuse, 167
Spouse Abuse Accommodation
    Syndrome, 167
Standards of Practice, 10
Standards of Practice for Family
    and Divorce Mediation,
    276
Stepparents, 96
Stipulation, 238
Subpoena duces tecum, 239
Subpoenaed Records, 228, 238
Substance Abuse, 90, 143, 164
Suggestion, 92–93
Suicidal Behavior, 71, 165–66,
    174, 182, 184, 231
Support, 53, 152, 239
Support Network, 218

T
Temporary Orders, 239
Tender Years Doctrine, 1

Termination of Parental Rights
    (TPR), 239
Test Integrity, 14
Testimony, 185, 217–18, 223, 231
    expert testimony, 210–11, 213
    hearsay, 29
    learned treatises, 6, 216–17,
        224, 226, 238
    narrative testimony, 220
    question and answer, 220
    Rorschach, 185
    ultimate issue, 221–22
Therapists, 97
Therapy, 206–207
Treatment, 145
    family therapy, 155
    psychiatric hospitalizations, 2,
        97
    psychiatric medication, 2, 83
    psychiatric treatment, 83
    psychological treatment, 83
    suicidal ideation, 71
Trier of Fact, 4, 211, 217, 238

U
Ultimate Issue, 22, 221–22, 238
Uniform Marriage and Divorce
    Act, 1

V
Violence, 59, 100, 164, 170
Violent Behavior, 164
    family, 165
Visitation, 40–44, 49, 55, 144,
        151–53, 175, 181, 205–07
    Christmas, 44, 143
    Easter, 44
    50/50 schedules, 43, 46, 56
    Fourth of July, 44
    holidays, 43, 45, 143
    supervised visits, 205, 207–08
    Thanksgiving, 44, 143
    therapeutic supervised visits,
        205
    unsupervised monitored visits,
        205
Voir dire, 239

W
Weight of Evidence, 239
Work Product, 8, 29, 225